Families and the European Union

In the first book to offer a comprehensive analysis of family law in the European Union, McGlynn argues that a traditional concept of 'family', which has many adverse effects – on individuals, on families (in all their diverse forms), and indeed on the economic ambitions of the EU – is forming the basis for the little-recognised and under-researched field of EU family law. This book examines three different aspects of family life – childhood, parenthood and partnerships – and critically analyses existing EU law in relation to each. It examines the emerging field of EU family law, providing a highly sceptical account of recent developments and a robust challenge to the arguments in favour of the codification of European civil law, including family law.

Clare McGlynn is Professor of Law at Durham University. She has previously taught at the University of Newcastle upon Tyne, was Visiting Professor of European Labour Law at Stockholm University in 1999, and qualified as a solicitor in the City of London. She is author of *The Woman Lawyer: Making the Difference* (1998).

The Law in Context Series

Editors William Twining (University College London) and
Christopher McCrudden (Lincoln College, Oxford)

Since 1970 the Law in Context series has been in the forefront of the movement to
broaden the study of law. It has been a vehicle for the publication of innovative scholarly
books that treat law and legal phenomena critically in their social, political and
economic contexts from a variety of perspectives. The series particularly aims to publish
scholarly legal writing that brings fresh perspectives to bear on new and existing areas of
law taught in universities. A contextual approach involves treating legal subjects broadly,
using materials from other social sciences, and from any other discipline that helps to
explain the operation in practice of the subject under discussion. It is hoped that this
orientation is at once more stimulating and more realistic than the bare exposition of
legal rules. The series includes original books that have a different emphasis from
traditional legal textbooks, while maintaining the same high standards of scholarship.
They are written primarily for undergraduate and graduate students of law and of other
disciplines, but most also appeal to a wider readership. In the past, most books in the
series have focused on English law, but recent publications include books on European
law, globalisation, transnational legal processes, and comparative law.

Books in the Series

Anderson, Schum & Twining: *Analysis of Evidence*
Ashworth: *Sentencing and Criminal Justice*
Barton & Douglas: *Law and Parenthood*
Bell: *French Legal Cultures*
Bercusson: *European Labour Law*
Birkinshaw: *European Public Law*
Birkinshaw: *Freedom of Information: The Law, the Practice and the Ideal*
Cane: *Atiyah's Accidents, Compensation and the Law*
Clarke & Kohler: *Property Law: Commentary and Materials*
Collins: *The Law of Contract*
Davies: *Perspectives on Labour Law*
Dembour: *Who Believes in Human Rights?: The European Convention in Question*
de Sousa Santos: *Toward a New Legal Common Sense*
Diduck: *Law's Families*
Elworthy & Holder: *Environmental Protection: Text and Materials*
Fortin: *Children's Rights and the Developing Law*
Glover-Thomas: *Reconstructing Mental Health Law and Policy*
Gobert & Punch: *Rethinking Corporate Crime*
Harlow & Rawlings: *Law and Administration: Text and Materials*
Harris: *An Introduction to Law*
Harris, Campbell & Halson: *Remedies in Contract and Tort*
Harvey: *Seeking Asylum in the UK: Problems and Prospects*
Hervey & McHale: *Health Law and the European Union*
Lacey & Wells: *Reconstructing Criminal Law*
Lewis: *Choice and the Legal Order: Rising above Politics*
Likosky: *Transnational Legal Processes*

Families and the European Union

Law, Politics and Pluralism

Clare McGlynn
Durham University

CAMBRIDGE
UNIVERSITY PRESS

CAMBRIDGE UNIVERSITY PRESS

Cambridge, New York, Melbourne, Madrid, Cape Town, Singapore, São Paulo

Cambridge University Press
The Edinburgh Building, Cambridge CB2 2RU, UK
Published in the United States of America by Cambridge University Press, New York

www.cambridge.org
Information on this title: www.cambridge.org/9780521613354

First published 2006

Printed in the United Kingdom at the University Press, Cambridge

A catalogue record for this publication is available from the British Library

ISBN-13 978-0-521-61335-4 paperback
ISBN-10 0-521-61335-3 paperback

Dedicated with love to Ian, Ross and Freya

Contents

Preface

When this book was first conceived, my aim was to analyse the concept of family employed in a number of different areas of substantive Community law. The thought of writing a book which also included a detailed discussion of the family law of the European Union never entered my head. If it had, I should have thought it would be a very short book indeed. However, in the late 1990s, when carrying out research for an article on the developing concept of family in European Union law, I came across references to family law in discussions regarding the prospects for a European civil code.[1] The deeper I delved, the more astonished I became. Not only was there already a Matrimonial Convention, but also a proposal to Communitarise it in the form of a regulation.[2] I was very surprised that I had not come across this material before then. Where was the discussion of these extremely important, and potentially very controversial matters, not just in the academy but in public debates more generally?[3] While academic scholarship has caught up with these developments, public debate remains scandalously absent. Indeed, in reality, it is only scholarship in common law countries and in the English language that has 'caught up'; there has been a long and detailed discussion of family law harmonisation in other European jurisdictions.

When writing, then, in 1999, about the possible creation of a family law for the European Union, I feared I was being too conspiratorial in suggesting such developments. I thought this would be yet another area of Community law in which proposals languished on bookshelves for years before being taken up and usually then radically amended and, if lucky, adopted. But I was wrong. With

1 This article became Clare McGlynn, 'A Family Law for the European Union?' in Jo Shaw (ed.), *Social Law and Policy in an Evolving European Union* (Oxford: Hart Publishing, 2000), 223–42.
2 See the Convention on Jurisdiction and the Recognition and Enforcement of Judgments in Matrimonial Matters, OJ 1998 C 221/1, 16 July 1998, which was Communitarised by the adoption of the Regulation on jurisdiction and recognition and enforcement of judgments in matrimonial matters and in matters of parental responsibility for children of both spouses, Council Regulation No. 1347/2000 of 29 May 2000, OJ 2000 L 160/19, 30 July 2000.
3 But see Paul Beaumont and Gordon Moir, 'Brussels Convention II: A New Private International Law Instrument in Family Matters for the European Union or European Community?' (1995) 20 *European Law Review* 268–88.

incredible speed, the Matrimonial Convention was Communitarised,[4] an amended version has also now been adopted,[5] and further proposals are in the pipeline.[6] These developments are supported at the highest political levels and it is clear that we are only in the first stages of the development of the Union's competence in the field of family law.

So, while this book began life by examining the concept of family, it now also encompasses the Union's family law. These two fields of inquiry are, of course, intimately connected. One of my major concerns with the Union's developing family law is that the existing Union concept of family is based on the dominant ideology of family, premised on the heterosexual married family and the sexual division of labour. For this reason alone, we should be worried about developing Union competence to regulate families and family life. But there are of course further concerns with such developments, as discussed later in the book.

Outline of the book

The discussion in the book proceeds as follows. The first two chapters aim to set the theoretical foundation for the rest of the book. In chapter 1, I consider recent thought on the jurisprudence of the European Union and conclude that the Union is more a postmodern than modern polity. I suggest that Rawlsian pluralism gives us a basis from which to develop the postmodern critique into something more positive and constructive and which meets the lack of a European public philosophy. The realistic, pragmatic, but still positive, basis for such a public philosophy, I suggest, is human rights. These ideas are developed in chapter 2, which examines the dominant ideology of the family, before going on to consider the realities of family life, the new sociological explanations for changes in family practices and the new and emerging ideals of family life. I argue that the Union must embrace a more diverse, pluralist concept of family than has hitherto been the case, based on human rights principles. It is this expanded concept of family which should form the basis for the European Union's regulation of families and emerging family law.

The following three chapters consider different aspects of the concept of family employed by European Union law. Chapter 3 examines the concept of the child and children's rights. The role and place of children within the dominant ideology of the family is considered, before going on to examine the newer ways of thinking about children and their rights and interests. While the European Union

---

4 Regulation on jurisdiction and recognition and enforcement of judgments in matrimonial matters and in matters of parental responsibility for children of both spouses, Council Regulation No. 1347/2000 of 29 May 2000, OJ 2000 L 160/19, 30 July 2000.

5 Council Regulation No. 2201/2003 of 27 November 2003 concerning jurisdiction and in recognition and enforcement of judgments in matrimonial matters and in matters of parental responsibility, repealing Regulation 1347/2000, OJ 2003 L 338/1, 23 December 2003.

6 For further discussion, see chapters 6 and 7.

(still) has no children's policy to speak of, European Union law is adapting to change and is beginning to reflect more modern approaches to children and their rights. Children's rights in the context of the free movement of persons, the reconciliation of paid work and family life and the evolving family law are analysed. The final section in this chapter examines how the Union's Charter of Fundamental Rights and a rights-based approach to children's law and policy provide the most appropriate way forward for the Union.

Parenthood is the subject of chapter 4. At first sight, it may not be obvious that European Union law and policy engages with the concepts of motherhood and fatherhood. However, as similarly discussed in the previous chapter regarding children, it became clear relatively early in the history of the Community that the impact of its economic policies extended far beyond the mere completion of a single market. In particular, the development of sex equality policies necessarily involved the concept of parenthood, regardless of what the Court of Justice first sought to claim. Thus, for so long as sex equality is an objective of Community policy, the concept of parenthood will be a focus for debate within Community law. Similarly, the Union's employment policy, with its aim to increase the labour market participation of women, must address the balance of paid work and family life, and therefore parental roles, if it is to be successful in achieving its aims. In terms of the future, it may be the Union's emerging family law that will in time have the most impact on the rights of parents and the nature of the parental role. As yet, the direction of these measures is not clear, although the first indications are not wholly positive.

This chapter argues, therefore, that the approach of the Union to parenthood is at best described as ambiguous. The concept of parenthood in the dominant ideology of family is critiqued, followed by a discussion of a more appropriate foundation for the legal regulation of the concept of parenthood. I argue that, if the Community is to achieve its goal of greater workplace participation by women, and if the Union is to receive the support of the European citizens for its incursions into the controversial field of family law, and if the Union is to meet its human rights commitments as detailed in the Charter of Fundamental Rights, it must embrace a concept of parenthood which is more gender neutral than gender distinctive and which furthers the ideals of equal parenting.

Chapter 5 considers the role of European Union law in the regulation of intimate relationships. As with parenthood, it may be desirable that there is no regulation of intimate relations at the Union level, but this is not realistic in view of the competence of the Union. In the fields of equality, free movement, immigration, asylum and judicial co-operation, to name just a few areas, it is simply not possible for the Union to avoid encroaching on personal relationships. Indeed, the very existence of the right to marry in the European Convention on Human Rights, and the transposition of a similar right into the Union's Charter of Fundamental Rights, precludes any attempt to eliminate marriage as a legal category, however desirable that might be. The Union, therefore, has to take a stance on the politically charged and controversial questions regarding the status of marriage, cohabitation and same sex relationships.

At present, the Union, and particularly the Court of Justice, remain faithful to a traditional ideology of the family, with life-long, monogamous, heterosexual marriage viewed, in practice, as the sole legitimate partnership. Nonetheless, the sands are shifting, albeit slowly. The dramatically changing nature and form of family practices are slowly being recognised. That most Member States are already acknowledging this changing landscape of family life in their law and policy is perhaps influencing the Union in turn to take an increasingly progressive approach. In addition, the Court of Justice is beginning to take seriously the application of human rights norms to Community law, at the same time as the Union legislature appears to be increasingly convinced by its own human rights rhetoric. While this remains a patchwork application of human rights principles, it provides a basis for further innovation. Finally, the Union's ambition of creating an area of freedom, justice and security is bringing about demands for further measures to facilitate movement both in order to secure political, integrationist objectives, but also to continue the economic ambition of eradicating obstacles to the free movement of Union citizens.

The final two chapters move from considering the concept of family to the European Union's emerging family law. Chapter 6 examines the background to and development of Union activity in this field and interrogates the justifications for such action. It also considers the detail of the legislation thus far adopted and examines the more immediate proposals for the future. The family law thus far adopted is criticised for its reliance on a dominant ideology of the family and for its instrumental nature. That is, family law has become a focus for legislative attention in the Union more to achieve the aims of greater integration and economic success, than for more appropriate motives regarding the easier and quicker resolution of cross-national family disputes.

Chapter 7 considers the long-term prospects for the development of family law in the Union. The chapter begins by outlining the harmonisation/codification debates in private law, leading to a discussion of recent developments regarding family law in particular. It then proceeds to consider the reasons for opposing greater convergence of family laws, including an analysis of debate as to whether or not European family laws are converging and an examination of the problematic jurisprudential foundation for any proposed code. I argue that the common human rights norms of Europe should form the bedrock of all national family laws, but, beyond this commonality, diversity should reign. Where convergence results from the normal interchange of ideas and policies, this is to be welcomed. This is indeed one of the benefits of diverse and plural legal systems: arguably the 'success' of family law requires an ongoing conversation between law reform approaches and possibilities. But convergence at the behest of ideological, political and jurisprudential commitments to universality, supposed jurisprudential coherence and rationality and deeper European integration should be opposed.

Accordingly, the chapter concludes by calling for more fluid and diverse approaches to any further co-ordination of the family laws of the Member States of the Union, warning that greater harmonisation may in fact promote disintegration, rather than greater European integration, contrary to the wishes of harmonisation/codification advocates.

This book, therefore, discusses some of the interstices of European Union law. The aim is to bring together these seemingly disparate aspects of Union law and to see them as a whole. To consider the concept of family employed across a spectrum of fields of substantive law. To consider the rights of children, or the regulation of intimate relationships, conceptually, and not just tied to a particular aspect of Community or Union law. To see the connections between discussions of the concept of family and the emergence of a European Union family law.

In doing so, no attempt has been made to examine the entire field of European Union law. Children's rights and interests, for example, are affected by many areas of law and policy not considered in chapter 3. It would simply not be possible within the confines of this book to have done so; nor was that the aim of a text which seeks to examine selected areas of Union law, conceptually. Equally, in terms of analysing the concept of family, there are other aspects of 'family' which could have been considered, but were simply beyond the scope of this study, including the right to family life, or not to have a family (with the impact of single market rules on access to infertility treatment and abortion especially pertinent). Accordingly, the focus of this book has been on seeking to establish a theoretical and conceptual framework for an analysis of 'family' and 'family law' in the European Union, using such insights in three case studies on different aspects of the family and to examine the emerging family law of the Union.

Acknowledgments

In writing this book, I have had the help, assistance and support of many people. Much of the preliminary research was carried out while I was Visiting Associate Professor at Stockholm University in 1999. I should like to thank Professor Ronnie Eklund both for inviting me to Stockholm and for his continuing support and interest in my academic work. Thanks must also go to Professor Barbara Hobson of Stockholm University for many stimulating discussions and seminars. My time in Sweden, and frequent return visits, also involving collaboration with colleagues at the universities of Lund and Umea, have greatly enhanced my understanding of issues of families, feminism and law. Working with Professor Kevat Nouisianen and Anu Pylkkänen of the University of Helsinki also helped to shape many of the ideas expressed in this book.

I have benefited from funding from the Arts and Humanities Research Council Research Leave Scheme and the British Academy Travel Fund. The Department of Law at the University of Durham has also been very supportive of my research and I should like to particularly thank Bob Sullivan and Colin Warbrick for their support for this project and my academic career generally. There are many others in the department whom I should like to thank for their friendship, wise counsel, sense of humour and collegiality, including Dapo Akande (now at Oxford), Ronan Deazley, Lorna Fox, Panos Koutrakos, Sonia Harris-Short and Claire McIvor. The support of the Durham European Law Institute and Rosa Greaves, especially in providing the excellent and the invaluable research assistance of Sebastian Harter-Bachmann, is much appreciated.

I have enjoyed discussion and debate on the themes considered in this book with many colleagues following seminars at the universities of Aberdeen, Cardiff, Kent, Manchester and Nottingham. I was also greatly assisted by comments from participants at the Law and Society conference in Budapest in 2001. I am grateful to Katharina Boele-Woelki and Masha Antokolskaia for inviting me to speak at the inaugural conference of the Commission on European Family Law, entitled 'Perspectives on the Unification and Harmonisation of Family Law in Europe', at the University of Utrecht in 2002. Discussions at that conference, and subsequently, have advanced my understanding of, and thinking on, this complex field of enquiry. Many other colleagues have happily shared ideas, sources and views, which I have much appreciated; so thank you to Mark Bell, Eugenia Caracciolo di Torella, Peter McEleavy and Ian Sumner. I have enjoyed many discussions with Helen Stalford, on a whole range of different subjects, including the subject matter of this book, and would like to thank her for all her help. I should also like to thank many other colleagues and friends with whom I have enjoyed academic debate and support over the years, not least Rosemary Auchmuty, Joanne Conaghan, Tammy Hervey and Celia Wells.

I would like to thank my parents, Archie and Leah, for their ongoing love and support; Ross and Freya for the joy and fun (and scallywaggery) they bring to my life. My final thanks are for Ian who has had to live with this project for far too long and without whom it could genuinely not have been realised. Thank you Ian for helping to shape the ideas advanced in this book, not only professionally through many lengthy discussions of various theories and approaches, but also personally, by demonstrating the true value of love, friendship and family.

Table of Cases

Table of legislation and documents

International documents

League of Nations / United Nation

Geneva Declaration of the Rights of the Child of 1924, adopted 26 September 1924, League of Nations OJ Spec. Supp. 21, at 43 (1924) 67

Universal Declaration of Human Rights, GA Resolution 217A (III), 10 December 1948, UN Doc. A/810 at 71 (1948) 13, 67

Art. 25 67

Art. 29 13

Declaration of the Rights of the Child, GA Resolution 1386 (XIV), 14 UN GAOR Supp. (No. 16) at 19, UN Doc. A/4354 (1959) 67–8

International Covenant on Economic, Social and Cultural Rights, GA Resolution 2200A (XXI), 16 December 1966, in force 3 January 1976, UN Doc. A/6316 (1966), 993 UNTS 3; (1967) 6 ILM 360 13

Art. 7 13

Art. 10 13

Art. 11 13

International Covenant on Civil and Political Rights, GA Resolution 2200A (XXI), 16 December 1966, in force 23 March 1976, UN Doc. A/6316 (1966), 999 UNTS 171; (1967) 6 ILM 368 13

Art. 23 13

Convention on the Elimination of All Forms of Discrimination Against Women, GA Resolution 34/180, 18 December 1979, in force 3 September 1981, UN Doc. A/34/46 (1979); (1980) 19 ILM 33 13

Preamble 13–14

Art. 5 14

Convention on the Rights of the Child, GA Resolution 44/25, 20 November 1989, in force 2 September 1990, UN Doc. A/44/49 (1989); (1989) 28 ILM 1456 14, 20, 21, 68–9, 76–7, 170

Preamble 14

Art. 2 68

Art. 3 68, 70

Hague Conference on Private International Law

European legislation and documents

EC Treaties

Resolutions

Communications

Actions

Council Joint Action 96/700/JHA of 29 November 1996 establishing an incentive and exchange programme for persons responsible for combating trade in human beings and the sexual exploitation of children, OJ 1996 L 322/7 22, 63

Council Joint Action 97/154/JHA of 24 February 1997 concerning action to combat trafficking in human beings and sexual exploitation of children, OJ 1997 L 63/2 63

Recommendations and Reports

Jenard Report, OJ 1979 C 59 155

Council Recommendation on childcare 92/241/EEC, OJ 1992 L 123/16 59–60, 61, 93, 94

European Parliament, Report on the situation as regards fundamental rights in the European Union (2000), A5-0223/2001 150

European Parliament, Annual report on respect for human rights in the European Union (1998–9), A5-0050/2000 150

Conclusions of the Council and of the Ministers responsible for family affairs meeting within the Council of 29 September 1989 regarding family policies, OJ 1989 C 277/2 153, 154

Council Act of 28 May 1998 drawing up the Convention on jurisdiction and the recognition and enforcement of judgments in matrimonial matters, OJ 1998 C 221/1 11–12, 156–7, 159, 160–1, 163, 167–71

Explanatory Report on the Convention on jurisdiction and the recognition and enforcement of judgments in matrimonial matters prepared by Dr Alegría Borrás Professor of Private International Law University of Barcelona, OJ 1998 C 221/27 157–8, 163

Presidency Conclusions, Tampere European Council 15–16 October 1999 159

Recommendation 1470 (2000) on the situation of gays and lesbians and their partners in respect of asylum and immigration in the Member States of the Council of Europe 150

Recommendation 1474 (2000) on the situation of gays and lesbians and their partners in the Council of Europe Member States 150

Draft programme of measures for implementation of the principle of mutual recognition of decisions in civil and commercial matters, OJ 2001 C 12/1 174

Council Report on the need to approximate Member States' legislation in civil matters, Council Report No. 13017/01 of 29 October 2001, adopted on 16 November 2001 174, 181, 184, 197, 198

National legislation

United Kingdom

Sexual Offences Act 2003 66

1

Pluralism and human rights: a legal foundation for the regulation of families and family law in the European Union

Any study of European Union law must be set within a theoretical framework. Accordingly, the aim of this and the following chapter is to establish just such a framework, laying the foundations for the subsequent examination of the concept of family and emerging family law of the Union. This chapter begins by offering a brief sketch of recent jurisprudential debates regarding the nature and future of European legal integration. This is an essential precursor to the subsequent section which proposes a human rights foundation for analysing concepts of family and as a basis for the Union's family law.

1.1   Positivism, pluralism and the jurisprudence of the European Union

During the previous decade or more, the impact of European integration on established jurisprudential paradigms has become ever more apparent. In simple terms, nothing really seems to fit any more. On the one hand, classical legal positivism, so dependent upon conceptions of unitary sovereignty, coherent systems, hierarchies and rules, suddenly appears to be hopelessly arcane. On the other, the more radical postmodern critique, whilst celebrating this apparent incoherence, rarely seems capable of answering the more pressing policy questions.

The aim of this section is to suggest that the way forward lies between these extremes, with a system of rules that is better able to address the questions of particularity and 'otherness' that underpin the postmodern critique and which moves away from the paradigms of positivism. This is a solution which caters to reality. The new Europe is very much a legalistic Europe. It is often proclaimed that the defining characteristic of the Union is the extent to which it was engineered by lawyers. Law, as one prominent European judge famously declared, is part of the Union's 'genetic code'.[1] Accordingly, families in Europe are regulated and constructed by law, and the evolving family law is described by rules and

---

1 Federico Mancini and David Keeling, 'From CILFIT to ERT: The Constitutional Challenge Facing the European Court' (1991) 11 *Yearbook of European Law* 1–13.

legal, moral and social norms, and any change, therefore, requires a legal theory and solution which can effect change.

1.1.1   Positivism and its critics

Classical positivism finds its most famous expression in the writings of jurists such as Jeremy Bentham, John Austin and Herbert Hart. All three were determined to do two things. First, they distinguished questions of law from questions of morality and therefore reduced the theory of law to a matter of distinguishing systems of legally credible and enforceable rules. Secondly, in order to give their systems of rules a necessary coherence, they were equally determined to identify ultimate sources of authority, or sovereign bodies.

The first argument of the classical positivist, that questions of law can be readily distinguished from questions of morality, has attracted considerable criticism for centuries. On the one hand, natural lawyers have long held that any law is infused with moral attributes and effects. More recent critics have added further fuel to the critical fire, by asserting that laws are also political, as well as moral, expressions. They denote, in simple terms, the locus, not so much of right, as of power. Indeed, it is not too much to say that it seems absurd today to suggest that law is devoid of political or ideological content. With regard to this first critique of classical legal positivism, the European experience is typical, but not particularly unique.

It is in regard to the second strand of the positivists' theories that the European experience has been more atypical, with the uncompromising destruction of all the pretences of unitary sovereignty. There is, in simple terms, no single source of legal or political authority in the new Europe, and nor is there, accordingly, any such authority in any of the constituent nation-states. As Neil MacCormick famously put it, Europe has moved 'beyond the nation-state'. And it has, accordingly, moved beyond the idea of a unitary sovereign authority; an idea that was intrinsically related to modern ideas of the unitary nation-state. MacCormick concludes that we have escaped from the 'idea that all law must originate in a single power source, like a sovereign', and in doing so we have the possibility to discover a 'broader, more diffuse, view of the law'.[2]

This admission has not led to the wholesale abandonment of classical doctrines of legal positivism.[3] There are still some who pine after coherent systems of rules and norms. According to Reinhard Zimmermann, for example, legal positivism, and only legal positivism, can provide the necessary intellectual sustenance to the idea of a 'European legal science'. There is, Zimmermann alleges, an irreducible

---

2 Neil MacCormick, 'Beyond the Sovereign State' (1993) 56 *Modern Law Review* 1–18 at 8.

3 See also the work of those who are seeking to revisit positivism for a new age, proposing a 'general' jurisprudence that would allow us to re-map our new world order, describing firm legalistic boundaries but also accommodating the substantive political, social and cultural differences that now exist. For a compelling argument along these lines, see William Twining, *Globalisation and Legal Theory* (London: Butterworths, 2000).

'internal coherence' to the law, understood as an 'autonomous discipline'. Zimmermann is desperate to address what he perceives to be the kind of 'higgledy-piggledy' jurisprudence which presently characterises European law.[4] Unsurprisingly, perhaps, Zimmermann is particularly enamoured by legal codes. The idea of a European code of private law has gained considerable currency in contemporary European debates. For some it appears to be the obvious next step in the process of legal integration, despite its resting on an arcane approach to legal theory. Others have suggested that this desire for codes and coherence represents something of a missed opportunity. As Pierre Legrand has suggested, the construction of a new Europe gives us the chance to reach 'beyond a mode of apprehending social relations which has traditionally been linked to the state'.[5] We should, he suggests, have the courage to take this opportunity.

Support for this idea of moving 'beyond' can be found in the ideas of cosmopolitanism, derived from the writings of the German philosopher Immanuel Kant, and applied to the European Union. Cosmopolitanism, recommended by the likes of Ian Ward and Pavlos Eleftheriadis, demonstrates the fallacy of the traditional positivist ideals when considering the context of Europe.[6] Cosmopolitanism deals in the relations between individuals, rather than in the relations between states: it is indeed a 'new kind of law'.[7] This has echoes for the European experience, with its Charter of rights and citizens' rights: it increasingly speaks to individuals and not to nation-states. This is, perhaps, more obviously a cosmopolitan than a Westphalian order which is concerned with relations between states. And it seems, as Eleftheriadis has rightly suggested, to fit the reality of the new Europe, the legal system of which 'is a synthesis of national constitutions, international treaties and an area of cosmopolitan law which applies regardless of hierarchies of sources or state sovereignty'.[8] Eleftheriadis confirms that this Kantian idea of cosmopolitan governance admits a conception of law that does not require firm boundaries or strong hierarchies. Indeed, it embraces the idea that the authority of law might be multidimensional. These ideas have attracted the support of many, including Jürgen Habermas who has argued the need for a 'future cosmopolitan order sensitive both to difference and to social equality'.[9]

4 Reinhard Zimmermann, 'Savigny's Legacy – Legal History, Comparative Law and the Emergence of European Legal Science' (1996) 112 *Law Quarterly Review* 576–605 at 582–5. See also Christoph Schmid, 'The Emergence of a Transnational Legal Science in European Private Law' (1999) 19 *Oxford Journal of Legal Studies* 673–89, who speaks of the 'chaotic situations' of Community law, at 674.
5 Pierre Legrand, 'Against a European Civil Code' (1997) 60 *Modern Law Review* 44–63 at 59.
6 Ian Ward, 'Kant and the Transnational Order: Towards a European Community Jurisprudence' (1995) 8 *Ratio Juris* 315–29; Pavlos Eleftheriadis, 'Cosmopolitan Law' (2003) 9 *European Law Journal* 241–63.
7 Eleftheriadis, 'Cosmopolitan Law', 242.
8 Eleftheriadis, 'Cosmopolitan Law', 259.
9 Jürgen Habermas, *The Postnational Constellation* (Cambridge: Polity Press, 2001), p. xix.

While cosmopolitanism seeks to chart a middle way between the perceived extremes of intergovernmentalism and federalism, it is the postmodern critique which is embracing the apparent incoherence that the experience of European integration has brought. In his essay, *The Other Heading*, Derrida famously suggested that the 'universal' of Europe was its respect for 'differentness' and it was this apparently ambiguous determinant that made the European project endemically postmodern.[10] It is a view that echoes Albert Camus' famous injunction, made half a century earlier: 'Unity and diversity, and never one without the other – isn't that the very secret of our Europe?'[11] At the same time, however, according to Derrida, the ever-present danger within the present project of 'integration' is that the pretences of uniformity might suppress particularity and respect for 'otherness'.[12]

A wave of European lawyers has followed the Derridean lead. It has been suggested that the 'European Union can be best understood as a postmodern text, and perhaps as a postmodern polity'.[13] Likewise, Deirdre Curtin has argued that the reality of a 'fragmented and fluid' Europe impels us to contemplate the complementary reality of a 'post-national', even 'post-modern', Europe.[14] James Caporaso has described a 'post-modern' Europe that is 'abstract, disjointed, increasingly fragmented, not based on stable or coherent coalitions of issues or constituencies, and lacking in a clear public space within which competitive visions of the good life and pursuit of self-interested legislation are discussed and debated'.[15] This latter thought resonates with the argument that what Europe really lacks today is a credible and inspiring public philosophy, a concern considered further below.

There are, perhaps, two potential problems with the postmodern critique. The first is that it might just be plain wrong. In this vein, Peter Fitzpatrick has suggested that the 'new' Europe is actually not that new at all, but rather a quintessentially modern phenomenon. Of course, the same implication lies behind Derrida's critique. But it is a conclusion that leads Fitzpatrick to doubt the bolder assertions that the new Europe might describe some kind of postmodern 'text'. All the plumage of modernity, he suggests, is proudly on display in Brussels,

---

10 Jacques Derrida, *The Other Heading: Reflections on Today's Europe* (Bloomington: Indiana University Press, 1992).

11 Albert Camus, *Resistance, Rebellion and Death* (London: Vintage, 1974), pp. 234–5. This has even been recognised recently by the European Parliament which noted that European unity was itself largely based on diversity: European Parliament Resolution on Cultural Co-operation in the European Union (2000/2323 (INI), OJ 2002 C 72E/142.

12 See Derrida, *The Other Heading*, pp. 11–12.

13 Ian Ward, 'Identity and Difference: The European Union and Postmodernism' in Jo Shaw and Gillian More (eds.), *New Legal Dynamics of European Union* (Oxford: Oxford University Press, 1995), pp. 15–28 at p. 15.

14 Deirdre Curtin, *Postnational Democracy: The European Union in Search of a Public Philosophy* (The Hague: Kluwer Law International, 1997), p. 16.

15 James Caporaso, 'The European Union and Forms of the State: Westphalian, Regulatory or Post-Modern' (1996) 34 *Journal of Common Market Studies* 29–52 at 45.

Strasbourg and Luxembourg: laws and charters of rights, courts and parliaments.[16] The presence of such institutions likewise counsels Jürgen Habermas to prefer the idea of a Europe that is intellectually 'post-metaphysical' if not politically postmodern.[17] There is an element of realism here; for, as Alan Dashwood has affirmed in much the same spirit, when all is said and done, for the present at least, the new Europe is still a Europe of constituent nation-states, even if it is overlaid by some kind of transnational economic, legal, and to a degree political, order.[18] In this way, the modern and postmodern do not have to be mutually exclusive. We are undoubtedly living in a more postmodern, than modern, Europe. There is indeed a diversity of legal structures, multiple sites of legal power, a post-national constitution. But there remain central elements of our more modern traditions, predominantly the trappings of nation-states. So, we must recognise the new legal and political environment of Europe, but not get lost in utopian or disutopian excurses on postmodernism.

The second problem with the postmodern critique of European legal integration is a variant of the wider general critique of postmodernism. Deconstructing things is easy; constructing something that can work in their place is altogether harder to do. And yet it must be done. The regulation of families by the European Union is relentless and a European family law is emergent. There are virtues and vices in these developments and, while it may be very well to identify each, what really matters is suggesting how there might be rather more of the former, and rather fewer of the latter. There are two compelling, and related, possibilities. The first lies in the more theoretical realm of legal pluralism. The second can be found in the idea of rights.

1.1.2   Pluralism

Pluralism has emerged as perhaps the most intriguing theoretical solution to the jurisprudential challenges posed by the experience of European integration. The idea of a 'constitutional pluralism' has been ventured by Neil Walker and also by Ingolf Pernice who refers to a constitutionalism that is 'multilevel' and in which there is a 'divided power system' with governance conducted at various levels.[19] It has also found a strong expression in Neil MacCormick's embrace of a 'new form of legal and plural order' in Europe, one that can accommodate both integration and differentiation. It is the idea of a legal pluralism that underpins MacCormick's vision of a 'broader, more diffuse, view of law'.[20] Such pluralism is

---

16 Peter Fitzpatrick, 'New Europe and Old Stories: Mythology and Legality in the European Union' in Peter Fitzpatrick and James Bergeron (eds.), *Europe's Other: European Law between Modernity and Postmodernity* (Aldershot: Ashgate, 1998), pp. 27–46.

17 Habermas, *The Postnational Constellation.*

18 Alan Dashwood, 'States in the European Union' (1998) 23 *European Law Review* 201–16.

19 See Neil Walker, 'The Idea of Constitutional Pluralism' (2002) 65 *Modern Law Review* 317–59 and Ingolf Pernice, 'Multilevel Constitutionalism and the Treaty of Amsterdam: European Constitution-Making Revisited' (1999) 36 *Common Market Law Review* 703–50.

20 MacCormick, 'Sovereign State', 153.

often presented in terms of multiplicity. Joseph Weiler's idea of 'multiple *demoi*', of a politics that is encountered and engaged in a variety of public spaces and at all levels in European governance, speaks to this idea of multiplicity in action.[21]

There is, of course, a resonance between aspects of legal pluralism and the kind of postmodern jurisprudence discussed above. Certainly the kind of pluralism recommended by Emilios Christodoulidis, one that embraces a consciously 'disorganised civil society, genuinely plural, resistant to dominant representation', seems to speak to a more radical idea of pluralism. It should, Christodoulidis argues, translate the Derridean urge to deconstruct into a 'constitutional irresolution' that can actually nourish genuine democratic engagement.[22] The same kind of postmodern rhetoric can also be heard in Christodoulidis' earlier suggestion, made with Zenon Bankowski, that the new Europe should be understood as being an 'essentially contested project', one in which there is a 'continuous process of negotiation and renegotiation'.[23] In this way, the postmodern critique and explanation of the new Europe feeds into a reconstructive jurisprudence of pluralism.

This jurisprudence of pluralism is perhaps best illustrated in the constructivist theories of law and society espoused by John Rawls.[24] Developing his earlier, and hugely influential, idea of 'justice as fairness' famously presented in *A Theory of Justice*, Rawls returned to Kantian ideas of moral constructivism in order to flesh out a more 'practicable' theory of justice in his series of essays entitled 'Kantian Constructivism in Moral Theory'.[25] As opposed to the potentially anarchic implications of radical postmodern scepticism, Rawls held that his revised 'Justice as Fairness tries to construct a conception of justice that takes deep and unresolvable differences on matters of fundamental significance as a permanent condition of human life'.[26] Thus, rather than chasing the illusory shadows of presumed ethical commonality, Rawls suggested that the role of a 'constructivist' legal theory is to secure mechanisms within which a plurality of moral positions might be accommodated. It should thus provide the 'formal condition' for a 'well-ordered society'.[27]

It is also liberating and democratic: for although 'a well-ordered society is divided and pluralistic, its citizens have nevertheless reached an understanding on principles to regulate their basic institutions'.[28] In practice, Rawls affirmed, it

21 Joseph Weiler, *The Constitution of Europe* (Cambridge: Cambridge University Press, 1999), p. 262.
22 Emilios Christodoulidis, 'Constitutional Irresolution: Law and the Framing of Civil Society' (2003) 9 *European Law Journal* 401–32.
23 Zenon Bankowski and Emilios Christodoulidis, 'The European Union as an Essentially Contested Project' (1998) 4 *European Law Journal* 341–54 at 342.
24 An idea suggested by Eleftheriadis, 'Cosmopolitan Law', 261–3.
25 John Rawls, 'Kantian Constructivism in Moral Theory' (1980) 77 *Journal of Philosophy* 515–72 at 518.
26 Rawls, 'Kantian Constructivism', 542.
27 Rawls, 'Kantian Constructivism', 516–19.
28 Rawls, 'Kantian Constructivism', 537–40.

presumes little, except the willingness of citizens to converse, to respect the different values of others, and to engage in constructing approximate and contingent models of the good society.[29] Alongside this pluralist idea of 'justice as fairness', Rawls advanced a complementary idea of an 'overlapping consensus'. The idea of such 'consensus', Rawls suggested, is that it 'enables us to understand how a constitutional regime characterized by the fact of pluralism might, despite its deep divisions, achieve stability and social unity by the public recognition of a reasonable conception of justice'.[30] It is a mechanism for promoting liberty and democracy, as well as demanding respect for cultural, moral and political difference. It recognises the 'fact of reasonable pluralism', whilst also providing the degree of political and social stability that a 'good society' requires.

In the final passages of his *Political Liberalism*, Rawls presented a compelling defence of his constructivist variant of legal pluralism:

> The conception of justice to which these principles belong is not to be regarded as a method of answering the jurist's questions, but as a guiding framework, which if jurists find it convincing, may orient their reflections, complement their knowledge, and assist their judgment. We must not ask too much of a philosophical view. A conception of justice fulfils its social role provided that persons equally conscientious and sharing roughly the same beliefs find that, by affirming the framework of deliberation set up on it, they are normally led to a sufficient convergence of judgment necessary to achieve effective and fair social cooperation.[31]

The attractions of Rawlsian pluralism are obvious. It provides a framework for the European legal and political order that is plural, that respects individual differences and different moral positions, that requires citizens to converse, respect each other and engage in dialogue in seeking an 'overlapping consensus' and that provides the foundations for a 'well-ordered' society, without a top-down imposition of moral standards. And, as Rawls' later work on international order emphasised, there is no compelling reason why they should not apply to a community as grand as the European.[32] Indeed, given the reality of such deep cultural, moral and political plurality in the new Europe, Rawlsian pluralism becomes ever more compelling.

1.1.3   The search for a public philosophy

While Rawls provides the basis for a legal and political order in Europe, it does not prescribe the content of those rules which might characterise the 'overlapping consensus'. It is such a vacuum which has been identified by many as representing a lack of public philosophy for the Union. Law, as Václav Havel rightly observed,

---

29 Rawls, 'Kantian Constructivism', 560–1.
30 John Rawls, 'The Idea of an Overlapping Consensus' (1987) 7 *Oxford Journal of Legal Studies* 1–25 at 2.
31 John Rawls, *Political Liberalism* (New York: Columbia University Press, 1993), p. 368.
32 John Rawls, *The Law of Peoples* (Cambridge, MA: Harvard University Press, 1999).

can only do so much. There has to be more: a 'legal relationship or legal order must be preceded by a connection to an order from the realm of morality, because only a moral commitment imbues the legal arrangements with meaning and makes them truly valid'.[33] Havel is blunt:

> To put it more succinctly, Europe today lacks an ethos; it lacks imagination, it lacks generosity, it lacks the ability to see beyond the horizon of its own particular interests, be they partisan or otherwise, and to resist pressure from various lobbying groups. It lacks a genuine identification with the meaning and purpose of integration. Europe appears not to have achieved a genuine and profound sense of responsibility for itself as a whole, and thus for the future of all those who live in it.[34]

It is a striking condemnation. The absence of a coherent and compelling public philosophy underpins the 'crisis of legitimacy' described by Weiler who came to the 'disconcerting realization that Europe has become an end in itself', and is, accordingly, 'no longer a means for higher human ends'.[35] The idea that Europe's present 'crisis of legitimacy' might be traced to the fatal absence of a public philosophy has been enjoined by the likes of Deirdre Curtin, Larry Siedentop and Ian Ward.[36] According to Ward, the crisis of legitimacy aligns questions of democracy, citizenship and rights. Seizing upon Romano Prodi's proclamation of a coming 'decade' of Europe made back in 2000, Ward suggests that:

> The success or failure of the prospective 'decade' of Europe will not lie in drafting more statutes, arguing more cases, or even making more money. If the 'decade' of Europe is actually to address the 'question' of Europe, it will have to engage once again with an intellectual tradition which champions democracy and humanity, tolerance and compassion.[37]

More recently, the search for a European public philosophy has been championed by Larry Siedentop, who argues that Europe's present 'crisis' is rooted in a mindset that is driven by the demands of 'economism' rather than 'moral consensus'. Where liberalism was once a philosophy of 'human flourishing' and of 'passion', it is now one of alienation and competition. The new Europe is a symbol of this morally impoverished and 'distorted' liberalism.[38] There is, indeed, precious little public philosophy to make sense of Rawlsian pluralism.

33 Václav Havel, *The Art of the Impossible – Politics as Morality in Practice* (New York: Fromm International, 1998), pp. 247–8.
34 Havel, *Art of the Impossible*, pp. 129–30.
35 Weiler, *Constitution of Europe*, p. 259.
36 See Curtin, *Postnational Democracy*; Larry Siedentop, *Democracy in Europe* (London: Penguin, 2000); and Ian Ward, 'The European Constitution, the Treaty of Amsterdam and the Search for Community' (1999) 27 *Georgia Journal of International and Comparative Law* 519–40.
37 Ian Ward, 'A Decade of Europe? Some Reflections on an Aspiration' (2003) 30 *Journal of Law and Society* 236–57 at 257.
38 Siedentop, *Democracy in Europe*, pp. 28–40, 230–1.

1.1.4   Human rights

This leads to a reconsideration of the role of human rights in the Union. Rights are the cornerstone of modern liberal legalism and of European Community and Union law. Indeed, rights have always existed at the heart of Europe and its legal order. The various rights of freedom of movement were a key dynamic in the creation of the common market, and there have always been some, if not too many, collateral social rights. But there has, equally, always been a sense that the Union has not taken rights 'seriously' for their own sake, but merely as tools for the pursuit of economic aspirations.[39] It is perhaps only with the adoption of the Charter of Fundamental Rights that any real commitment to human rights has been realised. A structure of rights, still more so a Charter of rights, presents itself as precisely the kind of structure that a Rawlsian pluralist would expect in any 'well-ordered society'. It should provide a frame of reference within which a discursive democratic society can operate. As such, it is only the beginning, a statement of broad, and contingent, values, not a presumed assertion of legalistic finality.

In this way, it should help to counter one of the most strident criticisms of those who are dismissive of rights and charters of rights, namely that rights are limited by interpretative indeterminacy. Rights, in short, can mean different things to different people. Such an argument was a centrepiece of Critical Legal Studies' critiques of liberal legalism during the 1980s. Scholars were quick to seize on the apparent incoherence of rights in political practice. And indeterminacy is not the only mooted problem with rights. There is also the tendency for the presence of rights to somehow construct the ideal rights-bearing citizen. This assertion of 'ideal citizen' models, with its consequent marginalisation and exclusion of the non-ideal, carries a particular resonance for feminists.

Alongside doubts regarding the ideal liberal rights-based citizen is the related critique of negativity. Classical liberal rights tend to be negative, in the sense that they accept the dominant influence of John Stuart Mill's famous 'harm principle'. Accordingly, following Mill, liberal rights protect people from harm, they rarely try to construct solutions. They might, thus, try to protect children from being beaten, but say little about the empowering rights children should enjoy. And a further variant of this negativity critique is the disutility critique. The presence of rights, in charters or even just in the minds of certain judges, brings out the Pangloss in all of us; we assume, just because we have some rights, that we do indeed live in the 'best of all possible worlds'.

Such criticisms again have been central to the feminist distrust of rights. Feminists have argued that a concentration on rights, and their enforcement, can divert attention away from the political sphere: law is limited in its capacity to

---

39 See Jason Coppel and Aidan O'Neill, 'The European Court of Justice: Taking Rights Seriously?' (1992) 12 *Legal Studies* 227–45.

bring about changes for women, and it is political reform which offers the best hope for change. Allied to this argument is the fear that rights may in fact lead to a reduction in the existing entitlements of women. Litigation is an inherently risky business, especially when the interpretation of rights is in the hands of a conservative, predominantly male, judiciary. Therefore, surrendering to rights may in fact increase women's disadvantages, rather than improve women's situation. Thus, the dominance of rights discourse is seen as yet another facet of the reifying of law over political and social activism. It is also often suggested that framing reform struggles in terms of rights tends to produce 'politically conservative' or 'classical liberal outcomes'.[40] Thus, more progressive political activism becomes 'channeled and neutralized through the turn to rights'.[41]

There is no doubt that such arguments have force. Sets of charters of rights can be indeterminate, as well as negative in tone. They do presume a degree of commonality amongst citizens and they can be enervating. But, all the same, they are the centrepiece of modern liberal political philosophy and they are the favoured currency in today's Union. And, perhaps most importantly, in the absence of any credible alternative mechanism for promoting the liberties of individuals, and thereby respecting differences, they remain compelling. This essentially pragmatic argument has been famously presented by the likes of Patricia Williams. Speaking as a black woman in the United States, Williams is quick to confirm that working with rights is dramatically more effective than pontificating about indeterminacy in law journals.[42] The insight is valuable. We live in a juristic world of rights, just as we do a world of rules and laws, and it is within this world that a European family law is emerging. Rather than merely casting brickbats at the edifice of rights, it is perhaps better to try to make our rights-mentality better equipped to accommodate the acute diversities and particularities of European communities and citizens.

1.2   Human rights and families

1.2.1   Families and international human rights

The deployment of human rights norms to regulate families and family law can be seen as the result of two converging trends. The first is the growth of human rights norms and consciousness generally in politics and law in recent years. Human rights have become trumps in political and legal debates and have come to occupy an unprecedented place in political and legal discourse. Concepts of family and family law have not been immune to such developments. At the same

---

40   Carl Stychin, *Governing Sexuality: The Changing Politics of Citizenship and Law Reform* (Oxford: Hart Publishing, 2003), p. 78.
41   Carl Stychin, *Governing Sexuality*, p. 78.
42   See Patricia Williams, *The Alchemy of Race and Rights* (Cambridge, MA: Harvard University Press, 1991), pp. 146–65.

time, the changes in family practices discussed in the next chapter, and the resulting sociological explanations, also emphasise an increasing respect for individuals and their needs and desires, alongside those of groups, such as 'the family', or 'society' more generally. Thus, there could be said to be a movement from 'family' to the 'individual'. In terms of concepts of family, and family law, these trends demand that we look beyond the surface of 'the family' and to the interests and needs of individual family members. These two trends are of course related as the claims to autonomy could increasingly be arising as a result of the dominance of human rights norms, particularly the ideals of freedom and equality.

This disaggregation of 'the family', or 'fragmentation', or 'destruction', depending on how such developments are viewed, is controversial. Some suggest that it runs counter to the supposed ideals of family life based on mutual love and respect, rather than legal duties and rights. Thus, Roberto Unger has suggested that the 'very process' by which the 'members of a family cast their relationships in the language of formal entitlement would confirm and hasten the dissolution of the family'.[43] Similarly, Mary Ann Glendon has argued that an 'overblown rights rhetoric and our vision of the rights-bearer as an autonomous individual' channels our thoughts away from 'what we have in common and focuses them on what separates us'.[44] And Martha Fineman argues that individual rights and responsibilities have 'impeded the development of a concept of collective responsibility for children'.[45] This critique is based on the assumption that respect and protection of individual rights undermines the collective nature of the family unit. Valuing individual autonomy is seen to run counter to valuing families, community and society more generally. It is also a critique premised largely on the idea of the 'private family'; that is, that the family should be a private space free from interference by the state. This is part of the ideology of the family based on a separation of the public and private spheres, with state regulation being legitimate only in the public domain.

Feminists have long challenged the argument that there exists a private sphere free from state intervention that is being challenged by law and rights. It is the nature of the state regulation of the private sphere that is challenged. Indeed, it is the very state regulation relating to marriage, for example, which is the foundation of the traditional nuclear family. Without such state privileging of this family form, there would be little substance to the ideology of the family. As Gillian Douglas suggests, there is no such thing as 'non-intervention' in family life, because 'where law and policy draw a line, they mark a judgment on what is to

43 Roberto Unger, *The Critical Legal Studies Movement* (Cambridge, MA: Harvard University Press, 1986), p. 65.
44 Mary Ann Glendon, *Rights Talk: The Impoverishment of Political Discourse* (New York: The Free Press, 1991), p. 143.
45 Martha Albertson Fineman, *The Neutered Mother, the Sexual Family and Other Twentieth Century Tragedies* (London: Routledge, 1995), p. 199.

be regarded as acceptable behaviour between family members'.[46] Thus, as well as state rules regulating and privileging marriage there are state rules regarding divorce, domestic violence and sexual behaviour, for example, all of which involve state sanctioning of certain forms of behaviour. For so long as there is mutual love and respect within families, there will be no need for rights, or even no knowledge that such rights exist. However, when the love is absent, or manifests itself in ways society deems inimical, there is a need for legal interventions in family life in order to reveal and punish exploitation, violence and abuse, as well as providing an escape from inequalities, dominance and destructive power imbalances.

Accordingly, while family rights are resisted by some, on the basis of there being some magical private sphere which should remain free from state intrusion, there is in fact considerable regulation of the private sphere. Debate should focus on the nature of that regulation and the positive benefits that rights can bring. Rights can be used to redirect state intervention into more appropriate channels which better benefit women, children and families in general. Rights strategies can be employed to expand the concept of family, edging it away from the dominant ideology discussed further in the next chapter. Indeed, rights represent the most immediate political tool for alleviating the oppression of women and children within families. This has been a particularly resonant claim by minority groups in the United States where the critique of rights has been rejected and rights strategies favoured as the means by which minority groups began to gain access to and acceptance within public life. This argument relates to the importance and rhetoric of rights in the Western political process: addressing claims in terms of rights ensures a hearing in the present political context and provides one way of seeking to satisfy such claims. Thus, as Claire Archbold rightly argues, in a pluralistic society, the 'explicit introduction of human rights into the law making process is one way of ensuring that the competing interests of everyone, especially minority groups and those without significant lobbying power, are taken into account as fully as possible'.[47]

It is also evident from an examination of recent Canadian jurisprudence that it is via rights-based strategies that meaningful gains have been made in the family law field.[48] The litigation under the Canadian Charter has led to the recognition of non-married heterosexual partnerships as equivalent to marriage, has granted same-sex partners many of the same rights as unmarried heterosexual partners and, most recently, it was held that the ban on same-sex marriage breached the Canadian Charter.[49] Madam Justice L'Heureux-Dube has stated that the Canadian Charter precipitated two main changes in Canadian family law: first, the

---

46 Gillian Douglas, *An Introduction to Family Law* (Oxford: Oxford University Press, 2001), p. 14.
47 Claire Archbold, 'Family Law-Making and Human Rights in the UK' in Mavis Maclean (ed.), *Making Law for Families* (Oxford: Hart Publishing, 2000), pp. 185–208 at pp. 203–4.
48 Nicholas Bala and Rebecca Jaremko Bromwich, 'Context and Inclusivity in Canada's Evolving Definition of the Family' (2002) 16 *International Journal of Law, Policy and the Family* 145–80.
49 *Halpern et al.* v. *Attorney General of Canada* [2003] 14 BHRC 687.

'refashioning of anachronistic public law to reflect private realities more accurately' and, secondly, the 'penetration of parts of the formerly private sphere in the interest of public values'.[50] While there are concerns expressed with the normalising and disciplinary effect of some of these rulings on gay and lesbian partnerships,[51] the momentum that they have generated towards equality for lesbians and gay men, albeit on the basis of assimilation, has been considerable and has resulted in legislative changes entrenching the judicial pronouncements.

Further, human rights norms are not inimical to families or to the promotion of the values associated with family life. Savitri Goonesekere has demonstrated that international human rights norms in fact represent a balance between individual rights and duties to family and community.[52] For example, the 1948 Universal Declaration of Human Rights, which is recognised today as part of customary international law, states in Article 16(3) that 'the family is the natural and fundamental group unit of society and is entitled to protection by society and the State'.[53] While it is likely that such a statement was intended to refer, at the time of drafting, to the nuclear family, no less so because of its reference to 'the' family, it nonetheless leaves room for a broader definition. Thus, in a Declaration that protects the rights of individuals, we can see that broader social units, families, are also to be cherished and respected. This is confirmed by Article 29(1) which states that 'everyone has duties to the community in which alone the free and full development of his [or her] personality is possible'.

This balance between individual rights and families continues in the International Covenants on Civil and Political Rights and on Economic, Social and Cultural Rights, both adopted in 1966. Both Covenants require states to give protection and assistance to families as the 'natural and fundamental group unit of society'.[54] In addition to the Covenants, the Convention on the Elimination of All Forms of Discrimination against Women adopted in 1979 recognises the role of women within families, while maintaining the central importance of equality between women and men. Thus, women's roles within families are recognised, but these are not to be given precedence over her individuality and capacity outside families. Further, the preamble recognises that the traditional role of men within society and families must change if there is to be full equality between women and men and that states must recognise the 'common responsibility of

---

50 Claire L'Heureux-Dube, 'What a Difference a Decade Makes: The Canadian Constitution and the Family Since 1991' (2001) 27 *Queen's Law Journal* 361–71.

51 See Carl Stychin, *Governing Sexuality.*

52 Savitri Goonesekere, 'Human Rights as a Foundation for Family Law Reform' (2000) 8 *International Journal of Children's Rights* 83–99.

53 Universal Declaration of Human Rights, GA Resolution 217A (III), 10 December 1948, UN Doc. A/810 at 71 (1948).

54 International Covenant on Civil and Political Rights, GA Resolution 2200A (XXI), 16 December 1966, in force 23 March 1976, UN Doc. A/6316 (1966), 999 UNTS 171; (1967) 6 ILM 638, Article 23; and International Covenant on Economic, Social and Cultural Rights, GA Resolution 2200A (XXI), 16 December 1966, in force 3 January 1976, UN Doc. A/6316 (1966), 993 UNTS 3; (1967) 6 ILM 360, Articles 10, 7(a)(ii), 11.

men and women in the upbringing and development of their children'.[55] The same argument can be made regarding the United Nations Convention on the Rights of the Child: the preamble recognises that the family is 'the fundamental group of society' and the 'natural environment for the growth and well-being of all its members and particularly children'.[56] Thus, the concept of children's rights does not seek to separate them from their families, but to ensure their individuality and protection *within* families.[57]

The 'family' is therefore recognised in international human rights instruments as being a fundamental group in society deserving of protection. At the same time, the very notion of human rights respects individuals and their autonomy. The rights of families, therefore, can be used not just to protect individuals from harm within families, but also to ensure that families themselves are given attention by states. Further, as Goonesekere argues, as the concept of human rights has developed to include social and economic rights, and to demand positive obligations from states, so it has become a useful tool to assist in the reform of family law. This mixing together of civil, political, social and economic rights means that international human rights challenge the 'idea that human rights respect an individualist ideology of personal autonomy which is anti-family and community'.[58] So, human rights norms are not necessarily the individualistic tool they were once considered to be and in fact have a positive role to play in balancing community, society, familial and individual interests.

1.2.2   Families and the European Convention on Human Rights

The more immediate European context to the debate on family rights centres on the European Convention for the Protection of Human Rights and Fundamental Freedoms.[59] This Convention forms the bedrock of human rights debates within Europe, representing a commonly agreed statement of the rights to be given primacy within Europe. It is also the human rights instrument which forms the basis of the European Union's understanding and promotion of human rights.

The Convention was not, of course, originally designed to be utilised in complex familial disputes. Instead, it was and largely remains a catalogue of rights aimed at the quintessential defence of the individual against the overbearing state. It is largely negative in its frame – the state must not interfere in the rights of

---

55 Convention on the Elimination of All Forms of Discrimination against Women, GA Resolution 34/180, 18 December 1979, in force 3 September 1981, UN Doc. A/34/46 (1979); (1980) 19 ILM 33, Preamble and Article 5(b).

56 Convention on the Rights of the Child, GA Resolution 44/25, 20 November 1989, in force 2 September 1990, UN Doc. A/44/49 (1989); (1989) 28 ILM 1456.

57 For a discussion of these international human rights instruments and the balance between individual and family rights, see Goonesekere, 'Human Rights as a Foundation'.

58 Goonesekere, 'Human Rights as a Foundation', 86.

59 European Convention for the Protection of Human Rights and Fundamental Freedoms (as amended by Protocol No. 11), Council of Europe CETS No. 5, Rome, 4 November 1950, in force 3 September 1953.

individuals, and the rights given priority are those most felt in need of defending after the atrocities of the Second World War. While the jurisprudence has moved on, towards the recognition of positive duties[60] and its impact on private, familial disputes, the emphasis remains negative, individualised and public-oriented. It is also a document of its time. There is no reference, for example, to the rights of the child, nor to what are often called second or third generation rights. Again, while the Convention has been upheld as a 'living instrument' to be interpreted according to the social and political conditions of the day, there remain limits on the possibilities offered by such a broadening of interpretative method. Thus, for example, the Article 14 non-discrimination provision, while it has been broadly interpreted, most recently, to include sexual orientation discrimination, also remains parasitic on the other rights of the Convention being invoked. Nonetheless, the Convention remains *the* primary human rights document in Europe and has an elevated status within the European Union.

Within the Convention, family relationships are examined for their closeness and similarities to what is perceived to be the norm of traditional marriage (however unlike the norm many marriages may be). Same-sex partnerships have yet to be recognised as comprising family life, though aspects of homosexuality are protected on the basis of the right to respect for private life. Again, while the boundaries of what constitutes a marriage are being eroded, as a result of challenges from transgendered individuals, the ultimate privileging of marriage and the traditional family remains.[61] Thus, while the Convention contains the right to marry in Article 12, there is no right to re-marry following a divorce where the state concerned does not sanction divorce.[62] Thus, the importance of marriage overrides any claim to autonomy and choice in relationships which may manifest itself in a desire for divorce and possible re-marriage. A more recent example of the privileging of the traditional family is to be found in *Karner* v. *Austria*.[63] While the substantive outcome of this case was positive, it being held that the term 'life companion' must be interpreted to include same-sex couples as well as heterosexual unmarried couples, at the same time the Court reaffirmed its valorisation of the traditional family. It held that, while the Austrian government had not offered sufficient evidence to justify the discrimination in the instant case, in principle, 'the protection of the family in the traditional sense' is a weighty and legitimate reason which might justify a difference in treatment on the grounds of sexual orientation.[64] Convention jurisprudence also continues to permit differential treatment of married and unmarried heterosexual couples,

60 See for example *Belgian Linguistics (No. 2)* (No. 1474/62), (1979–80) 1 EHRR 252.
61 *Goodwin* v. *United Kingdom* (No. 28957/95), (2002) 35 EHRR 18.
62 In *Johnston* v. *Ireland* (No. 9697/82), (1987) 9 EHRR 203, it was held that there was no right to divorce implicit in Article 12. While Ireland has reformed its laws on divorce, Malta still prohibits divorce.
63 *Karner* v. *Austria* (No. 40016/98), (2004) 38 EHRR 24.
64 *Karner* v. *Austria*, para. 40.

with the Commission having stated that marriage 'still continues to be characterised by a corpus of rights and obligations which differentiate it markedly from
the situation of a man and a woman who cohabit'.[65]

The concept of 'family life' in Article 8 is more malleable and has been the
focus of intense debates regarding its legitimate scope. The Court of Human
Rights has spelled out the complex nature of this right and the importance of
ensuring a 'fair balance between the competing interests of the individual and the
community as a whole'.[66] The jurisprudence on Article 8 indicates that not only
is it a negative right, in terms of protecting family life from interference, but it
is also positive in that it imposes obligations on states to provide an effective
private and family life. Article 8 has facilitated an examination of the content and
nature of relationships, to determine if they are familial, rather than relying on
the status or form of the relationship as in Article 12. However, the form of the
relationship has remained crucial. Thus, relationships based on marriage, even
after divorce, always constitute 'family life' for the purposes of Article 8.[67]

Where there is no marriage, the relationship is assessed on the basis of its
similarity to the functions that marriage *should* fulfill. Thus, the Court of Human
Rights has stated that 'the notion of "the family" . . . is not confined solely to
marriage-based relationships and may encompass other de facto "families" where
the parties are living together outside of marriage'.[68] Therefore, where a child is
born outside of marriage, there may still be a 'family unit'.[69] In order to make a
determination of whether a particular situation constitutes 'family life', the Court
has ruled that a number of factors may be relevant, including 'whether the couple
live together, the length of their relationship and whether they have demonstrated
their commitment to each other by having children together or by any other
means'.[70] Therefore, so long as the cohabiting relationship is closely assimilated to
marriage, it may gain some 'respect' and protection. Thus, while a marriage does
not have to fulfil the *ideals* of marriage for there to be 'family life', a non-marital
relationship has to be proven to be the match, at least in ideal terms, of marriage.
The marriage contract, therefore, acts as a barrier to further intrusion into the
relationship, and the functions of marriage are deemed to exist. However, no
matter how much a same-sex union meets the ideal, it remains excluded from the
protection of Article 8.[71] The Court also exhibits considerable scepticism of
family ties in an extended family situation.[72]

---

65 *Lindsay* v. *United Kingdom* (No. 11089/84), (1987) 9 EHHR 555; an approach recently confirmed in *Saucedo Gomez v. Spain* (No. 37784/97) (26 January 1998).
66 *Kroon* v. *Netherlands* (No. 18535/91), (1995) 19 EHRR 263 at para. 31.
67 *Berrehab* v. *Netherlands* (No. 10730/84), (1989) 11 EHRR 322.
68 *Keegan* v. *Ireland* (No. 16969/90), (1994) 18 EHRR 342 at para. 43.
69 *Keegan* v. *Ireland*, para. 43.
70 *X, Y and Z v. United Kingdom* (No. 21830/93), (1997) 24 EHRR 143 at para. 36.
71 *Kerkhoven* v. *Netherlands* (No. 15666/89) (19 May 1992).
72 For a discussion, see Jane Liddy, 'The Concept of Family Life under the ECHR' (1998) 1
European Human Rights Law Review 15–25.

The Article 8 protection of 'family life' has also been the scene of battles over the nature of the parent–child relationship and in particular which of such relationships require recognition and attendant rights. Again, we can see a hierarchy of protected relationships, in this case based on both marriage and genetics. Thus, although the Court of Human Rights has recognised the rights of unmarried fathers in relation to their children, it has held that legal differences between the rights of married and unmarried fathers do not breach the right to respect for family life.[73] Thus, unmarried fathers may be required to 'prove' their fitness to parent, unlike the married father. In this way, despite the differential treatment of children based on parental marital status, that is whether a child is deemed legitimate or illegitimate, being held to be contrary to the Convention,[74] differences do persist. The child of the unmarried father has potentially a different relationship to her or his father than the child of the married father. In the former case, the father may, lawfully, have fewer rights than the married father, which not surprisingly may impact on the child. Thus, 'no case has yet held that all the differences between mothers and fathers, or between married and unmarried fathers, are contrary to the Convention'.[75]

In general, therefore, while the Convention jurisprudence has slowly moved forward towards a pluralist and diverse approach to families, this definition remains tethered to heterosexual marriage as forming the foundation of 'the family'. Nonetheless, the requirement to interpret the Convention as a 'living instrument' has meant that the changing nature of social and family lives are being recognised and incorporated into the jurisprudence. Progress is, therefore, being made, and these developments may be utilised to move Union law towards a less formulaic, more nuanced and diverse approach to families and family law.

1.2.3   Families and the European Union Charter of Fundamental Rights

The adoption of the Charter of Fundamental Rights changed the landscape of rights protection in the Union.[76] Hitherto the Union and Community's rights regime was piece-meal and was dependent on the largesse of the Court of Justice in developing and protecting rights as part of the general principles of Community law. This ad hoc system had been the subject of sustained and trenchant criticism which, together with a desire to attempt – once more – to bring the Union closer to its citizens, led to the promulgation and adoption of the Charter of Fundamental Rights in 2000. The adoption of the Charter, as a Solemn Declaration attached to the Treaty of Nice, was met with equal amounts of acclamation and contestation. Its adoption was heralded by some as an 'historic

---

73 *McMichael* v. *United Kingdom* (No. 16424/90), (1995) 20 EHRR 205.
74 *Marckx* v. *Belgium* (No. 6833/74), (1980) 2 EHRR 330.
75 Hale J in *Re W; Re B (Child Abduction: Unmarried Father)* [1999] Fam 1; [1998] 2 FLR 146.
76 Charter of Fundamental Rights of the European Union, OJ 2000 C 364/1.

text'[77] which 'for the first time in the European Union's history'[78] sets out the civil, political, economic and social rights of European citizens. In a similar vein, it has also been argued that the Charter is an 'excellent' idea, which will place the European Union on a new foundation, a human rights foundation, and represents a 'further step forward on the road towards a common law of Europe'.[79] On the other hand, the Charter has been criticised for its legal ambiguity, its resort to the 'rusty and trusty formulae of yesteryear' around which consensus already exists and its success in distracting attention from the real human rights issues facing the Union.[80]

While the Charter claims to be a 're-affirmation' of existing rights,[81] it is in fact clear that the Charter's provisions relating to families and children signal a new and significant change in the Union's approach to its citizens and their private and home lives.[82] The Charter marks a shift away from the Union's preoccupation with economic actors and the regulation of markets, recognising for the first time its impact on families and the role which it plays in shaping, conceptualising and regulating families. The family provisions of the Charter, despite being scattered throughout the different chapters, are innovative, relatively detailed and may come to have a decisive impact on many aspects of Union law and policy, especially those provisions relating to families to be discussed in subsequent chapters. While not currently legally binding, the Charter's provisions nonetheless already play a significant role in the interpretation and development of Union law. The Charter has been considered by the advocates general on many occasions, with Advocate General Misho stating that the Charter 'constitutes the expression, at the highest level, of a democratically established legal consensus on what must today be considered as the catalogue of fundamental rights guaranteed by the Community legal order'.[83] Courts in the member states and the Court of Human Rights have also considered the Charter's provisions.[84] In

77 Jacques Chirac, Biarritz, 14 October 2001, quoted in the Commission's publication of the Charter, *Charter of Fundamental Rights of the European Union* (Commission: Luxembourg, 2001), at 6.
78 Chirac, *ibid.* at 2.
79 Aalt Willem Heringa, 'Editorial: Towards an EU Charter of Fundamental Rights?' (2000) 7 *Maastricht Journal of European and Comparative Law* 111–16 at 111, 116.
80 Joseph Weiler, 'Editorial: Does the European Union Truly Need a Charter of Rights?' (2000) 6 *European Law Journal* 95–7.
81 OJ 2000 C 364/1, Preamble and Article 51(2).
82 See further Clare McGlynn, 'Families and the European Union Charter of Fundamental Rights: Progressive Change or Entrenching the Status Quo?' (2001) 26 *European Law Review* 582–98.
83 Joined Cases C-20/00 and C-64/00, *Booker Aquacultur Ltd and Hydro Seafood GSP Ltd* v. *The Scottish Ministers* [2003] ECR I-7411; [2003] 3 CMLR 6 at para. 126 of the Opinion. See further Steve Peers and Angela Ward (eds.), *The European Union Charter of Fundamental Rights* (Oxford: Hart Publishing, 2004) and Tamara Hervey and Jeff Kenner (eds.), *Economic and Social Rights under the EU Charter of Fundamental Rights – A Legal Perspective* (Oxford: Hart Publishing, 2003).
84 Courts in Spain and Italy have considered the Charter: see Eugenia Caracciolo di Torella and Annick Masselot, 'Under Construction: EU Family Law' (2004) 29 *European Law Review* 32–51.

addition, the Commission routinely refers to the Charter in its legislative proposals. Most significantly, the new Union Constitution, if it is ratified by the member states, will incorporate the Charter into Union law.

Turning to consider the Charter's provision on families, it replicates the principal provisions of the European Convention, thus including Articles on the right to respect for family life (Article 7) and the right to marry (Article 9). The right to respect for family life included in the Charter is a close repetition of Article 8 of the European Convention and although the Court of Justice has referred to Article 8 of the Convention in its jurisprudence,[85] arguably with little effect, its inclusion in the Charter has cemented its place in the Community rights regime. The Charter Article on the right to marry also follows that in the Convention, although with potentially important textual differences.[86] Article 52(3) of the Charter states that, where its provisions 'correspond' to that of the Convention, the 'same' interpretation must be given to the Charter provision. However, the Charter further states that the jurisprudence of the Convention need not be followed where Union law offers 'more extensive' protection.[87] In addition, the Preamble to the Charter states that it aims to 'strengthen the protection of fundamental rights' in the light of 'changes in society' and 'social progress'.[88]

The important question, therefore, is whether an expanded concept of family and of marriage will constitute more 'extensive protection' justifying a departure from existing Convention jurisprudence. It is a principal argument of this book that the concept of family should be expanded beyond its current limited definition and that this is consonant with human rights norms. Thus, a broad concept of family would indeed constitute 'more extensive' human rights protection. Indeed, further provisions of the Charter could be employed to justify such an approach, most notably the non-discrimination provision in Article 21 which prohibits discrimination on a number of grounds including sexual orientation and birth. There are, therefore, some grounds for optimism that, while these Articles are borrowed from the Convention, in time, they may be used to more progressive ends.

As well as the provisions borrowed from the European Convention, the Charter includes its own family rights articles. Thus, Article 33(1) states that: 'The family shall enjoy legal, economic and social protection.' This Article represents the Union's first direct reference to its role regarding families, or rather 'the

---

The Court of Human Rights referred to the Charter as expanding the concept of what constitutes a marriage in *I* v. *United Kingdom* (No. 25680/94), (2003) 36 EHRR 53, para. 80; *Goodwin* v. *United Kingdom* (No. 28957/95), (2002) 35 EHRR 18.

85 For example, Case 249/86, *Commission* v. *Federal Republic of Germany* [1989] ECR 1263; [1990] 3 CMLR 540; Case 12/86, *Demirel* v. *Stadt Schwäbisch Gmünd* [1987] ECR 3719; [1989] 1 CMLR 421.

86 Discussed further in chapter 5.

87 OJ 2000 C 364/1, Article 52(3).

88 OJ 2000 C 364/1, Preamble.

family'.[89] This Article, therefore, is a recognition of the Union's impact on families, and expresses an aim to seek to 'protect' them. In particular, the focus is on 'the family' as a unit to be protected in its own right, rather than exploited in the pursuit of other goals. While this represents a positive step forward in many ways, the reference to 'the family' as opposed to 'families' may be indicative of a restrictive and limited approach to defining 'family', as is suggested in the chapters which follow. In fact, it may be the case that the specific text of this Article in fact entrenches the existing Community concept of family. Whereas, prior to the adoption of the Charter, a Community concept of family was only discernible from an analysis of a wide range of judgments and was therefore open to change, it has now been made more evident and perhaps therefore more fixed.[90] This potential for stagnation is of course one of the problems with rights and charters of rights alluded to above.

It may also be that Article 33(1) becomes a 'mainstreaming' provision of some sort. Mainstreaming aims to ensure that the person or theme, whether it be 'the family' or 'equality', is considered in the development, implementation and enforcement stages of all policies. Thus, whether any policy affects 'the family' would have to be considered at all times. While the mainstreaming or 'policy-proofing' of family issues was the aim of the Community family policy of the 1980s, such an approach was not limited to the heterosexual married family. Article 33(1) may therefore represent a step backwards, and, though it gives some recognition to the family dimension to Union law and policy, there is a danger that it may entrench existing exclusions and perpetuate its own forms of discrimination.

The Charter also includes provisions on the rights of the child in Article 24 which reproduce some of the central elements of the United Nations Convention on the Rights of the Child.[91] The best interests of the child are to be a primary consideration, children's rights to protection are to be balanced with their right to autonomy and self-expression and children are entitled to maintain a personal relationship with both parents. There is therefore a clear compromise between provisions which might be seen to undermine 'the family' and those which recognise that children are individuals in their own right and those which require the care and protection of children. Article 24 is supplemented by the inclusion of 'age' as one of the prohibited grounds of discrimination in Article 21. The provisions on the rights of the child are a substantive step forward in ensuring that children are no longer invisible in the Union.[92] These provisions will certainly provide support for those demanding a more integrated and thoughtful

---

89 The Treaty Establishing the European Community, OJ 2002 C 325/33, as amended by the Treaty of Nice, agreed at the same time as the Charter, also includes the first ever treaty reference to family law in Article 67.
90 Furthermore, the explanatory notes to the Charter state that there was no intention to extend the scope of Article 7 beyond that already given by the European Court of Human Rights: Charte 4473/00.
91 All member states and EEA members ratified this Convention.
92 See further chapter 3.

approach to children in the Union. Indeed, the children's provisions may be said to be the success story of the family provisions of the Charter.

Taken as a whole, the inclusion of family rights in the Charter is highly significant. As discussed in the chapters which follow, the Union's regulation of families is piecemeal and ad hoc and the development of family law is in its early stages. In this way, while international human rights documents and the constitutions of many member states have long accorded prominence to the role of 'the family', the inclusion of family rights in the Charter does represent a new stage for the Union. In terms of Community competence and legal basis, it is likely that the Charter will extend the interpretative scope of existing Community provisions. In this way, no longer will families and children be seen only as 'consumers' or appendages to economic actors, but they may be recognised as persons in their own right and granted rights on their own terms. The Charter, therefore, cements the developing process of family regulation, bringing families firmly within the rights rhetoric of the Union and ensuring that in the future family issues will be adjudicated on by the Community courts, rather than avoided, ignored or included at will. The Charter is not therefore likely to extend the legal basis for Community action per se, but will enable existing measures to be interpreted more broadly and in a more extensive fashion.

Furthermore, the Charter's provisions may create a climate in which the future inclusion of new legal bases relating to families in the treaties will not be seen as so radical, novel or dangerous. For these varied reasons, the Charter's family provisions can in no way be seen simply as a 're-affirmation' of existing rights, as no such rights or rhetoric previously existed. The Charter does therefore expand the interpretative scope of Union law and policy and perhaps even its competence. It provides the opportunity to argue for change, to reframe old questions and to achieve substantive reform in many areas of Union activity. Indeed, it is very much to be welcomed that the Union adopted its own Charter rather than acceding to the European Convention. Mere accession would not, for example, have provided the opportunity for rights relating to children, to families or to broadening the scope of existing Convention rights.

However, as with most bills of rights, the Charter offers mixed blessings. Despite the positive aspects of the family provisions noted above, there remain considerable concerns regarding the future development of the family rights of the Charter. The Charter employs a concept of 'family' which privileges marriage, with only a few exceptions. This replicates the status quo under the Convention and existing Community law jurisprudence, with the Charter offering only a few possibilities for future development. As will be considered in more detail in the following chapters, the Charter has so far been used to entrench the status quo.[93] This analysis brings to mind the warning words of Joseph Weiler, written before

---

93 Joined Cases C-122/99 P and C-125/99 P, *D* v. *Council* [2001] ECR I-4319; [2003] 3 CMLR 9, discussed further in chapter 5.

the final adoption of the Charter. He argued that, although the Charter could provide the possibility for the inclusion of new and radical rights, thereby updating older constitutional and international rights guarantees, it also has the downside of potentially sticking to the 'rusty and trusty formulae of yester-year' around which consensus already exists, thus avoiding innovation. This would not merely replicate the status quo, he argued, but could be retrogressive. He concluded that 'each time an innovative concept were argued before the European Court, it would be pointed out that such a proposal to that effect was considered in the drafting of the Charter and failed'.[94] This is indeed what has so far happened and lives up to Weiler's worst prediction that the adoption of the Charter would be a 'risky strategy' that may 'backfire'.[95]

Thus, although the Charter claims to be founded on the 'universal values' of 'human dignity, freedom, [and] equality',[96] it remains the case that this is only dignity, freedom and equality for some, not all. Thus, the Charter has only succeeded in bringing the Union closer to some of its citizens. Some children may benefit, but those living outside the traditional nuclear family remain marginalised and largely excluded from many of the entitlements and 'benefits' of Union membership. Therefore, as with other bills of rights, there will be gains and there will be losses. Overall, however, the Charter does provide a framework within which demands for further changes can be made, and crucially such demands can be based on human rights principles, rather than economic norms and priorities. The challenge, as with the European Convention, is to continue to engage with jurisprudential developments in order to secure, albeit slowly, greater recognition of a more diverse and fluid approach to families and family life.

1.3   Conclusions

The essence of my approach is, therefore, as follows. We live in a European Union that is more postmodern than modern, in which power is diffuse and fragmented, governance is multi-layered and the law is characterised by diversity, sometimes chaos and certainly a lack of unity and cohesion. We must embrace this reality of the European Union and use it for better ends. Rawlsian pluralism gives us a basis from which to develop the postmodern critique into something more positive and constructive and which meets the lack of a European public philosophy. The realistic, pragmatic, but still positive, basis for such a public philosophy is human rights. But this is a human rights which is embedded in the principles of pluralism, which therefore respects difference. It is also one which moves beyond freedom, liberty and equality, to encompass respect for dignity and compassion. If ever there was a field of law which required a jurisprudence of pluralism and of dignity and compassion it is the regulation of families and family law.

94 Weiler, 'Charter of Rights', 96.
95 Weiler, 'Charter of Rights', 95.
96 OJ 2000 C 364/1, Preamble.

2

Families, ideologies and value pluralism: towards an expanded concept of family

The 'dominant ideology of the family' is that of a white, heterosexual, married couple, with children, all living under the same roof, where the husband is the main breadwinner and the wife the primary carer of children and other dependants. In other terminology, this is, of course, the traditional nuclear family. This is 'the family' which frames debates on families and family law and it is the ideal against which other family forms and practices are measured. It is also 'the family' which bears little comparison to the realities of family life in Europe today, yet it continues to exert significant force over judicial reasoning and legislative activity. This chapter examines, first, the dominant ideology of the family, before going on to outline the realities of family life, the new sociological explanations for changes in family practices and the new and emerging ideals of family life. It is argued that the European Union must embrace a more diverse, pluralist concept of family which should then form the basis for its regulation of families and emerging family law.

2.1 The dominant ideology of the family

The dominant ideology of the family reproduces stereotypes and norms for women, men and families, which may not reflect reality, but which frame discussion of issues and against which the legitimacy of individual claims are judged. As Diana Gittins suggests, the ideology of 'the family' has 'influenced, and continues to influence, social policy and the ways in which laws are formulated and implemented for the population overall'.[1] In this way, the ideology is promoting a particular form of family which has 'enormous legal significance, so that other forms of family are treated less favourably, and thus rendered more difficult to sustain'.[2] This is the conservative force of the dominant ideology described by Martha Fineman. The dominant ideology, she suggests, serves to 'tame' and

---

[1] Diana Gittins, *The Family in Question – Changing Households and Familiar Ideologies* (2nd edn, Basingstoke: Macmillan, 1993), pp. 2–3.

[2] Alison Diduck and Felicity Kaganas, *Family Law, Gender and the State* (Oxford: Hart Publishing, 1999), p. 10.

'domesticate' new discourses and ways of seeing families, reducing the impact and effect of any radical ideas.[3]

The concept of the 'dominant' ideology of 'the family' is central to this analysis, as while there are many different ideologies, of both traditional and new families, it is the 'dominant ideology of the family' which pervades discussions of law and families and it is against this dominant ideology that the actions of all are measured, with varying disciplinary effects.[4] This dominant ideology is one which is 'transmitted through everyday discourse – through language, symbols and images as well as through the operations of formal institutions and structures of power'.[5] In other words, this dominant ideology of 'the family' is reproduced and legitimated, not just through law and legal policy, but also through politics, the educational system, the media, social policy generally and indeed most facets of society.

Two additional points need to be made before going further. It is not my argument that 'the family' of the type described by the dominant ideology is purely fictional. Indeed, the nuclear family is alive and well and an aspiration for many. But the language of the dominant ideology and its privileged status in law and policy, means that certain assumptions, supposed commonsense ideas, about families, take on the form of a set of dominant ideas such that they are generalised and applied to everyone. Secondly, no claim is being made that the dominant ideology is immutable. Indeed, we can see how it has evolved to take into account the part-time working of many mothers, so that full-time mothering is no longer an essential component to the 'ideal' family. However, the concept of ideology emphasises that once a set of ideas is rooted in a particular discourse it does become particularly difficult to dislodge.[6]

As noted above, the dominant ideology of 'the family' prescribes not just the ideal family form, namely heterosexual marriage, but also family roles, based on a gendered division of labour. Taking the form of 'the family' first, the 'ideal' of the heterosexual married couple clearly amounts to discrimination on the grounds of sexuality as it precludes same-sex couples not just from aspiring to the 'ideal', but from ever being considered truly 'family'. The dominant ideology is therefore a sexualised concept, embodying discrimination against gay and lesbian partnerships from the outset. It is also a concept which privileges marriage. Thus, unmarried heterosexual partnerships do not meet the required standard of the dominant ideology.

---

3 Martha Albertson Fineman, *The Neutered Mother, the Sexual Family and Other Twentieth Century Tragedies* (London: Routledge, 1995), p. 21.

4 Susan Boyd, 'Some Postmodernist Challenges to Feminist Analyses of Law, Family and State: Ideology and Discourse in Child Custody Law' (1991) 10 *Canadian Journal of Family Law* 79–113 at 94.

5 Fineman, *The Neutered Mother*, p. 22.

6 See further Boyd, 'Postmodernist Challenges', 105.

However, even were the 'ideal' family to include unmarried partnerships, same sex and heterosexual, the dominant ideology of 'the family' would remain premised on the sexual union between two people.[7] Thus, what unites many conceptions of family, both the dominant ideology and ideas of 'new families', is that they remain predominantly wedded to the idea of the 'sexual family'; the family revolves around the sexual tie of two of its members. In the dominant ideology, this sexual tie is heterosexual and marital; in ideas of 'new' families, it can be an unmarried heterosexual couple or a same-sex partnership. Thus, when we speak of the sexual partnership ending, we talk of 'family breakdown' or of a 'broken family'. The majority of what is traditionally conceived of as 'family law' revolves around the regulation of this sexual relationship, its ending and its potential impact on others. In this way, there is a presumed heterosexuality at the core of the dominant ideology of 'the family' and a presumption of a sexual tie even within newer conceptions of family.

Other forms of family are thereby marginalised, including most obviously the single parent family, but also familial relationships not based on the sexual dyad.[8] As Martha Fineman asserts, calls for the extension of the concept of 'family' to include same-sex and unmarried heterosexual unions merely reaffirm the 'centrality of sexuality to the fundamental ordering of society and the nature of intimacy'.[9] In doing so, these non-traditional unions are 'equated with the paradigmatic relationship of heterosexual marriage'.[10]

As already mentioned, the dominant ideology of 'the family' is based not just on particular family forms but also on the roles which individuals play within 'the family', most particularly the gendered roles of women and men. This is most immediately obvious in the role assigned to women as primary carer of children and other dependants. This is the expected role of women, despite their entrance into the paid labour force. A crucial part of the dominant ideology of 'the family', therefore, is a dominant ideology of motherhood which privileges the mother–child bond, it being held to be sacrosanct and pivotal to the emotional and physical well-being of the child. Thus, stress is also laid on the responsibility of the biological mother for raising her own children, with any paid work taking second place to her responsibilities within the home.[11]

The corollary of such roles for women is a similarly prescribed role for men and fathers within the dominant ideology of 'the family'. The father as breadwinner and provider, as authority figure and head of the family, remain dominant themes in discussions of fatherhood, even today: provision, protection and

7 Fineman, *The Neutered Mother*.
8 Note, however, that Advocate General Tizzano in Case C-200/02, *Chen and Zhu* v. *Secretary of State for the Home Department* [2004] 3 CMLR 48 described a mother and child who lived together as an 'economically self-sufficient family unit': Opinion of 18 May 2004, para. 20.
9 Fineman, *The Neutered Mother*, p. 143.
10 Fineman, *The Neutered Mother*, p. 144.
11 The dominant ideology of motherhood is discussed further in chapter 4.

authority, as described by Sara Ruddick.[12] These are roles for men which largely exempt them from any household or other care work. Fatherhood is seen as different from motherhood, less direct and immediate and more distant.[13]

But it is not just the gendered roles within families which are significant but the hierarchy attached to them. We know that so little public or societal value is placed on caring and that the work of household maintenance is largely invisible and denigrated. Thus, the ideology of separate spheres, of the masculine realm of the public, and of the private, feminine realm of the family, is hierarchical with the public being valued and accorded respect. Thus, the gendered roles of women and men within the dominant ideology of 'the family' are also hierarchical and differently valued.

As well as being a sexualised and gendered concept, the dominant ideology of 'the family' is also race and class based. The 'ideal' of the traditional family, which initially sprang up in the 1950s post-war, remains based on a particular economic structure that can only be financially sustained by the middle or upper classes. The poorer in society, the working classes, have never been able to afford the 'luxury' of women not working outside the home. In similar ways, the traditional family is also a 'raced' concept with ethnic minority families also often being among the more impoverished in society. Further, the idealised traditional family has often required help and assistance to maintain its façade, often coming in the form of the hired help of minority ethnic workers.

And economics underpins the dominant ideology of 'the family' in further ways. As Susan Boyd contends, the ideology of 'the family' has a 'clear material underpinning' in that it is allocated primary responsibility for the 'costs of producing and raising children, and caring for dependent family members'.[14] This is the 'privatisation' of 'the family', its location within the private, as opposed to public, sphere, and the consequent implications for law and policy. Locating the costs of care work within the private family absolves the state of responsibility. Within the European context, the extent to which care work is privatised varies considerably with the minimal welfare provision of some states, such as Greece, compared with the public provision of childcare in the Nordic states. Nonetheless, the idea of the private family, of care and household work within the home being beyond public view, remains a dominant notion: the sexual division of labour remains even in those countries with extensive welfare states.

The ascribed roles for women and men within the dominant ideology extend also to the role and place of children. While conceptions of children and child-hood have been changing in recent years, there remain strong elements of a

---

12 Sara Ruddick, 'The Idea of Fatherhood' in Hilde Nelson (ed.), *Feminism and Families* (London: Routledge, 1997), pp. 205–20 at p. 207, discussed in Alison Diduck, *Law's Families* (London: Butterworths, 2003), p. 85.

13 The concept of fatherhood is discussed further in chapter 4.

14 Susan Boyd, 'Family, Law and Sexuality: Feminist Engagements' (1999) 8 *Social & Legal Studies* 369–90 at 377.

'traditional' approach to children both in our everyday family practices, in law and thus in the dominant ideology of 'the family'. The Enlightenment view of the child, as 'becoming' an adult, rather than simply 'being' a child, remains a dominant conception of children.[15] Children, in this view, are incomplete adults, who are rightly excluded from the public realm of society, shielded by the protection of the private family. They are projects for adults to shape. Not for children are the ideas of individual autonomy, equality and democracy which can only come with the rationality which is achieved on adulthood. Thus, the paradigmatic child is the dependent child, shielded from the public realm by rightfully protective parents. As Alison Diduck describes, in this view, children must 'grow and mature into independence (individuation), being taught or guided (socialization) by loving carers attentive to their welfare'.[16] The dominance of the idea of family autonomy and privacy conspires against listening to children's wishes and feelings. Thus, in the dominant ideology, there is little room for the separate and individual views of the child.

It is this 'dominant ideology of the family' which frames the debates, cases, policy initiatives and laws which are the subject of this book. This is not to say that it is the dominant ideology which is always being reproduced: far from it. Indeed, an important aspect of this book is to trace how the concept of family is evolving. However, even an evolving concept of family, one which is more progressive and egalitarian, is developed as a response to the dominant ideology; the dominant ideology remains the framework and context.

Finally, the focus here on law does not seek to suggest or imply that law plays a special or dominant role in the construction of family ideology. Law does have coercive potential, but so do other facets of social life, such as religion, social mores, cultural expectations, the media and of course politics. Nonetheless, law remains important. It has symbolic value in sending out clear messages regarding appropriate norms and behaviours. It can be a tool for change, or can entrench the status quo. It can also facilitate positive remedies in individual cases. But law cannot be relied on wholesale to bring about changes in family ideology and family law. Thus, as Brenda Cossman argues, we must 'neither look to law as the exclusive site of the problem, nor the exclusive site of the solution'.[17]

2.2   From ideal to real: the changing nature of family life

The 'family', therefore, has long been defined in ideal terms. But this 'ideal' family bears little relation to real families in either the past or the present. Indeed, although social change has led to an increasing variety in family practices, it is

15 Nick Lee, *Childhood and Society: Growing up in an Age of Uncertainty* (Buckingham: Open University Press, 2001).
16 Diduck, *Law's Families*, p. 79.
17 Brenda Cossman, 'Family Inside/Out' (1994) 44 *University of Toronto Law Journal* 1–39 at 30.

also important to remember that a further dramatic change has been that
diverse family forms have become more *visible*. Non-traditional families were
once largely invisible in society due to social stigma and lack of official recognition.[18] Changes in society's mores has meant that non-traditional families are
now more evident and that others are more free to create and live in the families
that they choose.[19]

Thus, throughout Europe the marriage rate has declined: from an annual
average of eight per thousand inhabitants in 1970 to five by 2001.[20] There are
of course differences between the member states, with marriage remaining more
popular in some countries, such as Ireland, and less common in the Nordic
countries.[21] Similarly, while rates of cohabitation have increased across Europe
as a whole, this is more marked in some countries, such as Denmark, France and
the UK, than in others, such as the southern European countries and Ireland.[22]

As a consequence of the increase in cohabitation, there have also been increases
in births outside marriage.[23] Kiernan reports that in the Nordic countries well
over 40 per cent of births in the 1990s were outside of marriage.[24] This is matched
in the UK, with 39.4 per cent of births being outside marriage in 2000.[25] By
contrast, Italy records one of the lowest rates, with only 10.2 per cent of births
being outside of marriage in 1999.[26] But, in other countries with a traditionally
low rate of cohabitation and birth outside marriage, the picture is dramatically
changing. Hence, in Ireland, births outside marriage constituted only 5 per cent in
1980, a figure which rose to 30 per cent in 2000.[27] Similarly, in Portugal, the
figures were 9.5 per cent in 1981, increasing to 22 per cent in 2000.[28] While birth

---

18 As discussed in Nicholas Bala and Rebecca Jaremko Bromwich, 'Context and Inclusivity in
     Canada's Evolving Definition of the Family' (2002) 16 *International Journal of Law, Policy and
     the Family* 145–80 at 148–9.
19 It is important to be wary of general lists of statistics regarding the 'family'. As with the
     production and analysis of all statistics, the figures themselves do not reveal a truth: David
     Morgan, *Family Connections* (Cambridge: Polity Press, 1996), pp. 14–15. See also Carol Smart
     and Bren Neale, *Family Fragments?* (Cambridge: Polity Press, 1999), pp. 28–9.
20 European Commission, *The Social Situation in the European Union 2003* (Brussels: European
     Commission, 2003), pp. 7–8.
21 See further Rebecca Probert and Anne Barlow, 'Displacing Marriage – Diversification and
     Harmonisation within Europe' (2000) 12 *Child and Family Law Quarterly* 153–65.
22 Kathleen Kiernan, 'Cohabitation in Western Europe' (1999) 96 *Population Trends* 25–32, dis-
     cussed in Louise Ackers and Helen Stalford, *A Community for Children? Children, Citizenship
     and Internal Migration in the EU* (Aldershot: Ashgate, 2004), pp. 75–8. See also Kathleen
     Kiernan, 'The Rise of Cohabitation and Childbearing outside Marriage in Western Europe'
     (2001) 15 *International Journal of Law, Policy and the Family* 1–21.
23 The birth rate itself has also been falling: see Communication from the Commission, *Green
     Paper – Confronting Demographic Change: A New Solidarity between Generations*, COM (2005)
     94 final, 16 March 2005.
24 Kiernan, 'Cohabitation in Western Europe'.
25 Ackers and Stalford, *A Community for Children?*, pp. 75–8.
26 Ackers and Stalford, *A Community for Children?*, pp. 75–8.
27 Ackers and Stalford, *A Community for Children?*, pp. 75–8.
28 Ackers and Stalford, *A Community for Children?*, pp. 75–8.

rates outside of marriage have increased, overall there has been a general decline in fertility rates to below replacement levels.[29]

The incidence of divorce has also been increasing in member states over the last decades. Thus, for those who entered marriage in 1960, the proportion of divorces is estimated as 14 per cent. This figure has risen to 28 per cent for those married in 1980.[30] Nonetheless, there are again considerable divergences between the member states. For example, Denmark, over the last twenty years, has actually seen a decrease in the incidence of divorce.[31] The highest rates of growth can be observed in southern European countries, although this is partly due to their lower baseline. In the UK, Sweden, Germany and the Netherlands, the growth of divorce is slower, but then these countries have long divorce traditions. While it seems true to say that the incidence of divorce is certainly increasing, and those countries with hitherto low divorce rates are now 'catching-up' the others, the differences remain.

And these are not the only changes that are taking place. The ethnic composition of the population of the Union is also changing. Increased immigration has led to larger numbers of ethnic minorities within all member states, to varying degrees. There is, therefore, increasing diversity of religious and ethnic cultures which have impacts on different concepts of family.

This brief outline of the statistical changes in family practices does not seek to explain why such changes have taken place or to account for the differences between states. The purpose it does serve, nonetheless, is to demonstrate that the 'dominant ideology of the family' is out of step, to a greater or lesser degree depending on the member state under examination, with the realities of family life. While the dominant ideology is indeed normative, rather than descriptive, more and more people live in families which do not come close to the normative ideal. Thus, legal and social policies based on the dominant ideology marginalise, exclude and potentially discriminate against large numbers of people. It is also equally important not to see change as necessarily representing a new, progressive movement towards egalitarian and progressive family life.[32] Thus, statistics are here presented not as objective or demonstrating an irrefutable 'common sense', but as part of a picture of the changing nature of family life that deserves recognition and analysis and provides one part of an overall picture.

Indeed, as well as diversity, statistics also show remarkable continuity. While there are often cries of 'crisis' regarding families, it is important to remember that

---

29 For a detailed discussion, see Francis Castles, 'The World Turned Upside Down: Below Replacement Fertility, Changing Preferences and Family Friendly Public Policy in 21 OECD Countries' (2003) 13 *Journal of European Social Policy* 209–27.

30 Eurostat, *Living Conditions in Europe – Statistical Pocketbook* (Luxembourg: European Commission, 2000).

31 *Ibid.*

32 Carol Smart, 'Stories of a Family Life: Cohabitation, Marriage and Social Change' (2000) 17 *Canadian Journal of Family Law* 20–53.

most people have children at some stage in their lives and even that most people get married. Most children are therefore brought up within a family unit with two parents. Nonetheless, individuals are having fewer children, at later ages, and are often not married when they have children. Although marriage remains popular, many such marriages are second or third marriages and therefore divorce is increasingly commonplace. The children living with two parents, therefore, are often living in step-families. Thus, there is both continuity and diversity.

2.3   The 'new' family: changing ideals, but same old family practices?

While statistics may give us a partial view of what is happening within families, they do not tell us why these changes may be taking place or what might be the implications for law and policy. Sociological perspectives on the changing empirical realities of families and family life have highlighted a number of features which might explain recent trends and help us to understand the needs and demands of law and policies when dealing with families in the future.

Individualism, negotiation, democracy, equality and mutuality are all concepts which characterise modern relationships according to recent sociological theory on families.[33] Anthony Giddens speaks of a change from the standard roles and obligations of traditional marriage, to the fluid, constantly changing and contingent nature of today's relationships, including marriage.[34] He suggests that today we enter and continue in relationships for only so long as the relationship satisfies both parties: 'the relationship exists solely for whatever rewards that relationship can deliver'.[35] This is the 'pure relationship' in which 'external criteria have been dissolved',[36] resulting in personal autonomy, meaning that individuals 'determine and regulate the conditions of their association'.[37] It is also a vision of democracy in the family sphere. Modern intimacy, he suggests, is characterised by equality and democracy, not hierarchy and inequality.

In a similar vein, Ulrich Beck and Elisabeth Beck-Gernsheim suggest that relationships now vary considerably from relationship to relationship and individual to individual and it is therefore no longer possible to say what marriage, family or sexuality mean.[38] This is the 'normal chaos' of love. The meanings of relationships are determined and negotiated, in a spirit of intimate democracy, by individuals. There are no 'standard biographies' of individuals and few rules

---

33 Most particularly, Anthony Giddens, *The Transformation of Intimacy* (Cambridge: Polity Press, 1992); and Ulrich Beck and Elisabeth Beck-Gernsheim, *The Normal Chaos of Love* (Cambridge: Polity Press, 1995).
34 Giddens, *The Transformation of Intimacy*, discussed in Diduck, *Law's Families*, pp. 4–7.
35 Anthony Giddens, *Modernity and Self-Identity: Self and Society in the Late Modern Age* (Cambridge: Polity Press, 1991), p. 6.
36 Giddens, *Modernity and Self-Identity*, p. 6.
37 Giddens, *The Transformation of Intimacy*, p. 185, discussed in Diduck, *Law's Families*, pp. 4–7.
38 Beck and Beck-Gernsheim, *Chaos of Love*, discussed in Diduck, *Law's Families*, pp. 7–10.

governing behaviour or status. The new individualism which is apparent in these understandings of family life does not mean an end to family and family life as we know it. As Beck and Beck-Gernsheim contend, while individualisation *may* drive individuals apart, it also 'pushes them back into one another's arms'. As life becomes more fluid and change is a continuous part of life, the 'attractions of a close relationship grow'.[39]

In many ways, these new conceptualisations of family life represent a new 'ideal' in which the 'ideal' modern family is one characterised by equality and democracy, where roles are negotiated and relationships continue only for so long as individuals feel they have something to gain. This is a new 'ideal': for while these theories may begin to explain the changing nature of family practices, they do not yet represent a *description* of modern family life. As with the dominant ideology of 'the family', they too remain normative.

This is because the realities of family practices remain far from this idealised vision. Giddens' pure relationship and his description of individuals who are freely able to enter and exit relationships as they choose, without concern for others, especially children, is perhaps a vision more consonant with the lives of many men. In addition, Giddens' approach seems overly optimistic regarding gender equality and too reliant on individual change.[40] His ideas are based on gender equality, which seems to assume either that such equality exists, or that individuals are able to change the circumstances of inequality which pervade their relationships. For this reason, Lynn Jamieson expresses disbelief at how a change in the nature of heterosexual relationships 'would shatter the interconnection of gendered labour markets, gendered distributions of income and wealth and gendered divisions of domestic labour'.[41] Indeed, as she points out, empirical work on heterosexual couples 'routinely continues to find that men exercise more power than women in partnerships', for example by having greater choice regarding domestic work and childcare and by having greater control of family finances.[42]

So, these new families and relationships, characterised by equality and democracy, are also idealised and aspirational.[43] Indeed, they can often reinforce traditional gender stereotypes, even while attempts are made at justifying such actions and at naming them differently. Jamieson suggests that the idealised status of the new democratic and egalitarian relationship is evident in the attempts by heterosexual couples to describe their relationships within such a framework, while the lived experience suggests something different. She puts this forward as evidence that it is certainly difficult, if not impossible, for heterosexual couples

---

39 Beck and Beck-Gernsheim, *Chaos of Love*, p. 32.
40 Lynn Jamieson, 'Intimacy Transformed? A Critical Look at the "Pure" Relationship' (1999) 33 *Sociology* 477–94.
41 Jamieson, 'Intimacy Transformed?', 482.
42 Jamieson, 'Intimacy Transformed?', 482.
43 Smart, 'Stories of a Family Life'.

to renegotiate their relationships within prevailing social conditions. Thus, empirically 'intimacy and inequality continue to coexist in many personal lives' and these relationships remain 'highly gendered'.[44]

Nonetheless, what is interesting about much of this empirical work is that the discourses of which Giddens speaks, of equality, democracy and negotiation, have pervaded personal relationships to the extent that they are expressed as ideals. Researchers have found that the same couples who take for granted that a 'good' relationship is one which is equal and fair go to great lengths to construct their relationships as such, despite obvious gender inequalities. Indeed, as Jamieson suggests, it seems that the creative energy of the couples is deployed in disguising inequality, rather than in undermining it.[45] Similarly, others have found that the attributes of new relationships, of democracy, equality and negotiability, were cited as important aspects of a 'successful marriage'.[46] Jane Lewis has found that the 'culture of individualism' has also permeated relationships, though she rejects the argument that this is self-serving and destructive of relationships.[47] She discovered that commitment existed alongside individualism: modern relationships were simply being formed and continued on changed practices.[48] While for younger respondents, whose relationships continued and existed as a matter of choice, rather than prescription or compulsion, the nature of the expressed commitment differed. The relationships were governed by the internal norms agreed by the parties, rather than the imposed roles and expectations of traditions. Lewis suggests that relationships are being based on different, but no less moral or firm, foundations.[49]

Giddens suggests that high levels of dissolution of relationships is a result of the inherent fragility of the 'pure relationship'. However, Jamieson rejoins that it is more plausible to see this fragility 'as a consequence of the tension between strengthening cultural emphasis on intimacy, equality and mutuality in relationships and the structural supports of gender inequalities which make these ideals difficult to attain'.[50] Thus, what remains largely absent from these more idealised descriptions of family practices today is the continuing reality of women's economic disadvantage and vulnerability within both families and the

---

44 Jamieson, 'Intimacy Transformed?', 491.
45 Jamieson, 'Intimacy Transformed?', 485.
46 Jenny Reynolds and Penny Mansfield, 'The Effect of Changing Attitudes to Marriage and its Stability' in *Lord Chancellor's Department Research Series No. 2/99* (2 vols., London: Stationery Office, 1999), vol. I, discussed in Diduck, *Law's Families*, p. 32.
47 Jane Lewis, *Marriage, Cohabitation and the Law: Individualism and Obligation (Lord Chancellor's Department Research Series No. 1/99)* (London: Stationery Office, 1999), discussed in Diduck, *Law's Families*, pp. 32–3.
48 Jane Lewis, Jessica Datta and Sophie Sarre, *Individualism and Commitment in Marriage and Cohabitation (Lord Chancellor's Department Research Series No. 8/99)* (London: Stationery Office, 1999), discussed in Diduck, *Law's Families*, p. 33.
49 Lewis, Datta and Sarre, *Individualism and Commitment*, p. 90, discussed in Diduck, *Law's Families*, p. 33.
50 Jamieson, 'Intimacy Transformed?', 486.

labour market.[51] While family forms are undoubtedly changing, and gender relationships are the subject of change, there is much that remains the same. Thus, there is an idealisation of autonomy and change which often cannot be met by women, but the discourse and cultural expectations of such opportunities create additional tensions in families. In this 'negotiated' family, negotiations are often not taking place on an equal level. In consequence, there is a 'growing discrepancy between women's expectations of equality and continuity of gender inequality'.[52]

What seems evident here is a desire for a new form of relationship that is not matching reality. But this is not just because of the individuals' sense of their relationship and desires, but the social conditions under which individuals are living. Sara Arber and Jay Ginn suggest that there is a general disjunction between society's acceptance of equality, and policy demands for equality within the labour market, and the continuing reality of inequality within homes and families.[53] This is not just inequalities at the personal level, but continuing cultural norms about the importance of male breadwinners and childcaring roles: the dominant ideology of 'the family' remains a strong boundary on behaviour. The result is that women come to carry the 'double burden' of labour market participation and continued expectations in the home. Partly this is because the labour market participation of women has not generally led to substantial economic gains for women. While their labour market position has increased and improved, they remain trapped in largely low paid, low status work. Thus, while there is significant change in the rates of women's employment, there is also continuity of their disadvantaged position within the labour market.[54]

Ironically, therefore, while Giddens argues that the changes in family life he discusses have come about largely due to the success of women's demands for equality, autonomy and self-hood, and Beck and Beck-Gernsheim suggest that the opportunities created by these new forms of intimacy have been largely taken up by women, it seems that women remain disadvantaged. We may have new ideals and more opportunities than before, but, as Sarah Irwin rightly suggests, the 'new' family seems very much like the 'old' family where conventional divisions of labour remain intact.[55] Indeed, the gendered nature of family life, as prescribed by the dominant ideology of the family, continues to resonate, descriptively, in the lives of many.

51 Sarah Irwin, 'Resourcing the Family: Gendered Claims and Obligations and Issues of Explanation' in Elizabeth Silva and Carol Smart (eds.), *The New Family?* (London: Sage, 1999), pp. 31–45.
52 Irwin, 'Resourcing the Family', 37.
53 Sara Arber and Jay Ginn, 'The Mirage of Gender Equality: Occupational Success in the Labour Market and within Marriage' (1995) 46 *British Journal of Sociology* 21–43.
54 Irwin, 'Resourcing the Family', 42.
55 Irwin, 'Resourcing the Family', 42.

Furthermore, Carol Smart warns against seeing the increasing diversity of family forms as part of a vanguard movement for change.[56] Her empirical work demonstrates that individuals take up diverse family forms for a variety of reasons, often adverse economic circumstances, and only rarely as a reaction against the dominant ideology of 'the family'. Indeed, in her study of cohabiting relationships, she found they 'bore little relationship to a progressive, vanguardist movement dedicated to the transformation of intimacy at the start of the twenty-first century'.[57] Further, it was not possible to point to cohabiting relationships as being more progressive than married ones. She found that some of the 'worst aspects of traditional heterosexual marriage', such as domestic violence, a rigid sexual division of labour and the poverty of mothers, were reproduced in cohabiting relationships; while in other cohabiting relationships, there was a remarkable similarity to the ideal type of the heterosexual married family. Thus, she seeks to warn against the idealising tendency to view the increasing diversity of family forms as 'progress away from oppressive family forms and towards more desirable, egalitarian alternatives'.[58]

Nonetheless, despite such warnings, it is perhaps in other family forms that we can see a vanguard movement towards the new forms of intimacy and relationship described above. Jeffrey Weeks *et al.* suggest that it is in the gay and lesbian community that these new forms and ideals of relationships, of negotiation, fluidity, democracy and equality, can best be found.[59] Non-heterosexual relationships, it is argued, are 'less likely to be characterised by predetermined obligations, duties and commitments'.[60] Negotiation does, therefore, characterise such relationships.

As Alison Diduck highlights, while the same-sex families under study represented the new ways of being a family, they also expressed many of the ideals of the traditional family.[61] In this way, it may be that the gay and lesbian community is managing to embrace change in relationships, while maintaining some of the benefits of traditional relationships. For heterosexual couples, this is more difficult while marriage, with its clear roles and expectations, remains the idealised form of relationship. Nonetheless, the research referred to above by Jane Lewis also found that while relationships are being described and often characterised by individualism, commitment and other 'traditional' values continue alongside the new ideals, suggesting also a combination of new ways of thinking and doing relationships, combining with traditional elements.[62]

---

56 Smart, 'Stories of Family Life'.
57 Smart, 'Stories of Family Life', 51.
58 Smart, 'Stories of Family Life', 49.
59 Jeffrey Weeks, Catherine Donovan and Brian Heaphy, 'Everyday Experiments: Narratives of Non-Heterosexual Relationships' in Silva and Smart (eds.), *The New Family?*, pp. 83–114. See also Gillian Dunne, 'A Passion for "Sameness"? Sexuality and Gender Accountability' in Silva and Smart (eds.), *The New Family?*, pp. 66–82.
60 Weeks, Donovan and Heaphy, 'Everyday Experiments', 94.
61 Diduck, *Law's Families*, p. 31.
62 Lewis, *Marriage, Cohabitation and the Law*. See also Janet Walker, Noel Timms and Richard Collier, 'The Challenge of Social, Legal and Policy Change' in *Lord Chancellor's Department Final*

What then do the theories of Giddens and Beck and Beck- Gernsheim tell us about changes in family practices? An increasing emphasis on individualism and self-fulfillment perhaps means less willingness to remain in relationships which are no longer satisfying or fulfilling. Their ideas also suggest that traditions no longer constrain actions to the same extent. Such changes could point to an increasing selfishness, or indeed 'crisis', or may perhaps be better described as manifestations of greater freedom and equality. For, as Gillian Douglas has suggested, whereas women might once have been constrained by economic and social circumstances and mores to accept a life within the private sphere of the home and controlled by a male head of household, her husband, she is now at liberty to pursue her autonomous goals.[63] Women have gained some autonomy and individual fulfillment has become a valid ambition. This also has considerable implications for the nuclear family. One of the perceived strengths of the nuclear family, of the dominant ideology, was its prescribed form and roles. But, as Alison Diduck suggests, once these roles become negotiable, the supposedly beneficial nature of the nuclear family dissolves.[64]

However, there remains, as discussed above, a considerable disjuncture between the ideal and the lived reality of family life. Nonetheless, the ideals of democracy, equality, negotiation of shared goals and ambitions, and mutuality are desirable and legitimate ambitions for individuals and for law and policy. The question is, therefore, what measures can be taken at the societal level to ensure that the ideals move closer to becoming reality? Individual change is not sufficient to overcome the structural barriers and inequalities facing many families and particularly many women. One aspect of such required changes is to move away from the dominant ideology of 'the family' as the premise for law and policy, as suggested further below.

2.4   The lure of 'family'

Many have argued that, if we are to reject the dominant ideology of 'the family', then we must also discard the concept of 'family' in its entirety. Many lesbians and gay men have argued that 'the family' is an oppressive and exclusionary institution and that moves towards assimilation obscure the diversity of relationships within lesbian and gay communities, establish a hierarchy of socially legitimate relationships and negate the ways in which gay and lesbian relationships are different and subversive. The aim should be to decentre, deconstruct and/or otherwise destroy the concept of family.[65] For this reason, Brenda Cossman warns

---

Evaluation Report on Information Meetings and Associated Provisions within the Family Law Act 1996 (3 vols., London: Stationery Office, 1999), vol. I, pp. 5–16, discussed in Diduck, *Law's Families*, p. 34.

63 Gillian Douglas, *An Introduction to Family Law* (Oxford: Oxford University Press, 2001), p. 8.
64 Diduck, *Law's Families*, pp. 9–10.
65 For a discussion of the gay and lesbian debate regarding 'family', see Cossman, 'Family Inside/Out'.

that seeking to include gay and lesbian relationships within the concept of family makes sense only in the context of the 'continuing hegemony' of the 'ideologically dominant discourse of family' centred on the white, middle-class, heterosexual, nuclear family comprising a male breadwinner and an economically dependent wife and their biological children.[66] She continues that we cannot assume that this dominant ideology will be undermined simply by deconstructing and redefining it. Susan Boyd not only warns against the legitimating nature of assimilationist claims but suggests that this is in fact a move towards the 'domestication of deviant sexualities within a safe, useful and recognizable framework', rather than about transforming ideas about normative sexuality.[67] It is, therefore, about 'normalising' lesbian and gay relationships, but on heterosexual terms.

There are strong links between the lesbian and feminist rejection of 'family'. Didi Herman has cautioned against deploying the concept of family not just for the reasons given above but also in that, by 'appropriating familial ideology, lesbians and gay men may be supporting the very institutional structures that create and perpetuate women's oppression'.[68] This is a feminist position which sites the role of the family in the oppression of women: the argument is that 'the family' is a 'patriarchal arrangement, sustained by law, which ensures the social and economic insecurity of wives and mothers'.[69] Michelle Barrett has argued that the 'family-household constitutes both the ideological ground on which gender difference and women's oppression are constructed, and the material relations in which men and women are differently engaged in wage labour and the class structure'.[70] In this way, the traditional nuclear family reproduces a sexual division of labour, is based on the public/private distinction and favours the concept of a 'family wage', all of which work to women's detriment and disadvantage. For these reasons, feminist work in the 1980s sought to abandon use of the term 'family' altogether, replacing it with 'household'. This concept sought to cover shared residence and kinship ties, but without the ideological content and idealisation of 'the family'.

In these approaches, however, there is a clear and distinct air of unreality. Society is not going to stop using the term 'family' to describe our relationships. Despite the argument that 'family' has been an exclusionary concept and that the changing nature of families has not yet seen a decentring of the dominant ideology of 'the family', we need to work with the concept towards change. For this reason, many feminists have refused to give up the concept of family and have declined to accept that the existing inequalities within families are a natural and inevitable part of family practices. As a result, feminist strategy has focused

---

66 Cossman, 'Family Inside/Out', 29.
67 Boyd, 'Family, Law and Sexuality', 378.
68 Didi Herman, 'Are We Family? Lesbian Rights and Women's Liberation' (1990) 28 *Osgoode Hall Law Journal* 789–815 at 797.
69 Katherine O'Donovan, *Family Law Matters* (London: Pluto Press, 1993), p. 32.
70 Michèle Barrett, *Women's Oppression Today* (London: Verso, 1980), p. 211.

on the nature of family practices and has sought to open them up to scrutiny and to insist on equality and justice within families.[71] Thus, feminists have analysed and revealed the 'multiple interconnections between women's domestic roles and their inequality and segregation in the workplace' and have rejected the underlying assumption of most political theories, that the sphere of family life is so separate and distinct from the rest of social life that it can be ignored.[72]

So, many feminists maintain that 'family' is an important concept, but that it must be reformed. Martha Minow has argued, for example, that society gains through 'defining family membership broadly: the values signaled by "family" are worthwhile yet fragile; stability, nurturance and care should be promoted wherever possible, and people committed to taking on these tasks should be encouraged to do so'.[73] Thus, while 'the family', both as an institution and in practice, may sustain gender-based inequalities, 'it is often also the main source of love, identity and succour for many women'.[74] This means that gender inequalities must be eliminated, but the end of 'the family' is not necessarily going to bring this about and may even harm many women more than help them. More recent family theorists have also reached this conclusion. David Morgan rightly points out that people still use the term family.[75] Families do not need to live together, as households do. Family implies an emotional commitment that household does not. Indeed, with the deployment of the term 'families of choice'[76] for gay and lesbian relationships, it is perhaps the case that the 'ideological power of the term is changed'.[77]

Elizabeth Silva and Carol Smart contend that 'families remain a crucial relational entity playing a fundamental part in the intimate life of and connections between individuals'.[78] Thus, despite the debate about the utility of the concept of 'family', empirical studies confirm the growing consensus that, while diverse patterns of family life exist and are developing, 'people still define particular aspects of their lives as "family life" and feel committed to families'.[79] The major change here, argue Silva and Smart, is that the concept of 'family' has come to 'signify the subjective meaning of intimate connections rather than formal, objective blood or marriage ties'.[80] And this subjective meaning remains imbued

---

71 A paradigmatic example of this feminist approach is Susan Moller Okin, *Justice, Gender and the Family* (New York: Basic Books, 1989).
72 Moller Okin, *Justice*, pp. 125–6.
73 Martha Minow, 'All in the Family and in All Families: Membership, Loving and Owing' (1992–3) 95 *West Virginia Law Review* 275–332 at 304.
74 Gill Jagger and Caroline Wright, 'Introduction – Changing Family Values' in Gill Jagger and Caroline Wright (eds.), *Changing Family Values* (London: Routledge, 1999), pp. 1–16 at p. 5.
75 Morgan, *Family Connections*.
76 Kath Weston, *Families We Choose* (New York: Columbia University Press, 1991).
77 Smart and Neale, *Family Fragments?*, p. 21.
78 Elizabeth Silva and Carol Smart, 'The "New" Practices and Politics of Family Life' in Silva and Smart (eds.), *The New Family?*, pp. 1–12 at p. 5.
79 Silva and Smart, 'The "New" Practices', 7.
80 Silva and Smart, 'The "New" Practices', 7.

with notions of sharing of resources, caring, responsibility and obligations, those ideals which have always been consonant with 'families'. While family forms may be changing, and there are fewer normative constraints on family practices, bonds of love, commitment and responsibility continue to bind individuals together in their chosen families.

Equally, there is no agreement within the lesbian and gay community regarding the use or not of 'family'. Thus, Weeks *et al.* argue that the language chosen to express ways of living in the lesbian and gay community is that of 'family', meaning an 'affinity circle which may or may not involve children which has cultural and symbolic meaning for the subjects that participate or feel a sense of belonging in and through it'.[81] They suggest, therefore, that the debate is no longer about alternatives to the family, but 'alternative' families or 'families of choice', as they describe them.[82] The call to be included within the concept of family is generally made by reference to liberal norms of equality and non-discrimination and the language of human rights is utilised to seek law reform. In addition to these liberal claims to equality, some have argued that gay and lesbian relationships deserve the public legitimation that comes from acceptance as 'family' and/or that including gay and lesbian relationships within the concept of family could of itself be subversive. The argument here is that the idea of 'family' would be radically transformed were it to include gay and lesbian relationships. Finally, it has been argued that the emphasis on the family as oppressive is largely a white phenomenon; with the 'family' often being a haven from racism and a source of support in a hostile world.[83]

The idea of 'family' is so strong culturally and socially that individuals use the term to describe themselves and their relationships. Furthermore, in terms of law reform, again the concept of family remains deeply embedded in our legal system, not least in the field known as 'family law'. Finally, in relation to rights, as discussed in the previous chapter, the 'protection' to be offered to families and family life is already written into human rights treaties. It is already accepted as the norm and as a foundational principle. The strategy, therefore, that is most likely to lead to concrete results, and real improvements in the lives of individuals, is to argue for a broader definition of the concept of family employed in law, policies and human rights norms and discourse. While there is a legitimate concern that a focus on 'family' and extending the scope of the term may reproduce inequalities as it privileges those not in familial relationships, this must be the focus of attention in addition to expanding the concept of family, not at its expense. Finally, although the concept of 'family' should be retained, the idea

---

81 Weeks, Donovan and Heaphy, 'Everyday Experiments', 86, discussed in Diduck, *Law's Families*, pp. 26–7.
82 Weeks, Donovan and Heaphy, 'Everyday Experiments', 83.
83 bell hooks, *Feminist Theory: From Margin to Centre* (Boston: South End Press, 1984).

of 'family practices' better captures the fluidity, diversity and flux of family life and the active nature of family life, but also seeks to go wider to encompass all activities involving families.[84]

2.5   Towards an expanded concept of family

The lure of the concept of 'family', therefore, is strong and need not be resisted. Instead, we must embrace the concept of family and work to expand its meaning. The pluralist approach to understanding European law and integration, discussed in chapter 1, is the perfect foundation for an expanded concept of family. In the particular context of families and family law, Andrew Bainham has applied profitably the pluralist ideas of Joseph Raz, and particularly the idea of 'value pluralism', to demand a broader approach to families and the interpretation of family rights.[85] Bainham suggests that value pluralism implies that 'all those intimate and family relationships which can be considered valuable should be supported by the state in an even-handed way'.[86] Further, no particular form of relationship or arrangement should be officially promoted. Thus, whereas the state has always been interested in defining 'the family', both for the purposes of promoting certain norms and for administrative ease, these two ambitions for policy should be removed. The liberal state, Bainham argues, should not promote one equally valuable form of life over another and should certainly not do so purely for administrative ease.

But which relationships are 'valuable'? Bainham answers this by declaring valuable those relationships which are characterised by the values we associate with families, such as love, affection, support, commitment and permanence.[87] Bainham, therefore, suggests that 'value pluralism would require that the many alternative forms of family living, though different and perhaps incompatible, must be accorded equal respect'.[88] In this way, value pluralism rejects a hierarchy of family forms, such as marriage over same-sex partnerships, as well as a rejection of a hierarchy of familial roles, for example there would be no assumption that mothering is more important than fathering. In a similar vein, Janet Finch has argued that the aim of family policies should be to 'facilitate flexibility in family life, rather than to shape it into a particular form'. She continues that it is the proper role of the state to ensure that people have the 'maximum opportunity to work out their own relationships as they wish, to suit the circumstances

---

84 Morgan, *Family Connections* and David Morgan, 'Risk and Family Practices: Accounting for Change and Fluidity in Family Life' in Silva and Smart (eds.), *The New Family?*, pp. 13–30.
85 Andrew Bainham, 'Family Rights in the Next Millennium' (2000) 53 *Current Legal Problems* 471–503 and 'Family Law in a Pluralistic Society' (1995) 22 *Journal of Law and Society* 234–47.
86 Bainham, 'Family Rights', 475.
87 Bainham, 'Family Rights', 475.
88 Bainham, 'Family Rights', 476.

of their own lives. It is not the proper role of governments to presume that certain outcomes would be more desirable than others.'[89]

Another vital element of value pluralism is gender equality.[90] Thus, while value pluralism entails commitment to different forms of families, it also demands commitment to equality within families. This demand has of course been most keenly made by feminists over the years for whom the 'family' has been and continues to be a focus for analysis, critique and reform. As noted above, early feminist approaches to 'the family' subjected it to sustained attack as being a primary site of women's oppression. The very idea of the 'family' itself was to be rejected, with other diverse forms of association and household replacing the concept. Later feminist work recognised not just the overt simplicity of this approach but also its essentialist approach to women. Accordingly, a more complex approach is required, one which demands equality for women within families, not the wholesale rejection of the idea of family.

Closely related to gender equality is the more general principle of non-discrimination. Distinctions between and within families on the basis of characteristics such as sex, sexual orientation, race, religion, birth or other status, to name a few grounds, is also inimical to a pluralist approach to families. This is related to the concept of multiculturalism. Raz has argued that multiculturalism is an indication of respect for diversity within society and is a value in itself requiring recognition.[91] An approach to families which is based on principles of value pluralism must also therefore have a concern for multiculturalism and the diversity which it respects and promotes.

A pluralist approach to families, where all 'valuable' relationships are given equal respect, is also the logical outcome of the sociological approaches to families discussed above. Giddens and Beck and Beck-Gernsheim emphasised the importance of autonomy and equality in relationships today and of the ongoing negotiation regarding roles and forms of families. This means that there is an infinite variety of family practices which meet the differing needs and wishes of individuals. A pluralist approach should recognise these diverse family forms and familial roles as deserving of the respect and privileges which law and policy currently afford to only some families.

This approach does entail a greater focus on the nature and function of relationships, rather than their form. The dominant ideology, as well as prescribing specific familial roles, is principally based on privileging a particular family

---

89 Janet Finch, *The State and the Family*, lecture to inaugurate the Institute's Annual Theme for 1996–97, 30 October 1996 (Edinburgh, International Social Sciences Institute), at 13, quoted in Smart and Neale, *Family Fragments?*, p. 24.

90 Bainham, 'Family Rights'.

91 Joseph Raz, 'Multiculturalism' (1998) 11 *Ratio Juris* 193–205, discussed in the Union context in Chloe Wallace and Jo Shaw, 'Education, Multiculturalism and the Charter of Fundamental Rights of the European Union' in Tamara Hervey and Jeff Kenner (eds.), *Economic and Social Rights under the EU Charter of Fundamental Rights – A Legal Perspective* (Oxford: Hart Publishing, 2003), pp. 223–46.

form, namely heterosexual marriage. When a 'family' takes such a form, it is largely taken as given that this is a valid 'family' which should enjoy the protection and privileging of the state. An approach based on value pluralism would make no such assumptions based on the form of family life. There would be no presumption that children are best brought up within such a form of family life or that this form of family life is the most fulfilling. In this way, it seeks to recognise that violence, abuse, exploitation, solitude and misery exist in hetero-sexual marriages and the veil of the marriage certificate must not blind us to this reality. Equally, we cannot assume that more diverse forms of family life are necessarily more egalitarian or democratic.

Such a functionalist approach does require some measure of intrusion into the nature of family life.[92] The danger is that it sets up a new norm which exerts disciplinary power and, while perhaps being more inclusive, will by definition still exclude. However, while law and policy continue to privilege families, there needs to be a mechanism, a definition, for determining which relationships encompass 'family'. What is being suggested here is that a considerably broader definition be used than the dominant ideology of family, one that reflects the reality of today's relationships and families and which accords respect to the diverse ways in which people choose to live their lives. In this way, the Court of Justice is being urged to follow the Canadian example where the Supreme Court has declared that: 'Family means different things to different people, and the failure to adopt the traditional family form of marriage may stem from a multiplicity of reasons – all of them equally valid and all of them equally worthy of concern, respect, consideration and protection under the law.'[93]

---

92 On the benefits of a functional approach to defining 'the family', see Rebecca Bailey-Harris, 'Third Stonewall Lecture – Lesbian and Gay Family Values and the Law' (1999) 29 *Family Law* 560–70.

93 Claire L'Heureux-Dube in *Miron* v. *Trudel* [1995] 2 SCR 418, para. 102. In this case, the Supreme Court held that excluding long-term heterosexual cohabitants from the definition of spouse was discriminatory and contrary to section 15 of the Charter of Rights.

3

Children and European Union law: instrumentalism, protection and empowerment

The European Union has yet to create a fully fledged children's policy. It is, at present, a policy of 'bits and pieces' with no cohering theme or approach. Indeed, there has been little reflective thinking about children at all. In this policy vacuum, it is perhaps not surprising that the dominant ideology of the family, and children's roles within 'the family', has thoughtlessly shaped Union law and policy. Nonetheless, novel and more progressive ways of thinking about children, and their rights and interests, are beginning to be reflected in Union law. This chapter considers first these newer ways of thinking about children's rights and interests, before going on to examine the Union's laws and policies relating to children. The final section examines how the Union's Charter of Fundamental Rights and a rights-based approach to children's law and policy provide the most appropriate way forward for the Union.

3.1   Family ideology and children's rights

The dominant ideology of the family prescribes specific familial roles not just for men and women, but also for children. This is the hierarchical, private family in which the concept of parental autonomy affords parents sole charge over their children. In such a conceptualisation, the Enlightenment view of the child, as 'becoming' an adult, rather than simply 'being' a child, remains dominant. The paradigmatic child is the dependent child, shielded from the public realm by rightfully protective parents: they are projects for adults to shape. Not for children are the ideals of individual autonomy, equality and democracy which can only come with the rationality achieved on adulthood. Furthermore, in being viewed as 'embryonic persons' or 'projects', children are marginalised from society and deemed inferior to adults.[1] Children are also seen as synonymous with families; not independent beings who happen also to be part of families. This is the 'familialisation' of childhood where children are presumed to 'belong to' their parents. Children become 'fused with their parents into an idealised, inseparable

---

1 Carol Smart, Bren Neale and Amanda Wade, *The Changing Experience of Childhood – Families and Divorce* (Cambridge: Polity Press, 2001), p. 8.

family unit' and the diverse identities and interests of individual family members are concealed.[2]

However, recent shifts in sociological thinking, seeing children as 'being' rather than 'becoming', are emerging which challenge such conceptualisations of children and demand individual recognition of children and their interests, agency and rights.[3] Childhood here is understood as a socially constructed state, varying across societies and from child to child. There is no pre-ordained nature of children or their status in families. This approach treats children as competent autonomous individuals, whose choices, views and values are to be heard and respected. Carol Smart *et al.*'s research found that children viewed themselves 'not simply as children needing care but as young people who wanted to talk to others and be listened to, trust others and be trusted and engage in open and meaningful communications'.[4] In other words, children value a democratic style of family life. This is supported by Giddens and Pierson who suggest that family democratisation means that children are treated as individuals and can make important contributions to family decision-making.[5] Children, the subjects rather than objects of study, have expressed their desires to exercise choice; they want to be active participants in their lives. In such a context, the familialisation of children becomes inappropriate as the autonomy of individual family members should be recognised. Indeed, children need no longer be 'invisible' and 'emerge as fully fledged family members, actively engaged in negotiating their own family practices and relationships'.[6] They no longer just 'belong' to families. There are no presumptions that family members think or feel the same way, or that their interests and identities are merged within an inseparable or highly integrated unit.[7] This demands a change in the relationship between adults and children, moving away from the dominant ideology of the family.

But this is not to downgrade the importance of families. Children do require protection as they can be materially and physically vulnerable. They require adult support and supervision and parental love and attention. But, importantly, this new way of viewing children also recognises children's agency. Furthermore, research shows the enormous importance children 'attach to family life and relationships and the significance of family for their sense of well-being and for the formation of their identities. Family, it seems, is the setting above all others where children aspire to be treated as people in their own right.'[8] Families,

2 Smart, Neale and Wade, *Childhood*, p. 10.
3 This has been called a 'new sociology of childhood'. For a discussion of this work, see Alison Diduck, *Law's Families* (London: Butterworths, 2003), pp. 80–9; and Smart, Neale and Wade, *Childhood*.
4 Smart, Neale and Wade, *Childhood*, p. 58.
5 Anthony Giddens and Christopher Pierson, *Conversations with Anthony Giddens: Making Sense of Modernity* (Cambridge: Polity Press, 1998).
6 Smart, Neale and Wade, *Childhood*, p. 18.
7 Smart, Neale and Wade, *Childhood*, p. 18.
8 Smart, Neale and Wade, *Childhood*, p. 19.

therefore, remain extremely important, but the corollary is that within families children desire to be recognised as individuals.

These newer ways of thinking about children and childhood tie in with an approach to law and policy which respects, protects and promotes the individual rights of children. Thus, Tom Campbell has argued that 'the equal worth of all human persons, including children, is often best protected by ensuring that they have properly protected positive rights, justified in terms of their fundamental interests'.[9] Michael Freeman is equally clear in his support for children's rights, rejecting the argument that rights are not appropriate for children, as they may lead to conflict and do not allow space for the values of love, kindness and altruism.[10] He argues that conflicts already exist and, without rights, children's interests may not be recognised and protected. The existence of children's rights does not displace other values, it merely ensures that values which children may be in need of, for example protection, are ensured. Further, Freeman resists the idea that children's rights are not necessary because adults have their best interests at heart. This is the romantic ideal of family life which, Freeman rightly argues, is often absent. Indeed, as Tom Campbell further argued, it may be a symptom of the low status in which children are held that there is even a debate as to whether or not children should have rights.[11]

The political context to any discussion about children's rights is also important. Howard Cohen argues that the struggle for children's rights is part of the civil rights movements demanding rights for women, ethnic minorities and the like.[12] He argues that '"rights" is a militant concept to the extent that it is used as part of the ideology of a campaign for social change'.[13] This approach emphasises the pragmatic, political need to express claims in the language of rights, the language that will be successful in today's politics. To have a right is to have a trump card that is impossible to ignore. In the end it may be balanced with other rights, other trumps, but this balancing exercise must at least be carried out.

---

9 This is the 'interest' theory of rights, which suggests that, where an individual has certain interests, these interests may be protected by rights. For a discussion and justification of this approach, see Tom Campbell, 'The Rights of the Minor: As Person, as Child, as Juvenile, as Future Adult' in Philip Alston, Stephen Parker and John Seymour (eds.), *Children, Rights and the Law* (Oxford: Clarendon Press, 1992), pp. 1–23. For a classic exposition of the contrasting 'will' theory, see Neil MacCormick, *Legal Rights and Social Democracy* (Oxford: Clarendon Press, 1982).

10 Michael Freeman, 'Taking Children's Rights More Seriously' in Alston, Parker and Seymour (eds.), *Children*, pp. 52–71 at p. 55.

11 Campbell, 'Rights of the Minor', 3.

12 For a contrary view, see Onora O'Neill, who argues that the movement for children's rights is very different from other movements and as such parallels cannot be drawn: Onora O'Neill, 'Children's Rights and Children's Lives' in Alston, Parker and Seymour (eds.), *Children*, pp. 24–42 at p. 38.

13 Howard Cohen, *Equal Rights for Children* (Totowa, NJ: Littlefield, 1980), p. 45, quoted in Michael Freeman, 'The Limits of Children's Rights' in Michael Freeman and Philip Veerman (eds.), *The Ideologies of Children's Rights* (Leiden: Martinus Nijhoff, 1992), p. 31.

In the context of the European Union, these justifications for children's rights are extremely important. The rhetoric of rights has long been a legitimating force within the Union, as well as being deemed essential to its international status. Therefore, claims for children's rights fit neatly within the existing rhetoric and political values. In addition, as the Union has responded to the rights claims of women, ethnic minorities and other disadvantaged groups, generally in response to the international recognition of such claims, so too the Union has begun to recognise children's claims just as the international community has done. Nonetheless, while the international community has indeed taken steps to promote children's rights, this has not been without controversy.

It is the perceived attack on 'the family' which provokes the most resistance to children's rights. At root is the ideology of the 'private' family which should, it is argued, be free from state interference. This laissez-faire approach not only ignores children's claims but resists intervention in 'the family' on behalf of others who may be exploited or oppressed. Such an ideology, separating the public and private spheres and demanding no state intervention in the latter, has long been challenged by feminists who have demonstrated the detrimental effect of this concept for the autonomy and freedom of many within families, and such logic can equally be applied to the situation of children.[14]

It is the strong attachment to the ideology of the private family which means that claims for children's rights are often met with disdain. Ultimately, children's rights challenge the 'manner in which society organises family life and requires a reassessment of how it should respond to children's needs'.[15] Such a reassessment is a difficult exercise which requires a balance between the legitimate claims of families, the individual needs of children and the interests of society. Lifting the veil of family privacy does not necessarily mean state regulation of parenthood, or state parenting, but societal recognition that a child has interests which may conflict with parental wishes and which might therefore need to be protected. It may also signal that society takes an interest in the well-being of children, such that it does not surrender their care and attention to parents and parents alone. The corollary of such a conceptualisation may be a broader approach to the responsibility of children; that is, society as a whole has interests in and obligations towards children and therefore should play a part in their upbringing.

There are, of course, limits to rights.[16] The focus must be on action, not just on the rhetoric of rights. The adoption of a convention, or a charter, may be a valuable signal of intent, but it requires implementation. Equally, as feminists have long argued, law reform, and the adoption of charters of rights, do not

---

14 See further Jo Bridgeman and Daniel Monk (eds.), *Feminist Perspectives on Child Law* (London: Cavendish, 2000).

15 Jane Fortin, *Children's Rights and the Developing Law* (London: Butterworths, 1998), p. v.

16 For a discussion of the limits to the rights approach, see Michael Freeman, 'Taking Children's Rights More Seriously' (1992) 6 *International Journal of Law and the Family* 52–71 at 60–1.

always have the intended consequences: thus, rights can 'backfire'.[17] But this does not necessarily mean that a rights strategy should be abandoned. More, it reminds us that vigilance is required to monitor practices and demand change if necessary. Ultimately, as Michael Freeman argues, rights claims require a redistribution of resources. Without such a redistribution, the rights in the end will be 'meaningless'.[18] Nonetheless, without the rights claims, it may be more difficult to demand the resources. This is certainly the case in a political climate in which rights-rhetoric often trumps other discourses and in which being able to demand resources for the protection or enforcement of a 'right' is more likely to be successful than such a claim without the attendant right.

3.2   Children and European Union law

Having considered the approach upon which Union law and policy regarding children should be based, this section moves on to examine current Union law as it applies to children. The key area of free movement is considered first, followed by a discussion of the emerging family law of the Union, policies on childcare and co-operation regarding trafficking and violence against children.[19]

3.2.1   Children and free movement

It was in the field of free movement of persons that Community law first granted entitlements to children.[20] Secondary legislation detailed the rights to be extended to the families of migrant workers, including children, as a means of encouraging greater movement. Accordingly, from the very beginning, rights were granted to families and children in order to facilitate the free movement of economic actors: children were instrumental to the achievement of free movement and therefore the success of the single market. This instrumentalism remains the basis for children's entitlements in this field which, in large part, is due to a limited legal basis. In addition, a traditional norm of family life and children's dependent status within families restrict the opportunities for children to exercise their independence and autonomy and creates differences between children depending on their family status. Finally, the recently adopted Free Movement Directive fails to improve significantly the provisions relating to children, and thus represents a considerable lost opportunity.[21] Nonetheless, the Court of Justice has been

17 Freeman, 'Children's Rights', 60.
18 Freeman, 'Children's Rights', 61.
19 For a detailed discussion of the nature and extent of children's citizenship in the Union, see Louise Ackers and Helen Stalford, *A Community for Children? Children, Citizenship and Internal Migration in the EU* (Aldershot: Ashgate, 2004).
20 The rights do not apply in a wholly internal situation, thus creating division between children: Joined Cases 35–36/82, *Morson v. State of Netherlands* [1982] ECR 3723; [1983] 2 CMLR 221.
21 Directive 2004/58/EC of the European Parliament and of the Council of 29 April 2004 on the right of citizens of the Union and their family members to move and reside freely within the territory of the Member States, OJ 2004 L 229/35. Member states have until April 2006 to

innovative in its interpretation of existing entitlements and has extended the scope of children's rights in this field, though it ultimately remains constrained by the limits of its own competence. Accordingly, although steps have been made towards granting entitlements to children qua children, fundamentally, children and their rights remain a pawn in the single market game and the familialisation of children continues to be a dominant feature.

3.2.1.1   The 'child' of Community law

In *Lubor Gaal*, Advocate General Tesauro stated correctly that 'not one article and still less the preamble contains a definition of child' for the purposes of the free movement provisions.[22] Article 10 of Regulation 1612/68[23] provided that the worker's 'spouse and their descendants who are under the age of 21 or are dependants' are entitled to install themselves with the worker in the host member state. While this wording appeared to suggest that only joint children of the worker and spouse qualified,[24] it seems unlikely that the Court would interpret it in such a restrictive manner. Certainly, in *Baumbast* a step-child was treated as a member of the migrant worker's family for the purposes of the proceedings.[25] Similarly, Advocate General Stix-Hackl in the *Carpenter* case argued that the interests of step-children were protected by the 'right to family life' which is a fundamental right protected by Community law.[26] Again, although the Court did not make such an explicit finding, it did hold that there had been a breach of the right to family life by the deportation of a step-parent who was caring for the children of a citizen exercising free movement rights. In any event, the new Free Movement Directive clears up this point in providing that family rights are to be granted to the 'direct descendants who are under the age of 21 or are dependants and those of the spouse or partner'.[27] This clearly means that step-children will be included within the definition of family. However, this new definition does add a new source of ambiguity. The intention of including the qualifying term 'direct' of descendant is not apparent. It may be that this is intended to exclude

---

implement the terms of the directive. Accordingly, the discussion which follows considers both the existing law and the extent of any changes as a result of the new directive.

22 Case C-7/94, *Lubor Gaal* [1995] ECR I-1031; [1995] 3 CMLR 17, para. 7 of the Opinion.

23 Council Regulation 1612/68/EEC of 15 October 1968 on freedom of movement for workers within the Community, OJ 1968 L 257/2.

24 This may of course be an issue only in the English language. In addition, the relevant provision in Directive 73/148, governing the family entitlements of those establishing themselves or providing services, refers to 'the spouse and the children under 21', wording which would seem to cover children of one of the partners to the marriage from a previous relationship: Article 1(c) of Council Directive 73/148/EEC of 21 May 1973 on the abolition of restrictions on movement and residence within the Community for nationals of Member States with regard to establishment and the provision of services, OJ 1973 L 172/14.

25 Case C-413/99, *Baumbast and R* v. *Secretary of State for the Home Department* [2002] ECR I-7091; [2002] 3 CMLR 23, para. 17.

26 Case C-60/00, *Carpenter* v. *Secretary of State for the Home Department* [2002] ECR I-6279; [2002] 2 CMLR 64, para. 94.

27 Article 2(2)(c) of Directive 2004/58/EC, OJ 2004 L 229/35.

grandchildren, but doubtless they too are 'direct' descendants. It does, unfortunately, raise a question regarding adopted children or those born using fertility treatments where the child cannot be said to be a direct 'descendant'. However, it would surely be repugnant were the Court of Justice to exclude from the scope of these provisions an adopted child or a child born to parents by fertility treatment who may not be genetically related to them.

Article 10 of Regulation 1612/68 and Article 2(2)(c) of the new Directive also extend rights to the child of a worker/citizen who is over twenty-one years of age and 'dependent'. In *Lebon*, the Court held that dependency is a factual issue to be determined on a case-by-case basis and that national courts should not engage in an assessment of whether the individual *should* be dependent or not, or whether they *should* be able to support themselves by working.[28] Potentially, therefore, a child could be over twenty-one, be unemployed or in education, and, if continued to be supported by their migrant parent, will remain within the scope of Regulation 1612/68. Lorna Woods described this interpretation of dependency as 'relatively generous'[29] and indeed it suggests that children of migrant workers may remain within the scope of the free movement provisions for many years after the age of twenty-one.

However, before a child or dependent adult can begin to consider their entitlements under Regulation 1612/68, or the new Directive, the parent has to qualify. As will be discussed in more detail in the chapters that follow, the 'family' of Community law is largely based on the dominant ideology of the family. This clearly disadvantages children who are members of families who do not fall within this norm. For example, the child of unmarried parents has considerably fewer rights than the child of married parents owing to the judgment in *Netherlands* v. *Reed* where the Court held that the term 'spouse' is limited to married partners.[30] Further, the confusion over the rights of a non-working spouse on divorce, following *Diatta*,[31] translates into considerable uncertainty for any children of the marriage, especially where the primary carer is a non-working, third country national. The new Free Movement Directive does little to expand the concept of family, with children of families outside the norm continuing to be adversely affected. There are improvements in the rights of family members following the death or divorce of the Union citizen (discussed further in chapter 5), but even these provisions are subject to a number of conditions.

---

28 Case 316/85, *Lebon* [1987] ECR 2811; [1989] 1 CMLR 337. In Case C-200/02, *Chen and Zhu* v. *Secretary of State for the Home Department* [2004] 3 CMLR 48, the Advocate General opined that 'dependency' could not be interpreted to include 'emotional dependency', it clearly being 'material' dependency that is required: Opinion of 18 May 2004, paras. 84–5. The judgment of 19 October 2004 confirmed it is material dependency that is required: para. 43.

29 Lorna Woods, 'Family Rights in the European Union: Disadvantaging the Disadvantaged?' (1999) 11 *Child and Family Law Quarterly* 17–31 at 25.

30 Case 59/85, *Netherlands* v. *Reed* [1986] ECR 1283; [1987] 2 CMLR 448.

31 Case 267/83, *Diatta* v. *Land Berlin* [1985] ECR 567.

Accordingly, therefore, while it appears that who constitutes a 'child' is relatively broad, the personal scope of the provisions remains limited by the overall concept of family. Thus, as Louise Ackers and Helen Stalford have argued, children are the 'passive beneficiaries or victims of derived entitlement and their status is very much a consequence of their parents' employment status and relationships; they are the invisible appendages of the breadwinning migrant family'.[32] Moreover, the new Directive, while clearing up the status of stepchildren, raises new levels of confusion regarding other children, and has done little to improve the overall situation of children in families outside of the married nuclear family.

3.2.1.2   Entitlements granted to children: facilitating free movement?

In terms of the material rights extended to children, migrants are granted the same 'social and tax advantages' as nationals in order to facilitate free movement.[33] While the Court initially interpreted this provision to apply only to benefits related to employment,[34] in recent years it has extended its scope to a wide range of family and child benefits. Thus, migrants and their families are entitled to many independent family benefits,[35] such as subsidised child-birth loans,[36] family allowances and unemployment benefit for the children of migrant workers.[37] Helen Stalford argues that the extension in the scope of entitlements supports the Community's 'willingness to depart from following purely market-driven objectives towards a more socially-driven role'.[38] Nonetheless, although the link with the employment status of the migrant worker has diminished, there remains the requirement to demonstrate that payment of such benefits is necessary in order to 'facilitate free movement'. Thus, the social and tax advantages that are extended to the families and children of migrant workers may benefit them as individuals, but the benefits are granted on the basis that they encourage the *migrant's* free movement. The rights remain parasitic on the migrant; rights are granted to children instrumentally in order to ensure economic success.

---

32 Louise Ackers and Helen Stalford, 'Children, Migration and Citizenship in the European Union: Intra-Community Mobility and the Status of Children in EC Law' (1999) 21 *Children and Youth Services Review* 987–1010 at 1007.

33 Article 7(2) of Regulation 1612/68, OJ 1968 L 257/2.

34 Case 76/72, *S.* v. *Fonds national de reclassement social des handicapés* [1973] ECR 437.

35 Case 32/75, *Cristini* v. *Société nationale des chemins de fer français (SNCF)* [1975] ECR 1085; [1976] 1 CMLR 573.

36 Case 65/81, *Reina* v. *Landeskreditbank Baden-Württemberg* [1982] ECR 33; [1982] 1 CMLR 744.

37 Case 94/84, *Office national de l'emploi* v. *Deak* [1985] ECR 1873. In addition, the Court has held that the son of an Italian migrant worker residing in France could claim disability benefit from the French authorities by virtue of the fact that he was dependent on his parent-worker: Case 63/76, *Inzirillo* v. *Caisse d'allocations familiales de l'arrondissement de Lyon* [1976] ECR 2057; [1978] 3 CMLR 596.

38 Helen Stalford, 'The Citizenship Status of Children in the European Union' (2000) 8 *International Journal of Children's Rights* 101–31 at 108.

This instrumentalisation of children and their rights is, nevertheless, evolving into an approach which more readily recognises the autonomy of children. While the Court is constrained by the competence conferred on it by the treaties, and the scope of the relevant legislative provisions, in *Humer* it showed how it could use its interpretative imagination to expand the scope of the existing law.[39] In this case, following the divorce of her parents, Humer moved to France from Austria with her mother. Her father's subsequent failure to continue maintenance payments led to Humer commencing an action in the Austrian courts for recovery of the money owed. The relevant Austrian provisions insisted on a residence requirement before making such a claim, while the relevant Community provision, Regulation 1408/71,[40] entitles the migrant worker and spouse[41] to apply for family benefits, but no reference had been made to children.

The Court held that, although Regulation 1408/71 does not expressly cover entitlements post-divorce, there is nothing to justify excluding such situations from its scope.[42] This is particularly important here as it was following the divorce of her parents that Humer's mother moved to France, disentitling Humer, on the basis of the Austrian law, from claiming the maintenance payments. As the Court went on to say, it is entirely foreseeable that, following a divorce, the parent who has custody of the child may move to another member state to establish themselves or take up work.[43] In such a situation, if the Austrian law were allowed to stand, Humer would have been denied a benefit precisely because her mother exercised her rights of free movement.

Furthermore, there was technically no exercise of the right of free movement which would bring Humer within the scope of the Regulation. Her father, an Austrian national, had not exercised free movement rights as he remained in Austria. Humer's mother had exercised free movement rights, but the benefit being claimed was owed by the father to the child under Austrian law, not the law of the mother's new host member state. Nonetheless, the Court recognised that there was a Community element to this case and that it was the responsibility of the Community to ensure that this child was not disadvantaged because of the existence of Community law rights.

Thus, the Court recognised the reality of post-divorce family life and extended Community law to cover such situations, most importantly ameliorating any adverse impact the combination of divorce and free movement might have on children. In addition, the child's individual right to make a claim under the relevant provisions was recognised, going some way towards a concept of children

39 Case C-255/99, *Re Humer* [2002] ECR I-1205; [2004] 1 CMLR 41.
40 Council Regulation 1408/71/EEC of 14 June 1971 on the application of social security schemes to employed persons and their families moving within the Community, OJ 1971 L 149/2.
41 Extended to the spouse in Case C-78/91, *Hughes* v. *Chief Adjudication Officer, Belfast* [1992] ECR I-4839; [1992] 3 CMLR 490.
42 *Re Humer*, para. 42.
43 *Re Humer*, para. 43.

and their rights which focuses on their individuality and not only on their family context.

3.2.1.3   Rights to education: towards independence?

This more progressive approach is being replicated in relation to children's educational entitlements under the free movement provisions. Children benefit from Article 12 of Regulation 1612/68 which grants the children of migrant workers access to the educational system of the host state under the same conditions as nationals. In essence, the Court's jurisprudence under Article 12, combined with a broad interpretation of Article 7(2) covering fees and maintenance grants, has been sufficiently progressive for children's educational rights to be almost free-standing.[44] Thus, in *Echternach and Moritz*, the Court held that a child's education rights continue despite the parents returning to their home state.[45] A social justice explanation was given for such a ruling by the Advocate General, who stated that to hold otherwise would place a 'family in a highly precarious situation, quite often dependent on the father's behaviour'.[46] While this judgment was clearly far-reaching, the Court stuck to its 'facilitating free movement' justification, reducing the conceptual effect.[47] This ruling was extended in *Lubor Gaal*, where the Court dispensed with both the age (the child was over twenty-one) and dependency requirements (both parents were deceased).[48] As Louise Ackers and Helen Stalford point out, this ruling 'significantly enhances the independent status' of children, provided they can prove a biological link with a migrant worker.[49]

In *Baumbast*, the Court took very clear steps to recognise the child's right to education and the significance of such rights in the context of free movement.[50] The education of migrant children was deemed sufficiently important to grant continued residence to the children's carer, even after the lapse of the carer's independent right of residence, thereby enabling the children to continue their education in the host member state. To hold otherwise would have effectively deprived the children of their Community rights. The Court derived such an entitlement from Article 12 of Regulation 1612/68, rather than looking to the right to education found in the Charter of Fundamental Rights, or indeed the

---

44 For a recent example, see Case C-184/99, *Grzelczyk* v. *Centre public d'aide sociale d'Ottignies-Louvain-la-Neuve* [2001] ECR I-6193; [2002] 1 CMLR 19. For a discussion of this case and further examples of the development of the Court's jurisprudence in this field, see Castro Oliveira, 'Workers and Other Persons: Step-by-Step from Movement to Citizenship – Case Law 1995–2001' (2002) 39 *Common Market Law Review* 77–127.

45 Joined Cases 389–390/87, *Echternach and Moritz* v. *Minister van Onderwijs en Wetenschappen* [1989] ECR 723; [1990] 2 CMLR 305.

46 *Echternach and Moritz*, para. 43.

47 *Echternach and Moritz*, para. 49.

48 Case C-7/94, *Lubor Gaal* [1995] ECR I-1031; [1995] 3 CMLR 17.

49 Ackers and Stalford, 'Children, Migration and Citizenship', 1003.

50 Case C-413/99, *Baumbast and R* v. *Secretary of State for the Home Department* [2002] ECR I-7091; [2002] 3 CMLR 23.

educational rights in the European Convention. Thus, the child's right continues to be derived from the free movement provisions, rather than being based on broader human rights justifications.[51] Nonetheless, as Louise Ackers and Helen Stalford argue, the fact that the spouse and children's claims were considered in isolation from that of the migrant worker does represent a positive departure from the Court's previous emphasis on facilitating the mobility of the migrant worker.[52] Thus, *Baumbast* is a bold judgment which reaches beyond the traditional scope of the free movement provisions.[53] It broadens existing interpretations of the law, as well as expanding our approach to these provisions by emphasising the importance of the child's rights, albeit that they remain derived from a parent's entitlements. Most importantly, the *Baumbast* principle has now been given a legislative footing in the new Free Movement Directive which provides that the death or departure from the host state of the Union citizen shall not entail the loss of a right of residence of any children, or of the parent who has custody irrespective of their nationality, if the children reside in the host member state and are enrolled at an educational establishment for the purpose of studying there.[54]

The broad interpretation given to Articles 7(2) and 12 of Regulation 1612/68 by the Court, and the provisions of the new Directive, help to remove some concerns regarding education from the migration decision. However, the entitlements remain limited to access to education and are premised largely on an assimilationist model. There remain, therefore, considerable difficulties in terms of a child's language abilities and therefore ability to benefit from education in the host member state. It was due to the limitations of an access-only approach to children's educational entitlements that Directive 77/486 was adopted. This Directive applies only to compulsory education and is therefore considerably more limited than Regulation 1612/68. Nonetheless, it attempts to go beyond the assimilationist, non-discrimination model and attempts to recognise the different experience of migrant children. It therefore encourages, though not obliges, member states to provide special educational assistance for the children of migrant workers, especially regarding language training. However, empirical research has found that the implementation of this directive has been inconsistent and half-hearted.[55]

---

51 See further Holly Cullen, 'Children's Rights' in Steve Peers and Angela Ward (eds.), *The European Union Charter of Fundamental Rights* (Oxford: Hart Publishing, 2004), pp. 323–46 at pp. 325–6.

52 Ackers and Stalford, *A Community for Children?*, p. 94.

53 See further Norbert Reich and Solvita Harbacevica, 'Citizenship and Family on Trial: A Fairly Optimistic Overview of Recent Court Practice with Regard to the Free Movement of Persons' (2003) 40 *Common Market Law Review* 615–38.

54 Article 12(3) of Directive 2004/58/EC, OJ 2004 L 229/35.

55 Louise Ackers (director), *Children, Citizenship and Internal Migration in the European Community* (Project funded by the Nuffield Foundation and the European Commission, project reference 96-10-EET-0122-00), chapter 6.

Accordingly, while the Court has attempted to ensure that children of migrants are integrated into the education system of the host member state to a considerable extent, member states' implementation of measures to make that integration a reality has been negligible. This is regrettable for two main reasons. First, the education of migrant children is adversely affected and the individual child's right to education is not truly enforced. To recognise the child's rights means more than simply allowing access to education. There seems little that the Charter of Fundamental Rights can do to improve this situation. The Charter provides that 'everyone has the right to education' which 'includes the possibility to receive free compulsory education'.[56] Ultimately, therefore, the extent to which the individual rights of children are respected is improving but remains limited.

The second main reason why this limited approach to children's education rights is problematic is that education remains a key concern for migrant parents.[57] Empirical evidence suggests that education entitlements often constitute a decisive factor in decisions regarding migration and that in many cases children either remained in the member state of origin or returned there for periods of time in order to continue their education. Furthermore, the continued resort to 'international' schools for many migrant families demonstrates the lack of faith in the effectiveness of integration within the education system of the host member state and highlights the problems posed by migration in terms of the transferability of educational qualifications and progression. As Helen Stalford confirms, the ability to transfer skills and qualifications from one country's context to another is an essential prerequisite to the operation and exercise of free movement, but in the field of academic education has been largely ignored.[58] This is partly an issue of competence, with competence in relation to professional and vocational qualifications being clear, and children's education remaining tightly controlled by member states. The impact, however, of this situation is to leave the children of migrant workers with little security regarding their education. Helen Stalford refers to empirical research which demonstrates that the 'school environment provides an important arena for integration, and failure to adapt to this can serve to exacerbate the child's sense of dislocation and isolation, as well as significantly impeding academic progress'.[59] Thus, for so long as the Union is encouraging the free movement of persons, and thereby encouraging families to move within the Union, it is incumbent upon it to consider the effects which these policies have on children and to ameliorate any adverse impacts. Directive 77/486 on the education of the children of migrant workers may have

---

56 Article 14 of the Charter of Fundamental Rights, OJ 2000 C 364/1.
57 Ackers, *Children, Citizenship and Internal Migration*, chapter 6.
58 Helen Stalford, 'Transferability of Educational Skills and Qualifications in the European Union: The Case of EU Migrant Children' in Jo Shaw (ed.), *Social Law and Policy in an Evolving European Union* (Oxford: Hart Publishing, 2001), pp. 243–58.
59 Stalford, 'Transferability of Educational Skills', 244.

been a response to such concerns, but its non-compulsory nature and lack of implementation have meant that the Directive has been largely ineffective.[60]

Accordingly, while the educational rights of children do remain derivative, considerable steps are being taken to emphasise the importance of children's educational rights. As Helen Stalford points out, as 'economic, monetary, political and even cultural and linguistic barriers between member states are gradually eroded, there is a growing need for provisions which will accommodate the eventuality of an increasing number of young migrants'.[61] She argues that European and domestic education policy needs not just to take into account current migration trends, but also to envisage a more integrated and mobile Community future in which more young people will be pursuing an academic route in another member state.[62]

3.2.1.4   Free movement and third country nationals: privileging the nuclear family?

The preceding discussion has focused on the rights of children of Union citizens. With the adoption of the Family Reunification Directive, the Community extended residence and movement rights to third country nationals and their families.[63] However, there are considerable differences between the families of Union citizens and of third country nationals in terms of the concept of family adopted and the rights granted to 'children'. For a start, the preamble to the Directive states that its provisions are centred on the 'nuclear family, that is to say the spouse and minor children'.[64] This is an inauspicious start which is confirmed by examining the provisions of the Directive in detail.

The Directive provides for the admission of the sponsor's 'spouse' and their joint children which includes adopted children.[65] The explicit recognition of adopted children is welcome, especially in light of the possible concerns, discussed above, regarding the interpretation of the recently adopted Free Movement Directive. However, a clear distinction is drawn between joint children and step-children, with a dependency and custody requirement being imposed on the latter. The custody requirement is valid, but there are no grounds for distinguishing between joint children and step-children on the basis of dependency.

---

60 Council Directive 77/486/EEC of 25 July 1977, OJ 1977 L 199/32. For details of the lack of implementation, see the reports of the European Commission COM/88/787 and COM/94/80.
61 Stalford, 'Transferability of Educational Skills', 254.
62 Stalford, 'Transferability of Educational Skills', 257. See also Ackers and Stalford, *A Community for Children?*, chapter 8.
63 Council Directive 2003/86/EC of 22 September 2003, OJ 2003 L 251/12. The limited scope of the family rights in the Family Reunification Directive is mirrored in the Long-Term Residency Directive which grants rights of movement to legally resident third country nationals: Council Directive 2003/109/EC of 25 November 2003, OJ 2004 L 16/44. See further Steve Peers, 'Key Legislative Developments on Migration in the European Union' (2003) 5 *European Journal of Migration and Law* 387–410.
64 Preamble (para. 10) to Council Directive 2003/86/EC, OJ 2003 L 251/12.
65 Article 4(1)(a) and (b) of Council Directive 2003/86/EC, OJ 2003 L 251/12.

While dependency is likely to be easily demonstrated in most cases, it remains that there is a division drawn between children on the basis of the status of their parents and the nature of their family unit, a distinction which privileges the traditional, intact, nuclear family. Furthermore, the admission of step-children where there is joint custody is not required by the Directive, even where the co-parent consents.[66]

As a result of these provisions, the Directive has created a wholly discreditable hierarchy of rights dependent on the perceived proximity of the child and the family unit to the traditional nuclear family. Thus, at the top of the hierarchy is the joint child of the spouse and sponsor who must be admitted even if not materially dependent (though they must still be under the age of majority and unmarried). In second place is the step-child in respect of whom there is an order of sole residency, provided that child is dependent. The admittance of a step-child who is the subject of a joint residency order is left to the discretion of member states, even where the co-parent has consented (and provided they are dependent). Arguably, the difference between the child of sole custody and of joint custody is in perceived links to the family being unified in the member state, there being an implicit assumption that the child of joint custody is less integrated into the sponsor's family and therefore the requirements imposed on the member state may be more permissive. At the bottom of the heap is the child whose parents, or parent and step-parent, are not married. There is no obligation on member states to admit the unmarried partner of the sponsor, with Article 4(3) of the Directive only providing that member states 'may' authorise the entry and residence of an unmarried partner in a 'duly attested long-term stable relationship' or of a partner in a 'registered partnership'.

Thus, while the Union Charter declares the right of a child to maintain contact with both their parents, which might arguably be best achieved via a joint custody order, the existence of such an order may in fact work against the child's interests in other circumstances.[67] It does not seem that the child's best interests, which the Charter declares are to be a primary consideration, are being prioritised.[68] This is further evident in the derogation granted to member states to insist that children over twelve have to meet a condition of 'integration', relating to language and educational skills, if such legislation already exists in that member state. Finally, there is a clear incongruity between the provisions of the Directive which enable member states to set an age limit of twenty-one for both the sponsor and the spouse, but also to insist (if such legislation is already in existence in a member state at the time of adoption of the Directive) that the child must be under fifteen years of age, with different entitlements applying in respect of an older child. As Steve Peers rightly argues, it appears that 'while 20 year olds could be considered

---

66 Article 4(1)(c) and (d) of Council Directive 2003/86/EC, OJ 2003 L 251/12.
67 Article 24 of the Charter of Fundamental Rights, OJ 2000 C 364/1, discussed further below.
68 Also Article 24 of the Charter of Fundamental Rights, OJ 2000 C 364/1, discussed further below.

too immature to get married, 15 year olds could be considered too mature to enter as children'.[69]

3.2.1.5   Free movement and children's rights: from instrumentalism to individual rights?

Until the 2004 judgment in *Chen and Zhu*, it was clear that, despite the interpretative progress made by the Court of Justice, the rights and entitlements of children remained dependent on the exercise of free movement by their parents. Rights and entitlements were not granted to children as independent citizens, but rather were 'contingent upon their familial, dependent link with an adult who qualifies under the free movement provisions'.[70] It was assumed that a child could not, therefore, independently exercise rights of free movement (unless a worker in their own right) and could not access benefits unless they were deemed to 'facilitate' the free movement of the parent. This fortified 'children's dependency on their parents' and reinforced the '"partial" and "conditional" nature of their citizenship status within the EU'.[71] This market-driven context to children's rights enhanced their vulnerability by reinforcing their dependency on their parents.

While this remains largely the case, it was held in *Chen and Zhu* that a child can avail themselves of the rights accorded to Union citizens in Directive 90/364[72] to move and take up residence in another host member state so long as they have sufficient financial resources and the requisite medical insurance.[73] That such financial resources are in fact the resources of their parent is not material.[74] Furthermore, a right of residence must be granted to the child's primary carer, for the duration of the child's residence, even where that person is a third country national without an independent right of residence, as to hold otherwise would 'deprive the child's right of residence of any useful effect'.[75]

This is a significant judgment which finally recognises children's independent rights within the Union: a child has an independent right of movement and residence within the Union, regardless of their familial status and regardless of whether or not their parent is exercising free movement rights. The Advocate General considered in detail the attempts by the Irish government (the child being an Irish national) to restrict the scope of this Directive on the basis that the child was too young to be able to independently exercise her rights. Such claims go right to the heart of the debate about children's rights, with the Irish government effectively arguing that, as the child was so young, and could not independently

---

69 Peers, 'Key Legislative Developments on Migration', 403.
70 Stalford, 'Citizenship Status of Children', 110.
71 Stalford, 'Citizenship Status of Children', 110.
72 Council Directive 90/364/EEC of 28 June 1990 on the right of residence, OJ 1990 L 180/26.
73 Case C-200/02, *Chen and Zhu* v. *Secretary of State for the Home Department* [2004] 3 CMLR 48. Such entitlements are now incorporated into the new Free Movement Directive 2004/58/EC, OJ 2004 L 229/35.
74 *Chen and Zhu*, paras. 29–30.
75 *Chen and Zhu*, para. 45.

exercise her rights, she 'cannot be a person entitled to the rights accorded to nationals' by the Directive.[76] Just because the child cannot exercise the right independently, as she is dependent on her parents or another adult, does not, as the Advocate General contended, mean that she has no capacity to be an addressee of rights and therefore a holder of rights.[77] Children should, as indicated earlier in this chapter, be granted rights qua children, thereby recognising their independence and autonomy. This approach was endorsed by the Court, which held that the rights of free movement of persons 'cannot be made conditional upon the attainment by the person concerned of an age prescribed for the acquisition of legal capacity to exercise those rights personally'.[78]

However, while the recently adopted Free Movement Directive and the Court's jurisprudence have advanced the rights of children in important ways, and towards a more autonomous concept of the child, the approach of the Union to the rights of third country nationals reveals the limited scope of any genuine interest in promoting and protecting the rights of children qua children. No coherent approach to the rights of children has been taken in this area of law, with exceptions being made on arbitrary grounds based on the existing diverse provisions of national laws. Thus, we have derogations relating to twelve year olds and fifteen year olds, and a possible limitation on the rights of those under the age of twenty-one. There is no justified reason for such distinctions other than political compromises made to appease particular member states. The notion of children's human rights appeared to be far from the minds of the Union legislature.

Further positive developments may ensue as a result of the European Parliament's decision to challenge the adoption of the Family Reunification Directive[79] on the basis that the right to reunification for unaccompanied children over the age of twelve may be restricted.[80] This is contrary to existing international standards, particularly the UN Convention on the Rights of the Child. As Alison Hunter notes, the position of children who have been separated from their parents is particularly vulnerable as they are at risk of neglect, violence, sexual assault and many other abuses.[81] For the Union to be turning away from these children underlines the insecure foundations of children's rights within the Union.

---

76 *Chen and Zhu*, para. 42. This is the 'will' theory of rights, namely that only those who have the power to exercise their rights, to exercise their 'will', and are able to waive their rights, can be said to be rights bearers. As children, especially a child as young as the one in this case, are unable to exercise their will, they should not be granted rights. The 'interest' theory is preferable: where an individual has certain interests, as indeed children have, these interests may be protected by rights. One can have interests without having the rational capacity to know that this is the case and/or to waive such an interest. See further Campbell, 'Rights of the Minor'.
77 *Chen and Zhu*, para. 45.
78 *Chen and Zhu*, para. 20.
79 Article 4 of Council Directive 2003/86/EC, OJ 2003 L 251/12.
80 Case C-540/03, *European Parliament v. Council* [2004] OJ C 47/21.
81 Alison Hunter, 'Between the Domestic and the International: The Role of the European Union in Providing Protection for Unaccompanied Refugee Children in the United Kingdom' (2001) 3 *European Journal of Migration and Law* 383–410 at 383.

3.2.2   Children and the emerging European Union family law

In 2000, the Union adopted its first measure in the family law field, namely Regulation 1347/2000 on the jurisdiction, recognition and enforcement of judgments in matrimonial matters.[82] While this Regulation began to recognise the potential adverse impact of increasing free movement on relationships and children, it failed in its approach to children and their rights. The Regulation only dealt with parental responsibility disputes arising on the breakdown of the parents' marriage. No provision, therefore, was made for the children of cohabiting parents or for step-children. From the inception of the Union's family law, therefore, a hierarchy of relationships was established, with marriage being prioritised, and the concerns and needs of only some children being addressed. Further, while the Regulation made provision for the recognition of judgments relating to parental responsibility, there was no provision recognising the interests of children in these matters.

As a result of such criticisms, the Commission proposed a new Regulation dealing with matters of parental responsibility for all children which was adopted in November 2003.[83] The new Regulation provides for a common rule to determine which judge is competent to rule on matters such as parental responsibility, especially when a child is abducted from one of its parents and also seeks to ensure automatic and immediate recognition of decisions on visiting rights. This Regulation marks an important step forward as it is applicable to all children, regardless of the nature of the parental relationship and applies to all parental responsibility decisions, not just those made at the time of relationship breakdown. The Commission had justified its proposal on the basis of the need to guarantee 'equality of treatment for all children', thus taking into account 'social realities, such as the diversification of family structures'.[84] This principle of equality is written into the Preamble.[85] Further, the Preamble states that the Regulation 'seeks to ensure respect for the fundamental rights of the child' as set out in Article 24 of the Charter.[86] As discussed further below, Article 24 of the Charter includes the best interests principle, the right for a child to be heard and the right to maintain contact with both parents, all rights which are central in the area of parental responsibility decisions.

---

82 Council Regulation 1347/2000 of 29 May 2000 on jurisdiction and the recognition and enforcement of judgments in matrimonial matters and in matters of parental responsibility for children of both spouses, OJ 2000 L 160/19. See further chapter 6.

83 Council Regulation 2201/2003/EC of 27 November 2003 concerning jurisdiction and the recognition and enforcement of judgments in matrimonial matters and in matters of parental responsibility, repealing Regulation 1347/2000/EC, OJ 2003 L 338/1.

84 Commission Working Document COM (2001) 166 final: Mutual recognition of decisions on parental responsibility, p. 2.

85 Preamble (para. 5) to Council Regulation 2201/2003/EC, OJ 2003 L 338/1.

86 Preamble (para. 33) to Council Regulation 2201/2003/EC, OJ 2003 L 338/1.

Empirical research has highlighted how children may be adversely affected by family breakdown in families which have migrated, and highlights the inadequacy of legal protection for children in this context.[87] The legal impact of divorce is particularly important here, especially in terms of extinguishing a non-working or third country national's residency entitlement and potentially therefore the child's residency. There is indeed a greater propensity for family breakdown in migrant situations and therefore the responsibility of the Union is even greater.[88] Furthermore, the complex geography of migratory families, with many moves within a short space of time, simply exacerbates the problems and requires ever more sophisticated systems for dealing with family breakdown.[89] Thus, this new Regulation recognises the Union's role in making family life more complex by facilitating cross-border families and family breakdown and in this way the potentially adverse impact of Union policies on children is being addressed. Accordingly, while the Union's first entrance into the family law field raised many serious concerns, such criticisms are beginning to be addressed.[90]

3.2.3 Children, care and the right to parental time

In recent years, extensive policies on childcare and the reconciliation of family and professional life have been developed by the Union. However, what remains intriguing in this policy field is that, although measures on the reconciliation of paid work and family life intimately involve children, ironically children are often left out of the discussion. Debate focuses around the needs, desires and policy prescriptions for mothers and fathers, with little discussion of the interests, needs and wants of children. The childhood, or children's, perspective is largely missing from debate. If anything, children are viewed as 'obstacles' to labour market participation, or 'objects' for whom care has to be arranged, rather than subjects with their own needs. As in the field of free movement, this is partly a competence issue. However, policy is well developed in this area and if that policy is fuelled by economic and instrumentalist concerns then that will affect the nature and effect of the policy and therefore the impact on children. Despite such a gloomy picture, there are signs that change is afoot and that the future looks more child-oriented.

Since the mid-1970s, the Community has proclaimed the need for measures to ensure the reconciliation of the professional and family lives of parents.[91] Initially part of the sex equality programmes of the Community, in the late 1990s this area of policy became part of the more general employment policy of the Union.

---

87 Ackers, *Children, Citizenship and Internal Migration*.
88 Ackers and Stalford, *A Community for Children?*, p. 59.
89 Ackers, *Children, Citizenship and Internal Migration*.
90 However, there remain more general and serious concerns with the development of a family law for the Union. See further chapters 6 and 7.
91 For a detailed examination of the development of this field of policy, see Clare McGlynn, 'Reclaiming a Feminist Vision: The Reconciliation of Paid Work and Family Life in European Union Law and Policy' (2001) 7 *Columbia Journal of European Law* 241–72.

Under both of these policy 'umbrellas', the reconciliation of family and professional lives, and particularly the creation and maintenance of more childcare
services, was deemed necessary in order to encourage more women to (re-)enter
the labour market. Thus, the care of children became central to the achievement
of the economic ambitions of the Union. The principal policy measure relating to
childcare was the Recommendation on Childcare adopted in 1992.[92] The Recommendation proposed initiatives in the workplace, in childcare services, in leave
for parents and in the role of fathers. In relation to the care of children, therefore,
it envisaged a greater role for fathers and greater opportunities for both parents to
care for their children at home, together with greater provision of public childcare
services. The quality of those childcare services was given particular emphasis in
the Recommendation, not least because, if such facilities were not of high quality,
it was recognised that women would be reluctant to participate in the labour
market.

The adoption of the Recommendation was highly symbolic, as it suggested an
important role for the Union in the care of children. Nonetheless, the Recommendation was non-binding, and, although symbolically important, it is deba-
table whether it led to any measures of significance. In terms of allowing parents
time to care for their children, two further directives play an important role,
namely the Pregnant Workers Directive[93] and the Parental Leave Directive.[94]
These directives grant mothers the right to paid maternity leave of fourteen weeks
and both parents the right to twelve weeks of unpaid parental leave. Despite their
novelty in some member states, most notably the UK, the adoption of these
directives has done little to enhance existing national measures and therefore
achieves little from a children's perspective. The Union has not greatly enhanced
parents' opportunities to care for their young children, this being particularly so
as the Parental Leave Directive does not provide for any pay. Thus, although some
children may benefit from these measures, they were clearly not adopted with
children's interests and real needs at the fore. This again can be seen as a matter of
competence, but it underscores the point that measures which affect children are
being adopted but these measures do not have children's interests at heart, or even
as part of the equation.

This leads to a questioning of the purpose of childcare and the role of the
Union. The Union is proposing that childcare services be enhanced, with the aim
of integrating women into the labour market. What then is the future of this
policy field? Should childcare be seen as an educational issue, one of child
development, in which the provision of quality childcare and early education is

92 Council Recommendation on childcare 92/241/EEC, OJ 1992 L 123/16.
93 Council Directive 92/85/EEC of 19 October 1992 on the introduction of measures to encourage
    improvements in the safety and health at work of pregnant workers and workers who have
    recently given birth or are breastfeeding, OJ 1992 L 348/1.
94 Council Directive 96/34/EC of 3 June 1996 on the framework agreement on parental leave
    concluded by UNICE, CEEP and the ETUC, OJ 1996 L 145/4.

viewed as important for the development of creative, happy and confident children?[95] If this is the case, there is little competence for the Union, such a developmental concern rightly being viewed as within member state competence, except to the extent that the principle of non-discrimination would apply to migrant families. On the other hand, if childcare provision is to remain an element of economic policy, both in terms of enabling women to enter the labour market and in creating jobs in the childcare industry, it is very much within the competence of the Union. That this is the approach has been confirmed by the recent employment guidelines which set clear targets for the provision of childcare by 2010.[96] This is a significant move and is a long way on from the timid and apologetic suggestions of the 1992 Recommendation on Childcare. The provision of childcare is a key plank of a high-profile policy initiative, namely the employment guidelines. However, the danger is that this takes childcare policy further from a children's perspective.

The tensions between the different approaches to childcare are evident in all member states, at Community level and in international approaches to childcare. For example, Article 18(2) of the United Nations Convention on the Rights of the Child (UNCRC) provides that states shall render 'appropriate assistance to parents . . . in the performance of their childrearing responsibilities and shall ensure the development of institutions, facilities and services for the care of children'. This article clearly anticipates the provision of childcare services for children. However, Article 18(3) goes on to provide that states shall take all appropriate measures to ensure that 'children of *working* parents have the right to benefit from childcare services and facilities for which they are eligible'.[97] It is only the children of working parents who are to benefit here, which suggests an idea of childcare as a means of looking after children while parents engage in the paid workforce, rather than childcare as a necessary or positive part of a child's education and development. The divide between Articles 18(2) and 18(3) highlights the differences between different conceptions of children and children's rights. Arguably, Article 18(2) grants a right to a child to ensure that its parents are assisted in their task of childrearing, while Article 18(3) only grants a right to the parents of some children, which is not therefore a right granted to children per se. This approach is confirmed by considering Article 28 of the UNCRC which ensures that states must 'recognise the right of the child to education'. This is a right assigned directly to all children.

---

95 Advocate General Tissano in *Chen and Zhu* noted in passing that the recipient of childcare services 'would appear in fact to be' a parent, as opposed to the child (para. 58). However, were childcare to be viewed as educational, clearly it would be the child that would be the recipient. In this respect, different forms of childcare, for children of different ages, would need to be considered separately.

96 Para. 6 of Council Decision 2003/578/EC of 22 July 2003 on guidelines for the employment policies of Member States, OJ 2003 L 197/13.

97 Emphasis added.

This focus on parental rights is also reflected within Union law and policy. Early drafts of the Charter of Fundamental Rights bestowed a 'right to reconciliation' on parents.[98] This 'right' was removed from the final draft of the Charter and replaced with a simple provision reiterating the existing, limited scope of Community law on maternity and parental leave. Regrettably, therefore, the Charter goes no further than existing Community law. Thus, while a 'right to reconciliation', framed in terms of a parental right, has considerable shortcomings, it nonetheless had the potential to be developed to encompass many policy initiatives which would have benefited children. The Commission's fifth action programme on gender equality, for example, anticipated many of the policy prescriptions necessary for a genuine reconciliation, such as changes to 'working time, leisure, family responsibilities, paid and unpaid work including care work, access to goods and services, housing, transport, health services and social protection'.[99]

It is possible that Article 24 of the Charter of Fundamental Rights, on the rights of the child, may just reorientate the approach to the reconciliation of paid work and family life. Article 24 of the Charter requires consideration of the best interests of the child in all activities relating to their interests. As discussed above, the right of parents to time with their children is clearly an issue 'relating to' children. Moreover, if the 'best interests' of the child are to be considered, this orientates the issue away from the purely economic and as a 'right' of the parents, towards considering what might be best for the child in the particular circumstances, which is more often than not going to include time with their parents.[100] Whatever the final outcome of a policy or judicial decision, the mere fact that consideration is given to the child's interests may help to contextualise the issue beyond one of parental rights and economic considerations.

3.2.4   From instrumentalism to the protection of children from harm: trafficking and the sexual exploitation of children

In the policy fields so far considered, the rights and entitlements granted to children are generally instrumental to the achievement of objectives other than children's welfare. However, by the mid-1990s, the Union was developing policy

---

98 Resolution of the Council and of the Ministers for Employment and Social Policy of 29 June 2000 on the balanced participation of women and men in family and working life (2000/C218/02), OJ 2000 C 218/5, stated that both 'men and women . . . have a right to reconcile family and working life'. In addition, in an early draft of the Charter of Fundamental Rights, reference was made to a 'right to reconciliation': Charte 4422/00 of 28 July 2000. This was later amended. For a discussion, see McGlynn, 'Reclaiming a Feminist Vision', 261–3.

99 Communication from the Commission COM (2000) 335 final: Towards a Community framework strategy on gender equality (2001–2005).

100 See further Cathryn Costello, 'Gender Equalities and the Charter of Fundamental Rights of the European Union' in Tamara Hervey and Jeff Kenner (eds.), *Economic and Social Rights under the EU Charter of Fundamental Rights – A Legal Perspective* (Oxford: Hart Publishing, 2003), pp. 111–38 at pp. 126–8.

which had the welfare and protection of children at its core. These new initiatives, made possible by the creation of the Union in 1992 and the extension of competence to the field of justice and home affairs in the Treaty of Amsterdam, mark a significant step forward in the Union's approach to children. No longer are children passive accessories to the greater economic goals of the Community, but are the particular focus of new and, in Union terms, innovative policies focusing on their welfare and protection. In terms of policy development, what we see is a move away from instrumentalism towards a protectionist approach to children. While a focus on children which is predominantly protectionist raises many concerns, it does lay the groundwork for later movement towards a more progressive approach.

In the mid-1990s, the Union established the Stop programme,[101] followed later by the Daphne programme,[102] the aims of which were to develop co-operation between states, non-governmental organisations and law enforcement agencies to fight against the trafficking of human beings and the sexual exploitation of children. By 1997, a Joint Action had been adopted concerning trafficking in human beings and the sexual exploitation of children in which member states agreed to review their relevant criminal laws so as to ensure the criminalisation of certain behaviours and to encourage judicial co-operation.[103] Further concrete action was possible with the adoption of the Treaty of Amsterdam in 1997 and the first treaty reference to children. Article 29 of the Treaty on European Union stated that one of the objectives of the Union was to provide its citizens with a 'high level of safety' within the area of freedom, security and justice by developing common action regarding a number of matters, including 'offences against children'. This common action is to take the form of closer co-operation between police forces, customs authorities and judicial authorities and may lead to approximation of any rules on criminal matters where necessary. This provision was highly significant, representing the first explicit acknowledgment of the potentially adverse impact on children of the creation of the single market and the development of an area of freedom, security and justice.

In addition to continuing its activities in this field through the Daphne and Stop action programmes,[104] further measures have been adopted which seek to

---

101 Council Joint Action 96/700/JHA of 29 November 1996 establishing an incentive and exchange programme for persons responsible for combating trade in human beings and the sexual exploitation of children, OJ 1996 L 322/7.

102 Decision 293/2000/EC of the European Parliament and of the Council of 24 January 2000 adopting a programme of Community action (the Daphne programme) (2000 to 2003) on preventive measures to fight violence against children, young persons and women, OJ 2000 L 34/1.

103 Council Joint Action 97/154/JHA of 24 February 1997 concerning action to combat trafficking in human beings and sexual exploitation of children, OJ 1997 L 63/2.

104 The Daphne programme has been followed up by Daphne II which runs from 2004 to 2008, the aim of which is to help prevent and combat all forms of violence against children, young people and women: Decision 803/2004/EC of the European Parliament and of the Council of 21 April 2004 adopting a programme of Community action (2004 to 2008) to prevent and combat

enhance the criminal law sanctions against trafficking and the sexual exploitation of children. In 2002, a Council Framework Decision on combating trafficking in human beings was adopted, the aim of which is to ensure common 'definitions, incriminations and sanctions' against traffickers.[105] The Decision is aimed at all trafficking, but particular emphasis is placed on the fact that children 'are more vulnerable and are therefore at greater risk of falling victim to trafficking'.[106] The decision also supports international work in this field including the United Nations Protocol to the Convention against Organised Crime on Trafficking of Persons, Especially Women and Children.[107]

A Council Framework Decision on combating the sexual exploitation of children and child pornography was adopted in 2004,[108] following on from the Council's Decision on the need to combat child pornography on the internet.[109] The Framework Decision on sexual exploitation of children and child pornography places obligations on member states to ensure that certain specific offences relating to sexual exploitation (especially prostitution) and pornography are criminalised. The Decision also details minimum penalties and provisions on jurisdiction, criminal procedure, assistance to victims and judicial co-operation. The Decision must be seen in its international context, particularly the Second World Congress on the Sexual Exploitation of Children of December 2001, the United Nations Optional Protocol to the Convention on the Rights of the Child on the sale of children, child prostitution and child pornography and the Cyber-crime Convention developed by the Council of Europe which addresses child pornography in computer systems. The Preamble to the Decision does little to justify the need for Union action in this field, simply stating that the 'important work' performed by international organisations in this field 'must be comple-mented' by that of the European Union.[110] The Preamble also sets the Decision in the context of the creation of the area of freedom, justice and security, a primary

---

violence against children, young people and women and to protect victims and groups at risk (the Daphne II programme), OJ 2004 L 134/1.
105 Council Framework Decision 2002/629/JHA of 19 July 2002 on combating trafficking in human beings, OJ 2002 L 203/1.
106 Preamble, para. 5. See also Council Resolution of 20 October 2003 on initiatives to combat trafficking in human beings, in particular women (2003/C260/03), OJ 2003 C 260/4.
107 Protocol to Prevent, Suppress and Punish Trafficking in Persons, Especially Women and Children, Supplementing the United Nations Convention Against Transnational Organized Crime (UN Doc. A/55/383, not yet in force), GA Resolution 25, Annex II, UN GAOR, 55th Sess., Supp. No. 49, at 60, UN Doc. A/45/49 (vol. I) (2001), in force 9 September 2003. See further Anne Gallagher, 'Human Rights and the New UN Protocols on Trafficking and Migrant Smuggling: A Preliminary Analysis' (2001) 23 *Human Rights Quarterly* 975–1004.
108 Council Framework Decision 2004/68/JHA of 22 December 2003 on combating the sexual exploitation of children and child pornography, OJ 2004 L 13/44, 20 January 2004.
109 Council Decision 2000/375/JHA of 29 May 2000 to combat child pornography on the Internet, OJ 2000 L 138/1.
110 Council Framework Decision 2004/68/JHA of 22 December 2003 on combating the sexual exploitation of children and child pornography, OJ 2004 L 13/44, 20 January 2004, Preamble, para. 6.

Union objective. What is absent, therefore, is the recognition that it may be the Union's policies of freedom of movement and the creation of an area of freedom, justice and security which in fact have made the commission of crimes against children simpler to conduct and more difficult to detect. This is perhaps behind the proposals, but is not made evident. But such reticence does leave the specified justifications for action much weaker.

Interesting differences in approaches to children and their rights arose in the development of this Decision. The 'child' to be protected from pornography and sexual exploitation is any person under the age of eighteen.[111] The Commission stated that, although persons under the age of eighteen may have 'reached the maturity to take an informed decision about involving themselves in sexual activities', the depiction of such activities constitutes pornography and an offence against children.[112] Had the Commission's approach stood, a person under eighteen could have been engaged in lawful and consensual sexual activity, but the depiction of that activity may have constituted a serious criminal offence. There is clearly a risk here of undermining the autonomy of young people in making choices about sexual activity.

As a result of discussions within the Council, the Decision adopted allows member states to exclude from criminal sanction situations involving young people who have reached the age of sexual consent, but who are under eighteen, where the sexually explicit material has been produced with the individual's genuine consent and for their own private use.[113] An important balance has been struck here between different approaches to the autonomy of individuals under eighteen, but above the age of sexual consent. Thus, while member states may decide not to criminalise the consensual production and possession of pornography made for private use, material produced for public consumption is criminalised, even if there is valid consent from the individual. Thus, it will remain a criminal offence for an individual under eighteen, but above the age of sexual consent, to participate in pornography designed for public consumption.

There may also be concerns regarding the autonomy of young people in relation to the provisions on the sexual exploitation of 'children'. It is to be a criminal offence for a person to engage in 'sexual activities with a child' where 'abuse is made of a recognized position of trust, authority or influence over the child'.[114] While on its face this might sound reasonable and appropriate, particularly in relation to young children, in relation to a young person over the age of sexual consent, for example a seventeen year old, engaging in consensual sexual

---

111 Article 1 of Council Framework Decision 2004/68/JHA of 22 December 2003 on combating the sexual exploitation of children and child pornography, OJ 2004 L 13/44, 20 January 2004.
112 COM (2000) 854 final, p. 22.
113 Article 3 of Council Framework Decision 2004/68/JHA of 22 December 2003 on combating the sexual exploitation of children and child pornography, OJ 2004 L 13/44, 20 January 2004.
114 Article 2(c) of Council Framework Decision 2004/68/JHA of 22 December 2003 on combating the sexual exploitation of children and child pornography, OJ 2004 L 13/44, 20 January 2004.

activity with, for example, a trainee teacher who may be, say, twenty-one, it is less so. In other words, the ability of a young person over the age of sexual consent, but under eighteen, to give valid consent to sexual activity is seriously undermined by this Decision and again raises concerns about the concept of children's rights employed by Union law.[115]

It is important to recognise the significance of these proposals. In substantive terms, these measures ensure that the relevant provisions of national criminal law are approximated so that the coverage, sanctions and enforcement reveal a common approach and that judicial co-operation is considerably enhanced. Such action may go some way towards meeting the challenges of this area of policy. Keith Pringle has identified the differing ways in which the member states of the Union deal with child abuse and violence and the problems that this causes.[116] The approximation of approaches may help to ensure that such differences do not result in harm to children. Andrew Swithinbank argues that children continue to suffer harm as there is no 'European-wide definition of the concepts of child abuse and neglect' and that the 'level of identification and recognition of the problem varies enormously throughout Europe with taboos ensuring that abuse, particularly sexual abuse, is not revealed'.[117] Again, Union action may begin to meet such concerns. Finally, action in this field is welcome as it reveals a responsibility of the Union to take action in an area of activity which has become more prevalent in recent years. Due to its cross-border nature, these crimes are ones which the Union is uniquely situated to take action against.

3.3 Children and the Charter of Fundamental Rights

Accordingly, by the end of the 1990s, children's interests were slowly being recognised within the Union. Rights and entitlements under the free movement provisions were gradually being extended to encompass the diverse nature of modern family practices, with education rights almost becoming free-standing. Notwithstanding such important developments, however, the approach to children largely remains one in which children's status within 'the family' determines access to rights and moreover such rights are still granted to children often in the pursuit of other objectives, namely the economic objectives of free movement.

With the adoption of the Treaty of Amsterdam and the first treaty reference to children, this instrumentalist paradigm was giving way to an approach recognising the particular needs of children. However, while the Union's first family law

---

115 Similar concerns have been raised in the UK in connection with the Sexual Offences Act 2003 which criminalised similar activities to the example given. See further Andrew Bainham and Belinda Brooks-Gordon, 'Reforming the Law on Sexual Offences' in Belinda Brooks-Gordon *et al.* (eds.), *Sexuality Repositioned* (Oxford: Hart Publishing, 2004), pp. 261–96.
116 Keith Pringle, *Children and Social Welfare in Europe* (Buckingham: Open University Press, 1998).
117 Andrew Swithinbank, 'The European Union and Social Care' in Brian Munday and Peter Ely (eds.), *Social Care in Europe* (Hemel Hempstead: Prentice Hall, 1996), pp. 67–95 at p. 77.

measure was adopted in 2000, it was premised on a traditional concept of family, therefore only benefiting some children, and appears to have been adopted with wider integrationist objectives at heart. In addition, the Union's growing competence in the field of justice and home affairs, and in particular the drive towards creating an area of freedom, security and justice, was beginning to see policy innovations aimed at protecting children from trafficking, sexual exploitation and violence. Such measures are, however, largely based on a conceptualisation of children as vulnerable, passive individuals in need of protection. It was only with the adoption of the Charter of Fundamental Rights in 2000 that a more rounded and progressive approach to children and their rights entered Union law and policy.

The Charter of Fundamental Rights contains a number of references to children and their rights, and represents an attempt to balance competing conceptions of children's rights.[118] In terms of their overall impact, the rights in the Charter are highly significant. They represent the first recognition of children as independent subjects of Union law and policy, with their own particular needs and desires, separate from the interests of families, parents or other policy objectives. To this end, the Charter heralds an evolution in Union policy towards children, from the instrumentalism which characterises the fields of free movement, to the protectionism of policies on violence and trafficking, to a recognition of children's independence and autonomy. Nonetheless, this latter move towards a recognition of children's agency is only one element of the Charter's provisions which are also characterised by welfare concerns.

The inclusion of children's rights within the Charter is testament to the success of strategies to promote children's rights at the international level. As early as 1924, with the Declaration of Geneva,[119] the international community has promoted the interests and rights of the child, albeit that the emphasis was on the 'investment motive' behind specific measures for children, that is 'society's concern for the child is seen very much in terms of the child's usefulness to society'.[120] This instrumentalist view of children's rights was combined with a 'child-saving', protectionist approach in later international documents, including the 1948 Universal Declaration of Human Rights, which speaks of children requiring special care and assistance.[121] The later 1959 United Nations Declaration of the Rights of the Child,[122] which was arguably the 'first serious attempt to describe in

---

118 For a detailed discussion of the Charter's provisions on children, see: Clare McGlynn, 'Rights for Children? The Potential Impact of the European Union Charter of Fundamental Rights' (2002) 8 *European Public Law* 387–400; and Cullen, 'Children's Rights'.
119 Geneva Declaration of the Rights of the Child of 1924, adopted 26 September 1924, League of Nations OJ Spec. Supp. 21, at 43 (1924).
120 Discussed in Freeman, 'The Limits of Children's Rights', 30.
121 Article 25(2) of the Declaration of Human Rights refers to children as requiring special care and assistance, and the Preamble includes the statements on human dignity.
122 Declaration of the Rights of the Child, GA Resolution 1386 (XIV), 14 UN GAOR Supp. (No. 16) at 19, UN Doc. A/4354 (1959).

a reasonably detailed manner what constituted children's overriding claims and entitlements',[123] similarly remained largely 'child-saving' in its approach. Such documents failed to recognise what might be called the 'child's "individual personality" rights'.[124]

It was only in the 1970s, with the growth of the children's movement, and particularly the significant voice of children's liberationists, that the international community began to take the claims of children considerably more seriously. This pressure eventually led to the adoption in 1989 of the United Nations Convention on the Rights of the Child (UNCRC). The Convention is a comprehensive statement of children's rights and, as an international treaty, it has attracted record support, with only two countries refusing to ratify it.[125] At face value, therefore, the Convention represents a commonly agreed world standard for the treatment of children.

The Convention is a creature of negotiation, balancing competing visions of children's rights, resulting in a compromise between those who see protection and welfare as the most significant element in any children's rights programme and those who seek to promote children's self-determination. The 'general principles' of the Convention reflect these concerns: Articles 2 (non-discrimination), 3 (best interests of the child), 6 (right to life) and 12 (expression of child's views). Although the Convention is evidence of compromise, and criticisms can be made,[126] its existence and its inclusion of many autonomy rights for children remains remarkable. The early drafts of the Convention were protectionist in approach. It was only as the drafting process proceeded that the civil and political rights of children were included, that is the rights to free expression, to freedom of thought, to privacy and to association and assembly.[127]

In sum, therefore, the international community has progressed from its initial 'investment' motive in promoting children's rights, to a 'child-saving' approach with an emphasis on protection, to a combination of the latter with a recognition

---

123 Fortin, *Children's Rights*, p. 36.
124 Cynthia Price-Cohen, 'The Relevance of Theories of Natural Law and Legal Positivism' in Freeman and Veerman (eds.), *Ideologies of Children's Rights*, p. 61.
125 Although many doubt the importance of such a high ratification rate. Hans-Joachim Heinz argues that: 'The political will of states to ratify international human rights treaties is the result of a conviction of the uselessness of the standards laid down in these documents.' 'The UN Convention and the Network of International Human Rights Protection by the UN', in Freeman and Veerman (eds.), *Ideologies of Children's Rights*, p. 71.
126 See further: Freeman, 'Taking Children's Rights More Seriously'; and Kirsten Backstrom, 'The International Human Rights of the Child: Do They Protect the Girl Child?' (1996–7) 30 *George Washington Journal of International Law and Economics* 541–82.
127 Nonetheless, it is perhaps important to remember that these rights were not necessarily included due to a volte-face in how the international community views children and their rights. Cynthia Price-Cohen has argued that the majority of these rights were proposed by the US, largely as a response to the predominant focus of the early drafts on economic and social rights. The US was keen to put forward the 'Western' vision of civil and political rights, in response to the 'Eastern' emphasis on economic and social rights: Price-Cohen, 'The Relevance of Theories', 62.

of children's independence and autonomy. This is not to suggest that there is general agreement about such steps. As noted above, the Convention, despite being comprehensively ratified, requires implementation, on which there has been less progress. And it remains the controversial nature of granting children rights, particularly autonomy rights, that remains the barrier. Nonetheless, the progress through these different conceptions of rights remains significant and an important lesson for the Union's approach to children.

The Convention, therefore, represents an internationally agreed standard for children's rights and it has been ratified by all the member states of the European Union. It therefore forms an appropriate basis for the inclusion of the rights of the child within the Union's Charter. Accordingly, it is perhaps no surprise that the main provision on children's rights in the Charter, Article 24, reproduces some of the central elements of the UNCRC. The best interests of the child are to be a primary consideration, children's rights to protection are to be balanced with their right to autonomy and self-expression and children are entitled to maintain a personal relationship with both parents. There is therefore a clear compromise between provisions which might be seen to undermine 'the family', those which recognise that children are individuals in their own right and those which require the care and protection of children. Article 24(2) of the Charter states that: 'In all actions relating to children, whether taken by public authorities or private institutions, the child's best interests must be a primary consideration.' This is broadly the same text as that which forms the core of the UNCRC.[128] The inclusion of such a provision in the Charter means that for the first time the child's interests are to be considered in all areas of policy which 'relate' to children.[129] This represents a major step forward from the existing invisible position of children and, together with Article 21 of the Charter (considered below), may go some way towards creating the 'mainstreaming' or 'child-proofing' policy which many have recommended.[130]

However, the grant of only a 'primary' consideration to children's interests, as opposed to a paramountcy principle, may cause problems in Union law. This wording in the UNCRC was the compromise reached after much debate, it being considered that 'justice and society at large, should be of at least equal, if not

---

128 Article 3(1) of the UNCRC.

129 Note that in the UNCRC the child's best interests are to be considered in all actions 'concerning' children, as opposed to the Charter's text of 'relating to' children. It is not clear whether this is a deliberate and therefore substantive change. It could be that, in the other official languages of the EU, there is no difference between the texts of the UNCRC and the Charter. However, it is clearly arguable that the change from 'concerning' to 'relating to' is, at least in the English language, of significance. A measure may not have been adopted with children in mind, it might make no reference to children, but it might 'concern' children as it has an impact on them. Can it equally be said that the same measure 'relates to' children? This would seem to require a more explicit or direct consideration of children if it is to 'relate to' them.

130 See, for example, Sandy Ruxton, *A Children's Policy for the 21st Century: First Steps* (Brussels: Euronet and the European Commission, 1999).

greater, importance than the interests of the child'.[131] However, in the context of the Union, this balancing exercise may give rise to unforeseen and potentially adverse consequences. The development of a human rights jurisprudence by the Court of Justice has been plagued by criticism that the economic interests of the Union are often accorded greater weight than the human rights under consideration. The danger is that, where the best interests of children are only a primary consideration, an equally, or more, important element will be the commercial interests of the single market. That this may prove to be the case can already be seen from some areas of Community law impacting on children. Euronet argues, for example, that some single market directives and toy and television advertising policies of the Union demonstrate the privileged nature of commercial interests, over children's interests, in the Union.[132] Nonetheless, it is clear that the Charter now requires children's rights and interests to at least be considered alongside other competing demands.[133]

Article 24(1) of the Charter is a curious mix of what might loosely be termed children's 'protection' and 'empowerment' rights, which are often found to be in conflict. The inclusion of the two elements in the one paragraph would appear to be an attempt at compromise and to balance the competing interests of paternalism and autonomy. Article 24(1) of the Charter begins with the statement that children have the 'right' to such 'protection and care as is necessary for their well-being'. The phraseology of 'protection and care' replicates Article 3(2) of the UNCRC and, despite the wording being slightly different, it seems reasonable to assume that the standard expected is the same as that given to the interpretation of the UNCRC.

As noted above, the 'right' of a child to 'protection' is often seen to be in conflict with more liberationist approaches to children's rights which emphasise the importance of a child's autonomy and self-reliance, rather than need for protection. It is a reference to autonomy rights which are to be found in the second part of Article 24(2) of the Charter which provides that children may 'express their views freely'. The article goes on to state that the views of children shall be taken into account, in matters which concern them, in accordance with their 'age and maturity'. As with Article 24(2) of the Charter, this provision reproduces important elements of the UNCRC and emphasises the importance of children's participation in decision-making.[134]

---

131 As discussed in Philip Alston, 'The Best Interests Principle: Towards a Reconciliation of Culture and Human Rights' (1994) 8 *International Journal of Law and the Family* 1–25 at 12.

132 Euronet Submission to the Convention, Charte 4240/00, 19 April 2000.

133 See, for example, the inclusion of the best interests principles in the Council Directive laying down minimum standards for the reception of asylum seekers which states that the 'best interests of the child shall be a primary consideration for member states when implementing the provisions of this Directive that involve minors': Article 18 of Council Directive 2003/9/EC, OJ 2003 L 31/18.

134 On the difficulties, however, of operationalising the participation principle, see Louise Ackers, 'From "Best Interests" to Participatory Rights – Children's Involvement in Family Migration Decisions' (2000) 12 *Child and Family Law Quarterly* 167–84.

The final part of Article 24 of the Charter provides that the child has a right to maintain 'on a regular basis a personal relationship and direct contact' with both 'parents', unless that is contrary to her or his interests. This provision again balances interests between autonomy – the child's right to maintain contact – and welfare – the 'interests' of the child. In practice, this right will be balanced with the right to respect for private and family life in Article 7, drawn from the European Convention on Human Rights, which often involves claims regarding contact with children, though generally the right is framed in terms of the parent's right to contact.[135] Article 24(3) of the Charter is likely to be of relevance in a number of areas concerning children's relationships within families, especially in the areas of free movement, immigration and asylum concerning family reunification. Most immediately, it was cited as a justification for the extension of Regulation 1347/2000 to encompass all parental responsibility judgments to all children. It may also ensure that in future developments in the family law field, the interests of children are taken into consideration in the development of policy.

In addition to Article 24 of the Charter, there are a number of further provisions which relate to children's rights. Article 20 of the Charter states that '[e]veryone is equal before the law'. The inclusion of such a statement in a chapter which goes on to detail the rights of the child, the elderly, and the disabled, and which includes a general non-discrimination provision on the grounds of age, must be interpreted to include children. All children are equal before the law, and adults and children are equal before the law in the same measure. Such an interpretation is strengthened by the fact that an earlier draft of the Charter referred to 'men and women' being equal before the law, which would have posed problems for those wishing to interpret it to include children.[136] Perhaps, therefore, Article 20 of the Charter can be interpreted as a signal of a progressive approach to child–parent relations and to the child's status in society in general. Instead of the child being seen simply as an appendage to the parent, and her or his rights being parasitic on those of their parents, this provision might represent an independent, autonomous approach to children and their rights. Equally, if 'everyone is equal before the law', children might be viewed as rights-holders themselves, rather than just individuals in need of protection and over which other individuals and society have responsibilities.

Such an interpretation is supported by the provision in Article 21 of the Charter which prohibits any discrimination on a number of grounds, including age. It might be possible to argue that this general prohibition on discrimination can be used as a form of 'child-proofing' in that all policies and actions must not discriminate against individuals on the grounds of their age and therefore must

135 See Ursula Kilkelly, *The Child and the European Convention on Human Rights* (Aldershot: Ashgate, 1999), chapter 11.
136 Draft Charter of Fundamental Rights, Charte 4422/00, 28 July 2000, Article 20.

not discriminate against children.[137] These two provisions will also mean that all Charter rights, not just those which specifically relate to children, should be interpreted to include children.[138]

However, there is a potential clash between the prohibition on age discrimination in Article 21 of the Charter and a further provision which seeks to protect children, this time from employment. Article 32 of the Charter states that the 'employment of children is prohibited', though rules which are more favourable to children will be permitted. Such a protective right prima facie constitutes age discrimination and takes away choices from the child. No definition of child is given, though the article goes on to state that the minimum age of admission to employment may not be lower than the minimum school-leaving age. Although in practice this provision seems unlikely to demand much attention, mirroring the Young Workers Directive,[139] it emphasises the difficulties inherent in drafting a coherent set of rights for children, particularly one which attempts to balance competing conceptions of children and their rights.

The Charter also contains Article 14 which provides for a 'right to education' and the 'possibility to receive free compulsory education'.[140] The right to education is phrased in similar terms to Article 2 of Protocol No.1 to the European Convention on Human Rights.[141] In addition, as with the protocol, Article 14(3) of the Charter grants the right to *parents* to 'ensure the education and teaching of their children in conformity with their religious, philosophical and pedagogical convictions'. Accordingly, while Article 14 of the Charter proclaims a general right to education, a right which will inhere in children, it effectively qualifies this right by reference to the rights of parents to determine the nature of that education. Although such an approach is not surprising in view of its international pedigree, it remains the case that, where there is a possible clash of interests between children's claims to educational rights and parents' rights to determine the schooling of their children, the parents' claims are largely determinative. Nonetheless, it may be that the characterisation of a 'right to education' may enable developments in the field of free movement to advance along the path of

---

137 Note, however, that it is discrimination against older people which forms the main thrust of Community policy relating to age discrimination. This is apparent from the new Framework Directive on Equal Treatment (Council Directive 2000/78/EC of 27 November 2000 establishing a general framework for equal treatment in employment and occupation, OJ 2000 L 303/16). See further Clare McGlynn, 'EC Legislation Prohibiting Age Discrimination: "Towards a Europe for All Ages"?' (2001) 3 *Cambridge Yearbook of European Legal Studies* 279–99.

138 However, the focus here is limited to those provisions which specifically address children in a family context. For other provisions on children, see Articles 28 and 32 of the Charter which address children's concerns in the context of employment and education.

139 Council Directive 94/33/EC of 22 June 1994 on the protection of young people at work, OJ 1994 L 216/12.

140 See further Cullen, 'Children's Rights', who also discusses the prohibition on child labour and the protection of young people at work (Article 32).

141 On the right to education within Community law, see Gisella Gori, *Towards an EU Right to Education* (The Hague: Kluwer Law International, 2001).

children's individual entitlements, detached from family status. Thus, it might be possible that case law develops a right to education for migrant children. However, advances in this direction are not likely to be immediate. For example, despite the progressive nature of the Court's approach to the concept of family and family rights in *Baumbast*, it still characterised the children's claims for residence for educational purposes as one which involved the right to family life, rather than the child's right to education.[142]

Children's interests may also be developed where public policy supports families. Thus, the provisions in the Charter on the right to respect for private and family life (Article 7) and Article 33 which states that 'the family' shall enjoy 'legal, social and economic protection' and that, in order to reconcile professional and family life, workers are to be entitled to maternity and parental leave, may have a positive impact on children's rights. However, not only are the rights in Article 33 of the Charter themselves extremely limited,[143] but the emphasis on family, as opposed to children, will merely serve to emphasise children's status within families, rather than their independence.

In sum, therefore, the inclusion of provisions on the rights of children in the Charter is a substantive step forward in ensuring that children are no longer invisible in the Union. Children's interests are to be taken into consideration in all policies relating to them, their voices are to be heard in actions concerning them and they are to be extended protection where necessary. These provisions will certainly provide support for those demanding a more integrated and thoughtful approach to children in the Union. In addition, with the Union developing its competence in the family law field, these provisions ensure a necessary focus on children's rights within families.

However, courage is required on the part of the legislature and judiciary to employ these rights to good effect. While references have been made to the children's rights provisions of the Charter in a few legislative instruments, the judiciary is fighting shy. The children's rights in the Charter would have provided an excellent basis for the Advocate General's Opinion in *Chen and Zhu*. It seems that he was reluctant to engage with the human rights arguments, considering them unnecessary in that a positive outcome could be achieved by an interpretation of the relevant legislation relying on the aims and objectives of Union policy, rather than human rights norms. While this is in some ways understandable, it demonstrates the lack of confidence in human rights arguments and means that in future cases, where a traditional approach to interpretation of the relevant

142 Cullen, 'Children's Rights'.
143 Only certain children may benefit in view of the limited concept of family often employed by the Union and Court and the rights to leave merely replicate existing Community law. See Clare McGlynn, 'Families and the European Union Charter of Fundamental Rights: Progressive Change or Entrenching the Status Quo?' (2001) 26 *European Law Review* 582–98; and McGlynn, 'Reclaiming a Feminist Vision'.

law does not produce a positive outcome, there is little or no human rights jurisprudence on which to fall back.

3.4   Children's rights and European Union law: towards autonomy and independence?

The status of children within the European Union is at a turning point. Since the inception of the EEC, children have been noticed but not heard. They have been granted certain rights when necessary to achieve other policy ambitions. Latterly, as the competence of the Union has increased and the ambitions of the integration project have grown, children have become the focus of policy activity, most notably their protection from forms of international crime. Only with the Charter, and latterly the judgment in *Chen and Zhu*, has there been a recognition of children as persons in their own right, not just as members of families or victims of crime. The Charter grants rights to children which include their right to be heard and to express their views. The Union is on the cusp, therefore, of recognising children as independent citizens with their own interests and needs which must be protected and respected. The specific reference in the Union Constitution to the need to protect children's rights as one of the objectives of the Union may represent a significant opportunity to enhance still further the Union's approach to children and their individual rights.[144]

However, the mere expression of rights in the Charter, or the Constitution, is only a first step. The rights contained in the Charter are limited and represent an uneasy compromise between different conceptions of children's rights. Welfare and autonomy rights are included, but with little guidance as to how these sometimes competing claims are to be balanced. The Charter is not yet legally binding and will therefore have only a persuasive value in the development of policy and interpretation of law before the Court. Finally, the competence of the Union is necessarily limited in terms of the action it can take to directly improve the welfare and rights of children.

This latter point perhaps raises the question regarding the appropriate role, if any, of the European Union in the lives of children. Legal intervention in the 'private' sphere of the family and children is often considered to be not just unnecessary but unwelcome, even more so if the body of intervention is a supranational authority and not just the nation-state. But a laissez-faire approach to 'the family' and to children within families would mean little or

---

144 Article I-3(3) and (4). The Constitution also includes three further references to children: Article III-168 which covers the 'combating of trafficking in persons, in particular women and children'; Article III-172 which covers judicial co-operation in criminal matters including the 'sexual exploitation of women and children'; and Article III-182 which encourages co-operation between member states in the areas of education, youth and sport and is aimed at protecting the 'physical and moral integrity of sportsmen and sportswomen, especially young sportsmen and sportswomen'.

no protection of children from harm, let alone recognition of their independence and autonomy.

And there is here a particular role for the European Union. First, where existing Union activities impact on children, it is incumbent upon the Union to take action to ensure that children are not adversely affected. This is the current approach of the Union in the areas of free movement and family law. However, this must be only the first stage in developing a children's policy for the Union. Current laws and policies focus on protecting children from harm, but must move towards recognising the individual rights of children. Community law in the area of free movement and family law is on the cusp of taking such an approach, but it should become the foundation of all Union activities affecting children. One way to achieve this would be to adopt a 'children's policy' for the Union which is mainstreamed into all activities, in similar ways to the policy of gender mainstreaming. The prohibition on age discrimination and the general non-discrimination provisions within the Charter provide an ideal basis for the development of such an approach.[145] It might also be possible to adopt an age discrimination directive aimed at children which could ensure that children are not discriminated against by the mere fact of being children in the provision of certain public services, such as health and housing, as well as in relation to judicial services, as well as protecting religious and cultural diversity in education.[146]

Ultimately, however, it is the lack of competence in the treaties that limits the opportunities to enact legislation and promote policies for the benefit of children. To remedy this situation, the European Parliament has called for the introduction of a legal basis in the EC treaty to promote and protect the rights of the child and to involve children and young people generally in decision-making processes.[147] In addition, Euronet has called for a new article to be inserted into the treaties which will provide a specific legal basis for action relating to children, while respecting the member states' primary competence in this field.[148] However, a balance must be struck here between ensuring that children's rights are respected where Union laws and policies affect them and extending the power of the Union

145 Euronet have proposed the adoption of a comprehensive children's policy for the EU which would require the establishment of a clear legal framework in the EU treaties for the promotion of children's rights, the incorporation of the basic principles of the UNCRC into EU law, the strengthening of structures affecting children, the extension of citizenship and participation to children and the improvement of information on children: Ruxton, *A Children's Policy*, p. 17.
146 As suggested by Cullen, 'Children's Rights'. However, it seems unlikely that such a directive would ever be adopted. The General Framework Directive on discrimination (Council Directive 2000/78/EC of 27 November 2000 establishing a general framework for equal treatment in employment and occupation, OJ 2000 L 303/16) already includes age discrimination, though it is limited to the employment sphere and therefore caters little for the interests of children. In addition, there are question marks over the competence of the Union to adopt anti-discrimination measures beyond the employment sphere: see Gráinne de Búrca, 'The Drafting of the EU Charter of Fundamental Rights' (2001) 26 *European Law Review* 126–38 at 135.
147 Helen Stalford, 'The Developing European Agenda on Children's Rights' (2000) 22 *Journal of Social Welfare and Family Law* 229–36 at 231.
148 Ruxton, *A Children's Policy*, p. 8.

into even more fields of hitherto national competence. The emphasis in this book is on ensuring appropriate policies and laws aimed at families and children where they are already subject to the impact of Union policies or where the Union is best placed to take action in particular fields. It is not clear that this justifies more general expansion of Union competence in relation to children.

The second main role of the Union is in being an international organisation which can bring together member states to take joint action in relation to international problems. This aspect of the Union's role is clearly demonstrated in the action it has so far taken in relation to trafficking of children and protection of children from sexual exploitation. Activity in this field is at its early stages, but is slowly improving the co-ordination of member states' activities. In addition, the Union plays an important role in terms of its external relations not just with possible future members but also with countries which benefit from its development projects. As Holly Cullen has argued, it is in the Union's external relations that there exists considerable scope for the development of children's rights.[149] Of course this raises a legitimacy problem in that the Union is promoting children's rights abroad when its own competence to promote such rights is limited.

Allied to the Union's external role is its role in relation to the development of its human rights policies and jurisprudence. The Union has placed considerable emphasis on its human rights foundation in recent years, with significant changes to the treaties and to the competence of the Union. As this human rights competence develops, it is essential that the rights of children are not forgotten. In relation to the Charter, it has been noted that children's rights are included. However, the scope of human rights policy goes beyond the Charter. Of particular concern is the development of human rights as general principles of Community law, as developed, interpreted and enforced by the Court of Justice. Thus far, the Court has not made any specific reference to the rights of children in the promulgation of its general principles. The Court has made many references to the 'right to family life' protected by the European Convention, but this provision almost invariably protects parents' rights to family life, rather than children's rights. This is resonant of the European Convention as a whole which is not a document particularly favourable to children.

The Court has long held that in developing its general principles of law it will have regard to international instruments.[150] The UNCRC has been ratified by all member states and is therefore well placed to become a source of inspiration for the Court. The Court may now in addition choose to refer to the rights contained in the Charter. However, despite the progressive and welcome judgment in *Chen and Zhu*, both the Advocate General and the Court failed to refer to either the

---

149 See further Cullen, 'Children's Rights'.
150 In Case 4/73, *J. Nold, Kohlen- und Baustoffgroßhandlung* v. *Commission* [1974] ECR 491; [1974] 2 CMLR 338, para. 13, the Court held that general principles include 'international treaties . . . on which the member states have collaborated or of which they are signatories'.

UNCRC or the Charter in their Opinion and judgment.[151] Discussion of both or either rights document would have bolstered the arguments being made and would have helped begin a process of progressive development of children's rights based on principles of autonomy and independence.

The Court's approach to children's rights will be profoundly tested in a challenge by the European Parliament to the legality of the Family Reunification Directive.[152] The Directive provides that, in the case of children over twelve, the right to family reunification may be restricted, contrary to accepted international human rights standards, particularly provisions in the UNCRC. Most concerning is the fact that none of the member states currently has in place legislation preventing children below sixteen from being joined by their parents, hence the Directive represents a direct attempt to utilise European harmonisation measures to seriously weaken standards. The Court of Justice must use the opportunity of this case to uphold the Union's commitment to human rights and to the rights of the child. All the rhetoric of the Charter and numerous policy documents will mean little if, when faced with a direct challenge to children's rights, the Court backs down and panders to the securitisation and anti-immigrant agenda of the member state governments.

151 Though see *Carlos Garcia Avello* v. *Belgian State* [2004] 1 CMLR 1; [2004] All ER (EC) 740, in which the Advocate General (at para. 36) did refer to the UNCRC, though his Opinion was based on the application of Community law principles, it not being 'necessary' to examine any infringement of human rights norms (para. 66).
152 Case C-540/03, *European Parliament* v. *Council*, [2004] OJ C 47/21, 21 February 2004.

4

Parenthood and European Union law: old ideologies and new ideals

The concept of parenthood, the nature of parenting, even who is a parent, are all contested ideas. Many disciplines are grappling with changing realities in relation to parenting, attempting to map developments, contextualise them and examine their effects; the prospects for the future are analysed and prophecies made. In the context of European Union law, however, such rigorous and complex theoretical analyses are largely absent. Partly this is due to the limited competence of the Union to act in the controversial terrain of parenthood. Mostly, however, it is due to a fundamental theoretical failing, to an ignorance of the wider panoply of contexts and circumstances which affect parenthood today. Thus, to the extent that the concept of parenthood, and particularly ideas about motherhood, have come within the competence of Union law and before the Court of Justice, a remarkably narrow and traditional approach has been taken, premised on the 'dominant ideology of the family' discussed in chapter 2.

It is imperative that a reconsideration of this limited, atheoretical and apolitical approach to parenthood takes place. The Union must move away from a traditional ideology of motherhood and fatherhood. For law and policy to reproduce, legitimise and promote gender distinctiveness in parenting is to entrench existing patterns which are often discriminatory. The Union must embrace more modern approaches to parenting based on principles of gender neutrality. Although it might be right to wonder whether parenting can ever be gender neutral, it is important that law and policy proceed on the basis of seeking this ideal. Such a theoretical foundation will better equip the Union to deal with the complex issues it is – and will be – facing. It will also complement the Union's commitments to equality between women and men, non-discrimination and human rights.

This reconsideration of the concept of parenthood is both necessary and to some extent unavoidable. Traditional ideas regarding parenthood, as with childhood, are being challenged today by social and demographic changes in families. New biomedical technologies are influencing our ideas regarding parenthood and parenting, and political rhetoric and ideologies are evolving to take these complex changes into account.[1] At the same time, gender transformations and the ongoing (re)negotiation of the gender contract demand continual reconsideration of parenthood. In legal terms, this manifests itself in raising questions regarding the role of law in the regulation of parenting, the extent of appropriate state 'interference' in families, parenting, childcare and childrearing and the extent to which gay and lesbian families and parents face discrimination legitimated through law. The focus here is on the role of Union law in the organisation of parenting, with some additional analysis of the Union's approach to the child–parent relationship. Thus, although parenthood and parenting is more than a discussion about its organisation, the analysis is limited to the scope of Union law to influence certain aspects of parenthood.

Nonetheless, it may not be immediately apparent how or why the Union is engaged in fashioning the concept of parenthood. But, ever since the adoption of measures designed to eliminate discrimination on the grounds of sex, the EEC and now the Union have been implacably engaged in the production, reproduction and legitimation of ideas about parenting. This has not always been an explicit process, and part of the analysis of this chapter is aimed at revealing the implicit assumptions about parenthood. It is through an analysis of the case law of the Court that its assumptions about parenthood, and about the norm of motherhood in particular, are revealed. This pattern of case law exposes the traditional notions upon which the case law of the Court has been determined in the sex equality field. In doing so, the analysis suggests that the approach of the Court is based on an understanding of parenthood which is based on the 'dominant ideology of the family', which conceives of the 'family' as a married, heterosexual two-parent unit, with specific gendered roles for women and men. These roles assume a breadwinner father, with caregiver mother.

Further, as the Union's competence in the field of employment policy, as well as employment law, has increased, it has become more apparent that the organisation of parenting has economic effects and vice versa. In short, where childcare services are minimal or of poor quality, or where workplaces are insufficiently flexible to allow employees to balance their home lives with their professional lives, the labour market may lose highly skilled labour. Thus, the flexibility of the labour market, and the need to ensure a balance between home and professional lives, has become the focus of Union law and policy.

But it is not only in the field of employment law and policy that the Union has begun to engage with parenthood. As the Union has expanded its competence into the family law field, measures on the recognition and enforcement of judgments in the custody arena have become part of Community law. Although the first measure adopted in this field was based on the status of marriage, the latest

---

1 See further Andrew Bainham, Shelley Day Sclater and Martin Richards, 'Introduction' in Andrew Bainham, Shelley Day Sclater and Martin Richards (eds.), *What Is a Parent? A Socio-Legal Analysis* (Oxford: Hart Publishing, 1999), pp. 1–23 at p. 1.

Regulation moves away from status towards recognising parenthood as the basis for intervention. This approach is reinforced by a provision in the Union's Charter of Fundamental Rights which attests to the right of the child to have contact with both parents.

In addition to developments in the employment and family law spheres, the Union is belatedly addressing the changing realities of family life, and therefore the concept of parenthood, as part of its evolving free movement jurisdiction. As Helen Stalford argues, the very success of the free movement provisions, together with the changing nature of family life, means that the existing Community rules often aggravate, rather than facilitate, the organisation of cross-national families.[2] Thus, the Union is beginning to engage with the concept of parenthood and its regulation in order to deal with the consequences of its rules on free movement, particularly in the private sphere.

In essence, therefore, we see some contradictory messages arising from Union law and policy regarding parenting. The Court of Justice, particularly in its sex equality case law, replicates a traditional approach to parenthood, based on a traditional ideology of motherhood. Further, although the employment policy of the Union recognises the need to balance paid work and family life, and that this impacts on parenting, this policy also remains within a traditionalist paradigm. In other fields of law and policy, it appears that a more egalitarian, gender neutral, approach may be emerging. For example, family law measures have recently been expanded to include disputes regarding parental responsibility for all children, not just disputes regarding the joint children of married parents. However, before considering these different fields of law and policy in more detail, the following section examines the old ideologies on which much of the current law is based and suggests that new emerging ideals of gender neutral parenting are a more appropriate basis for Union law and policy.

4.1 Parenthood: old ideologies and new ideals

The concept of parenthood and ideas and expectations about parenting vary over time, from society to society, and are constantly changing.[3] Nevertheless, there appear to be certain constants, particularly the enduring desire of society generally to dichotomise sexual differences and to explain them as natural, not socially constructed. In the context of parenthood, this has led to the supremacy of the 'dominant ideology of the family', with specific roles for women and men. Thus, the model of the caregiving mother/wife and breadwinner husband/father

---

2 See further Helen Stalford, 'Regulating Family Life in Post-Amsterdam Europe' (2003) 28 *European Law Review* 39–52.

3 Parenthood has been defined as a 'fluid set of social practices and expectations that are historically and culturally situated and its meaning is contingent upon broader social, political and economic exigencies': Bainham, Sclater and Richards, 'Introduction', p. 1.

has been a dominant presence in all European states, albeit that it has been more ingrained in some countries than in others. Unfortunately, despite social and demographic changes, this normative vision of the family retains its purchase on law and policy making within the Union.

4.1.1   The dominant ideologies of motherhood and fatherhood

The concept of the 'dominant ideology of the family' views mothers as crucial to the emotional and physical well-being of any children, while the role of the father is to be the main/sole provider.[4] For women, these prescriptions on motherhood are based on an ideology of motherhood premised on the now-discredited theories of mother–infant bonding which privileges the mother–child relationship. The consequences of an ineffective attachment or bond were said to have devastating pathological consequences for children, ranging from restricted development, to emotional immaturity, to juvenile delinquency.[5] Some studies even recorded failure to bond in the first few hours after birth as the root cause of child abuse or neglect.[6] Accordingly, it was claimed that full-time employment of a mother was on a par with 'death of a parent, imprisonment of a parent, war, famine' and so forth, as a cause of family breakdown.[7] Despite the scientific criticism of this research, and the changes in society and families since the research was published, there remains a 'direct continuation' of these ideas leading to prescriptions of 'what constitutes the right family and what provides for the needs of an infant and child in order for it to become a physically healthy adult'.[8] Thus, the mother–child dyad is not seen as based on choice, individualism and equality, but on nature, self-sacrifice and altruism.

Fatherhood is similarly constrained, this time by an exclusion from care work and an emphasis on paid work as being the primary role for fathers. Thus, the father–child relationship is not characterised by a 'natural' bond, but is based on a social and legal reality. It is based on the ideas of proprietary rights over the child and is therefore more akin to considerations of rationality and rights. There is little flexibility here, just as there is little in relation to motherhood. The father as breadwinner and provider, as authority figure and head of the family, remain dominant themes in discussions of fatherhood, even today: provision, protection

---

4 For a more detailed analysis of the dominant ideology of motherhood employed in the jurisprudence of the Court of Justice, see Clare McGlynn, 'Ideologies of Motherhood in European Community Sex Equality Law' (2000) 6 *European Law Journal* 29–44.

5 Diane Eyer, *Mother Infant Bonding – A Scientific Fiction* (New Haven: Yale University Press, 1992), p. 47.

6 M. Lynch, J. Roberts and M. Gordon, 'Child Abuse: Early Warning in the Maternity Hospital' (1976) 18 *Developmental Medicine and Child Neurology* 759, discussed in Eyer, *Mother Infant Bonding*, p. 31.

7 John Bowlby, *Maternal Care and Mental Health* (Geneva: World Health Organization, 1951), p. 73, discussed in Eyer, *Mother Infant Bonding*, p. 50.

8 Juliet Mitchell and Jack Goody, 'Family or Familiarity?' in Bainham, Slater and Richards (eds.), *What Is a Parent?*, pp. 107–19 at p. 115.

and authority, as described by Sara Ruddick.[9] Thus, despite some acceptance of the changes taking place within families, there remains a continuing 'ideological emphasis on mother-as-carer and father-as-financial-provider that fixes the centrality of nuclear parenting, even where that is absent as a social reality'.[10] It goes without saying that this ideology of family is heterosexist, eschewing any scope for gay and lesbian families and parenting.

4.1.2   Towards gender neutral parenthood

The aim here is not to disparage any need for parental 'bonding' with children. Indeed, as Sandra Fredman has cogently argued, there remains 'insufficient recognition of the value of children and of active parenting' in European society.[11] The crucial point is the need to value *parenting*, not only mothering and not only parenting within the heterosexual nuclear family. My criticism, therefore, is directed at the privileging of the mother–child relationship, exclusive of the role of the father, and the consequences that this has for the organisation of childcare and families. An evolution in thinking is therefore required, away from the dominant ideology of motherhood towards a gender neutral approach to parenthood. A gender neutral approach attempts to depart from the dominant ideology of motherhood and family, seeking to free women and men to pursue the roles, both within families and in the public sphere, which suit them and their children best. In addition to different roles within families, this approach also acknowledges different forms of families as being equally viable and capable of fostering positive parenting. A 'gender neutral' perspective therefore seeks an end to the heterosexual norm of parenting and to the defined roles of 'mother' and 'father'. This is akin to Susan Moller Okin's vision of a 'gender-free' society which would result from a 'diminution and eventual disappearance of sex roles, of expectations that persons of different sexes think, act, dress, adorn themselves, feel, or react in ways supposedly representative of their sex'.[12] In such a society, there would be no assumptions about male and female roles and men and women would participate equally in all spheres of life, including infant care.[13]

In addition, to the extent that society would be free of gender, Moller Okin argues that this would contribute significantly to diminishing the stigmatisation of homosexuality and discrimination on the grounds of sexual orientation.[14] In relation to parenthood, therefore, this vision would see a gradual end to discrimination

---

9 Sara Ruddick, 'The Idea of Fatherhood' in Hilde Nelson (ed.), *Feminism and Families* (London: Routledge, 1997), p. 207, discussed in Alison Diduck, *Law's Families* (Butterworths: London, 2003), p. 85.
10 Mitchell and Goody, 'Family or Familiarity?', 115.
11 Sandra Fredman, *Women and the Law* (Oxford: Oxford University Press, 1997), p. 181.
12 Susan Moller Okin, 'Sexual Orientation and Gender: Dichotomizing Differences' in David Estlund and Martha Nussbaum (eds.), *Sex, Preference and Family – Essays on Law and Nature* (Oxford: Oxford University Press, 1997), pp. 44–59 at p. 45.
13 Moller Okin, 'Sexual Orientation and Gender', 45.
14 Moller Okin, 'Sexual Orientation and Gender', 46.

against gay and lesbian parents and families. Indeed, Moller Okin argues that 'in some important respects', gay and lesbian couples may provide a 'particularly good model of parenthood'.[15] The reason is that such couples are 'far less likely than heterosexual families to practise anything resembling a gendered division of labour'.[16] Thus, far from gay and lesbian families being seen as a threat to 'family values', such relationships 'may provide, in important respects, a very good model for heterosexual families to follow'.[17] This is borne out by empirical evidence demonstrating that, in lesbian parenting partnerships, there is a more egalitarian distribution of both care work and paid work than in the majority of heterosexual partnerships.[18] In particular, biological motherhood was found to be a poor indicator of employment differences between partners and non-biological co-mothers also participated to a greater extent than biological fathers in care and household work.[19] What this perhaps demonstrates is that gendered expectations regarding parental roles, as well as the dominance of existing patterns of work distribution, make it considerably more difficult for heterosexual partners to break free from existing constraints. The corollary is that lesbian partners may be better able to negotiate an egalitarian approach to parenting, due to their shared gendered histories and the lack of prescriptive family models.

4.1.3   Equal parenting

In a two-parent household, same sex or different sex, this gender neutral approach would be synonymous with 'equal parenting'. That is, the idea that parents share care work and paid work: a dual-breadwinner, dual-earner pattern.[20] Such a pattern is to be preferred to the 'full-commodification' strategy of early second wave feminism. Full commodification, that is, equality based on facilitating women working full time, with care work delegated to market or public services, in the end does little to foster gender neutral parenting, as the work of caring for children is generally delegated to other women. Fathers remain removed from childrearing and retain their primary role as financial providers. Furthermore, the pursuit of a full-commodification strategy is a largely class- and race-bound

---

15 Moller Okin, 'Sexual Orientation and Gender', 54.
16 Moller Okin, 'Sexual Orientation and Gender', 54.
17 Moller Okin, 'Sexual Orientation and Gender', 56. For a similar argument, see also Gillian Dunne (ed.), *Living 'Difference' – Lesbian Perspectives on Work and Family Life* (New York: Harrington Park Press, 1998).
18 See the studies discussed in Dunne (ed.), *Living 'Difference'.*
19 See the studies discussed in Dunne (ed.), *Living 'Difference'.*
20 The discourse on 'equal parenting' generally proceeds on the basis of debating the negotiation of paid and care work between a heterosexual couple. This is not just due to the numerical significance of such families, but also because of the centrality of discussing heterosexual parenting to the gender contract. In addition, as discussed above, evidence suggests that, in lesbian families, care work is already shared in a more egalitarian form: Dunne (ed.), *Living 'Difference'.*

strategy.[21] Access to paid work, and especially full-time paid work, does not necessarily bring liberation and fulfilment for women, where the options are limited and of poor quality.[22] The determined pursuit of full-time employment, with less reliance on families, is not therefore universally accepted.[23]

Indeed, Maria Rerrich argues that, in Germany, although there has been a move away from a female full-time carer norm of parenting, this has not resulted in changes in the activities of men, but in communities of women arranging and rearranging care in informal and market ways.[24] In this way, household work and caring becomes distributed not between women and men, but among women, creating new divisions of class and race between women, with men continuing as before.[25] The result is a growing 'marketized female domestic economy' with 'class closure' the result.[26] Rerrich further demonstrates that, in Germany, it is often non-Germans, often immigrant women, who take on the household caring work.[27] Accordingly, a full-commodification model, with care work taking place in the market, or to a lesser extent by the state, has adverse implications for many socially disadvantaged women. Dual earners in professional or managerial jobs may be able to pursue dual careers, together with family lives, but often only because household services are bought on the market, leading to 'polarization between women in societies'.[28]

What is required are changes to workplace structures and the activities of fathers such that women *and* men, of all social classes and ethnicities, are able to enjoy time at home to care for their children. This is what Joan Williams means when she aims to 'democratize' access to domesticity and care work.[29] Fundamental to this aim are radical changes in the structures of the workplace, to make it more flexible and amenable to workers with caring responsibilities, and

21 For an analysis from the US, see Joan Williams, *Unbending Gender – Why Family and Work Conflict and What to Do About It* (Oxford: Oxford University Press, 2000), especially chapter 5.
22 As Bell Hooks wrote: 'Among many poorer Americans, liberation means the freedom of a mother to finally quit her job . . . Of course work for her has meant scrubbing floors or scouring toilets.' bell hooks, *Feminist Theory: From Margin to Centre* (Boston: South End Press, 1984), quoted in Williams, *Unbending Gender*, p. 153. In the UK context, Sylvia Walby has pointed out that an increase in paid employment does not necessarily improve the position of women in society. In particular, paid work may not lead to greater equality for women who are working class or from ethnic minorities who 'only have opportunities to gain relatively poor forms of employment': *Gender Transformations* (London: Routledge, 1997), p. 23.
23 See further Dina Vaiou, 'Women's Work and Everyday Life in Southern Europe in the Context of European Integration' in Maria Dolors Garcia-Ramon and Janice Monk (eds.), *Women of the European Union – The Politics of Work and Daily Life* (London: Routledge, 1996), pp. 61–73.
24 Maria Rerrich, 'Modernizing the Patriarchal Family in West Germany' (1996) 3 *European Journal of Women's Studies* 27–37.
25 Sue Yeandle argues that evidence from the UK suggests similar patterns: 'Women, Men and Non-Standard Employment: Breadwinning and Caregiving in Germany, Italy and the UK' in Rosemary Crompton (ed.), *Restructuring Gender Relations and Employment – The Decline of the Male Breadwinner* (Oxford: Oxford University Press, 1999), pp. 80–104 at p. 95.
26 Yeandle, 'Women, Men and Non-Standard Employment', 103.
27 Rerrich, 'Modernizing the Patriarchal Family'.
28 Yeandle, 'Women, Men and Non-Standard Employment', 95.
29 Williams, *Unbending Gender*, p. 174.

in public services, particularly the provision of childcare and other caring services.[30] Feminist critiques of the structure and organisation of paid work are long-standing and focus on the dominance of a masculine norm of work. This is the norm of the 'ideal worker'[31] who works full-time, is continuously employed until retirement, works long hours and who, therefore, has no family commitments. To a considerable extent, the workplace remains structured around this norm which excludes and/or places at a disadvantage all those who do not conform. Joan Williams argues that embedded in the norm of the 'ideal worker' is a norm of 'mothercare': that is, the assumption that care work is and should be carried out by women and that paid work can and should remain structured around this assumption. Williams convincingly argues that this norm of mothercare should become a norm of 'parental care', with the assumption that all parents have caring responsibilities which limit their availability.[32] In time, this would encourage a move away from the norm of the 'ideal worker' and the assumption that the 'best' workers are those who work full-time continuously and who do not have parental responsibilities.[33] This would both facilitate time away from work, for those already in paid work, and encourage the further development of forms of work not based on the masculine norm of work, thus enabling others to enter the labour market.[34]

But time for parental care is not sufficient on its own. Childcare support is required, not least if lone parents are to be able to benefit from paid work. Child and other care services are widely available in some member states, but rare in others and can be a significant barrier to access to labour markets and facilitating time away from paid work, particularly for lone parents.[35] Lack of childcare facilities also has adverse effects on women's opportunities to pursue activities other than paid work and on equality within families. In the words of the European Commission's Network on Childcare: 'Childcare is an issue of the labour force, of family policy, of children's and women's welfare – as well as being an issue of equality.'[36] The public provision of care is important here; a governmental role

30 See further, Fredman, *Women and the Law*, especially pp. 206–44.
31 Williams, *Unbending Gender*, chapter 3.
32 Williams, *Unbending Gender*, p. 52.
33 Williams, *Unbending Gender*, p. 55.
34 See also Fredman, *Women and the Law*, p. 207, who argues that what is required is a social recognition of the value of parenting which in turn determines how labour markets are structured.
35 For an analysis of the nature of and support for family obligations in the member states, see Jane Millar and Andrea Warman, *Family Obligations in Europe* (London: Family Policy Studies Centre, 1996); European Commission Childcare Network, *Leave Arrangements for Workers with Children* (Brussels: European Commission, 1994). See also Heather Joshi and Hugh Davies, *Childcare and Mothers' Lifetime Earnings – Some European Contrasts (Discussion Paper No. 600)* (London: Centre for Economic Policy Research, 1991) who demonstrate the strong correlation between mothers' participation in the labour market and the availability of childcare, discussed in Fredman, *Women and the Law*, p. 215.
36 European Commission Childcare Network, *Childcare in the European Community 1985–1990* (Brussels: European Commission – Women of Europe Supplement, No. 31, August 1990), p. 2.

being vital due to the importance of its availability, quality and regulation.[37] In addition, a model of marketised care may achieve little for poorer women who are unable to avail themselves of market care, usually due to its high price; nor does the present structure of the workplace enable them to participate fully in caring. Further, without a formal public care service, care may become (remain) devalued and marginal, and workers more likely to be exploited. Although a widespread public care service may indeed lead to the 'universalisation of a female service economy',[38] as in some of the Nordic states, it remains less likely to lead to class closure where care and other household services are marketised and only then available to the middle and upper classes.

Facilitating equal parenting requires changes not only in the labour market and childcare services, but also in the behaviour and activities of men, particularly as fathers. Thus, change is required in the private sphere of the home and family. This is not a new argument. In 1978, Nancy Chodorow stated emphatically: 'It is politically and socially important to confront the organization of parenting.'[39] Care of children, she continued, should take place in 'group situations' and, were this to happen, children 'could be dependent from the outset on people of both genders'.[40] Chodorow's thesis was that cultural assumptions about women and men, the reproduction of gender, were achieved through parenting by women only. In a society in which both women and men cared for children, her hope was that this would radically transform all aspects of society. Thus, her purpose was to eliminate gendered assumptions and roles in society through changing parenting.

However, for many, a singular focus on sharing care within families was and remains extremely problematic. Denise Riley has argued that the principal problem with shared parenting is that it looks solely to the private sphere of the family for change.[41] Emphasis shifts from the public domain of the workplace and provision of childcare, to the private realm of relationships and the negotiation of family roles. Shared childcare, she argued, 'rests on private goodwill; but private goodwill cannot be relied on to sustain a whole politics'.[42] In particular, her concern is that shared parenting assumes an egalitarianism within families which is generally absent. Parents may begin their parenting with unequal access to work and money, and this is an imbalance which may be exploited in any later

---

37 As recommended by the Childcare Network, *ibid.*, p. 4.

38 Anneke van Doorne-Huiskes, 'Work–Family Arrangements: The Role of the State Versus the Role of the Private Sector' in Susan Baker and Anneke van Doorne-Huiskes (eds.), *Women and Public Policy – The Shifting Boundaries between the Public and the Private Spheres* (Ashgate: Aldershot, 1999), at p. 100.

39 Nancy Chodorow, *The Reproduction of Mothering, Psychoanalysis and the Sociology of Gender* (Berkeley: University of California Press, 1978), pp. 214–17.

40 *Ibid.*, pp. 214–17. See also Shulamith Firestone, *The Dialectic of Sex* (London: Paladin, 1972).

41 Denise Riley, '"The Serious Burdens of Love?" Some Questions on Child-Care, Feminism and Socialism' in Lynne Segal (ed.), *What Is to Be Done About the Family? Crisis in the Eighties* (London: Penguin, 1983), pp. 129–56, reprinted in Anne Phillips (ed.), *Feminism and Equality* (Oxford: Blackwell, 1987), pp. 176–97.

42 *Ibid.*, p. 196.

collapse of the goodwill which sustained the original sharing, or when the relationship breaks down. In either breakdown scenario, 'the structures of public inegalitarianism emerge harshly'[43] in terms of access to paid work, to public childcare and to financial and personal security on divorce. Equally, the ideal of shared parenting has nothing to say where there is no pair to share the care. That is, the single parent and others 'whose lives do not encompass potential sharers in the upbringing of children' are excluded and ignored from this vision and their needs forgotten.[44] Similarly, Martha Fineman has argued that the focus on equal parenting, and egalitarianism post-divorce, means that families not including both parents are demonised. She continues that this 'stigmatising process makes mothering outside the context of a two-parent, traditional family susceptible to extensive legal regulation and supervision'.[45] In other words, the privatisation of 'the family' prevails, and traditional norms about families and family life are in danger of being reproduced.

Increased public provision of childcare is clearly required to facilitate the reconciliation of professional and family lives, not least because not all parents can share care, but also because all parents need care support services. However, the focus must not be on public services at the expense of change in homes and families, as this could otherwise have the effect of reinforcing women's role as primary childcarers, as discussed above. Jan Windebank has demonstrated that, although social policy measures designed to facilitate paid work and family life can make some differences to some women's lives, this is generally in the form of a redistribution of work amongst women.[46] Thus, the ability of some mothers to move beyond traditional mothering roles relies on other women who are not in such an advantageous position. Changes are therefore required in families. It is only when change impacts on the private, as well as on the public, that radical transformations may come about. And this is particularly the case in the context of the EU.

As will be seen below, at the Union level, there is an over-emphasis on the public, losing sight of the personal, private aspect of parenthood. Demands for changes in the patterns of work are the meat and drink of Union discussions; a rhetoric which is acceptable and welcomed. Though to a lesser extent, even discussion regarding extending and developing childcare provision is a legitimate Union debate. The personal behaviour of men, and parents, however, is another matter. Though there are references to men's childcare patterns and responsibilities in Union law and policy, in effect the private is eschewed in favour of debate

---

43 Riley, '"The Serious Burdens of Love?"', 195.
44 Riley, '"The Serious Burdens of Love?"', 194.
45 Martha Albertson Fineman, *The Neutered Mother, the Sexual Family and Other Twentieth Century Tragedies* (London: Routledge, 1995), p. 68.
46 Jan Windebank, 'To What Extent Can Social Policy Challenge the Dominant Ideology of Mothering? A Cross-National Comparison of Sweden, France and Britain' (1996) 6 *Journal of European Social Policy* 147–61 at 160.

regarding the public sphere. In the Union context, the private dimension of change has been lost; it must be reclaimed, albeit not at the expense of the debate regarding the need for reform in the public sphere. Equal parenting, with its emphasis on the private and familial, is therefore an essential part of seeking to ensure more gender neutral parenting policies within the Union.

4.1.4   Parenthood and the new ideals of family practices

We can see the links, therefore, between the concepts of gender neutrality and equal parenting and the new ideals of family practices put forward by Giddens and by Beck and Beck-Gernsheim.[47] As will be remembered, these writers suggest that new family practices are emerging based on the ideals of equality, democracy and negotiation. Discrimination, on the grounds of sex or sexual orientation, has no place in these new ways of thinking about families, nor do prescribed forms of families and familial roles. Applying such ideas to parenthood, parenting should be based on equality, on democracy within families and on parental roles being negotiated and not based on some pre-ordained gendered division of roles and competences. It means an end to the dominance of parenting based on heterosexual family practices or on the gendered role of 'mother' or 'father'. Further, as no form of family life is prescribed, there is no presumption about two-parent families, with no consequent stigmatisation of single parents.

Nonetheless, it must not be assumed that a move towards gender neutral parenting practices is likely to be a smooth one, or that there are no objections to how some aspects of gender neutral parenting may be realised in practice. Most importantly, it is essential to recognise that what is described above is an ideal. While Giddens and Beck and Beck-Gernsheim put forward their ideas as descriptions of current changes in relationships, as discussed in chapter 2, they are more appropriately thought of as normative ideals, with reality yet to live up to such visions. Equally, the ideals of gender neutral parenthood and equal parenting are largely ideals, with everyday practice falling far behind. This disjuncture between ideals and practice does give rise to considerable problems.

This is particularly the case in parenting post-divorce. Whereas the negotiation of paid work and family life discussed above is not without its critiques, in the case of post-divorce parenting, changes are being sought in a context of conflict and considerable change. Thus, while gender neutral parenting in this context may be desirable, as Shelley Day Sclater and Candida Yates argue, it may in fact create a 'new opportunity for the expression of the old patriarchal powers'.[48] Their argument is that the rhetoric of gender neutrality in fact masks the colonisation by fathers of the traditional terrain of mothers, with little change in men's attitudes and activities in relation to the care of children, and consequently

---

47 See the discussion in chapter 2.
48 Shelley Day Sclater and Candida Yates, 'The Psycho-Politics of Post-Divorce Parenting' in Bainham, Sclater and Richards (eds.), *What Is a Parent?*, pp. 271–94 at p. 289.

increasing men's claims and 'rights', without the consequent positive changes for women.[49] Sclater and Yates argue that only when women obtain full substantive equality with men, and men recognise their own vulnerabilities, 'will the groundwork be laid for parenting to become truly gender neutral'.[50] Thus, considerable change is required – political, cultural and psychic – before the opportunity for real gender neutral parenting can arise, if indeed (as they query) it is in fact desirable.

Such concerns are borne out by empirical research in the UK which has shown that the policy and legal goals of equal parenting post-divorce are determining parents' relationships with their children.[51] The most significant impact of these goals is on fathers' relationships which have generally, prior to divorce, been mediated through the mother and thus there has not been an 'independent' relationship between the children and the father. Post-divorce, the mediating role of the mother diminishes or ceases and fathers, if they are to continue contact, must establish a new relationship with both the children and the mother. However, while society, in the form of legal and social policy and the courts, supports the father's new role as active father, little support or help is afforded to mothers. Thus, we have a situation where, post-divorce, equal parenting is promoted as the ideal and is supported in a myriad of ways; pre-divorce, in the 'intact' family, little or no support is given to equal parenting. On divorce, therefore, mothers commonly find themselves without the labour market skills or economic foundation necessary to support their lives as co-parents.

Accordingly, while equal parenting post-divorce remains an ideal, where it is not supported by equal parenting pre-divorce considerable hardship results, predominantly for women who were primary carers. They no longer have the role of primary carer, although even in the 'equal parenting' ideal post-divorce the final responsibility often rests with mothers,[52] yet they do not have the cultural or economic capital to benefit from this new independence and have little autonomy or choices. As Carol Smart notes, 'the current priority given by family law to children and to fathers after divorce does nothing to help the transition mothers have to make towards being treated as fully fledged citizens'.[53] Ultimately, therefore, the 'active pursuit – by family law – of equal, joint parenting *after* divorce combined with welfare and employment policies which make equal, joint parenting *during* marriage virtually impossible for the majority, gives rise to a form of disenfranchisement of motherhood rather than a new beginning for parenthood'.[54]

---

49 See also Carol Smart and Bren Neale, *Family Fragments?* (Cambridge: Polity Press, 1999).
50 Sclater and Yates, 'The Psycho-Politics of Post-Divorce Parenting', 289.
51 Smart and Neale, *Family Fragments?*. See also Carol Smart, 'The "New" Parenthood: Fathers and Mothers after Divorce' in Elizabeth Silva and Carol Smart (eds.), *The New Family?* (London: Sage, 1999), pp. 100–14.
52 Smart and Neale, *Family Fragments?*. See also Smart, 'The "New" Parenthood'.
53 Smart, 'The "New" Parenthood', 113.
54 Smart, 'The "New" Parenthood', 113.

Thus, while the reality of family practices does not yet match the ideals of gender neutral parenting, or of the legitimacy of diverse family practices, this does not mean that ambitions should be changed. The ideal of gender neutrality remains valid and must be the focus for law and policy, with careful attention being paid to the real situation of women and men while change is taking place. It is perhaps important, therefore, to see gender neutral parenting as a long-term strategy which may reap rewards in the longer term in terms of relationships between women and men, and parents and children. Such ideological shifts take time and the process of change is never easy. Sociologists Beck and Beck-Gernsheim have argued that, as the male breadwinner model of family life was one of the cornerstones of industrial society, it will not be transcended without conflict, over jobs, the domestic division of labour, childcaring and childrearing. In seeking change, they predict a 'long and bitter battle'.[55] At the European level, this is ever more so. The lowest common denominator, which pervades all policy making at the Union level, contributes to the continuation of outdated assumptions and ideologies about parenting. At best, small incremental steps can be taken which represent inroads into this dominant ideology, with the hope of changing the wider picture in the longer term.

4.1.5   Parenthood and children

What must also be remembered in this discussion of the organisation of parenting is the needs and desires of children. As Allison James has argued, there is a paucity of knowledge about what children think of parenting or family life in general, added to which there is an assumption that children are the passive recipients of 'parenting', a view which places parenting as essentially 'adult-centric'.[56] This view of parenting, as something which is 'done' to children, takes little account of children's own subjectivity and regards children as fundamentally vulnerable, dependent and in need of protection.[57] Furthermore, the discourse on reconciliation of professional and family life tends to see children as objects and obstacles, rather than as subjects in their own right with their own needs and expectations.[58]

In the absence of knowledge about children's experiences, policy prescriptions must be carefully made. Arguably, the gender neutral parenting approach advanced above meets what might be the interests of children in seeking to

---

55 Ulrich Beck and Elisabeth Beck-Gernsheim, *The Normal Chaos of Love* (Cambridge: Polity Press, 1995), p. 14.
56 Allison James, 'Parents: A Children's Perspective' in Bainham, Sclater and Richards (eds.), *What Is a Parent?*, pp. 181–96 at pp. 181–3.
57 James, 'Parents: A Children's Perspective', 181–3.
58 For a discussion of the adult-centric view of reconciliation, see Helmut Wintersberger, 'Work Viewed from a Childhood Perspective' in *Family Observer No. 1* (Luxembourg: European Commission, 1999), pp. 18–24.

ensure that parents are able to spend time with their children, rather than being constrained by a workplace culture which affords them little time, and therefore energy, to care for their children.[59] Policies, therefore, which support equal parenting may, in some small way, be advanced on the basis that they support children's needs and expectations, as well as the wishes of parents. In addition, therefore, it is arguable that the pursuit of equal parenting meets the instruction of the European Union's Charter of Fundamental Rights to pursue the best interests of the child. In addition, in the event of family breakdown, it is possible that more active parenting by fathers, as well as mothers, will enable a child's rights, as set out in the Charter, to maintain access to and contact with both parents, more likely to be fulfilled. But this does not detract from a recognition of the radical rethinking of our approaches to public policy and the organisation of working and family life which would be required for a truly child-centred approach.

Just as new ideas regarding parenthood are emerging, so are new understandings of children's relationships within families.[60] The ideals of family democracy have considerable implications for children, entailing their recognition as autonomous individuals. This has also affected parents' identities and expectations. Jane Ribbens found that these new concepts of children, of children as 'small people' as opposed to 'natural innocents' or 'little devils', while not common, are increasing and reveal new and different ways of conceptualising children's relationships with their mothers.[61] There is, therefore, a 'less explicit ideology which lays down pre-determined guidelines as to how mothers and children should interact. This is because mother and child are construed as different individuals of equal standing, without reciprocal obligations centred on the dependency needs of childhood.'[62] In this way, seeing the child as an individual, rather than a dependent element of the mother, leads to a relationship not based on the assumed 'naturalness' of motherhood or biological 'maternal bond'. Indeed, it creates a type of 'negotiated' relationship.[63] If children are 'small people', individuals to be treated as such, then mothers are more free to be individuals, rather than being bound by the natural, maternal bond. Ideas of fatherhood are also changing. Fathers' 'new' roles are, however, difficult to describe, being uncertain and ambiguous. Empirical evidence demonstrates that, as well as the role of

---

59 Even though parenting, as experienced by children, is often not gender neutral. Allison James discusses how, for children, the generalised concept of 'parent' or 'parenting' may have little meaning because for a child, his or her parents are regarded as gender specific, 'my mum' or 'my dad'. See James, 'Parents: A Children's Perspective', 190.
60 See further chapter 3.
61 Jane Ribbens, 'Mothers' Images of Children and Their Implication for Material Response' in Julia Brannen and Margaret O'Brien (eds.), *Childhood and Parenthood* (Institute of Education, University of London, 1995), discussed in Alison Diduck, *Law's Families* (London: Butterworths, 2003), pp. 87–8.
62 Ribbens, 'Mothers' Images of Children', 72, discussed in Diduck, *Law's Families*, pp. 87–8.
63 Diduck, *Law's Families*, p. 88.

fathers as 'providers', there is the expectation that fathers will 'be there' for their children, even though it was not clear what this meant.[64]

Nonetheless, there remain clear gendered divisions in the expectations of mothers and fathers discovered in this empirical evidence. Although the different expectations are not those of the traditional family, elements of such thinking remain. But, at the same time, the rhetoric of egalitarianism is emerging. The ideals, therefore, of egalitarianism and democracy are not yet being met in practice, but are being expressed as ideals – ideals which impact not just on parents' relationships vis-à-vis each other, but also in relation to their children.

4.1.6   A way forward

In conclusion, therefore, the 'dominant ideology of the family', with its normative prescriptions for family life and familial roles, must be eradicated from European Union law and policy. It must be replaced, in the context of parenthood, with a more modern, gender neutral approach, based on equal parenting and respect for the needs and rights of children. While such an ideal does not yet match reality, it is important that this remain the aim of law and policy. This is imperative if women are to be free to exercise choice in their lives, if men are to be released from their current strait-jackets of marketised automaton and principal bread-winner and if children are to be allowed to enjoy time with their parents.

4.2   Parenthood through the lens of sex equality law

It was through the Union's sex equality laws that its approach to parenthood was first developed. This section, therefore, investigates the institutional and judicial approach to parenthood, as played out in the field of sex equality law. It will be seen that there is a considerable disjuncture between the rhetoric employed at the institutional level regarding policies on the reconciliation of paid work and family life, which expresses commitment to equal parenting, and the jurisprudence of the Court of Justice, which reproduces traditional understandings of parenthood based on the dominant ideologies of motherhood and fatherhood.

4.2.1   The rhetoric of equal parenting: legislative and policy initiatives

Turning first to the positive aspects of the Union's approach and its policies on the reconciliation of paid work and family life, there is indeed much for an advocate of equal parenting to be pleased about.[65] Successive equal opportunity action

---

64 Jo Warin, Yvette Solomon, Charlie Lewis and Wendy Langford, *Fathers, Work and Family Life* (London: Family Policy Studies Centre, Joseph Rowntree Foundation, 1999), discussed in Ribbens, 'Mothers' Images of Children' and in Diduck, *Law's Families*, pp. 88–9.

65 See further: Clare McGlynn, 'Reclaiming a Feminist Vision: The Reconciliation of Paid Work and Family Life in European Union Law and Policy' (2001) 7 *Columbia Journal of European Law* 241–72; Eugenia Caracciolo, 'The "Family-Friendly" Workplace: The EC Position' (2001) 17 *International Journal of Comparative Labour Law and Industrial Relations* 325–44.

programmes have emphasised the importance of reconciliation and the need for change within families if that policy is to be effective. As long ago as 1989, the Social Charter included the non-binding commitment to enable 'men and women to reconcile their occupational and family obligations'.[66] Then, in 1992, the Recommendation on Childcare was adopted.[67] Although non-binding, it did represent a symbolic achievement, that being to 'encourage initiatives to enable women and men to reconcile their occupational, family and upbringing responsibilities arising from the care of children'.[68] One of the four key themes of the Recommendation was the need for measures to 'promote and encourage, with due respect for freedom of the individual, increased participation by men, in order to achieve a more equal sharing of parental responsibilities between men and women and to enable women to have a more effective role in the labour market'.[69] Peter Moss noted that this statement 'place[d] a clear commitment on member states to address the current unequal division of care and other family responsibilities' and was a 'formal recognition' at European level of the significance of the domestic division of labour.[70] Catherine Hoskyns equally welcomed the Recommendation, noting that it was the 'first EC equality measure actively to target male behaviour'.[71]

The promotion of gender neutral and equal parenting appeared, therefore, to be firmly on the Community agenda. The adoption of the Parental Leave Directive in 1996 seemed to set the seal on this approach.[72] The Directive, in providing for a twelve-week period of leave for mothers and fathers, is gender neutral in its treatment of parents. Furthermore, the Directive provides that the rights should be, in principle, non-transferable between parents, with the aim of ensuring a higher take-up by men. Finally, the Directive expresses the desire that 'men should be encouraged to assume an equal share of family responsibilities'. Similarly in 2000, the Council resolution on the balanced participation of women and men in family and working life declared that the 'de facto equality of men and women in the public and private domains' is a necessary condition for democracy. Furthermore, the resolution stated that both 'men and women,

---

66 Catherine Hoskyns notes that this 'commitment' was included at a 'fairly late date' in the negotiation and drafting of the Charter: *Integrating Gender – Women, Law and Politics in the European Union* (London: Verso, 1996), p. 154.

67 Council Recommendation on Childcare 92/241/EEC, OJ 1992 L 123/16.

68 *Ibid.*, Article 1.

69 *Ibid.*, Articles 3–6.

70 Peter Moss, 'Reconciling Employment and Family Responsibilities: A European Perspective' in Suzan Lewis and Jeremy Lewis (eds.), *The Work–Family Challenge* (London: Sage, 1996), pp. 20–33 at p. 25.

71 Hoskyns, *Integrating Gender*, p. 157.

72 Council Directive 96/34/EC of 3 June 1996 on the framework agreement on parental leave concluded by UNICE, CEEP and the ETUC, OJ 1996 L 145/4, as extended to the UK by Council Directive 97/75/EC, OJ 1998 L 10/24. For an analysis of the legislative process leading up to the adoption of the Directive, see Marlene Schmidt, 'Parental Leave: Contested Procedure, Creditable Results' (1997) 13 *International Journal of Comparative Labour Law and Industrial Relations* 113–26.

without discrimination on the grounds of sex, have a right to reconcile family and working life'.[73]

The rhetoric seems clear: equal parenting and an equal sharing of family work is the ambition of Community policy. The rhetoric appears to be supported by legislative action in the form of the Recommendation on Childcare and the Parental Leave Directive. However, beneath the rhetoric there is a far from dedicated commitment to equal parenting. Ultimately, the reconciliation policy is a means to an end. The end is the increased labour market participation of women, not equality in the home and more egalitarian family practices. Although the former may help assist the latter, that is not a foregone conclusion. Thus, at the same time that the rhetoric considered above was proclaiming a commitment to equal parenting, the same policy documents also emphasise what might be said to be the real agenda, that of increasing the labour market participation of women. Thus, the Commission, in its third equal opportunities action programme, stated that reconciliation was necessary to 'reduce the barriers to access to and participation in the labour market by women'.[74] Increased women's employment would help to 'reflate' local economies by, among other things, 'new demands on transport' and 'consumption of childcare'. The Commission stated that the reconciliation policy was necessary to 'harness the economic potential of women' and to meet their 'desire to enter or re-enter the labour market'.[75] Although in its implementation of the programme the Commission sponsored and developed many projects examining gender roles and men as carers, all of which are essential and welcome, such efforts were marginal to the main ambition of increasing women's labour market participation.

This emphasis on the labour market was confirmed with the inclusion of reconciliation as an essential element in the Union's employment policy, with the Commission stating that '[i]ncreasing female participation on the labour market, in view of impending demographic change, is an important objective of the European Employment Strategy'.[76] To this end, one of the original four pillars of the employment strategy was equal opportunities, an aspect of which was reconciliation. All references to reconciliation include women and men, but the *real* agenda is that reconciliation is a *woman's* problem and one that inhibits

73 Resolution of the Council and of the Ministers for Employment and Social Policy of 6 June 2000 on the Balanced Participation of Women and Men in Family and Working Life, Press Release No. 8980/00.
74 Council Resolution of 21 May 1991 on the third medium-term Community action programme on equal opportunities for women and men (1991–1995), OJ 1991 C 142/1. See also the Report from the Commission COM (95) 246 final, Equal Opportunities for Women and Men – Third Community Action Programme 1991–1995, p. 38.
75 Interim report of the Commission on the Implementation of the Medium-Term Community Action Programme on Equal Opportunities for Men and Women (1996 to 2000), COM (98) 770 final, p. 20.
76 Communication from the Commission COM (99) 347 final, A Concerted Strategy for Modernising Social Protection, p. 10.

increased labour market participation. Thus, the 1999 and 2000 Employment Guidelines stated that '*women* still have particular problems in . . . reconciling professional and family life'.[77] The 2003 Guidelines emphasise the need to increase the labour market participation of women, with particular targets set, and stress that particular attention must be given to 'reconciling work and private life' including the 'encouraging of sharing family and professional responsibilities'.[78] The Commission's explanatory document is even more explicit, highlighting the need to facilitate the participation of 'mothers with small children'.[79]

This approach is confirmed in the Commission's recent Communication on demographic change, which states that, to compensate for the predicted fall in the working age population, the 'Union advocates greater employment participation, particularly by women and older people'.[80] Furthermore, the Communication states that families must be encouraged to have more children through the enhancement of public policy 'incentives' such as family benefits, parental leave and childcare which, it claims, have been demonstrated to have a 'positive impact on the birth rates to increase employment, especially female employment'.[81] While the Communication does talk about the need to 'reconcile family life and work' for women and men, again it can be seen that the thrust of the argument is on increasing the birth rate *and* women's employment participation.

Viewed from this perspective, the last thing that is recommended is the withdrawal of men from the labour market to care for children. This would not solve the 'problem' which is the anticipated reduction in the working population due to the reduction in birth rates. Equally, the limited role which many fathers currently play in family life is not considered problematic per se and in need of transformation. Accordingly, it seems that the suggested changes in workplace structures are focused on women, which is simply a false panacea which enables a more basic change in the relations between women and men to be avoided. The point, therefore, is that, while the Commission does state that more favourable conditions are required for women *and* men to enter, re-enter and remain in the labour market, which include an 'equal share of care and household responsibilities' and an 'encouraged take-up of parental and other leave schemes by men', for so long as the focus is principally on the labour

77 Draft Council Resolution of 16 December 1998, quoted in Annual Report from the Commission on Equal Opportunities 1998, COM (99) 106 final, p. 14; Proposal for Guidelines for Member States' Employment Policies 2000, COM (99) 441, p. 10.
78 Council Decision 2003/578/EC of 22 July 2003 on guidelines for the employment policies of Member States, OJ 2003 L 197/13, para. 6.
79 Communication from the Commission to the Council, the European Parliament, the Economic and Social Committee and the Committee of the Regions – The Future of the European Employment Strategy (EES), COM (2003) 6 final, para. 2.2.9.
80 Communication from the Commission COM (2005) 94 final, Green Paper – Confronting Demographic Change: A New Solidarity between Generations, p. 3.
81 *Ibid.*, p. 5.

market participation of women, these suggestions are little more than cheap talk.[82]

In other words, while the increased participation of women in the labour force is important, serious concerns arise when the focus is solely on women's entry into the workforce. Without concomitant changes in the structure of family and household work, an increase in women's labour participation would simply add to women's existing responsibilities, creating and/or making worse women's 'double shift'. This situation has the likely effect of reproducing the very discrimination which an equal parenting policy might have originally tried to eliminate. In the short term, the increase in labour market participation will assist some women, facilitating their wish to participate in the labour market as well as continuing their caring responsibilities. However, in the longer term, it simply entrenches women's responsibilities within families, by confirming assumptions that such obligations are women's only, while doing little to change the marginalisation of women's paid work.[83]

Finally, although the Parental Leave Directive was highly symbolic in its grant of rights to mothers *and* fathers, it was ultimately a damp squib. There was no provision for paid leave and thus the Directive only required changes in a small number of member states. Similarly, the amended Equal Treatment Directive, while recognising the importance of paternity leave, simply promotes it as an option for member states to consider.[84] In contrast, the Pregnancy and Maternity Directive[85] provides for a minimum of fourteen weeks' paid leave, together with significant protection from discrimination. While maternity leave is essential, if not complemented by changes in the practices of men it simply cements women's relationship to the home.[86] And a directive which details considerable rights and entitlements for women on the birth of a child, but does not address men as fathers, is almost certainly likely to reproduce traditional approaches to

82 Communication from the Commission to the Council, the European Parliament, the Economic and Social Committee and the Committee of the Regions – The Future of the European Employment Strategy (EES), COM (2003) 6 final, para. 2.2.9.

83 There is a further danger of a strong link between women's equality and (un)employment in that, in times of high unemployment, women could be encouraged to leave the workplace, to (re)turn to caring duties. Their position as paid workers is therefore rendered marginal and dependent on the vagaries of the changing economic situation and labour market policies. Indeed, Jeanne Fagnani has argued that family policy has been used as a means of reducing unemployment: 'Recent Changes in Family Policy in France' in Eileen Drew, Ruth Emerek and Evelyn Mahon (eds.), *Women, Work and the Family in Europe* (London: Routledge, 1998), pp. 58–65 at p. 58.

84 Preamble (para. 13) to and Article 2(7) of Directive 2002/73/EC of the European Parliament and of the Council of 23 September 2002 amending Council Directive 76/207/EEC on the implementation of the principle of equal treatment for men and women as regards access to employment, vocational training and promotion, and working conditions, OJ 2002 L 269/15.

85 Council Directive 92/85/EEC of 19 October 1992 on the introduction of measures to encourage improvements in the safety and health at work of pregnant workers and workers who have recently given birth or are breastfeeding, OJ 1992 L 348/1.

86 Melissa Benn, *Madonna and Child – Towards a New Politics of Motherhood* (London: Jonathan Cape, 1998), p. 70.

parenthood. Although there is a need to be sex specific when considering pregnancy, this should not extend to rights post-birth which should be gender neutral. Accordingly, although the Directive brought an immediate improvement to the workplace rights of many women, its longer term consequences are problematic. In this way, Patrizia Romito has argued that, although such policies will seem to many women like the lifeline which keeps them afloat, they are in fact 'measures which rationalize the exploitation of the work mothers do both inside and outside the family'.[87]

Unfortunately, the Charter of Fundamental Rights simply reproduces the existing position in Community law, rather than attempting to map a more progressive approach to reconciliation and parenthood. Article 33(2) of the Charter states that: 'To reconcile family and professional life, everyone shall have the right to protection from dismissal for a reason connected with maternity and the right to paid maternity leave and to parental leave following the birth or adoption of a child.' It can be seen that this carefully crafted provision simply restates existing entitlements under the Pregnancy and Maternity Directive and the Parental Leave Directive. In particular, the omission of a reference to 'paid' parental leave is most notable. This provision, while recognising parenthood as distinct from marriage or a particular form of family life, does however reinforce a hierarchical gendered preference for motherhood over fatherhood, via the provision of paid maternity leave, followed only by (unpaid) parental leave and no provision for paternity leave.[88] Moreover, this 'right' is contained in the title on employment rights, not the title on equality. Its development, if there is to be any, will be bedevilled by the same problems identified above in pursuing reconciliation through an employment policy.

Faced with a challenge to existing Community provisions on reconciliation, it seems that there is little in this Article which an advocate general or the Court could use to develop and enhance the law. This inadequacy is all the more striking in view of an earlier draft which began with the bold statement: 'Everyone shall have the right to reconcile their family and professional lives.'[89] The grant of a 'right to reconciliation' may have had potentially far-reaching consequences. It could have been developed to cover not only paid parental leave, but also a wide range of policies which impact on the (im)balance between paid work and family lives, not least childcare and flexible working practices.

---

87 Patrizia Romito, '"Damned If You Do and Damned If You Don't": Psychological and Social Constraints on Motherhood in Contemporary Europe' in Anne Oakley and Juliet Mitchell (eds.), *Who's Afraid of Feminism? Seeing Through the Backlash* (London: Hamish Hamilton, 1997), pp. 162–86 at p. 183.

88 For a contrary interpretation, see Marzia Barbera, 'The Unsolved Conflict: Reshaping Family Work and Market Work in the EU Legal Order' in Tamara Hervey and Jeff Kenner (eds.), *Economic and Social Rights under the EU Charter of Fundamental Rights – A Legal Perspective* (Oxford: Hart Publishing, 2003), pp. 139–60 at p. 142.

89 Charte 4422/00, 28 July 2000, Article 31.

This earlier draft of the Charter did go on to qualify the 'right to reconciliation' by stating that the right 'includes in particular the right to protection from dismissal because of pregnancy and the right to paid maternity leave and to parental leave following the birth or adoption of a child'. It is, however, the words 'in particular' which would have been crucial: such words do not limit the scope of the right, but give examples of the possible manifestations of the right. Had this provision on reconciliation been included in the final text of the Charter, it is possible that the Court of Justice could have used it to develop a broad and progressive interpretation of the 'right to reconciliation'. As things stand, the final text of the Charter is limited and inadequate and is therefore unlikely to bring about any significant changes to the existing reconciliation policy.

Perhaps, however, a creative court could make use of Article 23 of the Charter, to be found in the equality chapter, which states that: 'Equality between men and women must be ensured in all areas, including employment, work and pay.' Is it possible that this could be interpreted broadly to include, for example, equality of parenting? The provision states that equality is to be included in 'all' areas, including those relating to the workplace, but not limited thereto. Therefore, although earlier jurisprudence of the Court suggests that, in terms of relations between women and men within the home and family, the preference is for the traditional sexual division of labour, perhaps the Court could be persuaded that this provision, in combination with the many statements of the Commission and Parliament in a similar vein, suggests that relations between women and men should be modernised and equalised.[90] However, in view of the Court's approach, further discussed below, this seems unlikely. Another potentiality is the general non-discrimination provision in Article 21. Marzia Barbera argues that this provision may provide the Court of Justice with the institutional capacity and competence to expand reconciliation rights beyond those found in Article 33, including the 'unequal distribution of discretionally attributed benefits, such as parental leave paid only to women workers and not to men workers as well'.[91] One final possibility is Article 24 on the rights of the child, which Cathryn Costello argues could facilitate a more gender neutral approach to parenting as it would be difficult to justify measures on the basis of the sex of parents, rather than on the best interests of the child.[92]

Generally, however, it is here, in the Charter, that the gap between the rhetoric and the reality of Union policy is clearest. The Council adopted its forward-thinking

---

90 It might even be that 'work' could be interpreted to include unpaid work in the home, albeit that this is again unlikely in view of the Court's existing jurisprudence. In the area of free movement of workers, the Court has rejected arguments that unpaid work in the home might constitute 'work' for the purposes of Community entitlements. See further Isabella Moebius and Erika Szyszczak, 'Of Raising Pigs and Children' (1998) 18 *Yearbook of European Law* 125–56.

91 Barbera, 'The Unsolved Conflict', 153.

92 Cathryn Costello, 'Gender Equalities and the Charter of Fundamental Rights of the European Union' in Hervey and Kenner (eds.), *Economic and Social Rights*, pp. 111–38 at pp. 126–8.

resolution on the balanced participation of women and men in public and private lives in mid-2000, with its somewhat radical policy proposals and commitment to equal parenting and a right to reconciliation. Later that year, however, the Charter of Fundamental Rights was adopted which bears little resemblance to the resolution and which will effectively restrict future opportunities and reinforce the status quo. A resolution is cheap talk: whereas it appears to be too much of a risk to include progressive proposals and statements in a (non-binding) Charter of Fundamental Rights. Rhetoric and reality could not be further apart.

4.2.2   The Court of Justice and the reproduction of traditional ideologies of motherhood and fatherhood

In the policy and legislative field, discussed above, measures which have been taken in the name of gender neutral parenthood are often merely exhortatory and generally require little or no action at member state level. Nonetheless, there are some moves towards equal parenting, and the rhetoric, at least, is moving in the right direction. In the jurisprudence of the Court of Justice even the positive rhetoric is largely absent. As discussed below, the Court of Justice has been reproducing a traditional ideology of motherhood, and parenthood, which owes little to the ideas of equal parenting. Although lip-service has been paid to the Union's policy objectives regarding the reconciliation of paid work and family life, this has yet to manifest itself in concrete decisions.

An explanation for this divergent approach is not easy to find. Perhaps the conservative nature of legal reasoning and precedent, the absence of dissenting opinions and the pressure of case loads, combined with the isolated disciplinary nature of judicial decision-making, account for the differences.[93] In addition, rhetoric is cheap. The Union institutions can afford to make bold claims, without there being many real consequences. On the contrary, the Court's judgments can have wide-ranging cultural and economic effects, which the Court is perhaps rightly shy of precipitating, particularly in a political climate of contested legitimacy of the Union. Notwithstanding such constraints on its activities, it is my argument that the Court should be exercising its interpretative power in a more progressive manner; in a way which is consistent with its own oft-stated commitment to equality between women and men and which reflects the principles of gender neutral and equal parenting.

The foundation of the Court's jurisprudence can be traced back to the *Commission* v. *Italy* and *Hofmann* cases of the mid-1980s.[94] The Court held in *Commission* v. *Italy* that Italian legislation which granted only women a right to

93 See further Giuseppe Federico Mancini and Siofra O'Leary, 'The New Frontiers of Sex Equality Law in the European Union' (1999) 24 *European Law Review* 331–53; and Siofra O'Leary, *Employment Law at the Court of Justice – Judicial Structures, Policies and Processes* (Oxford: Hart Publishing, 2002).

94 Case 163/82, *Commission* v. *Italy* [1983] ECR 3273; [1984] 3 CMLR 169; Case 184/83, *Hofmann* v. *Barmer Ersatzkasse* [1984] ECR 3047; [1986] 1 CMLR 242.

leave on the adoption of a child was not contrary to the Community's Equal Treatment Directive.[95] The Court held that the Italian government had been motivated by a 'legitimate concern' which led it 'rightly' to introduce legislation attempting to assimilate the entry of adoptive and biological children into the family, especially during the 'very delicate initial period'.[96] Underpinning this judgment was a belief that different treatment on account of motherhood (and not biological differences regarding the capacity to give birth) does not constitute unlawful discrimination. In so holding, the Court reinforced the sexual division of labour in which childcare is always the responsibility of mothers, ignoring any conception that the father may also have a legitimate need and/or desire for a period of leave. Fatherhood is thereby limited, by implication, to a breadwinning role, with the assumption that a father's primary commitment and identification should be with paid work, rather than childcare.[97]

This approach was followed in *Hofmann* which involved a challenge to German legislation which provided that only women were entitled to an optional period of maternity leave which took effect eight weeks after birth. Hofmann, the father of a newly born baby, argued that this leave was for childcare purposes and should therefore be available to mothers and fathers.[98] The German government justified the policy on the ground that it had 'favourable repercussions in the sphere of family policy, inasmuch as it enable[d] the mother to devote herself to her child', free from the 'constraints' of employment.[99] The Court agreed, holding that Community law was not designed to settle questions relating to the 'organisation of the family', or to 'alter the division of responsibility between parents'.[100] The Court suggested, therefore, that Community law stands outside the sexual division of labour in the home, thus absolving Community law of any responsibility for the 'social organisation' of family life.[101] However, in not intervening, the Court, and thereby Community law, effectively legitimated the status quo. The Court sanctioned legislation which helped ensure that women are, and should remain, primarily responsible for childcare.

---

95 Council Directive 76/207/EEC of 9 February 1976 on the implementation of the principle of equal treatment for men and women as regards access to employment, vocational training and promotion, and working conditions, OJ 1976 L 39/40.

96 *Commission* v. *Italy*, para. 16.

97 On the traditional conception of fatherhood and the part this plays in limiting opportunities for women, see Richard Collier, '"Feminising" the Workplace? Law, the "Good Parent" and the "Problem of Men"' in Anne Morris and Therese O'Donnell (eds.), *Feminist Perspectives on Employment Law* (London: Cavendish, 1999), pp. 161–81.

98 This view was supported by the fact that the second period of leave was withdrawn in the event of the death of the baby.

99 *Hofmann*, written observations to the Court, at p. 3061.

100 *Hofmann*, para. 24. A formula repeated in many subsequent cases: see, for example, Case C-345/89, *Re Stoeckel* [1991] ECR I-4047; [1993] 3 CMLR 673, para. 17.

101 This apparent neutrality was echoed in Case 170/84, *Bilka-Kaufhaus* v. *Weber von Hartz* [1986] ECR 1607; [1986] 2 CMLR 701, para. 43, where the Court stated that employers, and Community law, did not have to take into account the 'difficulties faced by persons with family responsibilities' when establishing entitlement conditions for occupational pensions.

This is confirmed by the Court's justifications for granting leave to women only. It declared that it was 'legitimate to protect the special relationship between a woman and her child'.[102] The language of the 'special relationship' inevitably recalls the discredited theories of mother–infant bonding in which the bonding of mother and child is seen as crucial to the future healthy development of the child and reinforces the 'notion that women's childcare obligations are "natural" and unchangeable'.[103] This is the 'special protection' of a particular conception of motherhood, one that perpetuates the assumption, based on the bonding research, that because 'women bear children they are therefore automatically the sex that is responsible for rearing them'.[104] The Court conceived, normatively, of a workplace in which only women take time off to care for children and was effectively encouraging 'women to stay at home with their children during the early months at least, while men continue with their uninterrupted careers'.[105]

After much condemnation of *Hofmann* by feminist activists, scholars and many others, not least in Germany, it was thought that the Court's judgment in *Commission* v. *France* in 1986 signalled a change of direction.[106] In this case, the Court rendered unlawful a range of rights granted to French women which included leave when a child is ill, the grant of an additional day's holiday in respect of each child, granting time off work on Mother's Day and payments of allowances to mothers for childcare expenses.[107] The Court held that these rights were incompatible with the Equal Treatment Directive as they were entitlements which should be available to women and men. The Court continued that the rights breached the principle of equality as they granted women special rights in their capacity as parents, which is a category 'to which both men and women equally belong'.[108] The Advocate General continued that a 'father, in modern social conditions, may just as much be responsible for looking after sick children or need to pay childminders' and should therefore be entitled to the same rights.[109]

The judgment in *Commission* v. *France* was greeted as heralding a sea-change in the Court's approach.[110] The Court had rejected special rights granted to

---

102 *Hofmann*, para. 26. The concept of the 'special relationship' has been reiterated in many subsequent cases, most recently in Case C-342/01, *Merino Gómez* v. *Continental Industrias del Caucho SA* [2004] 2 CMLR 3.
103 Fredman, *Women and the Law*, p. 195.
104 Christopher Bovis and Christine Cnossen, 'Stereotyped Assumptions Versus Sex Equality: A Socio-Legal Analysis of the Equality Laws in the European Union' (1996) 12 *International Journal of Comparative Labour Law and Industrial Relations* 7–23 at 19.
105 Sandra Fredman, 'European Community Discrimination Law: A Critique' (1992) 21 *Industrial Law Journal* 119–34 at 127.
106 Case 312/86 [1988] ECR 6315; [1989] 1 CMLR 408.
107 *Ibid.*, para. 8.
108 *Ibid.*, para. 14.
109 *Ibid.*, p. 6328.
110 For example, Cathryn Claussen suggested that, if Case 312/86, *Commission* v. *France* [1988] ECR 6315; [1989] 1 CMLR 408, is to be taken as an indication of how the Court will decide

mothers, arguing that parental rights should be available to women *and* men. Thus, by the late 1990s, with the reconciliation policy well established and the Parental Leave Directive[111] adopted, as well as the rapid increases in women's employment, it might have been thought that the traditional rendering of women's and men's roles within 'the family' would have given way to a more progressive and egalitarian response by the Court. Unfortunately, however, such optimism was misplaced and in *Abdoulaye, Hill and Stapleton, Lewen* and *Lommers* the Court has effectively reiterated its *Hofmann* jurisprudence.[112]

In *Abdoulaye*, the Court rejected a claim that a payment granted to women 'when taking maternity leave' constituted discrimination against men.[113] The men had argued that this was a payment equivalent to a child allowance to which women and men should be equally entitled, as it was made on top of women's full salary and, where a child was adopted, a payment was made to mothers or fathers. The Court justified its position by arguing that women taking maternity leave were in a unique position which made comparison between their rights and the rights of women and men at work impossible.[114] However, the appropriate comparison should have been women and men becoming parents and, as the Court stated in *Commission* v. *France*, this category applies to both women and men, and therefore they should both be entitled to equal rights.

The Court's ruling in *Abdoulaye* bears all the hallmarks of its earlier approach in *Hofmann* and its legitimation of the status quo. It sought to 'protect' women from having their existing rights diluted or removed. However, in doing so, it reinforced a traditional approach to women's responsibilities and capabilities. Although women may presently remain primarily responsible for childcare, the granting of rights to women to compensate therefor in fact entrenches their disadvantageous position. In effect, the Court's judgments reinforce the very discrimination that they are seeking to render unlawful. It is appropriate to ensure the continuation of women's employment rights whilst pregnant and giving birth, but such judicial enforcement should not extend beyond such biological and

similar issues in the future, it would 'represent a significant step forward': 'Incorporating Women's Reality into Legal Neutrality in the European Community: The Sex Segregation of Labor and the Work–Family Nexus' (1991) 22 *Law & Policy in International Business* 787–813 at 797.

111 Directive 96/34/EC, OJ 1996 L 145/4.

112 There are further cases which could be considered here, for example the Court's endorsement of a legislative prohibition on the night work of pregnant women: Case C-421/92, *Habermann-Beltermann* v. *Arbeiterwohlfahrt* [1994] ECR I-1657; [1994] 2 CMLR 681, and its reiteration of the 'special relationship' justification in many pregnancy discrimination cases, for example, Case C-32/93, *Webb* v. *EMO Air Cargo (UK) Ltd* [1994] ECR I-3567; [1994] 2 CMLR 729, para. 20. See also Tamara Hervey and Jo Shaw, 'Women, Work and Care: Women's Dual Role and Double Burden in EC Sex Equality Law' (1998) 8 *Journal of European Social Policy* 43–63.

113 Case C-218/98, *Abdoulaye* v. *Régie nationale des usines Renault SA* [1999] ECR I-5723; [2001] 2 CMLR 18. See further, Clare McGlynn, 'Pregnancy, Parenthood and the Court of Justice in *Abdoulaye*' (2000) 25 *European Law Review* 654–62.

114 In particular, the Court held that women suffer 'several occupational disadvantages inherent in taking maternity leave', para. 18, for which this payment is made in lawful compensation.

health requirements. Hence, the optional period of maternity leave in *Hofmann*, or the period of adoptive leave in *Commission* v. *Italy*, and, similarly, the payment in *Abdoulaye*, should not come within this field of protection. To do so, as these judgments have done, is to perpetuate stereotypes about the roles of mothers and fathers. To exclude men from a societal recognition of the significance (and financial expense) of the birth of a child perpetuates traditional assumptions that the birth and care of a child is a women's concern and responsibility. This not only does a disservice to women, ensuring the continuation of outdated assumptions about their familial and workplace roles, but means that men are not encouraged and facilitated in taking up new and expanding opportunities to play a significant role in the care and upbringing of their children.

The judgment in *Abdoulaye* confirmed that the Court's earlier ruling in *Hill and Stapleton* was not perhaps as progressive as it might have first appeared.[115] In the context of considering potential justifications for indirectly discriminatory employment conditions, the Court had stated that it was Community policy to 'encourage and, if possible, adapt working conditions to family responsibilities'.[116] It continued that such a policy aims to ensure the '[p]rotection of women within family life and in the course of their professional activities', adding that this was also the case for men.[117] In many ways, this statement could be seen as progressive and a move away from the *Hofmann* approach. It does recognise a familial dimension to equality law and refers to the need for measures to facilitate a reconciliation of paid work and family life.[118] However, the Court implies the need to adapt working conditions *to* family responsibilities, that is, to meet *existing* responsibilities: not that family responsibilities need to change in order to liberate women and men. Thus, the Court appears to assume a static position regarding family responsibilities and seeks to adapt working conditions to meet that reality. Although this does constitute a belated recognition of the need for some change, it is a limited vision.[119]

---

115 Case C-243/95, *Hill and Stapleton* v. *Revenue Commissioners and the Department of Finance* [1998] ECR I-3739; [1998] 3 CMLR 81. See further Clare McGlynn and Catherine Farrelly, 'Equal Pay and the "Protection of Women in Family Life"' (1999) 24 *European Law Review* 202–7.
116 *Hill and Stapleton*, para. 42.
117 *Hill and Stapleton*, para. 42.
118 See also Case C-1/95, *Gerster* v. *Freistaat Bayern* [1997] ECR I-5253; [1998] 1 CMLR 303, para. 38, in which the Court stated that: 'The protection of women – and men – both in family life and in the workplace is a principle broadly accepted in the legal systems of the member states as the natural corollary of the fact that men and women are equal and is upheld by Community law.'
119 It is also a principle which the Court did not apply in the later case, Case C-249/97, *Gruber* v. *Silhouette International Schmied GmbH & Co. KG* [1999] ECR I-5295, in which the Court rejected the argument that resigning from employment because of the absence of adequate childcare arrangements was equivalent to the other 'important' reasons for leaving employment. Her sex discrimination claim was therefore rejected. See O'Leary, *Employment Law at the Court of Justice*, pp. 221–2.

Such a limited approach was reinforced in the first case to consider the Parental Leave Directive. In *Lewen*, the Court held that the payment of a Christmas bonus was not a 'right' protected by the Parental Leave Directive, despite the clause stating that 'rights acquired or in the process of being acquired' must be maintained.[120] Accordingly, Lewen was not able to utilise the directive to challenge her employer's refusal to pay her a Christmas bonus while on parental leave. Although Lewen was granted a remedy in part, this was on the basis of indirect sex discrimination as 'female workers are likely . . . to be on parenting leave far more often than male workers'.[121] In this way, the potentially adverse impact of child-care responsibilities on employment opportunities is only recognised in the context of the existing sex equality laws, not the Parental Leave Directive, and only for women. This reinforces the assumption that such childcare commitments are the primary responsibility of women and it is only women whose employment rights require protection.[122] This ruling negates the purpose of the Directive in that, although men can take leave, their employment rights will not be protected to the same extent as those of women, as a man in a similar position to Lewen would not have been able to challenge the employer's actions. Moreover, as Lewen's rights were only protected by indirect discrimination, this means that as more men avail themselves of the right to parental leave, as is the explicitly stated aim of the legislation, the rights of women will be reduced as they will be less able to claim indirect discrimination. This is a preposterous situation in which the rights of women and men are pitted against one another. This is counter-intuitive as it means that the very ambition of many women, that men be more involved in childcare, will lead to a reduction in their own rights.

A further problematic aspect of this judgment was the fact that the Court held that, when calculating the amount of a bonus, compulsory periods of maternity leave must be taken into account, whereas time on parental leave could reduce the bonus payable.[123] This approach is explicable in view of the Court's pregnancy discrimination jurisprudence, but underlines the obstacles to encouraging greater parental care by men. If women's entitlements are protected in this way, but not men's, it is of little surprise that few men avail themselves of leave. Furthermore, it means that women's rights are best protected by sex specific, rather than sex neutral, provisions. Thus, rather than supporting a move away from *maternity* rights to *parenting* rights, the consequence of the Court's ruling may be to encourage the enactment of sex specific rights. This is because, where parenting rights are enacted in a gender neutral fashion, it in effect reduces the rights and entitlements of women where those would have been characterised as maternity

---

120 Clause 2(6) of the framework agreement annexed to Directive 96/34/EC, OJ 1996 L 145/4.
121 Case C-333/97, *Lewen* v. *Denda* [1999] ECR I-7243; [2000] 2 CMLR 38, para. 40.
122 See further Eugenia Caracciolo di Torella, 'Childcare, Employment and Equality in the EC: First (False) Steps of the Court' (2000) 25 *European Law Review* 310–16.
123 *Lewen* v. *Denda*, para. 47.

rights. In providing some protection for women, over and above rights for parents, the Court appears to be mimicking the approach to reconciliation considered in the section above. In other words, the reconciliation policy focuses attention on *women's* labour market position, rather than on a more general approach to the parenting rights of women and men.

This approach has been confirmed in the extraordinary case of *Lommers*.[124] A branch of the Dutch civil service reserved nursery places for its female employees, except in cases of emergency when they could be offered to men. Unsurprisingly, a male employee challenged this policy as constituting unlawful sex discrimination. The Court held that the scheme does 'create a difference of treatment on grounds of sex' and that the situations of a 'male employee and female employee, respectively father and mother of young children, are comparable as regards the possible need for them to use nursery facilities because they are in employment'.[125] However, the Court went on to state that the scheme was justified under Article 2(4) of the Equal Treatment Directive[126] as a measure designed to 'eliminate or reduce actual instances of inequality which may exist in the reality of social life'.[127]

The Court then considered the facts of the case and referred to the under-representation of women in the Ministry of Agriculture, the proven insufficiency of nursery facilities and the fact that this is more likely to induce female employees to give up their employment. Accordingly, the Court held that the reservation of nursery places for women, except in emergencies, is within the category of 'measures designed to eliminate the causes of women's reduced opportunities for access to employment and careers and are intended to improve their ability to compete on the labour market and to pursue a career on an equal footing with men'.[128] Of crucial importance, however, was the existence of the potential exception in favour of men. The Court held that a scheme such as the one under consideration which did not grant access to men who 'take care of their children by themselves' would go beyond the permissible scope of Article 2(4) of the Equal Treatment Directive. The scheme, therefore, was held to be lawful for so long as men who take care of children by themselves have access to places on the same conditions as women.

Although the judgment of the Court suggests that this ruling is positive for women, in that it is a legitimate measure of positive discrimination, in practice it reproduces the dominant ideology of motherhood which hinders women's

124 Case C-476/99, *Lommers* v. *Minister van Landbouw, Natuurbeheer en Visserij* [2002] ECR I-2891; [2004] 2 CMLR 49.
125 *Lommers*, para. 30.
126 Council Directive 76/207/EEC of 9 February 1976 on the implementation of the principle of equal treatment for men and women as regards access to employment, vocational training and promotion, and working conditions, OJ 1976 L 39/40.
127 *Lommers*, para. 32.
128 *Lommers*, para. 38.

progress in the workplace and reaffirms the inferior status of fatherhood. Indeed, the Court referred to academic opinion which considers that 'measures such as those' under discussion are 'likely to perpetuate and legitimize the traditional division of roles between men and women'.[129] And this is indeed what such measures and this judgment will do. Legitimating the grant of childcare places to women only simply serves to reinforce the fact that they are primarily responsible for childcare. As with *Abdoulaye*, this judgment seeks to deal with the symptoms of discrimination, rather than treating the cause. It is the case that women remain largely responsible for childcare and that they are more likely than men to leave work if childcare is in short supply or is of poor quality. The remedy for this, however, is not to grant places only to women, but to ensure that women are not primarily responsible for childcare and that good quality childcare places are widely available. The judgment may assist some women in the short term, but in the longer term it reinforces disadvantageous assumptions.

Furthermore, the emphasis placed by the Court on the exception in favour of fathers 'who take care of their children by themselves'[130] is equally problematic. This formulation suggests that only single fathers would come within the exception, whereas there is no such proviso in favour of women.[131] This is precisely because of the underlying assumption that women, whether in partnerships or not, will take primary responsibility for childcare, whereas men will only do so where they are on their own. Thus, the exception for men simply reinforces the assumptions about women's roles and the dominant ideology of fatherhood. It suggests that, in a partnership where childcare is shared, the father would not be eligible for a childcare place under this scheme. It is this result which ultimately demonstrates the adverse impact of this judgment.

Fortunately, there are some limits as to how far the Court will expand the scope of justifications for discrimination. In *Griesmar*, the Court held that a French government retirement scheme which granted credits to women with children, regardless of any time away from the workplace, constituted unlawful sex discrimination.[132] The Advocate General had held otherwise, suggesting that, following *Abdoulaye*, the credit was a legitimate measure designed to offset the disadvantages of raising children.[133] The French government had similarly claimed that the credits addressed a 'social reality', namely the disadvantages which women incur in the course of their professional careers by virtue of the 'predominant role assigned to them in bringing up children'.[134] The Court

---

129 *Lommers*, para. 22.
130 *Lommers*, para. 50.
131 It seems that this is the interpretation placed on the judgment by the Court in its press release which acclaims the judgment as representing 'progress for lone fathers' who are to be treated equally with lone mothers. *Agence Europe*, 21 March 2002.
132 Case C-366/99, *Griesmar v. Ministre de l'Economie, des Finances et de l'Industrie* [2001] ECR I-9383; [2003] 3 CMLR 5.
133 Opinion of 22 February 2001, [2001] ECR I-9383; [2003] 3 CMLR 5.
134 *Griesmar*, para. 51.

rejected the argument because there was no link made between the credit and any absences from work on maternity or parental leave,[135] holding that 'situations of a male civil servant and a female civil servant may be comparable as regards the bringing-up of children' so there can be no discrimination.[136] The Court here particularly emphasised the fact that there was no credit available for a man who had assumed the task of bringing up his children and was thereby exposed to the same career disadvantages.[137] The implication is that, had there been such an exception, this might have led to a different result.

The Court reached the correct judgment in this case. Credits should be granted to women and men who have taken time away from the workplace to care for children. This would ensure that those individuals do not suffer disadvantage when it comes to retirement. In addition, recognition is given that, when it comes to the upbringing of children, mothers and fathers should be treated the same. But they are not so treated in situations like *Abdoulaye* and *Lommers*. Therefore, we have a situation where parents are to be treated equally, except where they are legitimately not treated equally. The line drawn between the two situations is not sufficiently clear, and the confusion will simply hinder attempts to ensure equality for mothers and fathers. As Siofra O'Leary rightly argues, the Court's case law is 'riddled with confusion and contradiction'.[138]

It can be seen, therefore, that the Court's approach to parenting relies on the sexual division of labour and reproduces the traditional ideologies of motherhood and fatherhood. Despite the Union's perceived economic need to ensure greater participation of women in the labour market, it fights shy of the real measures that would need to be taken so that women would feel able and willing to increase their paid work. The Court of Justice, in particular, is confused in its jurisprudence regarding sex equality and the reconciliation of paid work and family life. It appears to flit between what it perceives as beneficial positive discrimination and gender neutrality, with little consistency and continuing adverse symbolic and practical effects.

4.3   Parenthood and the Union's evolving family law

In 2001, the Union adopted its first measure in the family law field, providing for the jurisdiction, recognition and enforcement of judgments relating to marital breakdown and parental responsibility.[139] However, this was no vanguard family law: no new opportunity was taken to establish modern laws reflecting changing social and conceptual realities. In fact, this first measure clearly reflected

---

135 *Griesmar*, para. 52.
136 *Griesmar*, para. 56.
137 *Griesmar*, para. 56.
138 O'Leary, *Employment Law at the Court of Justice*, p. 220.
139 For a detailed examination, see chapter 6. This section concentrates on the implications of this area of law specifically in relation to the concept of parenthood.

the dominant ideology of the family and hence a traditional conception of parenthood.[140]

At the national and international level, there has been an increasing separation of marriage from parenthood, with marriage fast being replaced by parenthood as the foundation of families. Historically, marriage was the basis for 'the family' in view of the factual difficulty of establishing paternity. Thus, legal presumptions were developed such that paternity may be assumed in certain situations, most notably marriage. In this way, parenthood became synonymous with marriage and fatherhood was assumed to exist only within the nuclear family. Thus, marriage became a key element in our understanding of what it means to be a father. This traditional perspective also conceived of biological children as the possessions of their parents, who had exclusive rights in relation to them and in whom all parental decisions should reside. The social reality of increasing numbers of children born to parents outside of marriage, often cohabiting, combined with increasing levels of divorce and the formation of step-families, necessitated changes in this approach, with parenting becoming separated from marriage. Furthermore, the emphasis placed by modern family law on the child's best interests requires consideration of non-biological and non-marital relationships which may be central to ensuring the child's welfare and interests.

For this reason, the social reality of parenting becomes more important than the civil status of the parents. A recognition of these changes is necessary to ensure that families which do not conform to the married nuclear norm do not suffer, either with fathers being excluded from parental rights, or children being prejudiced as a result of their parents' status, or lack of status. In addition, phases of family and relationship formation can be repeated throughout the lifecycle, for example through divorce, remarriage and reconstituted families, such that legal rules need to recognise such changes and reformations of families.[141]

It is lamentable, therefore, that the social and conceptual realities referred to above, and discussed elsewhere in this book, failed at first to make an impression on the Community legislature. Accordingly, the first family law measure adopted by the Community linked parenthood to marriage. Regulation 1347/2000 detailed new Community rules on jurisdiction and the recognition and enforcement of judgments in matrimonial matters and in matters of parental responsibility for joint children.[142] In relation to parents, therefore, the Regulation only dealt with disputes regarding the children of both spouses on the event of their divorce, separation or annulment. It excluded, therefore, disputes over the parental

---

140 See further chapters 6 and 7.
141 See Stalford, 'Regulating Family Life', referring to Wilfried Dumon, 'Recent Trends and New Prospects for a European Family Policy' in Henry Cavana (ed.), *The New Citizenship of the Family* (Aldershot: Ashgate, 2000).
142 Council Regulation 1347/2000/EC of 29 May 2000 on jurisdiction and the recognition and enforcement of judgments in matrimonial matters and in matters of parental responsibility for children of both spouses, OJ 2000 L 160/19 (repealed by Regulation 2201/ 2003).

responsibility for step-children, children of unmarried or same-sex partners and adopted children of only one partner, and therefore excluded many forms of social parenthood from its scope. Thus, the personal scope of the Regulation mirrored the highly restrictive dominant ideology of the family. Accordingly, the status of the parents appeared to be more important than the interests of the child or the child–parent relationship. It meant that there was one set of rules for children of married parents and another for those whose parents have not married. The arcane nature of such a distinction should not need emphasising. Not only did it go against any modern conception of parenthood, but it also restricted the rights of children, with their interests clearly not being a primary consideration and there being potential discrimination on the grounds of their birth, contrary to Articles 21 and 24 of the Union's Charter of Fundamental Rights.

The inadequacies of this regulation were very soon recognised and in 2003 a new Regulation was adopted which concerns all parental responsibility judgments, regardless of the status of the parents.[143] The Preamble states that its aim is to ensure 'equality for all children' with the Regulation covering parental responsibility decisions 'independently of any link with a matrimonial proceeding'.[144] The Preamble also refers to the Charter, in particular to the rights of the child in Article 24 of the Charter.[145] The 'hearing of the child' is said to play an 'important role' in the application of the Regulation, although this is not intended to modify existing national procedures. This emphasis on the rights of the child, and in particular the importance of their participation in decisions concerning them, where appropriate according to their age and maturity, represents an important move away from a paternalistic approach to the parent–child relationship in which the child's future is decided with little reference to him or her.[146] Nonetheless, the provisions on the rights of the child are considerably weaker than an earlier draft of the Regulation.[147] Helen Stalford argues that the concept of the child and their rights under these measures is based more on a 'welfare' approach to the children, rather than an 'agency' approach recognising the independence of the child.[148] There appears to be a general reluctance to endorse

143 Council Regulation 2201/2003/EC of 27 November 2003 concerning jurisdiction and the recognition and enforcement of judgments in matrimonial matters and the matters of parental responsibility, repealing Regulation 1347/2000/EC, OJ 2003 L 338/1.
144 Preamble (para. 5) to Regulation 2201/2003/EC, OJ 2003 L 338/1.
145 Preamble (para. 33) to Regulation 2201/2003/EC, OJ 2003 L 338/1.
146 Helen Stalford, 'Brussels II and Beyond: A Better Deal for Children in the EU?' in Katharina Boele-Woelki (ed.), *Perspectives for the Unification and Harmonisation of Family Law in Europe* (Antwerp: Intersentia, 2003), pp. 471–88 at p. 476.
147 For example, an earlier draft included an Article stating: 'A child shall have the right to be heard on matters relating to parental responsibility over him or her in accordance with his or her age and maturity.' This general provision has been replaced with one in which the scope of existing national rules is secured, with only a limited provision allowing the non-recognition where such national rules have not been followed. For a discussion, see Stalford, 'Brussels II and Beyond', 477.
148 Stalford, 'Brussels II and Beyond', 480.

children's active and direct rights within cross-national family law. This in turn underpins the paternalistic model of dependency that underpins traditional Union legislation relating to families, suggesting little ideological movement beyond the original 1960s free movement provisions. It also reinforces the hierarchical attitude to parenthood, rather than a more co-operative 'joint venture' approach which recognises the independence, autonomy and interests of the child.

There remains a final concern with the Community's family law measures in the context of parenthood. Concerns have been expressed regarding the potential for forum shopping resulting from these new measures.[149] Particular concern has been expressed regarding the potential for individuals seeking a divorce to seize jurisdiction in the member state which offers the divorce provisions best suited to their needs. But the issue may also arise in connection with parental responsibility issues. While it is true that the parent is required to establish a close connection with the state in which the parental rights are being challenged or enforced, there are possibilities for forum shopping especially where the practice of member states regarding parental responsibility varies so considerably. In addition, the considerable divergence between the practice of member states regarding gay and lesbian parenthood may become a focus for conflict.[150] Non-recognition of parental responsibility judgments is permitted where it would be 'manifestly contrary to the public policy' of the member state concerned.[151] Whether this would permit non-recognition in the case of orders in favour of gay and lesbian parents is perhaps unlikely, but nevertheless may be a focus for dispute.[152]

The Union's evolving family law has not, therefore, begun well. Its first measure reinforced the dominant ideology of the family, in particular reproducing a traditional approach to parenthood based on marriage and hierarchy over children. This is a law which reinforced the lowest common denominator in member state negotiations and in doing so wreaked havoc on those families and children which did not conform to the ideal norm. While the most recent Regulation is a significant move forward, the pattern has been established. We are now playing catch-up: the norm has been prescribed and forever after we will be engaged in complex and controversial negotiations to attempt to move the boundaries even slightly.

149 See David Truex, 'Brussels II – It's Here' (2001) 7 *International Family Law Review* 7–9; Nicolas Mostyn, 'Brussels II – The Impact on Forum Disputes' (2001) 31 *Family Law* 359–67.
150 See further Kate Griffin, 'Getting Kids and Keeping Them: Lesbian Motherhood in Europe' in Dunne (ed.), *Living 'Difference'*, pp. 23–34.
151 Article 23(a) of Regulation 2201/2003/EC, OJ 2003 L 338/1.
152 The judgment of the European Court of Human Rights in *Da Silva* v. *Portugal* (No. 33290/96), (2001) 31 EHRR 47 should ensure that non-recognition is not permitted on this basis.

4.4   Conclusions

At first sight, it may not be obvious that Union law and policy engage with concepts of motherhood and fatherhood. However, as discussed in the previous chapter regarding children, it became clear relatively early in the history of the Community that the impact of its economic policies extended far beyond the mere completion of a single market. In particular, the development of sex equality policies necessarily involves the concept of parenthood, regardless of what the Court of Justice first sought to claim. Thus, for so long as sex equality is an objective of Community policy, the concept of parenthood will be a focus for debate within Community law. Similarly, the Union's employment policy, with its aim to increase the labour market participation of women, must address the balance of paid work and family life, and therefore parental roles, if it is to be successful in achieving its aims. In terms of the future, it may be the Union's emerging family law that will in time have the most impact on the rights of parents and the nature of the parental role. As yet, the direction of these measures is not clear, although the first indications are not wholly positive.

The approach of the Union to parenthood is best described as ambiguous. Perhaps that is inevitable when faced with the wide scope of Union law and policy which encompasses this field. However, even within the scope of discrete fields of law, such as sex equality law, the Union's rhetoric and the reality of the Court's jurisprudence are far apart. In other areas, such as the emerging family law, the Union made an unfortunate start, but appears now to be moving towards a more egalitarian approach to parenthood. If the Community is to achieve its goal of greater workplace participation by women, and if the Union is to receive the support of the European citizens for its incursions into the controversial field of family law, and if the Union is to meet its human rights commitments as detailed in the Charter of Fundamental Rights, it must embrace a concept of parenthood which is more gender neutral than gender distinctive and which furthers the ideals of equal parenting.

5

European Union law and the regulation of intimate relationships: marriage, partnerships and human rights

Rates of marriage are declining in the European Union. Rates of divorce in some member states are increasing rapidly. Rates of cohabitation are escalating. It seems, in fact, that the institution of marriage is unpopular, and increasingly so. Or, is it? Both the Netherlands and Belgium have introduced marriage for same-sex couples, and a significant number of member states now provide some form of legal recognition of same-sex relationships.[1] Contradictions abound: the European Convention on Human Rights and the Union's Charter of Fundamental Rights both declare the 'right to marry' and prohibit discrimination on the grounds of sexual orientation. Yet, the Court of Justice and the Court of Human Rights refuse to define gay and lesbian partnerships as families and defend marriage as the preserve of heterosexual couples only.

In such a complex, controversial and empirically challenging context, what is the role of law and, in particular, the role of European Union law in the regulation of intimate relationships? The answer to such a question is not immediately apparent. It may be desirable that there is no regulation of intimate relations at the Union level, but this is not realistic in view of the competence of the Union. In the fields of equality, free movement, immigration, asylum and judicial co-operation, to name just a few areas, it is simply not possible for the Union to avoid encroaching on personal relationships. Indeed, the very existence of the right to marry in the European Convention on Human Rights, and the transposition of a similar right into the Union's Charter of Fundamental Rights, precludes any attempt to eliminate marriage as a legal category, however desirable that might be. The Union, therefore, has to take a stance on the politically charged and controversial questions regarding the status of marriage, cohabitation and same-sex relationships.

At present, the Union, and particularly the Court of Justice, remains faithful to a traditional ideology of the family, with life-long, monogamous, heterosexual

---

1 See further Robert Wintemute and Mads Andenas (eds.), *Legal Recognition of Same Sex Partnerships* (Oxford: Hart Publishing, 2001); and Katharina Boele-Woelki and Angelika Fuchs (eds.), *Legal Recognition of Same-Sex Couples in Europe* (Antwerp: Intersentia, 2003). In addition, Spain looks set to permit same-sex marriages, as reported in the *Guardian*, 22 April 2005.

marriage viewed as the sole legitimate partnership. However, the sands are shifting, albeit slowly. The dramatically changing nature and form of family practices are slowly being recognised. That most member states are already acknowledging this changing landscape of family practices in their law and policy is perhaps influencing the Union in turn to take an increasingly progressive approach. In addition, the Court of Justice is beginning to take seriously the application of human rights norms to Community law, at the same time as the Union legislature appears to be increasingly convinced by its own human rights rhetoric. While this remains a patchwork application of human rights principles, it provides a basis for further innovation. Finally, the Union's ambition of creating an area of freedom, justice and security is bringing about demands for further measures to facilitate movement in order both to secure political, integrationist objectives, and to continue the economic ambition of eradicating obstacles to the free movement of Union citizens.

Ultimately, however, the extent to which Union rights and entitlements are advanced to families, rather than to individuals, lies at the root of the problem. If, for example, all Union citizens and legally resident third country nationals were able to travel, live and work throughout the Union, without restriction, and were able to avail themselves of national tax and welfare provisions, there would be no need for detailed regulation about the rights extended to the families of those who are entitled to move and take up work. There would be less need for a tortuous definition of 'family'. Equally, if the couple, especially the monogamous, long-term, interdependent couple were not favoured in social policy, there would be little need to determine which couples or relationships could come within current definitions of 'marriage', 'partnership' or 'spouse'. However, the dominance of the 'family' as the touchstone for social and legal entitlements remains strong and it is therefore important to work within such an approach to ensure the broadest and fairest definition of 'family'. This argument will be considered further in the first section of this chapter which will also outline the human rights foundation which should inform Union law and policy. Subsequent sections examine the Union's regulation of intimate relationships in selected areas of substantive law.

5.1   Rights, relationships and 'the family'

The legal regulation of intimate relations is an area fraught with controversy, diverse opinion and fierce rhetoric. It is also an area in which there is considerable diversity between the member states, from the pro-marriage, anti-divorce culture of Ireland, to the Netherlands where lesbians and gay men can now marry on the same terms as heterosexual couples. Change also takes place at considerable speed. The Court of Justice referred to an English Court of Appeal decision refusing to define a gay partnership as 'family' to support its judgment not to extend benefits to gay and lesbian couples, only to see the superior House of Lords reverse the

Court of Appeal decision months later, but *after* the Court of Justice had handed down its judgment.[2]

I argue in this chapter that the approach of the European Union should be one based on the principles of value pluralism and respect for individual human rights.[3] Thus, in its inevitable regulation of intimate relationships, the Union should not privilege or valorise any one form of relationship. All relationships, whether they be same sex or opposite sex, married or unmarried, should be treated on a similar footing. Fundamental to this strategy is the opening-up of marriage to same-sex couples, entailing a recognition of gay and lesbian couples as 'family' and 'spouses'.

Such an argument is highly controversial among both the traditional right and the gay and lesbian community.[4] Many in the gay and lesbian community reject attempts to introduce same-sex marriage. For example, Nancy Polikoff states that the 'desire to marry in the lesbian and gay community is an attempt to mimic the worst of mainstream society, an effort to fit into an inherently problematic institution that betrays the promise of both lesbian and gay liberation and radical feminism'.[5] She continues that 'we will get what we ask for', namely a conservative, gendered institution of marriage, despite access to it by same-sex partners. More worrying still, she argues, is the possibility that gay and lesbian couples will become socially constrained to adopt the characteristics of the gendered heterosexual institution of marriage. As Kenneth Norrie suggests, this would reduce the possibility of heterosexual relationships learning from the diversity and equality of gay and lesbian partnerships.[6]

The problem being identified is that in challenging the heterosexual interpretation of spouse, the gay claimant 'attempts to demonstrate that their intimate relationship is qualitatively no different from that of the paradigmatic heterosexual couple'.[7] In doing so, the paradigm of heterosexuality and 'coupledom' is reinforced, the effect of which is to exclude further those that do not conform to such a norm. In this way, the law benefits those engaged in long-term, monogamous, stable relationships in which the parties are interdependent, share a home and finances and exhibit a public face of coupledom. Susan Boyd argues

---

2 Case C-249/96, *Grant* v. *South West Trains Ltd* [1998] ECR I-621; [1998] 1 CMLR 993.
3 See further the discussion in chapter 2.
4 For a discussion of the way in which traditionalist and progressive arguments against same-sex marriage appear to mirror each other, see William Eskridge, 'The Ideological Structure of the Same Sex Marriage Debate (And Some Postmodern Arguments for Same Sex Marriage)' in Wintemute and Andenas (eds.), *Same Sex Partnerships*, pp. 113–32.
5 Nancy Polikoff, 'We Will Get What We Ask For: Why Legislating Gay and Lesbian Marriage Will Not "Dismantle the Legal Structure of Gender in Every Marriage"' (1993) 79 *Virginia Law Review* 1535–50 at 1536.
6 Kenneth Norrie, 'Sexual Orientation and Family Law' in Jane Scoular (ed.), *Family Dynamics – Contemporary Issues in Family Law* (London: Butterworths, 2001), pp. 151–75 at p. 172.
7 Didi Herman, 'Are We Family? Lesbian Rights and Women's Liberation' (1990) 28 *Osgoode Hall Law Journal* 789–815 at 794.

that such recognition claims are an example of the 'domestication of deviant sexualities within a safe, useful and recognizable framework'.[8]

Feminists have also long identified the 'family' and particularly the institution of marriage as being a primary site of women's oppression.[9] Thus, Carol Smart once argued that marriage should not be reformed to include lesbians and gay men, but should be abandoned as a legal category. Instead, she continued, there should be a 'system of rights, duties, or obligations which are not dependent on any form of *coupledom* or quasi-marriage'.[10] On this analysis, marriage is the 'legal tie binding women to family', and 'spouse' derives from marriage; therefore neither 'marriage' nor 'spouse' are terms viable for lesbians and gay men.[11] Equally, family 'necessitates the productive, and reproductive, and sexual exploitation of women by men' and therefore precludes any extension for lesbians and gay men.[12] As Katherine O'Donovan argues, no matter the winning of women's personal autonomy, or attempts to avoid replicating patriarchal marital relations, these are reproduced in the institution of marriage.[13] The notion of what it is to be a 'wife' is enduring and difficult to circumvent. In the end, therefore, by 'appropriating family ideology, lesbians and gay men may be supporting the very institutional structures that create and perpetuate women's oppression'.[14]

This is not, however, the only story. As discussed in chapter 2, lesbians and gay men are increasingly adopting the language of family to describe their relationships. And, while the evidence of disadvantage facing women remains strong, this endures in cohabiting relationships as well as in those formalised by marriage. Indeed, there are strong arguments that opening marriage to gay and lesbian couples is not only appropriate in terms of principle, but may also positively affect the nature of marriage itself, thus effecting change in heterosexual relationships.

Compelling in this respect is the argument of Tom Stoddard that the issue is not 'the desirability of marriage, but rather the desirability of the *right* to marry'.[15] Similarly, David Richards argues that one may be personally moved by arguments against same-sex marriage, particularly in terms of the 'frigid stereotypes' generally on offer, yet find them inadequate as reasons to justify limiting the right to

---

8 Susan Boyd, 'Family, Law and Sexuality: Feminist Engagements' (1999) 8 *Social and Legal Studies* 369–90 at 377.

9 See for example Michèle Barrett and Mary McIntosh, *The Anti-Social Family* (London: Verso, 1982); Carol Smart, *The Ties that Bind: Law, Marriage and the Reproduction of Patriarchal Relations* (London: Routledge & Kegan Paul, 1984), discussed in Herman, 'Are We Family?', 795–7.

10 Smart, *The Ties that Bind*, p. 146, quoted in Herman, 'Are We Family?', 797.

11 Herman, 'Are We Family?', 797.

12 Herman, 'Are We Family?', 797.

13 Katherine O'Donovan, *Family Law Matters* (London: Pluto Press, 1993), p. 48.

14 Herman, 'Are We Family?', 797.

15 Tom Stoddard, 'Why Gay People Should Seek the Right to Marry' in William B. Rubenstein (ed.), *Sexual Orientation and the Law* (St Paul: West Publishing, 1997), quoted in Chai Feldblum, 'The Limitations of Liberal Neutrality in Favour of Same Sex Marriage' in Wintemute and Andenas (eds.), *Same Sex Partnerships*, pp. 55–74 at p. 56.

marry to heterosexual intimate life.[16] Thus, as rights discourse strengthens its hegemony in Western political culture and to claim a 'right' is to claim a 'trump', lesbians and gay men have come to rely on rights as a pre-eminent strategy aimed at securing their claims. So long as the institution of marriage exists, it remains unjustifiably discriminatory to restrict entry to heterosexual couples. This does not mean proselytising in favour of marriage, but is simply a recognition that to exclude lesbians and gay men is to perpetuate a discrimination which is no longer justified.

While the abolition of marriage may be ultimately desirable, it remains a utopian dream. Marriage is likely to continue to be regarded as a positive institution by many and forms the basis for the regulation of relationships. As Katherine O'Donovan argues, we are dealing with something which is 'deeply embedded' and, although its present form may be criticised, 'its continued survival must be acknowledged'.[17] Accordingly, Carlos Ball contends that marriage should be open to gay and lesbian partners in order that such relationships be recognised as 'normatively valuable'.[18] He continues that the recognition by the state of such relationships is essential for the attainment of 'personal autonomy'.[19] Arguably, therefore, for so long as society privileges marriage, but excludes same-sex couples from the institution, gay and lesbian relationships are deemed less worthy. Indeed, for so long as the European Convention on Human Rights, and now the Union Charter, includes a right to marry, the best that can be suggested is that the right to marry be extended to lesbians and gay men. Therefore, it is simply to recognise reality that marriage will continue and that therefore it should be open to all.

This rights-based argument would stand, despite any possible adverse consequences of such a move. Nonetheless, it is also possible that the advent of same-sex marriage would herald a number of positive consequences which make its promulgation more acceptable. Tom Stoddard has argued that 'marriage is . . . the issue most likely to lead ultimately to a world free from discrimination against lesbians and gay men'.[20] In other words, the pre-eminence of the institution of marriage means that its opening-up to lesbians and gay men could radically transform their lives.

But it could also transform the nature of marriage, leading to new forms of relationship for heterosexuals, as well as gay and lesbian couples. Tom Stoddard again makes this argument, suggesting that same-sex marriage may transform the

16 David Richards, 'Introduction – Theoretical Perspectives' in Wintemute and Andenas (eds.), *Same Sex Partnerships*, pp. 25–30 at p. 29.
17 O'Donovan, *Family Law Matters*, p. 44.
18 Carlos Ball, 'Moral Foundations for a Discourse on Same Sex Marriage: Looking Beyond Political Liberalism' (1997) 85 *Georgetown Law Journal* 1871–943 at 1875.
19 Ball, 'Moral Foundations', 1936.
20 Thomas Stoddard, 'Why Gay People Should Seek the Right to Marry' in Suzanne Sherman (ed.), *Lesbian and Gay Marriage: Private Commitments, Public Ceremonies* (Philadelphia: Temple University Press, 1992), pp. 13–19 at p. 17.

nature of marriage, particularly removing its gendered basis.[21] Similarly, Nan Hunter has suggested that what is most compelling about lesbian and gay marriage is its 'potential to expose and denaturalize the historical construction of gender at the heart of marriage'. She continues that the impact of lesbian and gay marriage will be nothing less than the dismantling of the 'legal structure of gender in every marriage'.[22] Because of the sexual nature of the marriage contract, and its basis in sexual difference, to admit same-sex couples to the institution of marriage would be to alter radically its constitution and assumptions. Further, Martha Nussbaum suggests that, as empirical evidence suggests that many lesbian and gay households adopt far more egalitarian approaches to domestic labour than heterosexual couples, their recognition in marriage may make 'valuable contributions' to our understandings of marital commitment and fairness.[23]

However, it is not just that same-sex couples disrupt the gendered norms of marriage, but that, even if same-sex couples adopt what may appear to be a traditional division of labour within the relationship, that too will alter gender relations. This point is made by William Eskridge, who points out that, in such circumstances, in each couple, one partner will be performing a role not associated with their gender, be it a woman doing the accustomed male role of working outside the home, or the male partner doing the accustomed role of keeping house.[24] Although the potentially transformative nature of gay and lesbian marriage is not inevitable, it is at least preferable to retaining the heterosexual exclusivity of the institution.

It is for these reasons that the option favoured by many states for the regulation of same-sex relationships, the registered partnership, is less preferable than same-sex marriage. The registered partnership simply institutionalises discrimination in that lesbians and gay men remain excluded from the institution of marriage. For example, the adoption of registered partnership legislation in the US states of Vermont and Hawaii was specifically adopted to meet the claims to equality, but importantly also to 'protect' marriage as a heterosexual institution.[25] The adoption of partnership legislation in France appears to have had a similar purpose, with the French government arguing that the legislation does not 'undermine marriage' as marriage remains 'fundamentally different'.[26] Equally,

21 Stoddard, 'Why Gay People Should Seek the Right to Marry' in Sherman (ed.), *Lesbian and Gay Marriage*, pp. 18–19.
22 Nan Hunter, 'Marriage, Law and Gender: A Feminist Inquiry' (1991) 1 *Law and Sexuality* 9–30 at 18–19.
23 Martha Nussbaum, *Sex and Social Justice* (Oxford: Oxford University Press, 1999), p. 202.
24 William Eskridge, 'The Ideological Structure of the Same Sex Marriage Debate (And Some Postmodern Arguments for Same Sex Marriage)' in Wintemute and Andenas (eds.), *Same Sex Partnerships*, pp. 113–32 at pp. 127–9.
25 Harry Krause, 'Marriage for the New Millennium: Heterosexual, Same Sex – Or Not at All?' (2000) 34 *Family Law Quarterly* 271–300.
26 Quoted in Eva Steiner, 'The Spirit of the New French Registered Partnership Law – Promoting Autonomy and Pluralism or Weakening Marriage?' (2000) 12 *Child and Family Law Quarterly* 1–14 at 4.

the Canadian experience suggests that the legislative adoption of forms of registered partnership was made in order to meet legal demands for recognition of same-sex relationships, but in an effort to maintain marriage for heterosexuals only. As Kathleen Lahey suggests, the 'creation of segregated legal structures, that parallel but do not touch existing marriage legislation, merely changes the way in which the simple right to marry continues to be denied'.[27]

The only possible basis for advocating, or accepting, the establishment of registered partnerships is that it constitutes a stepping-stone to same-sex marriage. Kees Waaldijk has argued that there is a 'standard sequence of steps' which takes states from a position of the criminalisation of gay conduct to, ultimately, same-sex marriage. He argues that, once virtually all the legal consequences of civil marriage have become available to same-sex partners through registered partnership, there will be no morally or politically acceptable arguments left to maintain that in law a same-sex partnership cannot be called a 'marriage'.[28] There is some evidence that this may be the case. In the Netherlands, where same-sex marriage is now legalised, there was first a form of registered partnership, and Kees Waaldijk argues that it was simply a 'small step' to same-sex marriage, as incremental changes had been made which led inevitably to same-sex marriage.[29]

Reform, though, must not be exclusively focused on same-sex marriage. To the extent that individuals form relationships, for which they do not seek the recognition of law, such relationships should be acknowledged in terms of the rights and entitlements which are extended to legally recognised couples. There are those who choose not to formalise their relationship, but who should not be denied social entitlements. There are others who have little choice or who are unaware of the consequences of inaction. Children, as we saw in chapter 3, should not be adversely affected by the civil status of their parents. Thus 'family' benefits should be extended to cohabiting couples. The values of mutuality, commitment and support should be fostered and recognised, rather than simple formal ties, through marriage or registered partnerships. The disadvantage of this approach is the potential decrease in certainty and the possible increase in judicial discretion.[30] It is also perhaps accompanied by greater intrusion into private lives as courts seek to understand the 'true' nature of a relationship, rather than simply accept a legal certificate. While this amounts to assessing the similarity of the relationship to traditional marriage, for so long as rights and entitlements are extended to couples, this seems necessary. As Kenneth Norrie argues, if the end

---

27 Kathleen Lahey, 'Becoming "Persons" in Canadian Law: Genuine Equality or "Separate but Equal"?' in Wintemute and Andenas (eds.), *Same Sex Partnerships*, pp. 237–78 at p. 274.

28 Kees Waaldijk, 'Civil Developments: Patterns of Reform in the Legal Position of Same Sex Partners in Europe' (2000) 17 *Canadian Journal of Family Law* 62–88 at 87.

29 Kees Waaldijk, 'Small Change: How the Road to Same Sex Marriage Got Paved in the Netherlands' in Wintemute and Andenas (eds.), *Same Sex Partnerships*, pp. 437–64.

30 See Rebecca Bailey-Harris, 'Law and the Unmarried Couple – Oppression or Liberation?' (1996) 8 *Child and Family Law Quarterly* 137–47.

result is 'justice and equality for gay men and lesbians, as well as a more equitable approach to all family disputes', then this is a price worth paying.[31]

In the end, this rights-based approach to the regulation of intimate relationships should ultimately ensure the recognition of same-sex marriage. Short of this, same-sex partnerships should be recognised as having equal status to heterosexual relationships and be granted the same social and legal entitlements. Further, unmarried couples, whether same sex or different sex, should enjoy the same rights as those whose relationships are formalised. This follows the approach of the Canadian Supreme Court which, in expanding the definition of spouse to include same-sex partners, stated that non-recognition 'perpetuates disadvantages suffered by individuals in same sex relationships and contributes to the erasure of their existence'.[32]

5.2   The free movement of persons and family rights

5.2.1   Free movement of partners?

The Community first entered the difficult terrain of regulating intimate relations when it adopted legislation extending rights of free movement to the families of migrants.[33] As this legislation was adopted in the late 1960s, it is perhaps no surprise that the 'family' to which rights were extended was the heterosexual married family of the migrant, specifically the migrant's 'spouse' and children. Dependent relatives in the ascending line were also granted residence, but member states were only required to 'facilitate' the entry of other 'members of the family' and only if they were dependent or were living under the same roof as the migrant. Subsequent legislation granted similar rights to migrants offering services or establishing themselves in other member states.[34] In the case of non-economic migration, permitted in a series of Directives in the early 1990s to those with sufficient means, only the spouse and children are entitled to move with the migrant, there being no residual category of 'member of the family'.[35] These provisions on migrants and their families apply not just to the existence of family ties while a migrant is exercising Community rights, but also to the rights of families in circumstances of the retirement or death of the migrant.[36]

---

31 Norrie, 'Sexual Orientation', 174.
32 *M* v. *H* [1999] 2 SCR 3, paras. 73–4.
33 Council Regulation 1612/68/EEC of 15 October 1968 on freedom of movement for workers within the Community, OJ 1968 L 257/2.
34 Council Directive 73/148/EEC of 21 May 1973 on the abolition of restrictions on movement and residence within the Community for nationals of Member States with regard to establishment and the provision of services, OJ 1973 L 172/14, Article 1.
35 Council Directive 90/364/EEC of 28 June 1990 on the right of residence, OJ 1990 L 180/26, Article 1; Council Directive 90/365/EEC of 28 June 1990 on the right of residence for employees and self-employed persons who have ceased their occupational activity, OJ 1990 L 180/28, Article 2; Council Directive 93/96/EEC of 29 October 1993 on the right of residence for students, OJ 1993 L 317/59, Article 2.
36 Regulation 1251/70/EEC of the Commission of 29 June 1970 on the right of workers to remain in the territory of a Member State after having been employed in that State, OJ 1970 L 142/42;

These rights granted to migrants and their 'families' were the foundation, together with the other freedoms, of the single market. They now form the core of the Union's concept of citizenship and are included in the Charter of Fundamental Rights.[37] Thus, the privileging of the heterosexual married family pervades not just the detailed rules on free movement, but is also a central component of the single market and the concept of Union citizenship. As Amy Elman concludes, integration within the Union has been accomplished 'in part, through the mutual recognition of privileges accorded exclusively to heterosexual EU nationals, their spouses and families'.[38]

Until very recently, the approach of the Court of Justice to interpreting concepts of family has been formulaic, perhaps the result of an initial desire to avoid courting publicity and opprobrium by engaging in an examination of such controversial concepts. For example, in *Diatta* v. *Land Berlin*, the Court held that the spouse of a migrant worker could continue to enjoy rights as a spouse, despite the fact that divorce was imminent and the couple no longer lived together.[39] The continued existence of the formal legal tie of marriage was held to be sufficient to trigger the rights of spouses and, until that tie had been formally ended, there would be no change in the situation. Although the technical, formulaic approach of the Court in this case can be criticised, it must also be noted that Mrs Diatta was a third country national and thus holding that she was no longer a 'spouse' for the purposes of free movement family rights may have prompted her deportation. Nonetheless, the reprieve was perhaps only temporary, as the implication of the ruling in *Diatta* is that, on divorce, the rights of the former spouse are extinguished.[40]

We have, therefore, an affirmation in *Diatta* that 'spouse' equals the partner to a formal legal marriage, without any need for investigation into the nature of the marriage, and that any rights cease on termination of the marriage. *Diatta* seems to underline the extent to which the Court has been reluctant to get involved in any real assessment of a relationship and whether the grant of rights in particular circumstances serves the purposes of Community law or complies with human rights norms. By sticking so strictly to the wording of Regulation 1612/68, the Court was able to disengage from the wider effects of the changing nature of

Council Directive 75/34/EEC of 17 December 1974 concerning the right of nationals of a Member State to remain in the territory of another Member State after having pursued therein an activity in a self-employed capacity, OJ 1975 L 14/10.

37 Article 15(2) of the Charter states that: 'Every citizen of the Union has the freedom to seek employment, to work, to exercise the right of establishment and to provide services in any Member State.'

38 R. Amy Elman, 'The Limits of Citizenship: Migration, Sex Discrimination and Same Sex Partners in EU Law' (2000) 38 *Journal of Common Market Studies* 729–49 at 734.

39 Case 267/83, *Diatta* v. *Land Berlin* [1985] ECR 567.

40 Although, in an earlier social security case, the Court had held that a divorced person could bring themselves within the definition of 'spouse' for the purposes of a particular benefit: Case 149/82, *Robards* v. *Insurance Officer* [1983] ECR 171 at 187.

family life in the member states and the effect this was beginning to have on Community law. The Court's formal approach in *Diatta* was confirmed in *Singh* where the couple had already been granted a decree nisi, the first formal step towards divorce, and the Court maintained that a spousal relationship still existed.[41] Thus, as d'Oliveira has pointed out, even marriages that are 'for all practical purposes dead and buried', can still be the basis for a 'dependent right of residence of the spouse of the worker'.[42]

The result in *Diatta* has most often been contrasted with the approach of the Court in *Netherlands* v. *Reed*, where a partner in a cohabiting relationship sought to bring herself within the concept of 'spouse'. The claim was rejected by the Court, which held that the term 'spouse' does not extend to unmarried cohabitees.[43] Thus, the partnership in *Netherlands* v. *Reed*, in which the couple had cohabited for approximately five years and were seeking to move to the Netherlands for one partner to take up employment, was held not to come within the Community concept of family rights, whereas the full panoply of family rights was granted to a partner where the couple had only been married and living together for just over one year, had separated and intended to divorce (*Diatta*).

The effect of *Netherlands* v. *Reed* is that unmarried partners, same sex or opposite sex, not being 'spouses', are excluded from the family rights attaching to migrants. The one exception is where a member state permits the entry of the unmarried partners of its own nationals, in which case it cannot refuse entry to the unmarried partner of a Community national.[44] Nonetheless, despite the strict nature of this ruling, the Court did hold out a glimmer of hope. In rejecting the claim in *Netherlands* v. *Reed*, the Court justified its position on the basis that there was no 'indication of a general social development [in the member states] which would justify a broad construction, and in the absence of any indication to the contrary in the Regulation, it must be held that the term spouse in Article 10 of the Regulation refers to a marital relationship only'.[45] It continued that a dynamic interpretation 'cannot be based on social and legal developments in only one or a few member states'.[46] Accordingly, although the Court ruled that unmarried cohabitees could not bring themselves within the definition of 'spouse', the Court did accept that such an interpretation may change in the future, where there is evidence of a 'general social development'. Thus, at least the principle of dynamic interpretation was acknowledged.

---

41 Case C-370/90, *R* v. *IAT and Singh, ex parte Secretary of State for the Home Department* [1992] ECR I-4265; [1992] 3 CMLR 358.

42 Hans Ulrich Jessurun d'Oliveira, 'Lesbians and Gays and the Freedom of Movement of Persons' in Kees Waaldijk and Andrew Clapham (eds.), *Homosexuality: A European Community Issue* (Dordrecht: Martinus Nijhoff, 1993), pp. 289–316 at p. 300.

43 Case 59/85, *Netherlands* v. *Reed* [1986] ECR 1283; [1987] 2 CMLR 448.

44 This meant that a remedy was granted to Reed in that, as Dutch law entitled the entry of an unmarried partner in an established relationship, the Dutch authorities could not deny the same right to a Community national.

45 *Netherlands* v. *Reed*, para. 15.

46 *Netherlands* v. *Reed*, p. 1300.

Netherlands v. *Reed* was decided in the mid-1980s, but was confirmed by the Court of First Instance in the early 1990s in *Arauxo-Dumay* v. *Commission*.[47] Since then, while it is clear that the social situation has indeed dramatically changed, there is as yet little movement towards broadening the concept of 'spouse'. However, in the recent case of *Eyüp*, the Court began to make inroads into these restrictive rulings. In essence, the Court ruled that periods of unmarried, as well as married, cohabitation 'must be taken into account in [their] entirety' for the purposes of calculating periods of legal residence for family members.[48] On its face, therefore, this case represents a small incursion into the hitherto limited scope of the concept of 'family': the Court treated unmarried (heterosexual) cohabitation as assimilated to that of married cohabitation. Nonetheless, the facts of *Eyüp* are peculiar and the Court made particular weather of the 'particular facts of the case'.[49]

Mrs Eyüp was permitted entry to Austria as the spouse of a Turkish worker who was lawfully resident there. The couple subsequently divorced, but continued to cohabit, later remarried and four of the couple's seven children were born during the period of unmarried cohabitation. Under the relevant provisions of the EC–Turkey Association Agreement, a 'member of the family' is entitled, after various years of lawful residence, to employment within the host member state. The question arose as to whether Mrs Eyüp's periods of unmarried cohabitation could be assimilated to her periods of married cohabitation in order to entitle her to take up employment.

The Court noted that Mr and Mrs Eyüp had lived together continuously and that their conduct was 'permanently in accordance' with the objectives of the provision, namely '*de facto* family unity in the host member state'.[50] In addition, the Court appeared to place significance on the nature of the relationship which subsisted during the period of unmarried cohabitation, namely that Mrs Eyüp 'devoted herself essentially to household tasks'[51] and only 'occasionally' took 'short-term jobs'.[52] Moreover, at all times, Mr Eyüp 'maintained his family'.[53] There appears, therefore, to be a number of central features upon which the Court based its ruling: the cohabitation closely resembled marriage; children were born during the period of cohabitation; Mr Eyüp maintained his family; and Mrs Eyüp was primarily engaged in caring for the children. It is not clear what weight was placed on each of these factors, but it is likely that each of them will

---

47 The applicant had been in a cohabiting relationship, followed by marriage, and tried to argue that the period of cohabitation should be assimilated to the period of marriage. The claim was rejected. Case T-65/92, *Arauxo-Dumay* v. *Commission* [1993] ECR II-597.
48 Case C-65/98, *Eyüp* v. *Landesgeschäftsstelle des Arbeitsmarktservice Vorarlberg* [2000] ECR I-4747, para. 36.
49 *Eyüp*, para. 36.
50 *Eyüp*, para. 34, emphasis in original.
51 *Eyüp*, para. 12.
52 *Eyüp*, para. 32.
53 *Eyüp*, para. 32.

be considered in subsequent cases. Following this examination of the facts, the Court simply stated that the period of cohabitation 'cannot be regarded as an interruption of their joint family life'.[54] As the relevant legislation provides that only 'members of the family' are entitled to take up work in the host member state, the implication must be that, during the periods of cohabitation, Mrs Eyüp was a 'member of the family'. Thus, at best, the judgment implies that a cohabitee may come within the concept of 'member of the family' and specifically does not affect the Court's interpretation in *Netherlands v. Reed* of the concept of 'spouse'. Indeed, the Court purposely emphasised that Mrs Eyüp had been granted entry to Austria on the basis of her marriage and that the ruling in this case does not affect the power of the member state to authorise entry of members of the family of the migrant.[55]

It seems likely that at least two factors have influenced the Court in its approach in *Eyüp*, which have been detailed and recognised in the Opinions of advocates general, but as yet are only just beginning to appear in the judgments of the Court. First, there is the rapidly and dramatically changing nature of family life. In particular, the rise in extra-marital cohabitation and its acceptance in society, together with the recognition and acceptance of gay and lesbian partnerships, render the privileging of marriage, and therefore heterosexuality, increasingly outmoded and reactionary. In recognition of such changes, Advocate General Geelhoed in his Opinion in *Baumbast* noted that Regulation 1612/68[56] dates back to a time when 'family relationships were relatively stable' and provision was therefore made for the 'traditional family'.[57] Thus, it was assumed that 'family' meant heterosexual marriage with the husband as breadwinner and the wife taking care of the household.[58] The *Baumbast* case exemplified these changes as it involved the rights of one family following divorce and another family which included a step-child and where the father worked away from the family home. The Advocate General continued that 'considerable social developments have occurred which are likely to have considerable influence on the view to be formed as to the nature and scope of the provisions of the Regulation' and that the Court must have regard to such social developments, else the 'relevant rules of law risk losing their effectiveness'.[59] Not least among these 'social developments' is the reality that under Article 8 of the European Convention 'relationships of sufficient permanence stand on the same footing' as marriage.[60]

54 *Eyüp*, para. 36.
55 *Eyüp*, para. 27.
56 OJ 1968 L 257/2.
57 Case C-413/99, *Baumbast and R v. Secretary of State for the Home Department* [2002] ECR I-7091; [2002] 3 CMLR 23, para. 23.
58 *Baumbast*, para. 23.
59 *Baumbast*, para. 20.
60 *Baumbast*, para. 59.

Advocate General La Pergola in *Eyüp* also recognised such changes in the nature of family life and tied this into the second factor that may be influencing the Court, namely the increasing adherence to the human rights jurisprudence of the European Court of Human Rights and its recognition of the changing nature of family life. The Court of Justice had stated in 1989 that Regulation 1612/68[61] must be interpreted in the light of the requirement to respect for family life as set out in Article 8 of the Convention.[62] However, this was largely a rhetorical aside, having little effect on the case law until the last few years. The Advocate General in *Eyüp* based his Opinion on a detailed analysis of the 'right to respect for family life' protected by the European Convention and opined that, as a 'general principle', including a cohabitee of a worker within the concept of 'member of the family', 'contradicts neither the spirit nor the purpose' of the relevant provision. Noting that the Court of Human Rights had held there to be family life deserving of respect in circumstances displaying a lesser degree of stability than the facts in question, the Advocate General opined that not to hold Mrs Eyüp to be a 'member of the family' would constitute a breach of her fundamental rights, as detailed in Article 8 of the European Convention. Advocate General La Pergola also emphasised the objective of the relevant provisions of the EC–Turkey Association Agreement, namely that they were designed to 'create conditions conducive to family unity in the host member state'. In such circumstances, he argued, it was justified to interpret those provisions in the light of the Convention's protection of the right to respect for family life.[63]

Although the Advocate General's Opinion in *Eyüp* went further than the Court of Justice's more reticent ruling, it is likely that the Court was influenced by the reasoning of the human rights aspects of the case, although its refusal even to refer to the Convention is perhaps surprising. In subsequent cases, the Court has shown less reluctance to refer expressly to Article 8 of the Convention and the right to respect for family life. Indeed, in *Carpenter*, also involving free movement family rights, not only did the Court reiterate the importance of Article 8, but it also specifically engaged in an analysis of the concept of 'family life' under Article 8, and whether the circumstances of that particular case came within the jurisprudence on family life and any potential justifications for breaching Article 8 and their proportionality.[64] By the time of the *Carpenter* judgment, the Union had adopted the Charter of Fundamental Rights, which includes the right to

---

61 OJ 1968 L 257/2.
62 Case 249/86, *Commission* v. *Federal Republic of Germany* [1989] ECR 1263; [1990] 3 CMLR 540.
63 *Eyüp*, paras. 17 and 23.
64 Case C-60/00, *Carpenter* v. *Secretary of State for the Home Department* [2002] ECR I-6279; [2002] 2 CMLR 64, paras. 38–44. See also Case C-459/99, *MRAX* v. *Belgium* [2002] ECR I-6591; [2002] 3 CMLR 25, para. 53, where the Court states that it is 'apparent' from the Community rules on free movement that the Community legislature has 'recognised the importance of ensuring protection for the family life of nationals of the member states in order to eliminate obstacles to the exercise of the fundamental freedoms guaranteed in the Treaty'.

respect for family life, reproduced from the European Convention, though the Court conspicuously failed to refer to it.

So, what can we conclude after the *Eyüp* case? The Court has implicitly recognised that a cohabitee may be considered to be a 'member of the family', with the Advocate General clearly stating this to be so. However, both the Court and the Advocate General stressed the particular nature of the facts of the case and several features of their relationship including the existence of children, the length of cohabitation and the economic dependence of Mrs Eyüp. There is a clear presumption of heterosexuality in this case, with the implication that a gay or lesbian couple would not find it as easy to bring themselves within the relevant definition. Partly, this would be due to the continuing reluctance of the Court of Human Rights to hold that gay and lesbian couples can constitute family life for the purposes of Article 8. It is also not possible to be entirely confident of the Court's approach to cohabiting couples who have never married each other, whose length of cohabitation is comparatively short, who do not have any children or who both work and are therefore financially independent. Accordingly, although *Eyüp* represents a success of sorts, it is a step on from *Netherlands* v. *Reed* and *Arauxo-Dumay*, the 'family' which has been recognised is one which, although it does not demonstrate the formal bond of marriage, does exhibit the features of a traditional marriage, most particularly a sexual division of labour and the inherent economic dependence of the woman partner.

Overall, in terms of extending the concept of 'member of the family' to include heterosexual cohabitees, the future has to be positive. For the Court of Justice to ignore both the changing realities of family life *and* the jurisprudence of the Court of Human Rights would be breathtaking indeed. The Court of Human Rights has made it clear that heterosexual unmarried relationships do enjoy the protection afforded by the right to respect for family life, as clearly recognised by the Advocates General in *Carpenter*, *Baumbast* and *Eyüp*.[65] The Union not only refers to the European Convention for its human rights inspiration, but it has also specifically incorporated such rights into the Union Charter. At the very minimum, therefore, so that the Union is compliant with the human rights norms of the Court of Human Rights, it must grant similar protection to heterosexual cohabiting relationships.

If heterosexual unmarried couples should clearly come within the concept of 'member of the family', what of gay and lesbian partnerships? It has long been argued that the concept of 'member of the family' should be interpreted to include same-sex couples.[66] In 1996, Kees Waaldijk commented that he would

---

65 This much is noted, without a fanfare, by Advocate General Geelhoed in *Baumbast*, where he notes that, under Article 8 of the European Convention, 'relationships of sufficient permanence stand on the same footing' as marriage: *Baumbast*, para. 59.

66 See Kees Waaldijk, 'Free Movement of Same Sex Partners' (1996) 3 *Maastricht Journal of European and Comparative Law* 271–85; Andrew Clapham and Joseph Weiler, 'Lesbians and Gay Men in the European Community Legal Order' in Waaldijk and Clapham (eds.), *Homo-*

be 'surprised' if such an argument did not convince the Court.[67] While there is no doubt that such an argument *should* succeed, it is not altogether clear that Waaldijk's optimism will be rewarded in the near future.[68] The Court of Human Rights has yet to hold that gay or lesbian couples can benefit from the right to respect for family life. Nonetheless, many other jurisdictions have held that not only opposite-sex, but also same-sex partners, constitute a 'family' for the purposes of various legislative provisions.[69] Furthermore, the Union's Charter states that its provisions may be interpreted to provide 'more extensive' protection than the European Convention. It is certainly arguable that, as a significant number of member states now provide for a form of legal recognition of same-sex relationships, and that many other jurisdictions interpret 'family' to include same-sex relationships, the Community rules on 'member of the family' should *at the very least* include such partnerships. I emphasise, *at the very least*, as it must be remembered that the free movement rights for 'members of the family' are considerably less than those granted to 'spouses'.

So, what prospect is there that 'spouse' will be interpreted to include unmarried partners? In *Netherlands* v. *Reed*, the Court clearly stated the possibility of a changing interpretation based on social developments. These social developments have occurred, yet there is little immediate prospect of change. As can be seen from *Eyüp*, the battle over the concept of 'member of the family' is not yet secure, let alone the concept of spouse. Unfortunately, the European Convention jurisprudence is little help in this respect. The Court of Human Rights continues to refuse to extend Article 8 of the Convention to same-sex relationships.[70] Nonetheless, in *Karner*, the term 'life companion' was defined to include a same-sex partnership, it being held that to preclude such an interpretation would constitute a breach of the right to respect for one's home.[71] However, the fact that the Court of Human Rights based its ruling on the right to respect for one's home, rather than the right to family life, demonstrates its hesitation regarding same-sex partnership rights. Furthermore, while it was held that insufficient justification

---

sexuality, pp. 7–69 at pp. 41–6. Nicholas Blake has argued that the concept of 'member of the family' should be interpreted to include unmarried partners, including same-sex partners: Nicholas Blake, 'Family Life in Community Law: The Limits of Freedom and Dignity' in Elspeth Guild (ed.), *The Legal Framework and Social Consequences of Free Movement of Persons in the European Union* (The Hague: Kluwer, 1999), pp. 7–19.

67 Waaldijk, 'Free Movement', 280.

68 The argument has so far been rejected in the English courts which rather dismissively described the argument as 'ingenious': *R* v. *Secretary of State for the Home Department, ex parte McCollum* [2001] EWHC Admin 40.

69 For example, the New York Court of Appeals, the Supreme Court of Israel, the Constitutional Court of Hungary, the Supreme Court of Canada, the UK's House of Lords and the Constitutional Court of South Africa, as discussed in Robert Wintemute, 'Strasbourg to the Rescue? Same Sex Partners and Parents under the European Convention' in Wintemute and Andenas (eds.), *Same Sex Partnerships*, pp. 713–32 at p. 727.

70 For a full discussion, see Loveday Hodson, 'Family Values: The Recognition of Same Sex Relationships in International Law' (2004) 22 *Netherlands Quarterly of Human Rights* 33–57.

71 *Karner* v. *Austria* (No. 40016/98), (2004) 38 EHRR 24.

for the different treatment of homosexual and heterosexual partnerships had been offered in this case, the Court of Human Rights went on to say that, in principle, 'the protection of the family in the traditional sense' is a weighty and legitimate reason which might justify a difference in treatment on the grounds of sexual orientation.[72] Hence, while the outcome of the case is of itself an advance in the acceptance of gay and lesbian relationships, it appears that the Court is exceptionally wary of the stance it is taking and feels the need to placate conservative forces, perhaps in the Court, and certainly in the member states of the Council of Europe.[73] What *Karner* does ensure is that unmarried heterosexual and homosexual partners enjoy the same rights, but such rights are likely to continue to preclude those granted to spouses. Accordingly, there seems little immediate prospect of significant change being demanded from either the Court of Justice or the Court of Human Rights.

5.2.2   The new Free Movement Directive: plus ça change?

For many years, the Commission had been proposing a new Community measure in the field of free movement, updating the directives considered above and bringing together in one document the rights of Union citizens to movement and residence.[74] Here was a legislative opportunity to update the concept of family in line with the developments discussed above. As Advocate General Geelhoed had recognised, the free movement rules on family rights have not 'kept pace with social, cultural and economic developments' since the 1960s when Regulation 1612/68[75] was adopted.[76] Further, this was the chance to review the judgment of *Netherlands* v. *Reed* in light of the social changes that have taken place since it was handed down. Indeed, the Commission's rhetoric appeared to understand the importance of expanding the concept of family. It stated in the explanatory memorandum to its original proposal that 'the right to preserve family unity' is 'intrinsically connected with the right to the protection of family life' which is a 'fundamental right forming part of the common constitutional traditions of the member states, which are protected by Community law and incorporated in the Charter of Fundamental Rights'.[77] However, the proposal demonstrated how little importance was attached to the rhetoric of fundamental

---

72 *Karner*, para. 40.
73 Indeed, such reticence is made explicit in the *Frette* case. In *Frette*, the Court was faced with a refusal by the French authorities to accept an application by a gay man to adopt. The Court upheld the judgment of the French courts stating that the refusal pursued a legitimate aim, namely the protection of the 'health and rights of children who could be involved in an adoption procedure': *Frette* v. *France* (No. 36515/97), (2004) 38 EHRR 21; [2003] 2 FLR 9, para. 38.
74 Proposal for a European Parliament and Council Directive on the right of citizens of the Union and their family members to move and reside freely within the territory of the Member States, COM (2001) 257 final, p. 4.
75 OJ 1968 L 257/2.
76 *Baumbast*, para. 34.
77 COM (2001) 257 final, p. 4.

rights or to the need to amend the legislation to reflect changing social mores. Only some partnerships and some families were to be entitled to the 'fundamental right to family unity'.[78] The privileging of marriage continued, even more remarkable in a draft directive which included a clause stating that the measures were to be given effect without discrimination on the grounds of sexual orientation.

But all was not lost. The European Parliament demanded valuable changes to the draft directive which would have significantly expanded the concept of family by requiring recognition of same-sex spouses, registered partners in accordance with the state of origin and non-married partners in accordance with the legislation or practice of the host member state.[79] However, the innovative and bold approach of the Parliament was not to last long. The Commission rejected most of the suggested changes,[80] and in the end the Parliament accepted the Council's version of the directive which virtually leaves intact the existing concept of family.[81] As two members of the European Parliament put it, for the 'umpteenth time, Parliament has given way to the Council, abandoning the political ideals set out at first reading in favour of a pragmatic approach – which is quite simply one of timidity and compliance – at second reading'.[82]

The definition of family in the new Free Movement Directive remains largely confined to a 'spouse' and minor children.[83] No reference is made to same-sex spouses. While ILGA-Europe suggests that post-*Karner* an exclusion of same-sex couples is unlikely from the definition of spouse, this seems too optimistic.[84] The Commission has stated that 'it should be concluded that same sex spouses do not yet have the same rights as traditional spouses'.[85] This is quite irrational,

---

78 In relation to partnership rights, the Commission proposal defined 'family member' as including a 'spouse' or 'unmarried partner, if the legislation of the host member state treats unmarried couples as equivalent to married couples and in accordance with the conditions laid down in any such legislation'. All that this proposal would have done is to enshrine in legislation the ruling in *Netherlands* v. *Reed*.

79 Santini Report, adopted on 11 February 2003, as reported in ILGA-Europe Newsletter, March 2003. For a more detailed analysis of the discussions within the European Parliament, see Helen Toner, *Partnership Rights, Free Movement and EU Law* (Oxford: Hart, Publishing 2004), pp. 63–5.

80 See amended proposal for a Directive of the European Parliament and of the Council on the right of citizens of the Union and their family members to move and reside freely within the territory of the member states, COM (2003) 199 final.

81 European Parliament, Recommendation for Second Reading on the Council common position with a view to the adoption of a European Parliament and Council directive on the right of citizens of the Union and their family members to move and reside freely within the territory of the Member States: A5-0090/2004, 23 February 2004.

82 Minority Opinion of Maurizio Turco and Marco Cappato.

83 Directive 2004/58/EC of the European Parliament and of the Council of 29 April 2004 on the right of citizens of the Union and their family members to move and reside freely within the territory of the Member States, OJ 2004 L 229/35, Article 2.

84 ILGA-Europe Newsletter March 2004, p. 7.

85 Communication from the Commission, Free Movement of Workers – achieving the full benefits and potential, COM (2002) 694 final, 11 December 2002, p. 8. This also seems to be the view of the Council: see Toner, 'Partnership Rights', pp. 62–3.

even if not surprising.[86] It also demonstrates new levels of textual confusion: the Commission admits that same-sex married partners are 'spouses', but just not 'traditional' spouses. Further, it seems unlikely that the Court of Justice will expand its interpretation of spouse when it has steadfastly refused to do so thus far. Indeed, it may well view the adoption of the Directive as evidence of a consensus among the member states against expanding the concept of spouse.[87]

While there is no movement regarding the concept of spouse, the Directive does acknowledge the existence of registered partnerships, though such recognition is largely symbolic. A Union citizen will be entitled to move with their registered partner only if the host member state 'treats registered partnerships as equivalent to marriage and in accordance with the conditions laid down in the relevant legislation of the host member state'.[88] Few states, however, treat registered partnerships as *equivalent* to marriage, though most provide similarity of treatment *in some respects*. Further, the Directive refers to the 'legislation' of the host member state, which may well be more restrictive than the 'practice'. It seems likely that this provision will occasion considerable litigation in order to determine its scope, surely the opposite intention of drafting a new measure aimed at simplifying the law. In effect, it means that registered partners will be entitled to movement rights in only a few states. While progress has been made, with registered partnerships being recognised, discrimination remains, despite the Preamble stating that the Directive respects 'fundamental rights and freedoms' and is to be implemented without discrimination on the ground of sexual orientation.[89]

In relation to unmarried partners, the Directive continues that the 'host member state shall, in accordance with its own national legislation, facilitate the entry and residence' of 'the partner with whom the Union citizen has a durable relationship, duly attested'.[90] Member states are to undertake an 'extensive examination of the personal circumstances' of such partnerships and 'shall justify any denial of entry or residence'.[91] The Preamble indicates that, in examining such

---

86 While the Commission considers itself to be describing the law, others suggest that this is the principle on which the law should be based, i.e. that there should be a distinction between same-sex and opposite-sex marriages: Michael Bogdan, 'Registered Partnerships and EC Law' in Boele-Woelki and Fuchs (eds.), *Legal Recognition*, pp. 171–7.

87 A challenge to the concept of spouse may also result from litigation arising from Brussels II*bis* which provides for the recognition and enforcement of judgments relating to divorce. The question which arises is whether Brussels II*bis* will be interpreted to include same-sex marriages and their dissolution, rather than just 'traditional' marriages, thereby expanding the concept of spouse and marriage. For a discussion of this possibility, see Peter McEleavy, 'The Communitarization of Divorce Rules: What Impact for English and Scottish Law?' (2004) 53 *International and Comparative Law Quarterly* 605–42 at 607–9. For a detailed discussion of Brussels II*bis*, see chapter 6.

88 Article 2(2)(b) of Directive 2004/58/EC, OJ 2004 L 229/35.

89 Preamble (para. 31) to Directive 2004/58/EC, OJ 2004 L 229/35.

90 Article 3(2) of Directive 2004/58/EC, OJ 2004 L 229/35. The reference to national 'legislation' is more limited than earlier drafts which referred to the legislation and 'practice' of host states.

91 Article 3(2) of Directive 2004/58/EC, OJ 2004 L 229/35.

cases, member states should take into consideration 'the relationship with the Union citizen or any other circumstances, such as their financial or physical dependence on the Union citizen'.[92] This provision effectively provides a legislative basis for *Netherlands* v. *Reed*, and in doing so at least acknowledges the existence of partnerships beyond marriage. However, the decision regarding entry and residence remains at the discretion of member states, albeit that the exercise of that discretion is to be justified after 'extensive examination' and, as noted above, the Directive is to be implemented without discrimination on a wide variety of grounds, including sexual orientation. It seems likely that, as with the provision on registered partnerships, these rules are going to engender considerable litigation as to the meaning and extent of the duty to justify and the scope of the concepts 'durable' and 'dependence'. While this is clearly the unsurprising outcome of a tortuous negotiation process, considerable uncertainty remains and little has been achieved beyond the symbolic to recognise the changing nature of family practices.

Where the Directive does develop the existing law is in relation to the rights of spouses and registered partners on the breakdown of the relationship. It will be recalled that *Diatta* implied that on divorce the rights of a spouse are extinguished. For Union citizens, the new measure provides few new safeguards, with the person being entitled to continued residence so long as they are workers, self-employed, have sufficient financial resources so as not to become a burden on the host member state or are in education.[93] Thus, a Union citizen who is not working, and whose relationship has broken down, will have no continuing right of residence unless he or she has sufficient resources or is able to take up work. It is not difficult to imagine individuals who will not be able to meet such requirements, though special provision is made for parents with the care of children who are exercising their education rights.[94]

The position of third country nationals on the death of the Union citizen will be measurably improved in that so long as they are in work, self-employed or have sufficient financial resources, they will retain a right of residence.[95] In relation to the dissolution of the marriage or partnership, the third country national must similarly demonstrate that they are in work, are self-employed or have sufficient financial resources. In addition, however, they must also show either that the marriage or registered partnership has subsisted for three years, with at least one year in the host member state, or that they have custody of any children, or access to any children so long as a court has ruled that such access must be in the host member state and for so long as is required, or that

---

92 Preamble (para. 6) to Directive 2004/58/EC, OJ 2004 L 229/35.
93 Articles 12 and 13 of Directive 2004/58/EC, OJ 2004 L 229/35.
94 This is the ruling in *Baumbast* written into the new Directive, Article 12(3) of Directive 2004/58/ EC, OJ 2004 L 229/35.
95 Articles 12 and 13 of Directive 2004/58/EC, OJ 2004 L 229/35.

continued residence is warranted by particularly difficult circumstances such as domestic violence.[96]

These new rules do at least facilitate the continued right of residence of a third country national, and the requirement for three years of marriage/partnership is shorter than the Commission's earlier draft which specified five years. However, the requirement for sufficient financial resources is likely to scupper the residence rights of many.[97] For example, while the Directive does recognise the difficult circumstances of domestic violence, a woman escaping domestic violence is quite possibly not going to have 'sufficient resources', especially in view of her desire to end contact with the violent partner. In addition, she may not be in a position to engage immediately in work, self-employment or education. Similarly, a parent who has custody of children again may not have sufficient resources, particularly if not supported by the former partner, and may not be able to engage in paid work because of their childcare responsibilities. The irony is that those relationships which are favoured in Community law, and in the definitions of 'family member' in legislation and jurisprudence, are precisely those relationships which exhibit traditional features of dependency and economic co-operation. Yet it is this very interdependence which may result in a former partner ceasing to enjoy residence and other rights on the breakdown of the relationship as they will not have independent resources. In addition, the Directive is very specific that these rights are granted on the dissolution of marriage or registered partnerships. Thus, there will be no continued rights, under the terms of the Directive, for those in unmarried partnerships, even were they to have been originally granted residence on the basis of the measures discussed above.

The adoption of the new Free Movement Directive clearly represents a wasted opportunity as regards the concept of family and rights of family members. While there is some recognition of the changing nature of family practices, with registered partnerships particularly being acknowledged, the concept of family remains primarily based on heterosexual marriage. The rights of third country nationals following divorce or the dissolution of a partnership have been improved, though the continued requirement for sufficient financial resources may hamper the practical effect of such improvements. In the end, what remains is a Directive which confirms the exalted status of marriage and which seeks more to ensure the continuation of a traditional concept of family than to open up free movement to even more people or to respect the fundamental rights of those in all forms of family. Depressingly, further legislative reform is now likely to be

---

96 Article 13 of Directive 2004/58/EC, OJ 2004 L 229/35.
97 The Court of Human Rights has held that 'family life' can continue after divorce and thus the protection of family life in Article 8 of the Convention can prevent deportation in certain circumstances. See *Berrehab* v. *Netherlands* (No. 10730/84), (1989) 11 EHRR 322 at 329, discussed in Helen Stalford, 'Concepts of Family under European Union Law: Lessons from the European Convention on Human Rights' (2002) 16 *International Journal of Law, Policy and the Family* 410–34.

many years away. Moreover, it is possible that the Court of Justice will employ the Directive as a bulwark against further innovation and modernisation of the concept of family.

5.3   Families, reunification and the harmonisation of asylum and immigration law

The 1997 Treaty of Amsterdam established the ambition of creating common asylum and immigration policies in pursuit of an 'area of freedom, security and justice, in which the free movement of persons is assured in conjunction with appropriate measures with respect to external border controls, asylum [and] immigration'.[98] The motivation behind this regime is a reduction in the number of persons seeking asylum,[99] which is partly to be achieved via a more consistent and efficient response to asylum applications and greater 'burden' sharing throughout the Union, together with a greater control and securitarisation of immigration. Thus, the impetus for policy development on one level relates to the pursuit of deeper integration and political union, while on another manifests itself in deliberate and detailed measures to reduce asylum and immigration and simplify procedures. Thus, despite the considerable rhetoric relating to individual rights and international obligations, there appears to be little genuine adherence to such concerns.[100] The continuing moves towards harmonisation, therefore, are more influenced by concerns regarding security of external borders, economic prosperity for those already within the Union's borders and political desires for greater integration, than respect for individual human rights. Clearly, this does not bode well for those individuals and families who fall outside the scope of the most basic of protections afforded by the Community and who are, therefore, seeking to extend the scope of existing measures to fit their circumstances. Partnerships outside the traditional norm of the nuclear family are likely to find the climate of harmonisation described above hostile to their claims. And indeed this has proven largely to be the case.

The drive towards greater harmonisation in this area, to create an area of freedom, justice and security, is being made at a time of rapid reform in the way in which member states define 'family' and in particular grant rights to unmarried partners. Not only have the Netherlands and Belgium introduced same-sex marriage, but most other member states have adopted some measures to recognise same-sex partnerships. While the solutions adopted at national level vary considerably, there is no doubt that there is some consensus towards changing

98 Article 2 of the Consolidated Version of the Treaty on European Union, OJ 2002 C 325/1.
99 For a discussion of recent trends and policies, see Elspeth Guild, 'Between Persecution and Protection – Refugees and the New European Asylum Policy' (2000) 3 *Cambridge Yearbook of European Legal Studies* 169–98.
100 See further Hannah Garry, 'Harmonisation of Asylum Law and Policy within the European Union: A Human Rights Perspective' (2002) 20 *Netherlands Quarterly of Human Rights* 163–84.

ideas of 'the family' and towards ending the axis between marriage and family. In this context, the Commission, in proposing measures in this field, has made attempts to recognise the changing national context. However, while alternatives to marriage are given some recognition, there remains a privileging of marriage and second-class status is granted to other unions.

5.3.1   Family reunification of third country nationals

In relation to legal immigration, the principal measure of interest is the Family Reunification Directive.[101] This Directive details the rules applicable to the entry of the families of lawfully resident third country nationals. It provides for a very limited right of reunification, centred on the 'nuclear family', that is to say the spouse and minor children'.[102] Thus, we have an explicit reference to the concept of the 'nuclear family' and a considerably more limited definition of family than that applicable to the free movement of persons provisions.

On the subject of partnerships outside marriage, the Directive does at least acknowledge their existence, specifically referring to registered partnerships.[103] However, the provisions relating to registered and unmarried partners are permissive, with Article 4(3) providing only that member states 'may' authorise the entry and residence of an unmarried partner in a 'duly attested long-term stable relationship' or of a partner in a 'registered partnership'. A distinction is drawn between unmarried partnerships, for which some evidence of the stability of the relationship is required, and registered partnerships for whom stability is assumed. This is symbolic in that recognition has been made of the status of registered partnerships, elevating it above unmarried partnerships, albeit that they do not have the status of marriage. The Commission, in its explanatory document, states that the distinction made between unmarried partners and those in a registered partnership means that, in relation to the latter, it is not a condition of entry that the relationship is stable and long-term because the partnership is registered.[104] Thus, while there is progress of sorts, in that unmarried partnerships are at least recognised on the face of the Directive, there is no requirement on member states to recognise such relationships.

Accordingly, the right to family reunification for third country nationals provides for a concept of family considerably more limited than that applied in relation to the family members of Union citizens exercising their rights of free movement. There is not even the reciprocal obligation required in the case of

---

101 Council Directive 2003/86/EC of 22 September 2003 on the right to family reunification, OJ 2003 L 251/12. The Directive on long-term resident third country nationals defines family in the same (limited) way as the Family Reunification Directive: Council Directive 2003/109/EC, OJ 2004 L 16/44, discussed in Steve Peers, 'Implementing Equality? The Directive on Long-Term Resident Third-Country Nationals' (2004) 29 *European Law Review* 437–60.

102 Preamble (para. 10) to Directive 2003/86/EC, OJ 2003 L 251/ 12.

103 Article 4(3) of Directive 2003/86/EC, OJ 2003 L 251/12.

104 Amended proposal for a Council directive on the right to family reunification, COM (2002) 225 final, p. 7.

Union nationals in *Netherlands* v. *Reed*.[105] This limited concept of family is the result of a failure of the member states to agree on any concept broader than the nuclear family. Indeed, the specific reference to the nuclear family in the Directive is a worrying trend. The only sunshine on the horizon is the recognition of registered partnerships and the implication that, for those who have been able to register their relationship, the intrusion required before acquiring rights is reduced.[106]

What is also alarming about the Directive is that, despite the nature of its provisions, it makes repeated references to its compliance with principles of fundamental rights and the importance of the right to family unity. The Preamble to the Directive states that measures concerning family reunification 'must be adopted in conformity with the obligation to protect the family and respect family life enshrined in many instruments of international law'. However, the formulaic approach taken in the Directive does not match the more fluid jurisprudence of the Court of Human Rights which, as discussed above, focuses on the reality of relationships, rather than on their form, when interpreting family rights. Further, the Preamble states that the Directive respects the fundamental rights laid out in the Union Charter, which includes not just the right to respect for family life but also non-discrimination on the ground of sexual orientation. If this Directive does comply with the Charter, it means that lesbians and gay men are excluded from the right to respect for family life and the concept of family does not extend beyond the nuclear family.[107]

It seems, in fact, that, instead of family reunification being viewed as a humanitarian or human rights issue, it is characterised as one of immigration and a potential strain on the labour market and social infrastructure of the member state.[108] This justifies the limited scope of the measures and has further consequential effects. Third country nationals who acquire the status of long-term resident under Directive 2003/109/EC are entitled to exercise certain rights of free movement to another member state, accompanied by their family.[109] Not

105 An earlier version of the draft directive did include such an obligation under which member states were obliged to authorise the entry of an 'unmarried partner living in a durable relationship with the applicant, if the legislation of the member state concerned treats the situation of unmarried couples as corresponding to that of married couples': Amended proposal for a Council directive on the right to family reunification, COM (2000) 624 final, OJ 2001 C 62E/99.

106 The Directive also states that member states may 'decide that registered partners are to be treated equally as spouses with respect to family reunification': Article 4(3) of Directive 2003/86/EC, OJ 2003 L 251/12.

107 As suggested in Clare McGlynn, 'Families and the European Charter of Fundamental Rights: Progressive Change or Entrenching the Status Quo?' (2001) 26 *European Law Review* 582–98.

108 For a discussion, see Gisbert Brinkmann, 'Family Reunion, Third Country Nationals and the Community's New Powers' in Elspeth Guild and Carol Harlow (eds.), *Implementing Amsterdam – Immigration and Asylum Rights in EC Law* (Oxford: Hart Publishing, 2001), pp. 241–66 at p. 243.

109 Council Directive 2003/109/EC of 25 November 2003 concerning the status of third-country nationals who are long-term residents, OJ 2004 L 16/44.

surprisingly, it is only the 'nuclear family' of the Family Reunification Directive who are entitled to move with the long-term resident. Furthermore, where a member state has authorised the family reunification of unmarried partners, other member states are not even obliged to then permit the residence of that partner.[110] Thus, even where a member state authorises the family reunification of unmarried partners, that family remains in a hierarchically inferior position to married partners as they are not entitled to the same rights of movement throughout the Union.

One final feature of the Directive worthy of note is its provisions on polygamous marriages. The Directive states that, where the sponsor already has a spouse living with him in the member state, the relevant member state 'shall not' authorise the family reunification of a further spouse, although states may permit entry of the minor children of a further spouse, though they are not obliged to do so.[111] This provision is ostensibly included in order to ensure the respect of the 'rights of women and of children' which, the Preamble provides, justifies the 'possible taking of restrictive measures against applications for family reunification of polygamous households'.[112]

The prescriptive nature of the provision is surprising. There is no discretion left to member states to permit the entry of multiple spouses (wives) where this might be compatible with the relevant national laws and/or may be appropriate in order to promote the rights of the particular woman and her children. Indeed, although provision can be made for the entry of minor children of further spouses, to do so without permitting entry of a further wife is indeed likely to seriously injure both the children's and woman's rights and happiness. This approach is stricter than that of the European Convention in that, while states 'cannot be required to give full recognition to polygamous marriages which are in conflict with their own legal order', there is no prohibition on their doing so.[113]

While concerns may be expressed that recognition of polygamous marriages may give rise to official recognition of the inequalities between women and men in such relationships,[114] non-recognition also entails considerable disadvantages for those women who have contracted polygamous unions. The non-recognition of polygamous unions means that many women and children in such families are denied recourse to many societal protections and benefits, including welfare, post-divorce financial protection and not least rights to family reunification.

---

110 Article 16 of Directive 2003/86/EC, OJ 2003 L 251/12.
111 Article 4(4) of and Preamble (para. 10) Directive 2003/86/EC, OJ 2003 No. L251/12.
112 Preamble (para. 11) to Directive 2003/86/EC, OJ 2003 L 251/ 12.
113 *RB* v. *United Kingdom* (also cited as *Bibi* v. *United Kingdom*) (No. 19628/92) (29 June 1992) (unreported).
114 See Susan Moller Okin, 'Feminism and Multiculturalism: Some Tensions' (1998) 108 *Ethics* 661–84, and Susan Moller Okin with respondents, *Is Multiculturalism Bad for Women?* (Princeton: Princeton University Press, 1999).

Prakash Shah therefore suggests that polygamous unions 'ought to be accepted as constituting one form of family arrangement within a plural society that may give rise to problems which require resolution by official fora'.[115] Indeed, to the extent that official recognition may prevent such practices being driven underground, and ensure that women in such relationships are at least officially recognised, it would help prevent the inequalities and vulnerabilities that many such women and their children face. Thus, just as a dominant ideology of the family has not and will not make all individuals adopt such a familial lifestyle, the non-recognition and criminalisation of polygamous unions is not going to prevent their continuation. The concern with the Family Reunification Directive, therefore, is its prescriptive nature. Rather than protecting the rights of women and children, it may in fact be to their detriment in some cases.

5.3.2   Adopting common rules on asylum

At the same time that measures are being taken to harmonise the member states' immigration rules, common approaches to asylum are also being adopted and proposed. The overall concern of the member states, translated into Union rhetoric, is to reduce the number of individuals seeking asylum within the Union as a whole and, in respect of those applications which are received, to deal with them on a more coordinated basis in order to reduce forum shopping, to facilitate 'burden sharing' and repatriation, and, overall, to control such 'security' threats.[116] In such an atmosphere of fear, particularly of 'others', it is not surprising, though still unwelcome, that the measures thus far proposed and adopted are limited in their scope regarding the concept of family. The lack of any attention to the person seeking asylum as an individual, and respect for her or his human rights, means that there has been no 'new' way of looking at this issue, despite the inclusion of the right to asylum in the Union Charter.[117] Instead, we have a rehashing of the limited scope of existing national measures and concepts at the Union level. Thus, any tension that exists between internal security considerations and human rights concerns has largely been decided in favour of security issues.

The definition of family being used in the asylum measures is slightly broader than that in the Family Reunification Directive. Thus, in the Council Directive on the laying down of minimum standards for the reception of asylum seekers, 'family' includes the spouse and minor children, as well as an 'unmarried partner in a stable relationship, where the legislation or practice of the Member State

---

115 Prakash Shah, 'Attitudes to Polygamy in English Law' (2003) 52 *International and Comparative Law Quarterly* 369–400 at 399.
116 See Theodora Kostakopoulou, 'The "Protective Union": Change and Continuity in Migration Law and Policy in Post-Amsterdam Europe' (2000) 38 *Journal of Common Market Studies* 497–518; Sandra Lavenex, 'The Europeanisation of Refugee Policies: Normative Challenges and Institutional Legacies' (2001) 39 *Journal of Common Market Studies* 851–74.
117 Article 18 of the Charter of Fundamental Rights, OJ 2000 C 364/1.

concerned treats unmarried couples in a way comparable to married couples under its law relating to aliens'.[118] The same definition is used in the Directive on minimum standards for giving temporary protection in the event of a mass influx of displaced persons[119] and in the Council Regulation establishing the criteria and mechanisms for examining asylum applications.[120] This is the *Netherlands* v. *Reed* formulation with an emphasis on 'comparability' and reference to the law of aliens. This means that only where the member state treats unmarried and married couples on a similar basis in relation to its law of aliens will the unmarried partner be accepted as a family member. It will not be enough, therefore, that other areas of the law, such as family law, assimilate married and unmarried partners. The reference to 'comparability' is more positive than earlier drafts which insisted that the legislation of the member state treat married and unmarried couples 'in the same way'.[121] However, it still leaves considerable ambiguity as to how the measure will be implemented in relation to interpretations of 'stable relationship', 'comparability' and exactly which laws constitute the 'law relating to aliens'.[122]

Furthermore, the rights of unmarried partners will vary from state to state.[123] As ILGA-Europe has argued, such a definition of family enshrines 'in law discrimination against lesbian, gay, bisexual and transgender persons and their families' as the rights of these individuals will vary depending on the state in which the applicant for asylum arrives.[124] Of particular note is the fact that an

---

118 Article 2(d) of Council Directive 2003/9/EC of 27 January 2003 laying down minimum standards for the reception of asylum seekers ('Dublin II'), OJ 2003 L 31/18.

119 Article 15(a) of Council Directive 2001/55/EC of 20 July 2001 on minimum standards for giving temporary protection in the event of a mass influx of displaced persons and on measures promoting a balance of efforts between Member States in receiving such persons and bearing the consequences thereof, OJ 2001 L 212/ 12.

120 Article 2(i) of Council Regulation 343/2003/EC of 18 February 2003 establishing the criteria and mechanisms for determining the Member State responsible for examining an asylum application lodged in one of the Member States by a third country national, OJ 2003 L 50/1.

121 Proposal for a Council Directive on minimum standards for giving temporary protection in the event of a mass influx of displaced persons and on measures promoting a balance of efforts between Member States in receiving such persons and bearing the consequences thereof, COM (2000) 303 final, OJ 2000 C 311E/251; European Commission proposal for a Council directive laying down minimum standards on the reception of applicants for asylum in Member States, COM (2001) 181 final, OJ 2001 C 213E/286, proposed Article 2(d).

122 For a detailed discussion, see Mark Bell, 'We Are Family? Same Sex Partners and EU Migration Law' (2004) 9 *Maastricht Journal of European and Comparative Law* 335–55.

123 In the Temporary Protection Directive (Directive 2001/55/EC, OJ 2001 L 212/12) there is a subsidiary category into which unmarried partners may fall, though it entails reduced rights compared with the provision above. Thus, whereas member states 'shall' reunite the family member discussed above, in Article 15(1)(b) the Directive states that the member state 'may' reunite a 'close relative' who lived as part of the family unit with the applicant. However, it seems likely that the wording 'relative', as opposed to 'family member', which was the wording of an earlier draft of the Directive, will preclude an interpretation extending to an unmarried partner.

124 The European Region of the International Lesbian and Gay Association, 'Position Paper on the Proposal for a Council Directive Laying Down Minimum Standards on the Reception of Applicants for Asylum in Member States', COM (2001) 181, October 2001.

earlier draft of Dublin II included a non-discrimination provision on the grounds of sexual orientation.[125] While the Directive does state in its Preamble that it complies with the fundamental rights recognised in the Charter, which includes non-discrimination on the grounds of sexual orientation, it is striking that a specific reference to sexual orientation has been deleted from the final text. Thus, despite the Commission's rhetoric that the cornerstone of the area of freedom, security and justice is 'freedom from discrimination',[126] discrimination is a central feature of these measures.

The limited scope of the concept of family and partnership employed in the field of asylum and immigration is significant in that how a state, or in this case a supranational organisation, deals with issues of migration, reveals much regarding notions of membership of the polity, its values, its concept of citizenship and its future orientations.[127] This being the case, the asylum and immigration laws of the Union reveal a concept of citizenship open only to some, a set of values based on a traditional nuclear family and a future which is characterised more by fear and the need for security, rather than the recognition of human rights and the necessity of modern approaches to inclusion and belonging. Indeed, as Theodora Kostakopoulou has argued, instead of the Union adopting a more relaxed, liberal and enlightened approach to migration flows, what we have seen and what appears to be on offer is the Union's uncritical adoption of the member states' paranoia regarding migration, their closed definition of who are 'Europeans' and their pre-occupation with securing existing national identities.[128] What remains of even greater concern is that this agenda, which characterises Community and Union action regarding immigration and asylum, may well come to define the free movement of persons within Community law, as these fields of policy are considered as a whole.[129] Nonetheless, it should be acknowledged that, at the very least, these new measures do depart from a sole focus on marriage as the basis for family rights. There is a recognition of partnerships without marriage, albeit of a second-class status, and it might be hoped that this recognition could form the basis for incremental development towards a more egalitarian and pluralist definition of family in the future.

5.4   Partnership rights and employment law

While the concept of family and the extent of partnership rights were first considered in the context of the Community's free movement rules, challenges

125 Proposed Article 32.
126 Communication from the Commission COM (1998) 459: Towards an area of freedom, security and justice, p. 5.
127 See Kostakopoulou, 'The "Protective Union"', 499.
128 Kostakopoulou, 'The "Protective Union"', 509.
129 As is now suggested by their coming together within a new Title IV of the Treaty of Rome entitled 'Visa, Asylum, Immigration and Other Policies Related to the Free Movement of Persons'.

have also been made to these concepts in the Community's anti-discrimination laws. At issue here is the remuneration package offered to employees which often extends benefits granted to that person's partner, most often a spouse, and/or family. So long as such benefits have been granted to husbands or wives, they have not been challenged as constituting a breach of the Community's sex equality laws. However, it was when the British company South West Trains granted benefits to an employee's unmarried opposite sex partner, as well as to a husband or wife, specifically excluding a same-sex partner and possibly a transgendered partner, that a challenge came before the Court of Justice.

In *Grant* v. *South West Trains*, the employer refused a request for the relevant employee benefit to be granted to the employee's same-sex partner.[130] The relevant company regulations extended such benefits only to spouses and opposite-sex partners, thereby specifically excluding gay and lesbian partners. During the course of the litigation, the company plainly stated that it excluded same-sex partners from its benefits package because this is not the 'sort of relationship which the company's regulations aim to encourage'.[131] Lisa Grant brought her claim alleging discrimination on the ground of sex, as her predecessor, a man, had been granted the relevant concession for his female partner. Arguably, therefore, this was a simple case of sex discrimination: the only difference between the situation of Ms Grant and her predecessor was Ms Grant's sex. The Court refused to adopt such an approach and treated the matter as a question of whether sexual orientation discrimination came within Article 141 of the EC Treaty. Furthermore, as the case involved the grant of benefits to the partners of employees, the Court decided that this case involved issues of civil status and family law.

The Court rejected the claim, holding that sexual orientation discrimination did not fall within existing Community law. Of particular significance were the Court's findings relating to the lack of any requirement for Community law to take cognisance of the discrimination facing same-sex partners. After the briefest of examinations of the approaches of the member states to same-sex partnerships, the Court stated that 'in the present state of the law within the Community, stable relationships between two persons of the same sex are not regarded as equivalent to marriages or stable relationships outside marriage between persons of the opposite sex'.[132] The Court stated that member states held this position 'for the purpose of protecting the family'.[133] The Court also justified its position by referring to the jurisprudence of the European Convention on Human Rights which has continued to hold that stable gay and lesbian relationships do not fall within the scope of the right to respect for family life under Article 8 of the Convention.[134]

---

130 Case C-249/96, *Grant* v. *South West Trains Ltd* [1998] ECR I-621; [1998] 1 CMLR 993.
131 South West Trains, quoted in 'Lisa – A Woman Uncoupled', Independent, 9 July 1997.
132 *Grant*, para. 35.
133 *Grant*, para. 33.
134 *Grant*, para. 33.

The judgment in *Grant* has been roundly condemned and the reasoning subject to detailed critique.[135] Most interesting, from the perspective of this chapter, is the attitude the Court displays towards same-sex relationships and the implications this had and continues to have for future developments. The Court in *Grant* pointed to a number of factors as demonstrating that there was no consensus regarding the treatment of same-sex couples and opposite-sex couples. However, many of its justifications are no longer valid, which should lead to change. The Court noted, first, that the Community has not adopted any rules prohibiting discrimination on the grounds of sexual orientation.[136] The General Framework Directive does now prohibit such discrimination.[137] The Court then referred to the laws of the member states, noting that, while some member states recognised same-sex relationships as equivalent to marriage, 'most' member states only treat them as equivalent with respect to a 'limited number of rights, or not at all'.[138] It is now the case that a majority of member states offer some form of legal recognition of same-sex relationships, albeit to varying degrees. The Court also noted that the Court of Human Rights had interpreted Article 12 of the European Convention, the right to marry, as applying only to 'traditional marriage between two persons of opposite biological sex'.[139] The Court of Human Rights has moved beyond such a conception in the *I* and *Goodwin* cases in which the right to marry was extended to transgendered people.[140] The only aspect of the Court's survey which remains accurate is its examination of the Court of Human Rights' approach to the notion of family life which it has not yet extended to same-sex relationships.[141] While this remains true, there have been inroads into this position, most particularly in *Da Silva* in which the Court held there to be family life between a gay father and his child.[142]

Accordingly, when the Court of Justice stated that 'it follows' from its discussion of the laws of the member states, the Community and the Court of Human Rights that there was no equivalence between heterosexual and homosexual relationships, this no longer rings true. In addition, the Court's purported survey of national laws was cursory, and its selection of cases/laws revealed much

---

135 Andrew Koppelman has argued that the *Grant* case represents not only a 'major defeat for lesbians and gay men', but has also 'damaged' human rights law at 'its core'. Andrew Koppelman, 'The Miscegenation Analogy in Europe, or, Lisa Grant Meets Adolf Hitler' in Wintemute and Andenas (eds.), *Same Sex Partnerships*, pp. 623–34 at p. 623. See also Mark Bell, 'Shifting Conceptions of Sexual Discrimination at the Court of Justice: from *P* v. *S* to *Grant* v. *SWT*' (1999) 5 *European Law Journal* 63–81.

136 *Grant*, para. 31.

137 Council Directive 2000/78/EC of 27 November 2000 establishing a general framework for equal treatment in employment and occupation, OJ 2000 L 303/16.

138 *Grant*, para. 32.

139 *Grant*, para. 34.

140 *Goodwin* v. *United Kingdom* (No. 28957/95), (2002) 35 EHRR 18.

141 *Grant*, para. 33.

142 *Da Silva* v. *Portugal* (No. 33290/96), (2001) 31 EHRR 47.

regarding the conclusion for which the Court was searching.[143] Indeed, there is much in the national laws of the member states to demonstrate increasing acceptance of gay and lesbian partnerships, revealed in the progressive elimination of discrimination on the grounds of sexual orientation. The device of the Court, looking to the laws of the member states, was a rhetorical strategy which can be used by the Court for extending or limiting the scope of Community law, rather than an objective methodology. Indeed, as Iris Canor has argued, the Court could just as easily have acknowledged an emerging consensus among member states regarding the need to extend equality to gay and lesbian individuals.[144]

However, had the Court done so, what might have been the effect? Carl Stychin has argued that the facts of *Grant* fit rather well with the Court's ideological approach to the family.[145] I have already argued that the Court reproduces and privileges the heterosexual nuclear family, a 'breadwinner' conception of family based on 'coupledom'. As Stychin argues, the facts of *Grant* tap into this ideology in which perks are granted for the employee's 'family', being based on a couple and the idea of a breadwinning wage.[146] Lisa Grant and her partner portrayed themselves as a couple, as interdependent as a married couple, and therefore on a similar footing. Amy Elman similarly argues that *Grant* is an example of the gay and lesbian movement embracing 'patriarchy's principal institution, the family'.[147] Thus, far from challenging the 'family' and, in this particular case, the distribution of privileges to couples, the case seeks to assimilate same-sex and heterosexual relationships. Thus, there is no challenge to the granting of perks to those not in a traditional spousal-type relationship, leaving individuals, and other forms of families, particularly single parent families, without such benefits. Similarly, Momin Rahman contends that these strategies endorse, rather than challenge, institutionalised heterosexuality as a model for human relationships.[148]

---

143 Furthermore, there was no evidence of the Court engaging in a survey of member state laws in Case C-13/94, *P* v. *S and Cornwall County Council* [1996] ECR I-2143; [1996] 2 CMLR 247. The Court simply stated that the discrimination in issue fell within the relevant Community law, as a matter of interpretation. In a similar vein, Kenneth Armstrong has pointed out that, while the Court's deference to the need for legislation before ruling on such a matter seems legitimate, the Court has not done so in regard to other concepts, such as the concept of worker, for which the Court maintains a strict hold on a Community interpretation. Kenneth Armstrong, 'Tales of the Community: Sexual Orientation Discrimination and EC Law' (1998) 20 *Journal of Social Welfare and Family Law* 455–79 at 463.

144 Iris Canor, 'Equality for Lesbians and Gay Men in the European Community Legal Order – "They Shall Be Male and Female"' (2000) 7 *Maastricht Journal of European and Comparative Law* 273–99 at 283.

145 Carl Stychin, '*Grant*-ing Rights: The Politics of Rights, Sexuality and European Union' (2000) 51 *Northern Ireland Legal Quarterly* 281–302.

146 Stychin, '*Grant*-ing Rights', 291.

147 Amy Elman, 'Familiar Orientations: Sex Discrimination, Same Sex Partners and Migration in European Law', paper presented to the American Political Science Association Annual Conference, 1999, quoted in Stychin, '*Grant*-ing Rights', 291.

148 Momin Rahman, 'Sexuality and Rights: Problematising Lesbian and Gay Politics' in Terrell Carver and Véronique Mottier (eds.), *Politics of Sexuality: Identity, Gender, Citizenship* (London: Routledge, 1998), pp. 79–88, discussed in Stychin, '*Grant*-ing Rights', 291–2.

Hence, as Carl Stychin maintains, a decision in favour of Lisa Grant would have fitted very well the ideological grounding of Community rights discourse, in terms of the nuclear family and particularly the privatised responsibility of care within the private sphere.[149]

However, notwithstanding such attractive reasoning, it would still have been preferable for the Court to have ruled in Lisa Grant's favour. As argued above, recognition of same-sex partnerships, while entailing some acceptance of heterosexual norms, remains important in terms of valuing such relationships and recognising the rights of individuals. As Mark Bell rightly suggests, the discrimination evident in *Grant* constitutes a 'symbolic representation of disapproval of same sex relationships'.[150] Indeed, at the more practical level, Bell continues that this is also an issue of remuneration where benefits are extended to married or opposite-sex couples, but not to same-sex couples.[151] Indeed, it is the lack of any real commitment to fundamental rights which is of most criticism in *Grant*. In the earlier *P* v. *S* case, the Court held that discrimination on the grounds of transsexuality did come within the Community's sex equality laws, explaining that to 'tolerate such discrimination would be tantamount, as regards such a person, to a failure to respect the dignity and freedom to which he or she is entitled and which the Court has a duty to safeguard'.[152] Clearly, lesbians and gay men are not entitled to similar respect for their freedom and dignity.[153]

The unsatisfactory nature of the ruling became ever more clear when the Court considered an appeal from a judgment of the Court of First Instance in *D* v. *Council*.[154] In this case, the Court of Justice refused to treat a Swedish registered partnership as equivalent to marriage for the purposes of an employee benefit. The Court of First Instance had rejected the claim and cited the interpretation of Article 12 of the European Convention, on the right to marry, in its favour.[155] In rejecting D's claim, Advocate General Mischo referred to the Charter of Fundamental Rights as a source of inspiration and confirmation of the fundamental rights to be protected by the Union. He noted the inclusion of the 'right to marry' in the Charter and went on to state that this provides no explicit requirement to recognise same-sex relationships, so the right to marry cannot

149 Stychin, '*Grant*-ing Rights', 294.
150 Mark Bell, 'Sexual Orientation Discrimination in Employment: An Evolving Role for the European Union' in Wintemute and Andenas (eds.), *Same Sex Partnerships*, pp. 653–76 at p. 666. For a more detailed discussion, see Mark Bell, *Anti-Discrimination Law and the European Union* (Oxford: Oxford University Press, 2002).
151 Bell, 'Sexual Orientation Discrimination', 666.
152 Case C-13/94, *P* v. *S and Cornwall County Council* [1996] ECR I-2143; [1996] 2 CMLR 247, para. 22.
153 In *Grant*, the Court simply stated that its ruling in *P* v. *S* is 'limited to the case of a worker's gender reassignment and does not therefore apply to differences of treatment based on a person's sexual orientation'. Case C-249/96, *Grant* v. *South West Trains Ltd* [1998] ECR I-621; [1998] 1 CMLR 993, para. 42.
154 Joined Cases C-122/99 P and C-125/99 P, [2001] ECR I-4319; [2003] 3 CMLR 9.
155 Case T-264/97, *D* v. *Council* [1999] ECR IA-1 and II–1, para. 28.

be interpreted as requiring some form of recognition of such relationships.[156] Although the Advocate General was right to the extent that the explanatory notes to the Charter do not state that the 'right to marry' should be extended to gay and lesbian couples, it does not, however, state that such an extension should be prevented. Indeed, it is neutral in its approach. The notes state that: 'This Article neither prohibits nor imposes the granting of the status of marriage to unions between people of the same sex.'[157] It continues that the right is therefore 'similar to that afforded by the ECHR', but its scope 'may be wider where national legislation provides'. It would have been possible for the Advocate General, and subsequently the Court, to have provided 'more extensive' protection, by also relying on the Preamble to the Charter, which states that one of its aims is to strengthen protection of rights in the 'light of changes in society'.[158] Furthermore, Article 21 of the Charter prohibits discrimination on the ground of sexual orientation, and the continued exclusion of gay and lesbian couples from the right to marry may clearly constitute just such discrimination. However, the Advocate General failed even to refer to Article 21 of the Charter.

The Court of Justice stated that: 'It is not in question that, according to the definition generally accepted by the Member States, the term marriage means a union between two persons of opposite sex.'[159] Further, it 'cannot disregard the views prevailing within the Community as a whole' in which the recognition of unmarried relationships 'reflects a great diversity of laws and the absence of any general assimilation of marriage and other forms of statutory union'.[160] And, 'according to the definition generally accepted by the Member States, the term "marriage" means a union between two persons of the opposite sex'.[161] The Court drew a particular distinction between this traditional concept of marriage and forms of same-sex relationship recognition. It noted that 'since 1989 an increasing number of Member States have introduced, alongside marriage, statutory arrangements granting legal recognition to various forms of union between partners of the same sex or of the opposite sex' and that these arrangements are 'regarded in the Member States as being distinct from marriage'.[162] In this way, the fact that some states have afforded recognition to same-sex relationships was in fact used against the applicant in this case as confirming the differential status between marriage and registered partnerships.

The Court's reference to rights highlights the fact that the Court of Human Rights has yet to declare same-sex relationships as coming within Article 8 of the European Convention (on the right to family life) or Article 12 of the European

---

156 Opinion of Advocate General Mischo, para. 97.
157 Charte 4473/00, at 12.
158 Preamble to the Charter of Fundamental Rights, OJ 2000 C 364/1.
159 *D* v. *Council*, para. 34.
160 *D* v. *Council*, paras. 49–50.
161 *D* v. *Council*, para. 34.
162 *D* v. *Council*, paras. 35–6.

Convention (on the right to marry). While this remains true, the recent cases of *I* and *Goodwin* challenge the complacency of the Court of Justice and will require a reconsideration of the concepts of 'spouse' and 'family'.[163] In these cases, the Court of Human Rights ended the privileging of a traditional concept of marriage, ruling that preventing a transgender male to female from marrying a man constituted a breach of her human rights, including Article 8 of the Convention, on the protection of private life, but most especially a breach of Article 12 of the Convention, which states that: 'Men and women of marriageable age have the right to marry and to found a family, according to the national laws governing the exercise of this right.' The Court of Human Rights stated that, in interpreting the Convention, it must have 'regard to the changing conditions' in contracting states generally and respond to 'any evolving convergence as to the standards to be achieved'.[164] The Court continued that it is of 'crucial importance' that the Convention is interpreted and applied in a manner which renders its rights 'practical and effective, not theoretical and illusory', and that a failure by the Court to maintain a 'dynamic and evolutive approach' would risk rendering it a bar to reform or improvement.[165]

In this respect, the interpretation of the 'emerging consensus' is also important. In considering the question of the evolution of standards among contracting states, the Court of Human Rights stated that it was less concerned with whether there was agreement as to the resolution of the practical and legal issues, but 'to the clear and uncontested evidence of a continuing international trend in favour not only of increased social acceptance of transsexuals but of legal recognition of the new sexual identity of post-operative transsexuals'.[166] In other words, there was general agreement that there was an issue which needed some form of resolution that was important, rather than the exact method of resolution. This allows for different approaches to the same issue. This is of particular interest in that the Court of Human Rights noted that fewer countries permit a transgendered person to marry, than recognise the change of gender itself.[167] The Court, however, was not persuaded that this was a sufficient basis for leaving the matter entirely within the margin of appreciation of the contracting states as this would be tantamount to saying that one of the permitted options was an effective bar on the exercise of the right to marry.[168]

The Court continued that there have been 'major changes in the institution of marriage' since the adoption of the Convention. In this regard, the Court noted that Article 9 of the Union's Charter of Fundamental Rights departs from the wording of

---

163 *I* v. *United Kingdom* (No. 25680/94), (2003) 36 EHRR 53; *Goodwin* v. *United Kingdom* (No. 28957/95), (2002) 35 EHRR 18.
164 *I* v. *United Kingdom*, para. 54.
165 *I* v. *United Kingdom*, para. 54.
166 *I* v. *United Kingdom*, para. 65.
167 *I* v. *United Kingdom*, paras. 78, 83.
168 *I* v. *United Kingdom*, para. 78.

Article 12 of the Convention, 'no doubt deliberately', by removing the reference to men and women.[169] Thus, the Union Charter was cited as an example of one of the changes to the institution of marriage. Ironically, therefore, while the Charter was employed by the Advocate General in *D* v. *Council* in order to *limit* the right to marry, it was cited by the Court of Human Rights as evidence of changing views regarding marriage, particularly its biological opposite-sex basis. Thus, the Court held that the refusal to allow a transgendered person to marry in their adopted gender constituted a breach of the 'very essence' of the right to marry.[170]

Nonetheless, the judgment in *Goodwin* cannot be viewed as an unmitigated success. We can see in it the dangers suggested by others in the continued use of family, that of the 'domestication of deviant sexualities within a safe, useful and recognizable framework'.[171] Thus, the Court talks of Goodwin and I in terms that they would 'only wish to marry a man'.[172] In this way, we see a continued dominance of the binary approach to marriage, between a man and a woman. There is no sense here of being transgendered as in some way on a continuum between woman and man, of a diverse approach to gender.[173] It is, rather, a reinforcement of dominant ideas of there being only two genders. Thus, while the Court shows 'genuine radicalism',[174] particularly in its talk of there being a general human right for all people to 'live in dignity and worth in accordance with the sexual identity chosen by them', which is not limited by the Court to any specific group, we also see the reinforcement of the binary divide of gender and the reiteration of the 'good' in relationships as being between a man and a woman. Ralph Sandland suggests, therefore, that, while there may be hope in the judgments, they should 'properly be read as homophobic'.[175]

Returning to the impact of these rulings on Community law, it will be recalled that the Court of Justice in *D* v. *Council* stated that it was relying on the 'views prevailing within the Community as a whole', which it said do not recognise gay and lesbian relationships, even those which are registered, as equivalent to marriage.[176] More recent case law suggests that a less restrictive interpretation may be possible in the future and the cases of *Goodwin* and *I* are part of that changing context. However, we have been here before. In reaching its judgment in *Netherlands* v. *Reed* in 1986, the Court said that the term 'spouse' may need to be reinterpreted in the light of social changes.[177] Fifteen years on, with considerable changes in society, there is still no movement.

---

169 *I* v. *United Kingdom*, para. 80.
170 *I* v. *United Kingdom*, para. 81.
171 Boyd, 'Family, Law and Sexuality', 378.
172 *Goodwin*, para. 101; *I* v. *United Kingdom*, para. 81.
173 Discussed in Ralph Sandland, 'Crossing and Not Crossing: Gender, Sexuality and Melancholy in the European Court of Human Rights' (2003) 11 *Feminist Legal Studies* 191–209.
174 Sandland, 'Crossing and Not Crossing', 196.
175 Sandland, 'Crossing and Not Crossing', 204.
176 Joined Cases C-122/99 P and C-125/99 P, *D* v. *Council* [2001] ECR I-4319; [2003] 3 CMLR 9.
177 Case 59/85, *Netherlands* v. *Reed* [1986] ECR 1283; [1987] 2 CMLR 448.

The principles established in *Grant* and *D* v. *Council* built on those already detailed in the area of free movement of persons. Thus, while *Netherlands* v. *Reed* denied recognition to an unmarried heterosexual partnership, *Grant* extended this to unmarried gay and lesbian relationships and *D* v. *Council* extended this further still to include relationships registered under national law as equivalent to marriage. The only acknowledgment from the Court of Justice that change is not just the right course of action, but also demanded by social reality, came in *Eyüp*. The Community legislature, however, has taken steps which may in time lead to a broader approach to relationships and their legal recognition, namely the adoption of the General Framework Directive on equal treatment.[178]

For present purposes, what is of most interest is the extent to which the Directive will eliminate practices such as that in *Grant* where partnership benefits are withheld from employees who are in same-sex relationships.[179] The position is not entirely clear as the legislature has made some attempts to limit the scope of the Directive. The Preamble states that: 'This Directive is without prejudice to national laws on marital status and the benefits dependent thereon.'[180] This appears to suggest that any benefits granted to married employees do not come within the scope of the Directive.[181] Yet it seems obvious that to grant benefits only to married employees constitutes discrimination on the grounds of sexual orientation as lesbians and gay men cannot get married (except in the Netherlands and Belgium). Mark Bell has argued that such discrimination is most likely to be construed as indirect discrimination, allowing justification, and it will therefore be up to the Court to determine the scope of justifications for this form of discrimination. An employer would have to demonstrate that the discrimination was 'objectively justified by a legitimate aim and the means of achieving that aim are appropriate and necessary'.[182] Bell argues that there are three potential grounds of justification – the different social value accorded to married relationships, economic reasons and the potential risk of abuse by fraudulent relationships – although only the former having any likely mileage.[183]

It was the social value attached to married relationships which was the justification presented by the employer in the *Grant* case. Despite Advocate General Elmer's comment that the employer's justification amounted to little more than the employer's 'own private conceptions of morality' overriding the fundamental

178 Council Directive 2000/78/EC of 27 November 2000 establishing a general framework for equal treatment in employment and occupation, OJ 2000 L 303/16.
179 See further Mark Bell, *Anti-Discrimination Law and the European Union* (Oxford: Oxford University Press, 2002), pp. 112–18.
180 Recital 22 of the Preamble to Directive 2000/78/EC, OJ 2000 L 303/16.
181 Mark Bell suggests that it is possible that the wording of the recital, not affecting benefits *dependent upon* national laws, could mean that public sector benefits are excluded, as being more closely related to national law, but not benefits offered in the private sector. Bell, 'Sexual Orientation Discrimination', 668.
182 Article 2(2)(b)(i) of Directive 2000/78/EC, OJ 2000 L 303/16.
183 Bell, 'Sexual Orientation Discrimination', 669.

principle of non-discrimination,[184] the Court held that 'stable relationships between two persons of the same sex are not regarded as equivalent to marriage'.[185] Thus, following *Grant*, there appears to be some mileage in this justification. However, there has been an evolution in the recognition of same-sex relationships since *Grant* both at the level of national law and under the European Convention on Human Rights, as discussed above, such that the context is not the same as it was at the time of *Grant*. Mark Bell concedes, however, that, although there should be change, the principle of subsidiarity suggests a degree of deference towards the member states, especially on such sensitive issues, and that the most likely outcome is that the Court 'will wait for a consolidation of national laws on the recognition of same sex partners before making any far-reaching decisions for the whole of the European Union'.[186] While such a negative prediction is perhaps accurate, it is arguable that such a consolidation has already taken place, and, by the time any case comes before the Court, this is certainly going to be so.

It also appears likely that, after *D* v. *Council*, discrimination between opposite-sex married couples and registered same-sex couples will be allowed to continue. Marriage was not defined in the relevant staff regulations and it was therefore open to both the Court of First Instance and then the Court of Justice to interpret marriage, under Community law, as including a registered partnership. Indeed, rejecting such a contention, the Court extended the scope of permitted discrimination in *Grant*, discrimination against a same-sex cohabiting couple, to discrimination against a same-sex couple in a registered partnership. Because of this judgment, discrimination against a registered partnership will have to be considered as indirect discrimination, as discussed above, as opposed to direct discrimination, thereby permitting justification.

While the extent of any prohibition of discrimination between married couples and same-sex couples is perhaps unclear, the form of discrimination in the *Grant* case, discrimination between an unmarried opposite-sex couple and an unmarried same-sex couple, would appear to be prohibited under the Directive, as it would constitute direct discrimination on the grounds of sexual orientation. The only possible exemption for such discrimination would be Article 2(5) of the Directive, which states that the Directive shall be without prejudice to national laws which are necessary in a 'democratic society' for the 'maintenance of public order and the prevention of criminal offences, for the protection of health and for the protection of the rights and freedoms of others'. In such a case, the employer would have to show that the discrimination was justified on this basis which appears unlikely, especially in the light of the judgment of the Court of Human Rights in *Karner*. Accordingly, at the very least, the discrimination in *Grant* is

184 *Grant*, p. 642.
185 *Grant*, p. 648.
186 Bell, 'Sexual Orientation Discrimination', 670.

now prohibited. The hope must be that in time the impact of the Directive will be to ameliorate the discrimination facing lesbians and gay men and that this will in turn have a positive impact on all relationships not conforming to the married heterosexual norm. In this light, the adoption of the Directive could be viewed as one of the many steps leading inexorably towards full recognition of lesbian and gay partnerships.[187]

Indeed, the recent case of *KB* v. *NHS Pension Agency* has required the Court of Justice to acknowledge the changing concept of marriage under European Convention case law such that laws precluding transgendered individuals from marrying in their chosen gender are 'in principle' in breach of Article 141 of the EC Treaty.[188] This case concerned an employer's refusal to pay a survivor's benefit to the (female to male) transgender partner of its female employee. The benefit, for a 'widower', was not to be paid on the basis that the partners were not married. The Court of Justice gave one of its more opaque judgments, clearly feeling compelled by *Goodwin* not to dismiss the case outright, but mindful of issuing a wide-ranging and progressive judgment. It held that, 'in principle', Article 141 precludes legislation which prevents a couple from fulfilling the marriage requirement which must be met for one of them to benefit from part of the pay of the other.[189] It then said that it was up to the national court to determine whether a person in KB's situation could rely on Article 141.

What seems clear from this judgment is that the human rights norms at issue in *Goodwin* have been held to infuse the law relating to Article 141, though the extent and scope of such infusion is not clear and is here left to the national court. Had there not been the judgment in *Goodwin*, it is almost inevitable that the case would have been decided differently. The implications of the case do, however, appear to be somewhat limited. In terms of the concept of family and the regulation of intimate relationships, the case is perhaps most significant for the intrusion of human rights norms directly into the Court's jurisprudence and the implicit censure of national legislation which limited the rights of transgendered individuals to marry. Europe-wide this means that legislation which prohibits the marriage of a transgendered person in their chosen gender may fall foul of Article 141. While the Court seeks to steer clear of intruding on the family laws of member states, as stated in *Grant* and reiterated in *KB*, it has done so in as timid a manner as it could. Its effects are also likely to be time-limited: once member states have complied with *Goodwin*, transgendered individuals will be able to marry and therefore avail themselves of benefits linked to marriage.

Missing from the Court's judgment is the type of emphatic statement offered by the English Employment Appeal Tribunal which considered this case. It declared itself exasperated by the nature of the law and employer provisions in

187 Waaldijk, 'Legal Position of Same Sex Partners in Europe', 62.
188 Case C-117/01, *KB* v. *NHS Pensions Service Agency* [2004] 1 CMLR 28.
189 *KB*, para. 36.

situations such as this, and stated that: 'We can think of no good social reason why travel facilities or derived pension benefits should not be available where there is a stable long-term relationship between two unmarried people, whatever the reasons for not being married.'[190] Indeed.

5.5   Conclusions

Amy Elman argues that the 'matrimonial bias' of Union policy reproduces three forms of discrimination: the disadvantages women face under conventional notions of family, the difficulties cohabiting couples face in a system which privileges state-sanctioned unions and the specific hardships facing same-sex couples to whom the protections and privileges of marriage have not been made available.[191] Ultimately, Elman argues that the heterosexism of Union law and policy will be more effectively undermined through its repudiation, rather than through an extension of its privileges to those who can be assimilated to the heterosexual married family.[192] Similarly, Kristen Walker argues that seeking entry into marriage does not 'challenge the economic status quo' and that therefore 'we need to fight more generally for social justice'.[193]

However, while it remains true that there are pressing economic issues which require immediate resolution and that there is a 'matrimonial bias' in Union law, the recognition of diverse relationships and particularly lesbian and gay equality should not need to wait until the halcyon days of economic equality arrive before being extended rights and entitlements on the same basis as heterosexual married couples. It is not likely in the foreseeable future that policy will focus on individuals and move away from its familial bias. More likely and more achievable is a broadening of the concept of family, making it less discriminatory. This should be the immediate focus of law reform strategies, while at the same time heeding the advice of Susan Boyd who demands, at least, that recognition strategies must be accompanied by 'trenchant critiques of the limits of such recognition in delivering a redistribution of economic well-being'.[194]

Important strides forward in recognising non-marital relationships have been made in recent years within Union law and policy. The concept of registered partnership is recognised in a number of measures, as is the comparability principle of *Netherlands* v. *Reed*. The impact of *Goodwin* is such that in *KB* v. *NHS Pensions Agency* the Court of Justice took the important step of declaring national laws

190 *Bavin* v. *NHS Trust Pensions Agency* [1999] ICR 1192, para. 19.
191 Elman, 'The Limits of Citizenship', 731.
192 Elman, 'The Limits of Citizenship', 745. See also Paula Ettelbrick, 'Since When Is Marriage a Path to Liberation?' in Sherman (ed.), *Lesbian and Gay Marriage*, pp. 20–7, quoted in Polikoff, 'Gay and Lesbian Marriage', 1535–6. See also Kristen Walker, 'United Nations Human Rights Law and Same Sex Relationships: Where to from Here?' in Wintemute and Andenas (eds.), *Same Sex Partnerships*, 743–58.
193 Walker, 'United Nations Human Rights Law and Same Sex Relationships', 748 and 751.
194 Boyd, 'Family, Law and Sexuality', 381.

which prohibit transgendered persons from marrying in their chosen sex to be, in principle, in breach of Article 141. However, while these changes are significant, there remains a clear and consistent privileging of heterosexual marriage over other forms of intimate relationship. Neither the Court of Justice nor the Court of Human Rights has yet taken the progressive step forward of the Canadian Supreme Court in interpreting spouse to include same-sex partners.[195] The Supreme Court emphasised the social importance of recognising same-sex relationships, stating that non-recognition 'perpetuates disadvantages suffered by individuals in same sex relationships and contributes to the erasure of their existence'.[196] Most significantly, the Supreme Court went on to say that the 'human dignity of individuals in same sex relationships is violated' by legislation excluding them from its scope.[197]

This is a jurisprudence from which both the Court of Justice and the Court of Human Rights have much to learn. Indeed, the Council of Europe's Parliamentary Assembly recommended in 2000 that its member states review their 'policies in the field of social rights and protection of migrants in order to ensure that homosexual partnership[s] and families are treated on the same basis as heterosexual partnerships and families'; take 'such measures as are necessary to ensure that bi-national lesbian and gay couples are accorded the same residence rights as bi-national heterosexual couples'; and that member states 'adopt legislation which makes provision for registered partnerships'.[198] The European Parliament has been making similar calls since 1994 when it demanded an end to the 'barring of lesbians and homosexual couples from marriage or from an equivalent legal framework'.[199] In 2001, it called on the member states to 'legally recognise same sex marriages', to 'decrease the discrimination between opposite sex marriages and same sex life partners' and to 'introduce legislation which prohibits discrimination for long term co-habitants and provides the same judicial protection as for legally married couples'.[200]

---

195 *M* v. *H* [1999] 2 SCR 3. It was held in this case that lesbian partners could bring themselves within the definition of 'spouse' on the basis of the equality clause of the Canadian Charter of Rights and Freedoms. Although this judgment extended the concept of family, and in particular 'spouse', to include same-sex partnerships, it sustained the functions of relationships akin to marriage and engaged in an exercise seeking to assimilate same-sex partnerships to marriage.

196 *M* v. *H* [1999] 2 SCR 3, paras. 73–4.

197 *M* v. *H* [1999] 2 SCR 3, paras. 73–4.

198 Recommendations 1470 (2000) on the situation of gays and lesbians and their partners in respect of asylum and immigration in the Member States of the Council of Europe and Recommendation 1474 (2000) on the situation of lesbians and gays in the Council of Europe Member States, discussed in Wintemute, 'Strasbourg to the Rescue?', 724–5.

199 European Parliament Resolution on equal rights for homosexuals and lesbians in the European Community, OJ 1994 C 61/40, para. 14.

200 European Parliament, Report on the Situation as Regards Fundamental Rights in the European Union (2000), A5-0223/2001, 21 June 2001, paras. 82–4 (adopted 5 July 2001). These recommendations are similar to those made the previous year in European Parliament, Annual Report on Respect for Human Rights in the European Union (1998–1999), A5-0050/2000, 29 February 2000 (adopted 16 March 2000).

Unfortunately, the Charter of Fundamental Rights has failed to bring about any real change in this area. Indeed, as we saw in *D* v. *Council*, the Charter has been used to entrench the status quo, as a bulwark against further change. The inclusion of provisions on the right to marry and the protection of 'the family' effectively exert priority over the non-discrimination provisions which are rarely acknowledged. Change is most likely to come as a result of pressure from the European Convention as it adapts its case law to reflect changing mores. The Union may prefer not to regulate intimate relationships, but it has no choice, due to its granting of rights to families of migrants, third country nationals, equality laws and now emerging family laws. Thus far, it has shown itself to be singularly lacking in any institutional imagination and has instead opted at all times for the lowest common denominator. There are signs of change; the picture is much brighter than a few years ago. But there remains a long way to go until the non-discrimination provisions of the Charter are put into practice and until the principles of value pluralism underpin the regulation of intimate relationships.

6

The emergence of a European Union family law

In 2000, the European Union adopted its first measure in the field of family law. This was an historic moment. The European Union had crossed the Rubicon: a legal measure had been adopted in a field of law so precious to individuals, families, politicians and so significant in terms of national power and sovereignty. Yet there was no fanfare, nor public protest. Indeed, hardly anyone knew this had happened, even family lawyers. This probably remains the case, even amongst scholars of European Union law. Why? This was because Regulation 1347/2000 on the recognition and enforcement of judgments in matrimonial matters[1] had been adopted as part of a raft of measures designed to facilitate 'judicial co-operation' between states in an effort to create an 'area of freedom, justice and security'. It sounds as anodyne as it was portrayed. While the focus – the fanfares and the protests – are on the immigration and asylum measures of the area of freedom, justice and security, the supposedly more technical field of judicial co-operation gets little attention.[2] This is a terrible error.

The adoption of the Regulation, known as Brussels II, was only the first of a number of family law measures, and for some it represents the first step towards a harmonised or even unified family law for the member states of the European Union. The fact that such developments are proceeding largely unnoticed, not just by the European public, but by legal scholars of national family law and European Union law, is tremendously disturbing. European Union action in this field of law raises crucial questions about the nature of the Union, its future form and scope, the reach of national sovereignty, methods of law-making and many more general issues. In addition, of course, there are many doubts about the nature of the family law being promulgated, the concept of family on which it

---

1 OJ 2000 L 160/19 (repealed by Regulation 2201/2003).
2 For a similar argument that proposals for the codification of contract law have been sheltered from political and media interest due to their characterisation as a technical field of Community law, see Study Group on Social Justice in European Private Law, 'Social Justice in European Contract Law: A Manifesto' (2004) 10 *European Law Journal* 653–74. In the case of contract law, the Commission's communication on this subject talked of 'non-sector-specific measures', which, translated, means a code of private law: European Commission, A More Coherent European Contract Law: An Action Plan, COM (2003) 68 final, para. 92.

relies, its lack of respect for diversity and the ultimate endeavour to harmonise European family laws.

This chapter considers the background to the development of Union activity in this field and interrogates the justifications for such action. It also considers the detail of the legislation thus far adopted and examines the more immediate proposals for the future. The following chapter examines the long-term prospects for further development of family law in the Union.

6.1   First steps: the development of a Community family policy

While families were mentioned in the free movement regulations adopted in the 1960s, it was not until the 1980s that the Community began to pinpoint 'family policy' as a distinct focus for policy action.[3] Thus, in 1983 the European Parliament adopted a resolution advocating the adoption of a 'comprehensive family policy'[4] which was to be developed by encouraging member states to take account of the needs of families when introducing legislation and, where appropriate, harmonising policies at Community level. Furthermore, the Parliament recommended, where appropriate, harmonisation of all policies relating to the family, and highlighted the need for further research to determine the need for Community action relating to the *laws* on adoption, custody of children, rights of access to children and maintenance obligations.[5]

The Commission largely endorsed the approach of the Parliament in its Communication on a Community family policy,[6] which was followed by a Council resolution on the same theme.[7] The resolution of the Council was considerably more limited than the proposals of the Parliament and the Commission, recommending only that the exchange of information regarding family policies be strengthened and that the 'family dimension' should be taken into account when adopting policy. While these resolutions were vague, and had a somewhat limited effect in practice, they remain symbolic in terms of their early recognition that the 'family', and the intimate relationships of all individuals, both have an impact on, and are affected by, Union activity. In addition, they gave a foretaste of what was to come, not least the Parliament's interest in the harmonisation of family laws. Finally, the adoption of a 'Community family policy' strengthened the legitimacy of Community action regarding families, beyond the limited policy field of free movement, to encompass the 'family' impact of all Community activities.

---

3 For a discussion of the concept of 'family policy' and analysis of the different policies of the member states, see Linda Hantrais, *Family Policy Matters: Responding to Family Change in Europe* (Bristol: Policy Press, 2004).

4 Resolution on Family Policy in the EEC, OJ 1983 C 184/116.

5 Emphasis added. Resolution on Family Policy in the EEC, OJ 1983 C 184/116.

6 Communication from the Commission on Family Policies, COM (89) 363 final.

7 Conclusions of the Council and of the ministers responsible for family affairs meeting within the Council of 29 September 1989 regarding family policies, OJ 1989 C 277/2.

While this 'Community family policy' declared its commitment to the welfare and concerns of families, further justifications for Community action were advanced. These further justifications raise the first questions about the motives of Community institutions for the development of, in this instance, family policy and later family law. In essence, the Community family policy is clearly instrumental to other, perhaps more dominant, aims and objectives of the Community and its institutions.

The Commission's interest in family policy appeared to spring largely from its anxiety about the changing demographic situation in Europe, in particular decreasing fertility rates and the problems this poses for the 'labour market', 'social security systems' and the 'realisation of the single market'.[8] In addition, the Commission argued that 'the family' is important for the future of European society as it is 'part of the economic sector, for it raises future producers and is a unit of consumption'.[9] For these (largely economic) reasons, Community-level action regarding 'the family' was deemed necessary. National-level action is apparently insufficient as it is 'relatively slow in adapting to the pace of change' in this area.[10]

The Council was similarly concerned with the 'demographic outlook' which raised no less than the 'question of Europe's political, economic and cultural future in the world'.[11] In addition, the Council endorsed the Commission's justification for Community action as springing from the 'economic role of the family', as well as its role in the care of children and 'solidarity between the generations'.[12] The concerns here are evident enough. Too few 'Europeans' are being produced in order to care for the growing elderly population, to act as consumers in the single market and to ensure the future of Europe as a politically and economically viable polity.

The Parliament reiterated its call for an 'integrated family policy' in 1994, this time stressing the need to 'adapt family *law*', at both national and European levels.[13] Most recently, in 1999, the Parliament targeted its proposals towards the need for a family policy on cross-border disputes. It demanded a 'co-ordinated mechanism among our European countries in the area of family law in order to avoid penalising children in the event of divorce between partners of different nationalities'.[14] Two features of these resolutions are particularly illuminating. First is the revelation of the extent to which the jurisdiction of the Community in the family *law* field is considered legitimate and, secondly, the integrationist turn

---

8 Communication from the Commission on Family Policies, COM (89) 363 final, para. 29.
9 *Ibid.*, para. 37.
10 *Ibid.*, para. 43.
11 Conclusions of the Council and of the ministers responsible for family affairs meeting within the Council of 29 September 1989 regarding family policies, OJ 1989 C 277/2.
12 *Ibid.*
13 Resolution on protection of families and family units at the close of the International Year of the Family, OJ 1995 C 18/96, emphasis added.
14 Resolution on the protection of families and children, OJ 1999 C 128/79.

of the Parliament's recommendations should be noted, particularly the considerable emphasis on future harmonisation of laws in this field.

The adoption of a family policy for the Community, now Union, sends mixed messages. While it is to be welcomed that the Community recognised the impact of its policies on families, and legitimated action relating to families as early as the 1980s, few steps were taken to give effect to these concerns. Thus, the resolutions and sentiments expressed were largely symbolic. However, while being welcomed, the family policy also raises considerable concerns, particularly in relation to the justifications offered for Community action. This is a point to which I will return when considering the development of a European family law. Suffice it to say here that the impression gleaned is that a family policy may be a useful vehicle for raising and potentially resolving very different economic and political issues from those of the needs and interests of families.

6.2   From family policy to family law: the Brussels Convention and the Treaty of Maastricht

While the Community institutions were debating the development of a family policy, there did already exist one measure of Community law which had a family law dimension, namely the Brussels Convention on the Jurisdiction and Enforcement of Judgments in Civil and Commercial Matters.[15] This Convention, now known as Brussels I, expressly excludes matters relating to the 'status or legal capacity of natural persons' or 'rights in property arising out of a matrimonial relationship', but does cover maintenance agreements.[16] Thus, in general, family law matters are excluded. The explanatory report to the original Convention recorded that family matters were so excluded due to the considerable 'disparity' in the laws of the member states, with the effect that agreement on common jurisdictional rules would have been extremely difficult.[17] In addition, as Paul Beaumont and Gordon Moir have noted, it is also likely that these matters were excluded because the then EEC was not seen as a 'body aimed directly at the regulation of family law matters'.[18] Nonetheless, it must not be forgotten that, in this small area of family disputes, the Community already had a foothold.

Despite this foothold, however, further action in the family law field was not contemplated until the 1990s and the creation of the European Union. The Maastricht Treaty created the conditions for deeper integration within Europe and, in the family law area specifically, it ushered in a new era of intergovernmental

---

15 Convention on jurisdiction and the enforcement of judgments in civil and commercial matters (consolidated version) (the Brussels I Convention) OJ 1990 C 189/2.

16 Article 1 of the Brussels I Convention, OJ 1990 C 189/2.

17 Jenard Report, OJ 1979 C 59, at p. 10, quoted in Paul Beaumont and Gordon Moir, 'Brussels Convention II: A New Private International Law Instrument in Family Matters for the European Union or European Community?' (1995) 20 *European Law Review* 268–88 at 270.

18 Beaumont and Moir, 'Brussels Convention II', 270.

co-operation beyond the single market. Power was granted to the Union to take action in the field of 'judicial co-operation' in civil and criminal matters.[19] Translated, this meant further co-operation and possible measures in the field of private international law, building on the Brussels Convention.

As a result, at the end of 1993, following discussions between the member states, the German government proposed the adoption of a new convention, extending the scope of the Brussels Convention, to cover marriage, divorce and separation.[20] It seemed that so-called 'limping marriages', where divorces and related orders are not recognised by other states, were causing concern, particularly in France and Germany.[21] The new provisions of the Maastricht Treaty provided a means for the Union to take action in this sphere and reduce the individual hardship which such cases undoubtedly cause.

However, despite the obvious personal anguish of such 'limping marriages', the political dimension to this initiative must be emphasised. Action in the family field constituted a powerful signal that the creation of a European Union did indeed mean more than just an economic union. Indeed, the problems of 'limping marriages' could easily have been resolved had France and Germany ratified the 1970 Hague Convention on the Recognition of Divorces and Legal Separations.[22] The Hague Convention not only provides a potentially global solution to the problems under discussion, rather than being limited to the member states of the Union, but it was already in existence, in force in many countries and ready to be ratified. But some member states lack commitment to the Hague Conference with Community/Union solutions being preferred, as was clearly the case here.[23]

After many years of negotiations, a Convention on Jurisdiction and the Recognition and Enforcement of Judgments in Matrimonial Matters was finally agreed.[24] The Convention applied to civil proceedings relating to divorce, legal separation, marriage annulment and to disputes regarding parental responsibility

---

19 Title VI of the Treaty on European Union (Maastricht), Provisions on Co-operation in the Fields of Justice and Home Affairs, included as matters of common interest, 'judicial co-operation in civil and criminal matters', Article K.1, OJ 1992 C 191.

20 Peter McEleavy, 'The Brussels II Regulation: How the European Community Has Moved into Family Law' (2002) 51 *International and Comparative Law Quarterly* 883–908 at 889–90.

21 Paul Beaumont and Gordon Moir indicate that the issue of recognition of divorce was the major concern of the German government after the judgment in Case 145/86, *Hoffmann* v. *Krieg* [1988] ECR 645 which highlighted the problems caused by a Dutch divorce not being recognised in Germany: Beaumont and Moir, 'Brussels Convention II', 269.

22 1970 Hague Convention on the Recognition of Divorces and Legal Separations, 11th Session of the Hague Conference on Private International Law, 1 June 1970, in force 24 August 1975; see McEleavy, 'The Brussels II Regulation', 888.

23 Other political motives were also in operation. Peter McEleavy suggests that the then UK government supported the adoption of the Convention as it wished to see the intergovernmental third pillar succeed, hopefully foreclosing Communitarisation at a later stage: McEleavy, 'The Brussels II Regulation'.

24 Council Act of 28 May 1998 drawing up the Convention on Jurisdiction and the Recognition and Enforcement of Judgments in Matrimonial Matters, OJ 1998 C 221/1.

for the children of both spouses and provided for the recognition and enforcement of such judgments. One of the major issues for debate, and the cause of the delay from the original proposal, was whether to include matters relating to children.[25] Some member states argued that not to do so might lead to unnecessary complications if litigation had to be divided up into different substantive issues. Other member states, including the UK, argued that there was no evidence that there were problems relating to child custody arrangements, that there was already a Hague Convention covering such matters which was being updated and that to include the ongoing issue of custody may lead to fewer ratifications of the final convention. The majority in favour of including custody arrangements was victorious and custody issues, at least those decided at the time of the divorce/separation and which related to the children of both spouses, were included in the Convention.

Peter McEleavy has suggested that there was little to be gained by the Union acting in the child custody field.[26] Not only was there a Hague Convention which would have solved the problems of 'limping marriages', but the Hague Conference was also negotiating a new convention which culminated in the 1996 Hague Protection of Children Convention.[27] This Convention could have provided a complete solution to private international law issues affecting children and was potentially worldwide in its scope. Contrast this with the limited scope of the Union convention and to the few countries to which it would apply and it is clear that there were other, political, agendas at work. It was suggested above that the desire to see the Union succeed, as a political and not just economic enterprise, was strong. Peter McEleavy suggests further that this was also an example of the 'Community staking a claim to this area, possibly for internal political motives and for reasons of future external competence'.[28]

Further rationales were offered for the Union entering into the family law arena in the Explanatory Report to the Convention (the Borrás Report).[29] The Borrás Report stated that European 'integration is now no longer purely economic and is coming to have an increasingly profound effect on the life of the European citizen'.[30] The idea of Union citizenship had also only just been introduced by the Maastricht Treaty. However, its limited and exclusionary scope was and continues to be roundly criticised. It seems that it was thought that the grant

---

25 McEleavy, 'The Brussels II Regulation', 892–4.
26 McEleavy, 'The Brussels II Regulation', 893.
27 1996 Hague Convention on Jurisdiction, Applicable Law, Recognition, Enforcement and Co-
    operation in Respect of Parental Responsibility and Measures for the Protection of Children,
    18th Session of the Hague Conference on Private International Law, 19 October 1996, in force 1
    January 2002.
28 McEleavy, 'The Brussels II Regulation', 894.
29 Explanatory Report on the Convention on Jurisdiction and the Recognition and Enforcement of
    Judgments in Matrimonial Matters prepared by Dr Alegría Borrás, Professor of Private Inter-
    national Law, University of Barcelona (the 'Borrás Report'), OJ 1998 C 221/27.
30 Borrás Report, OJ 1998 C 221/27, para. 1.

of family rights from the Union would strengthen a concept of Union citizenship. Accordingly, the report continued, 'family law therefore has to be faced as part of the phenomenon of European integration.'[31]

The adoption of this Convention was remarkable. Here was the Union adopting a measure in the family law arena, albeit in relation to the private international law of the family. Family law matters had hitherto been expressly excluded from Community/Union competence, but now, through the backdoor of 'judicial co-operation', the first steps were being taken towards a family law for the Union. But what is also striking is the political agenda at work. Arguably, the personal concerns of individuals who were suffering at the lack of agreement between states regarding cross-national family matters was not high on the member states' agendas. The Convention, as with the earlier Community family policy, could be seen as instrumental to wider political demands; for the Union to succeed, for intergovernmentalism to flourish, for Union citizenship to feel real and valuable. There were no empirical studies highlighting either the need for action, or the appropriate form of such action. There was little consultation beyond the corridors of the Union bureaucracy. There was little external knowledge and understanding of the momentous nature of this measure.

Nonetheless, the agreement remained in the form of a Convention between the member states, rather than a form of Community law. This left the discretion to member states as to whether and when to adopt the Convention into national law. Thus, although the measure had been adopted under the auspices of the Union, it remained a form of law outside of the traditional Community law structure. All this was, however, to change with the adoption of the Treaty of Amsterdam.

6.3   The Communitarisation of family law

There was no reference to family law in the Treaty of Amsterdam. Nonetheless, it was this Treaty which provided *Community* competence to adopt measures in the area of private international family law. In detail, the Treaty of Amsterdam committed the Union to the objective of maintaining and developing the Union as an 'area of freedom, security and justice.'[32] The legal competence to meet this objective was included in the EC Treaty, with Article 61 providing that, in order to 'establish progressively an area of freedom, security and justice', the Council shall take measures in the field of judicial co-operation in civil matters as further detailed in Article 65 of the EC Treaty. Article 65 of the EC Treaty provides that measures in the field of judicial co-operation, which have 'cross-border implications' and which are 'necessary for the proper functioning of the internal market', shall include, inter alia, the 'recognition and enforcement of decisions in civil and

---

31 Borrás Report, OJ 1998 C 221/27, para. 1.
32 Article 2 of the Treaty on European Union commits the member states to the objective of maintaining and developing the Union as an area of freedom, security and justice.

commercial cases', promoting the compatibility of the rules concerning conflicts of laws and eliminating obstacles to the 'good functioning' of civil proceedings.[33]

It was certainly not immediately clear that Article 65 of the EC Treaty would provide the legal basis to transfer the Matrimonial Convention into a Community regulation, especially as any such measures had to be necessary for the proper functioning of the internal market.[34] Indeed, one commentator considered that Article 65 of the EC Treaty would be unlikely to provide competence for the transfer of even Brussels I, on civil and commercial matters, to a Community regulation.[35] Others thought differently, considering the criteria general in nature which gave the Council a 'certain level of discretion' in their interpretation.[36] It was the latter approach which was ultimately successful.

While Article 65 of the EC Treaty provided the technical competence for the transfer of the Matrimonial Convention into Community law, it was the political impetus to the project of creating the 'European judicial area' which ensured that this was to become a focus of attention and action. The European Council stated in 1999 that the realisation of the 'European judicial area' was at the 'very top of the political agenda'.[37] This is a project, it proclaimed, which 'responds to the frequently expressed concerns of citizens and has a direct bearing on their daily lives'. A 'shared area of prosperity and peace' was the expressed aim, building on the already 'firm commitment to freedom based on human rights, democratic institutions and the rule of law'. The enjoyment of 'freedom' required a 'genuine area of justice, where people can approach courts and authorities in any Member State as easily as in their own'. Thus, in the European judicial area, 'individuals and businesses should not be prevented or discouraged from exercising their rights by the incompatibility or complexity of legal and administrative systems in the Member States', and this may require '[b]etter compatibility and convergence between the legal systems of Member States'.[38] In addition, the Council stated that there was a need for 'special common procedural rules for simplified and accelerated cross-border litigation',[39] as well as common rules

---

33 The legislative method for adopting measures under Article 65 of the EC Treaty is detailed in Article 67 of the EC Treaty which provides for unanimity for an initial period of five years, followed by the co-decision procedure.

34 See the discussion in McEleavy, 'The Brussels II Regulation', 896–8. See also Paul Beaumont, 'European Court of Justice and Jurisdiction and Enforcement of Judgments in Civil and Commercial Matters' (1999) 48 *International and Comparative Law Quarterly* 223–9 at 227.

35 Jorg Monar, 'Justice and Home Affairs in the Treaty of Amsterdam: Reform at the Price of Fragmentation' (1998) 23 *European Law Review* 320–35 at 324.

36 Mario Tenreiro and Monika Ekström, 'Unification of Private International Law in Family Matters within the European Union' in Katharina Boele-Woelki (ed.), *Perspectives for the Unification and Harmonisation of Family Law in Europe* (Antwerp: Intersentia, 2003), pp. 185–93 at pp. 186–7. The authors are members of the Commission, though writing in their personal capacities.

37 Presidency Conclusions, Tampere European Council, 15–16 October 1999, 16 October 1999, para. 5.

38 *Ibid.*, para. 5.

39 *Ibid.*, para. 30.

granting 'enhanced access to law', including the taking of evidence, time limits and orders for money payment.[40] The particular focus of these ambitions, in substantive law terms, was greater harmonisation in the criminal law field and in the development of common rules of asylum and immigration. In addition, however, one of the fields in which new common procedural rules were thought to be necessary was in the area of maintenance claims.[41] Further, the Council envisaged that some decisions in the field of 'family litigation', including 'maintenance claims and visiting rights', should automatically be recognised in all member states without the need for further legal proceedings.

The political impetus behind the establishment of the area of freedom, justice and security can perhaps best be viewed as akin to a new 'internal market' project.[42] Just as in advance of 1992 there was immense political activity in favour of 'completing' the internal market and a concerted drive to make it work, for it to be a beacon for a developing Community, so the area of freedom, justice and security is perceived as signifying a new ever closer political union, which has moved beyond the singular demands of the market.

6.4   Brussels II: the birth of Community family law

These changes in the Amsterdam Treaty were acted on with relative speed, to the considerable surprise of both family law and Community law specialists. Thus, in 2000, the Community adopted a Regulation on jurisdiction and recognition and enforcement of judgments in matrimonial matters and in matters of parental responsibility for children of both spouses.[43] This Regulation transformed the Matrimonial Convention, adopted under the Maastricht Treaty, into a binding Community measure and represented a significant expansion in the scope of the Community's activities. Indeed, this Regulation, known as Brussels II, was communitarised *before* Brussels I, which deals with the bread and butter issues of the Community, civil and commercial matters.[44]

---

40 *Ibid.*, para. 38.
41 *Ibid.*, para. 30.
42 See Jo Shaw, 'Process and Constitutional Discourse in the European Union' (2000) 27 *Journal of Law and Society* 4–37 at 13. See also the Commission Communication 2004 at 17, which states that, in developing the establishment of an area of freedom, justice and security, the Union 'must continue to show the same degree of ambition and determination as it did for the completion of the internal market'.
43 Council Regulation 1347/2000/EC, OJ 2000 L 160/19.
44 The Brussels Convention was transposed into a Community Regulation by the end of 2000 and retains the scope of the original convention, thus excluding family law matters except as regards maintenance: Council Regulation 44/2001/EC of 22 December 2000 on jurisdiction and the recognition and enforcement of judgments in civil and commercial matters, OJ 2001 L 12/1, which entered into force on 1 March 2002. The Regulation does not apply to Denmark. For a detailed discussion, see Helen Stalford, 'Old Problems, New Solutions? – EU Regulation of Cross-National Child Maintenance' (2003) 15 *Child and Family Law Quarterly* 269–78 at 277, who notes that the Communitarisation of Brussels I did include some changes in respect of maintenance payments, not all of which were welcome. Stalford comments that the 'economic-

Accordingly, in relation to both Brussels I and the Matrimonial Convention, what was once private international law now became Community law. It must be remembered that transposition into a Community measure came with the consequent implications for the supremacy of Community law, the reduced power of amendment, the impossibility of derogation, and overview by the Court of Justice; whereas the Maastricht Treaty had been limited to intergovernmental co-operation. Thus, whereas Brussels I and the Matrimonial Convention were adopted and proposed as *conventions*, in the sense that they were international agreements between the member states which happened to be regulated by the Court of Justice, they were now binding *Community* measures.

Brussels II came into force on 1 March 2001, and introduced uniform standards for jurisdiction on annulment, divorce and separation, and aimed to facilitate the rapid and automatic recognition among member states of judgments on these issues. It also provided for uniform rules of jurisdiction regarding parental responsibility for joint children and the recognition and enforcement of judgments relating thereto.[45] To a certain extent, the scope of Brussels II is limited. It covers only proceedings relating to the end of the marriage tie and not to ancillary matters such as the division of property or maintenance. Nor does it encompass grounds for divorce or findings of fault. Equally, it only deals with a small number of proceedings relating to parental responsibility, namely only those arising at the time of the proceedings to end the marriage and only those matters relating to the children of both spouses. But even this limited scope gives rise to considerable questions about the reasons behind its adoption, its scope, its technical provisions and its future impact.

Perhaps the first question to ask in relation to Brussels II is why it was ever enacted? Was the Union really the body best placed to adopt measures in this area? Arguably, it was not. The Community is not the only institution which has the power and desire to introduce rules for the more harmonious settlement of international disputes. The Hague Conference on private international law has, since 1893, been promulgating rules to unify conflicts of laws.[46] And, indeed, in the field of activity of Brussels II, there were already Hague conventions operating.[47] It was noted above that the problems of 'limping marriages', which the original Matrimonial Convention and now Brussels II were designed to prevent, could have been solved by the ratification of the Hague Convention on the

---

ally driven' nature of Brussels I is inappropriate to matters of child maintenance and has resulted in the Convention being 'haphazardly' adapted to accommodate such an important and litigious area of family law.

45 For a detailed discussion of Brussels II, see Helen Stalford, 'Regulating Family Life in Post-Amsterdam Europe' (2003) 28 *European Law Review* 39–52; and McEleavy, 'The Brussels II Regulation'.

46 Maarit Jänterä-Jareborg, 'Unification of International Family Law in Europe – A Critical Perspective' in Boele-Woelki (ed.), *Unification and Harmonisation of Family Law*, pp. 194–216 at pp. 198–9.

47 Jänterä-Jareborg, 'Unification of International Family Law in Europe', 200–1.

Recognition of Divorces and Legal Separations.[48] Further, the French–Spanish proposal to include questions of parental responsibility within the original Convention proposal pre-Amsterdam had been opposed by other member states[49] on the basis that the Hague Conference had already adopted several measures in this area.

Hence, there was in practice no need for a separate Community measure. Furthermore, Community action actually creates a number of anomalies and disadvantages. The benefits of the Hague conventions are that they provide potentially global solutions, rather than ones limited to the member states of the Union (with the exception of Denmark). Cross-border disputes do not just arise within the Community and in respect of Community nationals. Community nationals live all over the world; millions of third country nationals live within the member states. Accordingly, the 'best' solution would be one which would apply to all individuals. Subsidiarity gets a casual reference in Brussels II and the appropriate box is ticked. But, when there is a potentially global solution on offer through the Hague Conference, it is arguable that the principle of subsidiarity would suggest that the measure is better dealt with outside the Community, at a higher level. Furthermore, as Helen Stalford argues, part of the definition of subsidiarity is that the Community shall not go beyond what is necessary to achieve the objectives of the Treaty and it is questionable whether this measure is really necessary to achieve those objectives.[50]

Peter McEleavy raises additional concerns about the policy development and legislative processes involved in the adoption of Union family law measures, compared with the Hague Conference, and not surprisingly finding the Union wanting.[51] The democratic deficit and the lack of transparency within the Union are long-standing concerns.[52] Nonetheless, in a field of policy which is new to the Union, such as family law, and therefore in relation to which one might expect the highest levels of debate, consideration and reflection, these familiar failings of the legislative processes are rightly highlighted anew.[53] This is a point endorsed

---

48 McEleavy, 'The Brussels II Regulation', 888.
49 Principally the Nordic member states and the UK.
50 Stalford, 'Regulating Family Life in Post-Amsterdam Europe', 50–1. By contrast, Commissioner Vitorino has stated that harmonisation of private international law necessarily respects the principles of proportionality and subsidiarity, as it leaves the substantive laws of member states intact, as discussed in Oliver Remien, 'European Private International Law, the European Community and Its Emerging Area of Freedom, Justice and Security' (2001) 38 *Common Market Law Review* 53–86 at 64.
51 Peter McEleavy, 'First Steps in the Communitarisation of Family Law: Too Much Haste, Too Little Reflection?' in Boele-Woelki (ed.), *Unification and Harmonisation of Family Law*, pp. 509–26.
52 McEleavy notes in particular that the introduction of various of the Brussels II*bis* (see further below) proposals are 'shrouded in a high degree of secrecy' and moreover there are no minutes of relevant meetings to facilitate understanding: McEleavy, 'First Steps in the Communitarisation of Family Law', 518.
53 For a similar concern that the development of proposals to codify European private law is taking a largely technocratic approach, thus ignoring the need for democratic participation in these

by Maarit Jänterä-Jareborg who finds serious faults not just in the choice of topics for Union activity, but also in how the new rules are being organised and carried out.[54]

Ultimately, however, the Hague conventions were not seen as viable options by some Member States which lack commitment to the Hague Conference and which were instead determined to develop Community competence in this field. Some justifications for Union action were set out in the original explanatory memorandum to the Matrimonial Convention. This memorandum set the proposed convention very clearly within the framework of the continuing integration of the Union:[55] family law was seen as the next, logical, step forward in the onward march towards an ever closer Union.

Further, more specific, justifications were offered for the adoption of the Brussels II Regulation, but they too were generally weak and unconvincing.[56] Brussels II was adopted on the basis of Article 65 of the EC Treaty which is in the title of the treaty relating to common immigration policies and free movement of persons and enables measures to be taken promoting 'compatibility of the rules of conflicts of law and jurisdiction' which are 'necessary for the proper functioning of the internal market'. Not surprisingly, therefore, the Preamble to the Regulation stated that it was necessary in order to ensure the 'sound operation of the internal market' which created a need to 'unify the rules of conflict of jurisdiction in matrimonial matters and in matters of parental responsibility'.[57] Furthermore, it is stated that the 'proper functioning of the internal market' entailed the need to improve and simplify the 'free movement of judgments in civil matters'.[58]

However, these purported justifications are in fact mere assertions and fail to explain why the 'sound operation' of the internal market requires uniform rules relating to the dissolution of marriage and child custody judgments. The only possible explanation offered is that the present rules 'hamper the free movement of persons', though there is no explanation as to how or why this might be the case.[59] For example, no empirical evidence supporting such an assertion is offered by the Commission in its initial proposal.[60] Moreover, although it is plausible that a divergence in conflicts of law rules may prevent some individuals from

---

developments, see Martijn Hesselink, 'The Politics of a European Civil Code' (2004) 10 *European Law Journal* 675–97.

54 Jänterä-Jareborg, 'Unification of International Family Law in Europe', 211.

55 Borrás Report, OJ 1998 C 221/27.

56 See further Haimo Schack, 'The New International Procedure in Matrimonial Matters in Europe' (2002) 4 *European Journal of Law Reform* 37–56.

57 Preamble (para. 4) to Council Regulation 1347/2000/EC, OJ 2000 No. L160/19.

58 *Ibid.*, Preamble, para. 2.

59 *Ibid.*, Preamble, para. 4.

60 The research on which the measures are based appears to be largely based on comparative studies of national family laws, rather than on the experiences of those in cross-border family relationships. Helen Stalford has criticised the lack of empirical evidence supporting the need for the Union to engage in these family law issues: Helen Stalford, 'Brussels II and Beyond: A Better

exercising their free movement rights, can it really be said that Community rules are 'necessary' for the proper functioning of the single market? In support, Beaumont and Moir have argued that '[d]iscrepancies in the status of a person within the Member States can have implications for that person's freedom of movement within the Community', though notably they do not suggest that harmonisation of family laws, not even of private international family law, is necessarily the appropriate way to resolve these potential problems.[61] Peter McEleavy suggests that the best that can be said for the justifications is that they were based on a 'singularly creative interpretation which is intended to mould the legal basis to facilitate the desired result'.[62]

Related to the free movement justifications, the Commission suggested that the regulation would represent a 'fundamental stage' in the development of the 'European judicial area'.[63] This may indeed be so, but again did not provide an adequate justification as to why this measure in particular should have been adopted, beyond the assumption that the development of the European judicial area is axiomatically a good thing. In a similar vein, the Commission stated that the introduction of European citizenship requires 'additional work to be carried out in respect of certain aspects of the citizens' family life'.[64] In this way, regulation of private international family law is considered important not for the purpose of achieving more efficient or equitable resolution of cross-border disputes, but for the development of the concept of European citizenship. Related to the idea of Union citizenship is the perceived need to engender a 'European identity'. This is supported by Katharina Boele-Woelki who suggests that the divergences in family laws of the member states of the EU 'forms a serious impediment to attaining an actual European identity'.[65] It is not clear how such measures are to create a sense of European identity. Indeed, it is perhaps the very hierarchical, top-down nature of the imposition of common rules which may have the opposite effect. As Jo Shaw notes, debates about the constitution and governance of Europe are having to respond to the 'rise of identity politics and the idea of constitutionalism from the "bottom-up" driven by struggles for recognition and claim making, rather than elite conceptions of the nature of the polity'.[66] Jürgen Habermas also sees the need for a new European identity, but this is a 'participatory' and 'deliberative' democracy which requires citizens not just to vote but to be active participants.[67]

Deal for Children in the EU?' in Boele-Woelki (ed.), *Unification and Harmonisation of Family Law*, pp. 471–88 at p. 482.
61 Beaumont and Moir, 'Brussels Convention II', 276.
62 McEleavy, 'The Brussels II Regulation', 898.
63 Explanatory Memorandum, COM (99) 220, at para. 1.1.
64 *Ibid.*, para. 1.2.
65 Katharina Boele-Woelki, 'The Road Towards a European Family Law' (1997) 1 *Electronic Journal of Comparative Law*, available at http://www.ejcl.org/11/art11-1.html.
66 Shaw, 'Process and Constitutional Discourse', 6.
67 Jürgen Habermas, *Between Facts and Norms: Contributions to a Discourse Theory of Law and Democracy* (Cambridge: Polity Press, 1996), p. 25.

What was striking about all these purported justifications was their conse-quentialist nature. The measures were justified, not in order to eradicate perceived problems regarding the enforcement and recognition of divorce and child custody arrangements, but in order to promote other goals such as European integration, the creation of a common judicial area, the operation of the single market and the development of European citizenship.[68]

Such criticisms of Brussels II might have been immaterial were the provisions enacted appropriate, useful and effective. Maarit Jänterä-Jareborg has argued that Brussels II did bring some improvements on a general level in respect of matri-monial proceedings.[69] For example, Brussels II set aside exorbitant rules on jurisdiction and prevents concurrent divorce proceedings from taking place in different member states. Also, judgments dissolving a marriage are now valid in all member states. However, for her, the advantages are outweighed by the disadvantages. In particular, the inclusion of parental responsibility was a 'mis-take'.[70] She also details the considerable problems in relation to the enforcement of judgments once they are recognised that will remain.[71]

Peter McEleavy has argued that flexibility was sacrificed in favour of certainty which, while having benefits, may encourage pre-emptive litigation.[72] In a field of law and policy in which trepidation, time for reflection and alternative forms of dispute resolution are all encouraged, this encouragement of haste is regrettable.[73] Nigel Lowe shares such misgivings, together with concerns relating to the choice of jurisdictional rules as opposed to a clear hierarchy, the reference to nationality as a connecting factor and the lack of possibility for declining jurisdiction in favour of a more appropriate forum.[74]

A further concern relates to the role, or rather likely lack of role, for the European Court of Justice. By Article 68 of the EC Treaty only courts of last resort may make references to the Court of Justice in relation to measures under this title, thus including Brussels II. There is no rational reason for this provision. It simply reflects a political compromise to limit the power of the Court of Justice in sensitive asylum and immigration issues (also covered by this title) and an aim to 'protect' the Court from excessive numbers of references. So, again, in the family law arena, the principles which should be applied when legislating, are

---

68 This is perhaps due to the fact that the legal basis demands such justifications. However, this simply serves to demonstrate that 'family law' proper does not clearly fall within the competence of the EU, but has to be implied from other legal bases.

69 Jänterä-Jareborg, 'Unification of International Family Law in Europe', p. 202.

70 *Ibid.*, p. 202.

71 *Ibid.*, 202–4.

72 McEleavy, 'The Brussels II Regulation', 887.

73 For similar concerns, though not specifically regarding this provision, see Nigel Lowe, in 'The Growing Influence of the European Union on International Family Law – A View from the Boundary' (2003) 56 *Current Legal Problems* 439–80.

74 Nigel Lowe, 'New International Conventions Affecting the Law Relating to Children – A Cause for Concern?' (2001) *International Family Law Journal* 171–81 at 174–5.

ignored in favour of the familiar, though lamentable, Union political compromises. In relation to family law, this limit on references will mean that few cases will come before the Court. In some ways this negates one of the justifications for Union action in this field which was based on the credit which the Court of Justice has rightly obtained for ensuring the uniform and smooth operation of Brussels I. If cases rarely reach the Court of Justice, there will be little room for common principles and interpretations to be laid down. Furthermore, requiring references from only the court of last resort will lead to inordinate delays in cases which in the field of family law, especially cases regarding children, is potentially very damaging.[75]

Perhaps the most important criticism of Brussels II was the limited scope of the rights of children. The personal scope of the Brussels II Regulation,[76] being limited to biological or adopted children of the married couple seeking divorce, annulment or legal separation, denied any protection to step-children or the children of unmarried parents. Indeed, there were only two references to children in the entire Regulation. Article 3(2)(b) provided that the child's best interests will be taken into consideration in determining which jurisdiction is competent to decide on matters of parental responsibility. The only other reference was in Article 15(2) which sets out the grounds for non-recognition of a parental responsibility order between member states: '(a) ... such recognition is manifestly contrary to the public policy of the Member State in which recognition is sought taking into account the best interests of the child' and '(b) ... except in the case of emergency, without the child having been given the opportunity to be heard, in violation of fundamental principles of procedure of the Member State in which recognition is sought'.

Helen Stalford concludes that the lack of primacy accorded to the interests of the child in Brussels I[77] and II means that the European family law to have emerged thus far is 'firmly entrenched in the traditional notion that divorce is primarily concerned with regulating the lives of adults and of only incidental importance to the child'.[78] This contrasts with more modern approaches in which the ongoing relationship between the parents and child is prioritised. Ultimately, the child's status is conflated with that of the family and thus the regulations are based on an assumption that the interests of the child and parents are coterminous. Thus, the Regulation not only 'disregards the symbolic importance of

---

75 Nigel Lowe suggests that an expedited version of Article 234 should be established to deal with family law references and that specialist panels of the Court of First Instance, if it is to hear Article 234 references, be established: Lowe, 'The Growing Influence of the European Union on International Family Law'.

76 Regulation 1347/2000/EC, OJ 2000 L 160/19.

77 Specific provisions relating to the rights and interests of children remain absent from Brussels I. Although this reflects the original Convention, the adoption of that Convention in the form of a Regulation provided the opportunity to consider the interests and rights of children. See further Stalford, 'Brussels II and Beyond', 475.

78 Ibid., 475.

acknowledging that children do indeed represent a distinct category of citizens with an independent voice and differing needs', but more disturbingly, argues Stalford, it also 'ignores the very real personal dangers inherent in dispensing with children's views when making vital, life-changing decisions about custody and access'.[79]

Accordingly, therefore, there are many criticisms to be made of the Brussels II Regulation. The justifications offered for its adoption were weak and unconvincing and were predominantly based on broader integrationist and political demands, rather than on the perceived failings of international family law. As well as concerns regarding the technicalities of the provisions, in broader terms the Regulation is open to criticism due to its focus on a narrow concept of family. Only some children benefited from the Regulation and then only those who were part of a traditional nuclear family. Moreover, even those children who did fall within the scope of the Regulation were offered limited rights to take part in these fundamental decisions. Finally, although in some ways the Regulation was limited in its scope, involving only the harmonisation of private international law and not the legality of divorce and child custody per se, it did constitute the first direct Community regulation of the status of individuals, rather than just the rights which are accorded to a particular status.[80] Further, it laid the groundwork for more far-reaching measures.

6.5   Brussels II*bis*: the development of Community family law

Peter McEleavy has protested that 'scarcely had the ink dried on the Brussels II regulation but work began on a new series of family law initiatives'.[81] Indeed, following the adoption of Brussels II, the French Presidency submitted a proposal aimed at facilitating cross-border children's access rights. However, the scope of the provision was limited to that of Brussels II which only catered for children of both spouses and in relation to access decisions made at the time of the divorce or separation. Accordingly, the Commission later proposed a regulation on parental responsibility, extending the scope of Brussels II to all decisions on parental responsibility and including provisions on jurisdiction and the return of the child in cases of child abduction.[82] As a result of heated discussions, particularly regarding the provisions on child abduction, the Commission withdrew its proposal and presented a new proposal in May 2002. This proposal brought into one text the Brussels II Regulation, the French initiative on access rights and the

79 *Ibid.*, 476.
80 That is, the difference between Community law granting certain rights to married persons, thus recognising an existing status, and under the new proposals, Community law determining the married or other status of persons.
81 McEleavy, 'The Brussels II Regulation', 901.
82 Proposal for a Council Regulation on jurisdiction and the recognition and enforcement of judgments in matters of parental responsibility, COM (2001) 505 final, OJ 2001 C 332E/269.

Commission's earlier proposal.[83] Thus, only one year after Brussels II had been adopted, another proposal was on the table.

This new text, known as Brussels II*bis*, was adopted in November 2003 and came into force in March 2005.[84] The adoption of this Regulation marks an important step forward for Community action in this field. The competence of the Community is extended to cover the mutual recognition and enforcement of all judgments relating to the attribution, exercise, delegation, restriction or termination of parental responsibility.[85] The Regulation covers court judgments, decisions issued by relevant authorities and out-of-court agreements provided that they are enforceable in the member state in which they were concluded. In addition, for the first time in the field of judicial co-operation in civil law, the exequatur procedure is suppressed for judgments relating to visiting rights and to the return of a child following an abduction. This means that those judgments will no longer be subject to additional procedures before they are recognised in another member state.[86]

The Regulation also introduces new provisions in the complex and often controversial field of child abduction.[87] It was the area of child abduction that led to some of the more protracted negotiations leading to the adoption of the Regulation and tells us much about the future of Union family law. Many member states considered that Community action in this field was unnecessary because of the existence of the 1980 Hague Convention on Child Abduction.[88] Speculation at the time had it that France was unhappy with the manner in which the Hague Convention was being applied to it by Germany, hence the desire for new Community rules: a clear case of déjà vu after Brussels II.[89] No specific evidence was ever produced as to why Community action was needed. Indeed, all evidence points to the Hague Convention being very successful within the Union.[90] Nonetheless, with strong political backing to the proposal from dominant member states, Community action was almost inevitable and thus a compromise was finally reached by the end of 2002.[91]

---

83 6 June 2002, COM (2002) 297 final.

84 Council Regulation 2201/2003/EC of 27 November 2003 concerning jurisdiction and the recognition and enforcement of judgments in matrimonial matters and the matters of parental responsibility, repealing Regulation 1347/2000/EC, OJ 2003 L 338/1.

85 See further Peter McEleavy, 'Brussels II*bis*: Matrimonial Matters, Parental Responsibility, Child Abduction and Mutual Recognition' (2004) 53 *International and Comparative Law Quarterly* 503–18; and Mario Tenreiro and Monika Ekström, 'Recent Developments in EC Judicial Co-operation in the Field of Family Law' (2004) *International Family Law Journal* 30 at 30–2.

86 Provided certain conditions are met, as discussed in Tenreiro and Ekström, 'Recent Developments in EC Judicial Co-operation', 31–2.

87 For a detailed discussion, see Andrea Schulz, 'The New Brussels II Regulation and the Hague Conventions of 1980 and 1996' (2004) *International Family Law Journal* 22–6.

88 1980 Hague Convention on the Civil Aspects of International Child Abduction, 14th Session of the Hague Conference on Private International Law, 25 October 1980, in force 1 December 1983.

89 Jänterä-Jareborg, 'Unification of International Family Law in Europe', 206.

90 McEleavy, 'The Brussels II Regulation', 903–4.

91 For a discussion, see Lowe, 'The Growing Influence of the European Union on International Family Law'.

In effect, the 1980 Hague Convention was to continue to operate within the Community, but supplemented by a number of rules to be contained in Brussels II*bis*.[92] Thus, despite the opposition, a Community dimension to child abduction cases had been secured. Ultimately, therefore, the battle to maintain a role for the Hague conventions has been largely lost. It seems inevitable that in due course the Community will adopt an ever increasing number of regulations in this field which encroach on the activities of the Hague Conference. Peter McEleavy has criticised the provisions on child abduction, declaring them 'wasteful and short-sighted'.[93] Far better, he suggests, to work with the existing Hague Convention which has proved valuable, though not without its shortcomings, and which provides a more global solution. He concludes that a 'fixation' with ephemeral goals such as a European 'judicial space' risks destroying the achievements that have been made thus far in this field, primarily by the Hague Convention.[94]

Maarit Jänterä-Jareborg has argued that Brussels II*bis* is 'illustrative of the EU's lack of ability (or will) to identify the real key issues'.[95] In particular, she highlights the problems that will remain relating to enforcement, due to the continuing differences between member states' willingness to accept the final outcomes of proceedings. She argues that real progress can only be made when the Community is prepared to enter into discussion in sensitive areas where member states' outlooks may differ from each other.[96] For others, there is a resignation that Community action is inevitable and that at least Brussels II*bis* will iron out some of the problems arising from Brussels II.[97] Nigel Lowe also recognises that, while a Hague solution may have been preferable, given the length of time such texts take not just to negotiate, but to ratify and come into practice, the involvement of the Union is broadly welcome.[98]

Certainly, Brussels II*bis* improves on its predecessor in terms of its approach to children. Importantly, Brussels II*bis* encompasses all parental responsibility decisions relating to all children, thus including step-children and children of unmarried parents. This is indeed a welcome change, at last embracing the realities of family life. However, the Regulation is weaker than an earlier draft in relation to its declarations regarding the rights of the child. The draft had included specific provisions declaring the child's right to 'maintain on a regular basis a personal relationship and direct contact with both parents, unless this is contrary to his or her interests', and the statement that: '[a] child shall have the right to be heard on matters relating to parental responsibility over him or her in accordance with his

---

92 As discussed in Tenreiro and Ekström, 'Unification of Private International Law in Family Matters'; and in Tenreiro and Ekström, 'Recent Developments in EC Judicial Co-operation'.
93 McEleavy, 'The Brussels II Regulation', 904.
94 *Ibid.*, 908.
95 Jänterä-Jareborg, 'Unification of International Family Law in Europe', 205.
96 *Ibid.*, 205.
97 Lowe, 'The Growing Influence of the European Union on International Family Law'.
98 *Ibid.*

or her age and maturity'.[99] These provisions were drawn from the Union Charter which in turn followed the UN Convention on the Rights of the Child. Helen Stalford argued that this draft represented a 'much more genuine endeavour to engage with children's rights issues' than previous Community measures.[100]

It seems likely that these provisions were removed from the final text because of concerns over 'substantive law creep', that is, requiring changes in the substantive laws of member states regarding children's rights. Hence, in the Preamble to the Regulation, there is reference to the rights of children to be heard, but with the specific caveat that this 'instrument is not intended to modify national procedures'.[101] However, the inevitable consequence of this is that children's rights are not being prioritised. There appears to be a general reluctance to endorse children's active and direct rights within cross-national family law. This in turn underpins the paternalistic model of dependency which is the basis of much Union legislation relating to families, suggesting little ideological movement beyond the original 1960s free movement provisions. Thus, while the new Regulation is a clear improvement on the original Brussels II, it still seems that it is based more on a 'welfare' approach to children, rather than an 'agency' approach recognising the independence of the child.[102]

The promulgation and adoption of Brussels II*bis* represented a successful attempt to capitalise on the momentum gained with the initial adoption of Brussels II. The original Brussels II had only been in effect for a couple of years before the expansion in competence contained in Brussels II*bis* was approved by the member states. The new Regulation takes the Community deeper into the field of family law and particularly international child law. The expanded scope of the Regulation, to include all children, while broadening the reach of Community law, does at least ensure that children will not be treated differently on the basis of their parents' status. Nonetheless, concerns remain regarding the political ambitions of the Regulation. The first sentence of the explanatory memorandum relates the proposal to the creation of a 'genuine' judicial area based on mutual recognition of decisions.[103] There is no great acclaim here for Community measures to solve family law disputes and to make life better for the Union's citizens. It is the political objective of integration that is dominant. Although, as noted above, such justifications can be explained by reference to the need to establish a legal basis for the measure, this simply serves to emphasise the fact that, as yet, there is no clear legitimate legal basis for family law. The

---

99 Articles 3 and 4 of the Proposal for a Council Regulation concerning jurisdiction and the recognition and enforcement of judgments in matrimonial matters and in matters of parental responsibility repealing Regulation 1347/2000/EC and amending Regulation 44/2001/EC in matters relating to maintenance, COM (2002) 222 final/2.
100 Stalford, 'Brussels II and Beyond', 478.
101 Preamble (para. 19) to Regulation 2201/2003/EC, OJ 2003 L 338/1.
102 See further Stalford, 'Brussels II and Beyond', 480.
103 COM (2002) 222 final, p. 2.

memorandum does go on to state that it is responding to a 'real social need', namely that 'children need a secure legal environment for maintaining relations with persons who have responsibility over them and who now live in different Member States'.[104] The memorandum ties in this demand to the provisions of the Union Charter and the objective of protecting the child's best interests. This is an interesting development. It seems that the Charter has provided sufficient justification for advancing aims and objectives beyond the limited legal basis of the existing treaties. In this way, the Charter is indeed being used to reinterpret the treaties in a new way; here based on a human rights principle.

Indeed, a striking feature of Brussels II*bis* is the absence of justifications based on principles of free movement, in contrast to its predecessor. While the legal basis remains the same, there is obviously a perception that the specific links between free movement, the operation of the single market and this measure do not need to be expressly made. It is almost as if the mere existence of Brussels II provides the justification for further measures being taken. There is clearly much confidence that any question marks over the legal competence to enact measures such as this have been removed. Indeed, the inclusion of family law in the text of the Treaty of Nice, which was the first treaty reference to family law, represents a clear acknowledgment of the competence of the Union in this field.[105] Following the Treaty of Nice and the adoption of Brussels II*bis*, the family law of the Union is well established and its existence has to be accepted. There will no longer be a debate regarding whether the Union should have a family law; now the debate will only be able to engage with questions of scope.

6.6   Into the future: the further development of Community family law

The Commission has stated that the progressive establishment of an area of freedom, justice and security is 'one of the Union's priority policies'.[106] For this reason, further action must be taken to make 'tangible improvements to the daily lives of individuals'.[107] In this way, the further development of family law is viewed as a 'strategic priority'.[108] This is not an area of policy where proposals gather dust, long forgotten and ignored. It seems likely, therefore, that the proposals discussed below will become law, in some shape or form, in the near future.

---

104 *Ibid.*, p. 4.
105 The new Article 67 of the EC Treaty states that the co-decision legislative procedure will apply in all cases under Article 65 of the EC Treaty 'with the exception of aspects relating to family law'.
106 Communication from the Commission to the Council and the European Parliament, Area of Freedom, Security and Justice: Assessment of the Tampere Programme and Future Orientations, p. 4.
107 *Ibid.*, p. 11.
108 *Ibid.*, p. 5.

Following on from Brussels II*bis*, the Commission has presented a proposal to authorise the member states to ratify the 1996 Hague Convention on Jurisdiction, Applicable Law, Recognition, Enforcement and Co-operation in Respect of Parental Responsibility and Measures for the Protection of Children.[109] The Hague Convention will apply to those matters not covered by Brussels II*bis*, such as the question of applicable law. This decision regarding the Convention highlights the significance of the inclusion of the child custody arrangements in Brussels II: the Community now has external competence in this field. The member states are no longer free to ratify, negotiate or adopt international measures in the field of child custody. There are many issues raised by these proposals. Not least is the potential overlap, again, with the Hague Conference. Nigel Lowe highlights the plethora of measures being negotiated and adopted relating to international family law by the Union, the Council of Europe and the Hague Conference.[110] He rightly suggests that this international law relating to families is becoming 'hopelessly complex', the very antithesis of the measures being negotiated and adopted.[111]

The Commission's response to such claims is the adoption of further Community measures. In its Green Paper on the future of maintenance obligations, the Commission accepts that some member states consider that priority should be given to work at the Hague Conference over Community efforts.[112] It rejects such arguments, however, on the basis that the member states have agreed, via the Amsterdam Treaty, to empower the Community to act in the field of judicial co-operation and thus the member states have now agreed that the Community is the appropriate forum for greater co-operation in this field. Accordingly, in the area of maintenance, while the Hague Conference is undergoing extensive negotiations to produce a new text responding to the challenges of this field, the Commission is pressing ahead with its own consultation with a view to further Community legislation. It is more than likely that, in view of the more protracted (though ultimately more democratic and transparent and producing more global solutions) nature of negotiations in the Hague Conference, the Community will be adopting legislation in advance of the solutions being proposed by the Hague Conference. This seems inevitable, but still regrettable for reasons discussed

---

109 As discussed in Tenreiro and Ekström, 'Recent Developments in EC Judicial Co-operation'. The member states signed this Convention in 2003 following authorisation by the Union: Council Decision 2003/93/EC of 19 December 2002 authorising the Member States, in the interest of the Community, to sign the 1996 Hague Convention on jurisdiction, applicable law, recognition, enforcement and cooperation in respect of parental responsibility and measures for the protection of children, OJ 2003 L 48/1.
110 Lowe, 'New International Conventions Affecting the Law Relating to Children', 179.
111 *Ibid.*, 179.
112 Green Paper on Maintenance Obligations, COM (2004) 254 final, p. 9. For a detailed examination of the different arrangements for maintenance between spouses, see Katharina Boele-Woelki, Bente Braat and Ian Sumner (eds.), *European Family Law in Action, Volume II: Maintenance Between Former Spouses* (Antwerp: Intersentia, 2003).

above. The exact extent of future measures regarding maintenance is the subject matter of the consultation, but the ambit of the consultation and the apparent preference for considerably detailed rules, suggests an ambitious programme of action.[113]

Further measures being considered include a unification of choice of law rules relating to marriage dissolution, a project generally known as Rome III. The rationale for such a proposal is that the current rules under Brussels II*bis* encourage both forum shopping and forum racing, as the first court seized of jurisdiction is the application court which has exclusive competence. In the case of divorce, the forum in which proceedings are instigated can make a considerable difference to the outcome of the proceedings.[114] However, were courts to apply the same law to the marriage dissolution, that is, if there were unified choice of law rules, then these problems would not occur; hence the Rome III proposals.

However, although such reasoning may appear convincing, on closer examination, it is less so.[115] Uniform choice of law rules would require a state to apply the law of another state against which it might have strong objections. The clearest example is the divergence in divorce laws between Sweden and Ireland. Swedish law permits divorce on the application of either party, with a delay of six months if the other party objects. There is no question of guilt, nor proof of irretrievable breakdown, nor a requirement to finalise financial arrangements. By contrast, in Ireland, the spouses must have lived apart for four years, the court must be convinced that there is no opportunity for reconciliation and financial provision must have been determined. As Maarit Jänterä-Jareborg makes clear, unless a new European notion of public policy were to be enforced, application of foreign law is likely to be blocked on the ground of national public policy.[116] Swedish courts would not give effect to foreign rules requiring the establishment of fault prior to marriage dissolution; and presumably vice versa in Ireland. Accordingly, therefore, there is little to be gained simply from uniform choice of law rules on divorce. It is the whole panoply of rules determining the legal consequences of divorce which matter to the parties and which would require harmonisation. Furthermore, Maarit Jänterä-Jareborg argues, were such rules to be introduced, they would undermine a central principle of Brussels II*bis* which iterates the equality of laws on marriage dissolution between the member states. This was included at the insistence of Finland and Sweden because of their liberal divorce laws.[117] Indeed, a study funded by the Commission into possible problems arising

---

113 Green Paper on Maintenance Obligations, COM (2004) 254 final. See further Stalford, 'Old Problems, New Solutions?'.
114 On the different divorce laws of the member states see Katharina Boele-Woelki, Bente Braat and Ian Sumner (eds.), *European Family Law in Action, Volume I: Grounds for Divorce* (Antwerp: Intersentia, 2003).
115 Jänterä-Jareborg, 'Unification of International Family Law in Europe', 208–10.
116 *Ibid.*, 209.
117 Discussed in *ibid.*, 210.

from national choice of law rules reported that the different approaches to divorce in the member states constitutes a 'serious obstacle' to any unification of choice of law.[118] Nonetheless, we await the Commission's response.

Action on the Hague Convention, maintenance and Rome III are not the only measures in the offing. The Commission's action programme on mutual recognition of judgments envisages further action in the family law field.[119] In particular, the programme envisages future measures on jurisdiction, recognition and enforcement of judgments relating to property rights arising out of separations between married and unmarried couples and to wills and succession. In the longer term, the Commission suggests that measures to facilitate the mutual recognition of the civil status of individuals, family or civil relations between individuals (partnerships) and paternity should be considered.

6.7   Conclusions

Following the Nice Treaty in 2001, the European Council received a report on the need to approximate the laws of the member states in civil matters which specifically highlighted the harmonisation of family law.[120] No clear legal base for such measures was considered, although it was recognised that economic considerations do not apply to areas of civil law such as family law, in the same way as to areas of, say, contract law. The Council stated that family laws are 'very heavily influenced by . . . culture and traditions'.[121] Nonetheless, the report declared that the free movement of persons and the desire to establish an area of freedom, justice and security can provide justifications for further harmonisation in the family law field.[122] Walter Pintens has suggested that the adoption of the report by the Council suggests that the Council has 'realised that a unification, which is exclusively restricted to private international law, will not be sufficient to realize its goal of a uniform area of freedom, justice and security'.[123] Indeed, Katharina Boele-Woelki has suggested that Brussels II makes it 'necessary to make a start on the harmonisation of national divorce law'.[124] While the Commission

---

118 TMC Asser Instituut, *Practical Problems Resulting from the Non-Harmonization of Choice of Law Rules in Divorce Matters* (The Hague: TMC Asser Instituut, 2002), p. 59.

119 Draft programme of measures for implementation of the principle of mutual recognition of decisions in civil and commercial matters, OJ 2001 C 12/1.

120 Note 45 of the Presidency Conclusions, cited in Walter Pintens, 'Europeanisation of Family Law' in Boele-Woelki (ed.), *Perspectives for the Unification and Harmonisation of Family Law*, pp. 3–33 at p. 26.

121 Draft Council Report on the need to approximate Member States' legislation in civil matters, Council Report No. 13017/01 of 29 October 2001, adopted on 16 November 2001, cited in David Bradley, 'A Family Law for Europe? Sovereignty, Political Economy and Legitimation' in Boele-Woelki (ed.), *Perspectives for the Unification and Harmonisation of Family Law*, pp. 65–104 at p. 69.

122 Draft Council Report 13017/01 of 29 October 2001, adopted on 16 November 2001.

123 Pintens, 'Europeanisation of Family Law', 27.

124 For a discussion, see Katharina Boele-Woelki, 'Comparative Research-Based Drafting of Principles of European Family Law' in Michael Faure, Jan Smits and Hildegard Schneider (eds.),

has not yet gone so far, in 2004 it did declare that 'further and deeper' development of judicial co-operation was a priority, 'in particular as regards family law'.[125] The adoption of Brussels II*bis* is clear evidence of this momentum in the field of family law and there is undoubtedly institutional support for further measures at the highest level of the Union. Thus, there seems a very real possibility that the proposals discussed above will be adopted, in some form, in due course. There is therefore a clear future for a Union family law. The ultimate scope of such ambitions is the subject of the next chapter.

Towards a European Ius Commune in Legal Education and Research (Antwerp: Intersentia, 2002), pp. 171–89 at p. 184.

125 Commission Press Release IP/04/702, 2 June 2004.

7

Harmonisation, codification and the future of family law in the European Union

> Unity and diversity, and never one without the other – isn't that the very secret of our Europe?
>
> Albert Camus[1]

> [A] European civil code . . . will one day replace the Euro as the symbol of European integration.
>
> Walter Pintens[2]

Unity and diversity. That is indeed what Europe has been and *should* be about. At present, however, there is a grand debate taking place within the Union over just this theme. To be specific, the question is whether or not we should unify the private laws of Europe, effectively erasing the present diversity and pluralism. That is the extreme end of the debate, with more nuanced approaches focusing on harmonisation, as distinct from unification, and some speaking of a reform of 'legal science' such that harmonisation and perhaps unification will come about organically through the work of scholars, teachers and judges. While these debates were initially confined to the fields of tort, contract and commercial law, they are now a feature of family law discussions.

Despite the differences, what remains common to each of these approaches is the belief that some form of greater commonality, on a continuum from harmonisation to unification, is to be encouraged and welcomed. Existing shared norms, in the form of universal human rights principles, are not enough, but are indeed merely the basis, and for some the rationale, for greater assimilation. Thus, Walter Pintens suggests that the jurisprudence of the European Court of Human Rights has 'served as a catalyst for harmonisation through its decisions and judgments, which have given a rough sketch of European family law'.[3]

These trends towards harmonisation and codification will be resisted in this chapter. I will argue that the common human rights norms of Europe should

---

1 Albert Camus, *Resistance, Rebellion and Death* (London: Vintage, 1974), pp. 234–5, quoted in Ian Ward, *A Critical Introduction to European Law* (2nd edn, London: Butterworths, 2003), pp. 272–3.
2 Walter Pintens, 'Europeanisation of Family Law', paper presented to the conference entitled 'Perspectives on the Unification and Harmonisation of Family Law in Europe', organised by the Commission on European Family Law, University of Utrecht, December 2002.
3 Walter Pintens, 'Europeanisation of Family Law' in Katharina Boele-Woelki (ed.), *Perspectives for the Unification and Harmonisation of Family Law in Europe* (Antwerp: Intersentia, 2003), pp. 3–33 at p. 17.

form the bedrock of all national family laws, but, beyond this commonality, diversity should reign. Where convergence results from the normal interchange of ideas and policies, this is to be welcomed. This is indeed one of the benefits of diverse and plural legal systems: arguably the 'success' of family law requires an ongoing conversation between law reform approaches and possibilities. But convergence at the behest of ideological, political and jurisprudential commitments to universality, supposed jurisprudential coherence and rationality and deeper European integration should be opposed.

This chapter begins by outlining the harmonisation/codification debates in private law, leading to a discussion of recent developments regarding family law in particular.[4] It then proceeds to consider the reasons for opposing greater convergence of family laws, including an analysis of the debate as to whether or not European family laws are converging and an examination of the problematic jurisprudential foundation for any proposed code. The chapter concludes by calling for more fluid and diverse approaches to any further co-ordination of the family laws of the member states of the Union, warning that greater harmonisation may in fact promote disintegration, rather than greater European integration, contrary to the wishes of harmonisation/codification advocates.

7.1   Towards a European civil code: from academic utopia to institutional support

7.1.1   From academic utopia . . .

The development of the European Union's family law must be understood as part of a larger movement advocating greater harmonisation of the civil laws of the member states of the Union. There can already be said to exist considerable harmonisation of aspects of private law within the Community. Indeed, this is the whole purpose of moves towards an internal market; a harmonisation of laws to ensure fair and open competition and trade. The primary method of single market harmonisation is via the directive which is intended to be binding only 'as to the result to be achieved', thus leaving to member states the 'choice and form of methods' of implementation. This inevitably results in diversity of implementation; the directive is not designed to impose a uniform approach on all states. As a result of these harmonisation steps, and because of the inevitable diversity that has occurred, a strong movement towards greater harmonisation of private law has developed. Although such debates have a long pedigree,[5] it is only

---

4 There is clearly no set definition of what constitutes 'family law'. If every law which affected families were included within such a term, its scope would be wide indeed. Family law will be taken here to mean those laws which have a more direct impact on family relationships, such as laws relating to divorce, marriage, parenting and children.

5 A book published in 1976 on a common law for Europe was entitled '*New* Perspectives for a Common Law of Europe' (my emphasis) talked about the 're-born trend towards a *jus commune*':

in the last ten or so years that they have taken off in any viable sense and have gained both considerable academic and institutional support.

The academic work on harmonisation and codification began in the 1980s, when the Lando Commission on European Contract Law began its work. It has now produced its 'Principles of European Contract Law',[6] which was followed in 2000 with a document setting out general rules in further areas.[7] Similar work in the field of contract law has been carried out by the Institute for the Unification of Law (Unidroit) which in 1994 published its Principles for International Commercial Contracts.[8] The Unidroit principles have met with some success, being employed in some arbitral awards and influencing legislation in central and eastern Europe.[9] As well as the Lando and Unidroit groups, the other principal association working on contract law is the Trento Common Core project. This seeks, as its name suggests, to distil the common core of European contract law.[10] In addition to the work on contract law, similar academic groups are working on other fields of private law. Tort law has provided much focus of attention and to a lesser extent trust law and procedural law.[11] Most recently, in 1998, a Study Group on the European Civil Code was established, the aim of which, unsurprisingly, is to draft a comprehensive codification of European private law.[12]

Each of these academic projects has generally been working on the production of general principles of European private law in their particular areas.[13] The use to which their work should be put differs between authors and academic groups. For example, there are those who would support the drafting and then the imposition

Mauro Cappelletti (ed.), *New Perspectives for a Common Law for Europe* (Florence: European University Institute, 1976), p. 1.

6 Ole Lando and Hugh Beale (eds.), *Principles of European Contract Law – Part I* (Dordrecht: Nijhoff, 1995).

7 Ole Lando and Hugh Beale (eds.), *Principles of European Contract Law – Parts I and II* (The Hague: Kluwer, 2000).

8 Unidroit, *Principles for International Commercial Contracts* (Rome: Unidroit, 1994). See further Michael Bonell, *A New Approach to International Commercial Contracts – The Unidroit Principles of International Commercial Contracts* (The Hague: Kluwer, 1999).

9 As discussed in Ewoud Hondius, 'Towards a European *Ius Commune*: The Current Situation in Other Fields of Private Law' in Boele-Woelki (ed.), *Unification and Harmonisation of Family Law*, pp. 118–39 at pp. 123–5.

10 See Reinhard Zimmermann and Simon Whittaker, *Good Faith in European Contract Law* (Cambridge: Cambridge University Press, 2000) and James Gordley, *The Enforceability of Promises in European Contract Law* (Cambridge: Cambridge University Press, 2001). There are further groups involved in drafting common principles of contract law, the approaches of which differ in small ways, but which generally approach the matter with broadly similar methods. See further Hondius, 'Towards a European *Ius Commune*', pp. 128–9.

11 Discussed in Hondius, 'Towards a European *Ius Commune*', 128.

12 See Christian von Bar, 'Paving the Way Forward with Principles of European Private Law' in Stefan Grundmann and Jules Struyck (eds.), *An Academic Green Paper on European Contract Law* (The Hague: Kluwer, 2002), pp. 137–45 at pp. 139–42, and Masha Antokolskaia, 'The Harmonisation of Family Law: Old and New Dilemmas' (2003) 11 *European Review of Private Law* 28–49 at 30 and 46.

13 There are many more groups engaged in this type of work than those briefly referred to above: see further Martijn Hesselink, 'The Politics of a European Civil Code' (2004) 10 *European Law Journal* 675–97 at 685–6.

of a private law code on all member states. This is followed by those who support a code, but perhaps instituted via the 'closer co-operation' provisions of the Treaty; that is, only being applicable in consenting member states. Still others seek to draft a 'restatement' of the law in a particular area which can work as a guide for both national and Community legislatures when enacting law in the particular field. All in all, however, these are largely 'top-down' approaches; the drafting of common principles which can then be used in their entirety and if desired adopted and implemented en masse. And, as will be seen below, family law harmonisation is included within the sights of some of those advocating codification, largely on the basis that, if a code is meant to be as comprehensive, coherent and rational as possible, it must include family law. Thus, Jürgen Basedow is convinced that: 'A European civil code, which would follow the model of various continental codes, would at least include a comprehensive regulation of the law of persons and succession, of family relations and property.'[14]

These 'top-down' approaches can be contrasted with a more 'bottom-up' methodology which seeks to bring about a gradual realisation of common principles via a common legal education and the work of scholars, lawyers and judges in incorporating these principles into their own work and eventually making them a reality. This is an ambition to create a 'European legal science'. Thus, casebooks have been published in the fields of tort and contract law the purpose of which is to reveal the similarities between jurisdictions.[15] The aim here is more organic and non-coercive and the idea of a code may even be rejected entirely.[16] There is a strong commitment, amongst the authors of such work, to the need to reform legal education by introducing European approaches and perspectives and to encourage the legal profession and judiciary to appreciate and utilise European approaches; the end result being a European legal tradition which harmonises from 'bottom-up'.[17]

This latter approach is a valid scholastic enterprise in the tradition of comparative law. The search for commonality itself is revealing and the explication of differences and the reasons therefor contribute to a better understanding of law and better solutions to legal problems. Ideologically, the enterprise differs considerably from the attempts to draft common principles or a code. The

14 Jürgen Basedow, 'A Case for a European Contract Act' in Grundmann and Struyck (eds.), *Green Paper on European Contract Law*, pp. 147–58 at p. 148 and discussed in Antokolskaia, 'The Harmonisation of Family Law', 46–7.

15 See, for example, Walter van Gerven *et al.* (eds.), *Tort Law: Scope of Protection* (Oxford: Hart Publishing, 1998); Walter van Gerven, Jeremy Lever and Pierre Larouche (eds.), *Tort Law – Casebooks for the Common Law of Europe* (Oxford: Hart Publishing, 2000); Hugh Beale, Arthur Hartkamp, Hein Kötz and Denis Tallon (eds.), *Contract Law – Casebooks for the Common Law of Europe* (Oxford: Hart Publishing, 2002).

16 Walter van Gerven, for example, has stated that he is not in favour of codification: Walter van Gerven, 'The ECJ Case Law as a Means of Unification of Private Law?' in Arthur S. Hartkamp *et al.* (eds.), *Towards a European Civil Code* (2nd edn, The Hague: Kluwer, 1998), pp. 91–104.

17 For a discussion of these different trends, see Christoph Schmid, 'The Emergence of a Transnational Legal Science in European Private Law' (1999) 19 *Oxford Journal of Legal Studies* 673–89.

codification attempts rely on a specific ideological approach to law which fails to meet the reality of the European integration project, arguments which will be discussed further below. Nonetheless, while this 'bottom-up' strategy is less coercive, there remains a commitment to some form of harmonisation and thereby greater integration, albeit at a considerably slower pace.

And, indeed, there are some more forceful elements in this strategy. We must be teaching our students about European cases, we are told. We should be learning to express ourselves in other European languages. We should be 'promoting' the work of the harmonisers, together with the development of a common stock of European cases.[18] Indeed, Reinhard Zimmermann declares that the 'juristic nationalism' which characterises our consciousness must be 'overcome' and in its place a 'comprehensive Europeanisation of legal scholarship has to be brought about'.[19]

7.1.2   . . . to institutional support

For many years, it was only the European Parliament which gave any public support to the harmonisation and codification work discussed above. Thus, in 1989, 1994 and 2001, the Parliament called for a common European Code of Private Law.[20] In more recent times, however, both the Commission and the Council have come to support and encourage this work. The impetus for this greater institutional enthusiasm was the adoption of the Amsterdam Treaty and the Union's ambition to create an area of 'freedom, justice and security'. As discussed in the previous chapter, this political ambition, on a par with the 1992 internal market project, has generated a formidable desire for further legal integration, not just in the traditional commercial fields of Community law, but in asylum, immigration, criminal and family laws. Under the rubric of 'judicial co-operation', and the 'free movement of judgments', the Council and the Commission have been supporting the efforts of those engaged in scholarly enterprises to facilitate such harmonisation, as well as promulgating various measures and proposals on the same theme.

Hence, in 2001, the Commission published a Communication on Contract Law regarding the desirability, feasibility and necessity of a European law of obligations.[21] While many advocates of codification were disappointed with the Communication,[22] it did place the discussion of a European civil code firmly on the Union's agenda. No more was such discussion to be confined solely to

---

18 Hondius, 'Towards a European *Ius Commune*', 134.

19 Reinhard Zimmermann, 'Roman Law and European Legal Unity' in Hartkamp *et al.* (eds.), *Towards a European Civil Code*, pp. 21–39 at p. 26.

20 OJ 1989 C 158/400; OJ 1994 C 205/518; OJ 2002 C 140E/538.

21 Communication from the Commission to the Council and the European Parliament on European Contract Law, COM (2001) 398 final. For a discussion, see Walter van Gerven, 'Codifying European Private Law? Yes, If . . . !' (2002) 27 *European Law Review* 156–76.

22 See, for example, Hondius, 'Towards a European *Ius Commune*'.

academic circles (and the European Parliament). Furthermore, it was less than two years after the Commission Communication that it published its Action Plan for a more 'coherent' European contract law.[23] This is a much more explicit document in which the Commission declared that differences in national systems of contract law and the incoherence of existing Community law posed impediments to the further development of the single market. It made a number of recommendations for further action including the funding of an academic project to compile a 'common frame of reference', also known as a code of European contract law.[24]

The Council's generally positive response to the Commission Communication further entrenches the institutional support for these moves and discussions.[25] Moreover, the Council's response is not just important for its general endorsement of the Communication and the further development of harmonisation measures, but also for its ground-breaking discussion of family law, which was not even considered in the Commission's Communication. Not only, therefore, do we now have institutional support for harmonisation measures in the field of contract law, but we also have it explicitly and forcefully in the field of family law.

7.2   Into the terrain of family law

Until relatively recently, discussion of family law harmonisation was largely unheard of, let alone the subject of Council approval. The oft repeated explanation was that family law was too close to the 'culture' of individual states to permit comparison and harmonisation.[26] It is said to be a 'political' subject unlike the other 'technical' areas of private law. And, indeed, there was little economic impetus for harmonisation, unlike commercial law and aspects of private law. Thus, the first edition of the seminal 1994 text, *Towards a European Civil Code*, did not include a chapter on family law, it being considered that family and inheritance law were unsuitable for inclusion in a European civil code.[27] However, by the time of the second edition, in 1998, an entire chapter was devoted to the subject and the debate on harmonisation of family law was truly up and

---

23 Communication from the Commission to the European Parliament and the Council – A More Coherent European Contract Law – An Action Plan, COM (2003) 68 final, OJ 2003 C 63/1.
24 For a discussion of the Action Plan, see Hesselink, 'The Politics of a European Civil Code' 685–9 and Study Group on Social Justice in European Private Law, 'Social Justice in European Contract Law: A Manifesto' (2004) 10 *European Law Journal* 653–74 at 659–64.
25 Council Report on the need to approximate Member States' legislation in civil matters, Council Report No. 13017/01 of 29 October 2001, adopted on 16 November 2001.
26 See, for example, Schmid, 'Transnational Legal Science in European Private Law', 675. For a rejection of the 'cultural constraints' argument, see Antokolskaia, 'The Harmonisation of Family Law'.
27 Ewoud Hondius, 'Towards a European Civil Code' in Arthur S. Hartkamp *et al.* (eds.), *Towards a European Civil Code* (1st edn, The Hague: Martinus Nijhoff, 1994), p. 4.

running.[28] By the end of the 1990s, there were publications in many languages, taking many different perspectives, and the issue was firmly on the table.[29]

Interestingly, however, this is a debate which has been taking place largely among continental scholars. Thus, the vast majority of work in this field has been written in languages other than English and by scholars of the civil law tradition. This is perhaps symbolic of the nature of the debate: it was, and still is, largely unknown in common law jurisdictions and the Anglo-American debate on Europe and European law. While this situation is now changing, with more common lawyers writing about family law harmonisation, it is perhaps also revealing that the substantial majority of such work is generally against greater harmonisation,[30] and, even where some benefits of greater harmonisation are perceived, considerable concern is expressed regarding the methods and processes of reform.[31] This is an issue which will be further addressed below as it arguably reflects different traditions and perspectives on law.

Despite the steady growth of interest in family law harmonisation,[32] there was perceived by some to be a lack of academic organisation and drive, in comparison to the activities of private lawyers in other fields. Family law harmonisation was still viewed as a marginal subject.[33] Hence, in 2001, a group of academics estab-lished the Commission on European Family Law (CEFL).[34] The CEFL comprises a group of academics from the member states and prospective member states and has the aim of promoting and co-ordinating research activities in this field. Its stated aim is to distil common rules, although there will be situations where alternatives are proposed and 'better law' solutions advocated. Ultimately, the plan is to produce 'Principles of European Family Law' that can 'directly serve as a model for both national and European legislators elaborating new family laws

28 Dieter Martiny, 'Is Unification of Family Law Feasible or Even Desirable?' in Hartkamp *et al.* (eds.), *Towards a European Civil Code*.
29 For a discussion of the development of academic interest in this field, see Katharina Boele-Woelki, 'Comparative Research-Based Drafting of Principles of European Family Law' in Michael Faure, Jan Smits and Hildegard Schneider (eds.), *Towards a European Ius Commune in Legal Education and Research* (Antwerp: Intersentia, 2002), pp. 171–89, which includes a bibliographical index of relevant work in the field.
30 See, for example, David Bradley, 'A Family Law for Europe? Sovereignty, Political Economy and Legitimation' in Boele-Woelki (ed.), *Unification and Harmonisation of Family Law*, pp. 65–104.
31 Peter McEleavy, 'The Brussels II Regulation: How the European Community Has Moved into Family Law' (2002) 51 *International and Comparative Law Quarterly* 883–908.
32 See also the work by Walter Pintens and Koen Vanwinkelen which is one of the first casebooks on European family law and seeks to create a 'European consciousness in the field of family law' through education and legal doctrine: Walter Pintens and Koen Vanwinkelen, *Casebook – European Family Law* (Leuven: Leuven University Press, 2001), p. 27.
33 In 1997, Katharina Boele-Woelki made a 'plea' for 'fundamental academic research' into the 'convergence of family law regulation within the EU Member States' in 'The Road Towards a European Family Law' (1997) 1 *Electronic Journal of Comparative Law*, available at http://www.ejcl.org/11/art11-1. html.
34 For a discussion, see Boele-Woelki, 'Drafting of Principles of European Family Law' and Antokolskaia, 'The Harmonisation of Family Law'. The CEFL has a website at http://www.law.uu.nl/priv/cefl/.

and in that way can facilitate voluntary evolutionary harmonisation of family law within the EU'.[35] The CEFL plans to draft these principles with the assistance of comparative studies from the member states, starting with studies of the grounds of divorce and the maintenance obligations of former spouses.

The foundation of the CEFL clearly marks an important stage in the harmonisation of European family law. Its establishment gives greater academic credibility to the debates on family law harmonisation and provides considerable exposure for the ideas generated. In addition, family law can no longer be said to be outside the mainstream of harmonisation deliberations, the CEFL being funded initially by the European Commission. Its establishment is also politically and ideologically significant. The establishment of such a body, and the prospective publication of its 'Principles of European Family Law', clearly gives credence to arguments in favour of harmonisation. The debate has imperceptibly, but definitively, shifted from whether there should be harmonisation, to how and in what forms.

Other bodies, most notably the European Commission, will without doubt use the very existence of the CEFL as evidence of a perceived need within the academic community for harmonisation and of course can use its deliberations as the basis for its work. While the 'Principles' to be drafted are to be 'voluntary' and designed to facilitate an 'evolutionary' harmonisation, they will clearly exert considerable influence. It is these principles which will be examined by institutional bodies of the Union when contemplating greater harmonisation. Thus, it will be the ideological choices made by the CEFL and the drafters of its 'Principles' which will hold considerable sway on the future development of European family law.[36] Furthermore, while the CEFL states that there is no explicit aim of top-down unification, were this to become more likely, it is clear that the CEFL's 'Principles' would provide a basis for such developments.

The work of the CEFL and others is not, of course, taking place within a vacuum. There is already evidence of greater commonality among European states in the family law field. Previous chapters detailed the progress within the Community, most particularly with the adoption of Brussels II*bis*, but also the Charter of Fundamental Rights with its provisions on children's rights and other family rights. But it is also important to note the other forms of international co-operation in the family law field, the most obvious being the jurisprudence of the European Court of Human Rights. Family and children's rights have been developed and protected by the Court through its interpretation of Articles 8, 12 and 14, as discussed in previous chapters. While one judge of the Court of Human Rights accused his fellow judges of creating a 'whole code of family law'

---

35 For a discussion, see Boele-Woelki, 'Drafting of Principles of European Family Law', 182.
36 As is the case in the development of common principles of European contract law supported by Commission funding: see Hesselink, 'The Politics of a European Civil Code', 687–8.

through its interpretation of these articles,[37] it is more realistic to describe the Convention jurisprudence as providing a basic minimum of family and children's rights, below which states cannot fall. Other bodies, most notably the Hague Conference and the Council of Europe, have also been involved in the drafting and adoption of numerous international conventions and agreements on family law.[38] These are voluntary international agreements which are the result of years of collaborative and deliberative work. Their fundamental premise is to improve the lives of those who find themselves in cross-border family disputes and the focus remains on private international law.

On the contrary, in its report on the approximation of civil laws, the Council concluded that any obstacles to the principle of the free movement of persons 'generated by differences in national laws' should be 'queried'.[39] This is a potential reform based not on empirical demands to improve the quality of family laws to make the lives of individuals better, nor on the perceived need to conform to agreed human rights standards, but on a largely economic and ideological crusade to eliminate so-called obstacles to free movement, thereby creating a successful area of freedom, justice and security, leading to deeper European integration. It is this which marks out the endeavours of the European Union from the Council of Europe and the Hague Conference and which prompts opposition to greater harmonisation and ultimately a European civil code.

7.3   Opposing a European civil code

7.3.1   A code as an end to 'legal nationalism'?

As discussed in chapter 1, the European Union is suffering a jurisprudential crisis: it defies explanation on traditional grounds and comparisons with other political entities inevitably and necessarily fail. Nonetheless, this has not prevented some scholars from attempting to reinvigorate the old ideas of state-building, statehood and ultimately federation for the Union. The progress towards a European civil code is one of the clearest examples of this trend. Thus, proponents of a code unashamedly hark back to another era, to the time when codes were first being adopted on the continent in the nineteenth century, and suggest that this is a movement which needs to be reborn in the Union context.[40] The code, they argue, would form the basis of a federal Europe, or at least a Europe with explicit sovereign bodies, clearer and hierarchical lines of authority and a common

37 Dissenting Opinion of Judge Sir Gerald Fitzmaurice, in *Marckx* v. *Belgium*, ECHR, 13 June 1979, Series A No. 13.
38 For a comprehensive collection of such materials, see Carolyn Hamilton and Alison Perry (eds.), *Family Law in Europe* (2nd edn, London: Butterworths, 2002).
39 Draft Council Report on the need to approximate Member States' legislation in civil matters, Council Report No. 13017/01 of 29 October 2001, adopted on 16 November 2001, para. 19.
40 See, for example, Ole Lando, 'The Rules of European Contract Law' in the European Parliament Working Paper, *The Private Law Systems in the EU: Discrimination on the Grounds of Nationality and the Need for a European Civil Code* (Luxembourg: European Parliament, 1999), pp. 123–32.

statehood. This line of reasoning is plainly related to the nature of the state and the supranational state. While the French and German codifications of 1804 and 1900 differed in important respects, in one essential detail they were the same. Their purpose was distinctly ideological, that is, to put an end to legal differentiation and to 'contribute to the shaping of a centralized nation-state' and in Germany to lay the basis for 'political unification'.[41] Thus, Martijn Hesselink concludes that a 'Civil Code has always been a symbol of a new (or renewed) unity. And a European Civil Code would certainly have the same symbolic value.'[42]

The code is, in this way, seen as a symbol of a new Europe that is integrated to a considerable degree: witness the Walter Pintens quote at the head of this chapter. For Reiner Schulze, part of the rationale behind this retrospective approach is an aspiration to 'revive' the idea of a 'shared European identity', in support of the 'development of a body of common European law'.[43] Schulze argues that the studies of legal historians into the (supposedly) shared common identity of Europeans, contribute to a 'consciousness of a shared European identity', which was almost destroyed by the rise of the nation-state and which needs to be reclaimed. Presumably, this reclamation will take place at the expense of the nation-state in the promotion of not just a shared identity but also a shared polity. For Jan Smits, the historical roots of the codification movements provide support for current proposals, implying that the aim of Europe is axiomatically political and economic integration and that this necessitates uniform law.[44] Reinhard Zimmermann shares this need to look back, arguing that the role of the legal historian is to reveal the 'common systematic, conceptual, doctrinal and ideological foundations which are hidden under the debris piled up in the course of the legal particularization over the last two hundred years'.[45] It seems that we are to all but erase the last 'two hundred years' in search of a supposedly common law which can be used as a basis for a new common law for Europe.

For many, the original ideas of the founders of the Community, to establish a 'United States of Europe' to use Jean Monnet's phraseology, continue to resonate and a code appears to embody these ideals.[46] Schumann echoed these sentiments,

---

41 Van Gerven, 'Codifying European Private Law?', 159–60. See also Reinhard Zimmermann, 'Civil Code and Civil Law – The "Europeanisation of Private Law Within the European Community and the Re-emergence of a European Legal Science' (1994–5) 1 *Columbia Journal of European Law* 63 at 65. As Christian Joerges further explains: the 'German Civil Code put into effect the uniformity of the German *Reich* and thus symbolizes the emergence of a German nation state. A European Civil Code could play a similar part, as contribution towards European state-building, supplementing the political constitution of Europe': 'Europeanization as Process: Thoughts on the Europeanization of Private Law' (2005) 11 *European Public Law* 63–84 at 67.
42 Hesselink, 'The Politics of a European Civil Code', 684.
43 Reiner Schulze, 'European Legal History – A New Field of Research in Germany' (1992) 3 *Journal of Legal History* 270–95.
44 Jan Smits, 'A European Private Law as a Mixed Legal System' (1998) 5 *Maastricht Journal of European and Comparative Law* 328–40 at 328–9.
45 Zimmermann, 'Roman Law and European Legal Unity', 38.
46 Jean Monnet, *Memoirs* (London: Doubleday, 1978), pp. 522–3.

suggesting that Europe would be built by 'practical actions',[47] again a code being perceived as just such an action. In the context of such strong political ambitions, harmonisation or codification of law, to include family law is a tantalising prospect and one which appears to offer a way of uniting the member states in a way that citizenship, the euro and other laws and policies have not done. It would enable comparisons with other federalist states to be more meaningful and real. It would, therefore, enable traditional ideas of sovereignty, authority and the regulation of legal power to be resurrected and applied to Europe. It would, for Reinhard Zimmermann, remove 'legal nationalism' which, he argues, is essential for the eventual achievement of 'European unity' which he claims is the undoubted aim of the Treaties.[48]

And the family law dimension to such a code would also appear to be crucial. It is because family laws are so closely allied to the social, political and economic principles and ideologies of states that to secure the adoption of Union family laws would be so significant in terms of the nature and future of the Union. Family laws are indeed closely allied to state-building; witness the links between family policy, family law and the population of states. Thus, as David Bradley suggests, the project of family law harmonisation is of keen interest to those who desire ever greater integration among the member states of the Union.[49]

Further, family law harmonisation or codification is crucial to the political end-game of deeper integration because of the perceived need to create a 'European identity'. This has long been a project of the European institutions, with suggestions for anthems, flags and such like and most recently the introduction of the concept of European Union citizenship. Codification efforts are thus justified on the basis of their promotion of a European identity.[50] The wish to establish a new European identity, a common identity based on harmonisation and unity, is a very specific political project and one that necessarily includes family law. Katharina Boele-Woelki argues that the 'absence of harmonized family law creates an obstacle to . . . the creation of a truly European identity and an integrated European legal space'.[51] Boele-Woelki continues that economic and political integration within Europe will 'finally make it necessary to integrate family law, or at least attune the family law regulations to a considerable degree'.[52]

7.3.2   The role of law and legal positivism

Codification proposals exhibit a strong desire to use law to meet the political ambitions of a more integrated Europe. Ian Ward rightly notes that it was the lack

---

47 Quoted in Ward, *European Law*, p. 247.
48 Reinhard Zimmermann, 'Savigny's Legacy – Legal History, Comparative Law and the Emergence of European Legal Science' (1996) 112 *Law Quarterly Review* 576–605 at 581.
49 Bradley, 'A Family Law for Europe?'.
50 See, for example, Christoph Schmid, 'Legitimacy Conditions for a European Civil Code' (2001) 8 *Maastricht Journal of European and Comparative Law* 277–98 at 280 and 287.
51 Boele-Woelki, 'Drafting of Principles of European Family Law', 172.
52 Boele-Woelki, 'The Road Towards a European Family Law'.

of any clear political blueprint which 'invited a distinctive reliance on law' in the early stages of building the Community: that is, 'the idea that law would provide the cement that could keep the edifice of the Community from crashing to the ground'.[53] However, as Ward continues, the imposition of 'more and more laws' provides no solution to the crisis affecting the European project.[54]

It is indeed this reliance on law, as the motor of integration, which has led scholars to look back, as is so common in legal scholarship, to models of the past to employ for the Europe of the future. Ward observes that, rather than looking at the 'new' Europe as indeed new, such approaches presume that 'this Europe could be described by recourse to established theoretical models and strategies'.[55] Thus, Konrad Zweigert and Hein Kötz write that: 'One particular product of the Enlightenment is the idea of *codification*, the idea that the diverse and unmanageable traditional law could be replaced by comprehensive legislation, consciously planned in a rational and transparent order'.[56] It is indeed the diverse and unmanageable nature of European law which has given rise to many proposals for codification. Christian von Bar echoes these sentiments, stating that 'the artificial territorialisation of private law within the European Union must be overcome'.[57] In more trenchant form, Reinhard Zimmermann has deplored the state of 'European legal unification', it being 'not at all reassuring' because of its fragmented nature.[58] He castigates the 'higgledy-piggledy fashion' of law reform, complaining that, rather than gaining 'coherence, rationality and predictability', the law has tended to become 'disjointed'.[59] The solution to this problem is 'codifying European private law'.[60] Zimmermann suggests that this is the path laid out by legal scholars at the beginning of the nineteenth century. His perspective is also clearly of the legal positivist law tradition. He bemoans the fact that the 'internal coherence' of the law is no longer wholly recognised; faith in law as an 'autonomous discipline' is waning; and new fields of legal scholarship are rejected out of hand.[61] 'European legal science', Zimmermann argues, is based on the belief that law 'can be reduced to a rational and organised system' and can be presented as a 'logically consistent whole'.[62] He deplores the idea of law as an 'indigestible and arbitrary mass of individual rules and cases'.[63] Finally, he argues that the idea of 'European legal science' needs to 're-emerge', together with the demise of juristic nationalism.

53 Ward, *European Law*, p. 248.
54 *Ibid.*, p. 247.
55 *Ibid.*, p. 248.
56 Konrad Zweigert and Hein Kötz, *An Introduction to Comparative Law*, translated by Tony Weir (3rd edn, Oxford: Clarendon Press, 1998), pp. 135–6.
57 Christian von Bar, 'The Study Group on a European Civil Code' in the European Parliament Working Paper, *The Private Law Systems in the EU*, pp. 133–8 at p. 134.
58 Zimmermann, 'Savigny's Legacy', 581.
59 *Ibid.*, 582.   60 *Ibid.*, 582.   61 *Ibid.*, 583.
62 *Ibid.*, 585.   63 *Ibid.*, 585.

Zimmermann's approach is emblematic of many who favour harmonisation and codification. The unpredictability of law is to be removed; its disjointed nature to be reformed; and rationality and organisation is to replace the multi-level legal system that is the present Community and Union. This approach to 'the law', Pierre Legrand argues, is one of the major impulses behind the codification projects, all of which emanate from the continent.[64] The civil law system is one familiar with codes and for which codes are almost a prerequisite for what is deemed necessary – a sensible and rational legal system. Indeed, this is the argument offered in favour of codification by Christoph Schmid.[65] He argues that the 'big national codifications of the previous century' which have outlasted numerous political systems have achieved a legitimation and acceptance and are part of a 'collective consciousness' on the continent. He continues that jurists have been familiar with codes in their studies, their living is based on their expertise in them, as is their professional self-perception.[66] The affinity for codes is, therefore, Schmid suggests, not just rationally, but also emotionally, based.

Similar candid revelations are given by Walter van Gerven, who suggests that the decision as to 'how much fragmentation a legal system can tolerate is very much influenced by one's legal background'.[67] He continues that, as he was trained in a system of codified law, and is therefore 'naturally' imbued with the 'ideals of rationalization, unification and legal certainty', his own gut reaction is towards codification.[68] Nonetheless, he recognises that his gut reaction may not be correct.[69] Indeed, in the same way, this may influence my own thinking, coming from a common law background.

However, there is more to it than just familiarity. There are two further elements to the impulses towards codification which need to be challenged. To reiterate the first, it is that the desire for harmony and legal unity harks back to another era, as Pierre Legrand confirms, to an age of faith in centralised political authority and in formalist truth; the idea that the law governing the daily lives of citizens can be reduced to a set of neatly organised rules.[70] Thus, it is a traditional vision based on a 'universal and rationalistic ideal' belonging to the nineteenth century.[71] As discussed further in chapter 1, we have entered the era of 'complexity', where the supremacy of the nation-state has given way to a multiplicity of

---

64 Pierre Legrand, 'On the Unbearable Localness of the Law: Academic Fallacies and Unreasonable Observations' (2002) 10 *European Review of Private Law* 61–76 at 66.

65 Schmid, 'European Civil Code', 284–5.

66 *Ibid.*, 285.

67 Van Gerven, 'Codifying European Private Law?', 164.

68 This echoes Legrand's comment that those versed in the civilian tradition will look to the establishment of codes and sets of rules as a means of furthering European integration: Legrand, 'Academic Fallacies and Unreasonable Observations', 66.

69 Van Gerven, 'Codifying European Private Law?', 164.

70 Pierre Legrand, 'Against a European Civil Code' (1997) 60 *Modern Law Review* 44–63 at 58.

71 Ugo Mattei and Anna di Robilant, 'The Art and Science of Critical Scholarship. Post-Modernism and International Style in the Legal Architecture of Europe' (2002) 10 *European Review of Private Law* 29–59 at 56.

national and international powers. There is no longer a place for such an anti-quated approach to law. For this reason, Hugh Collins asks: 'Why transplant a tool fashioned by nineteenth century nationalist and positivist legal science to the context of a multi-level, post-national system of governance?'[72] Of course, the problem is that many advocates of codification either do not recognise that we do indeed inhabit a legal system of complexity, multi-levels and post-nationalism or, where they do, the aim of the code is to remove such complexity and return to the era of hierarchy, authority and clear legal sovereignty.

The second aspect which demands that codification is rejected is that the approach to law discussed above, and exemplified by Zimmermann, rests on a political and ideological belief in legal positivism. This is an approach to law which is largely divorced from its wider social, political and economic context. Legal positivism has the effect of being an ideological protection of the status quo. The law is professed to be an objective and neutral science upon which economics, politics and society have little influence or impact. But this is not the case. Laws are naturally a product of their environment; they are shaped by social, economic and political pressures. While this may seem axiomatic to many, the particularly strong legal science tradition in some member states, evident in the approaches of those demanding harmonisation and then codification, holds dear to such claims. It is this scientific approach to law which prevails in the discussions about convergence, unification and harmonisation of European law generally, including family law. This methodology does not see the divergent political and social cultures of the member states as problematic to codification, as it sees law as largely separate from politics and culture. In the civil law tradition, Pierre Legrand contends, 'context', be it historical, sociological, economic, political or psychological, is simply not law.[73] On the contrary, Legrand argues, 'the law cannot be captured by a set of neatly organised rules' and that there is 'much "law" to be found beyond the rules'.[74]

This is the case for all law, but the case can be made even more explicitly for family law. David Bradley emphasises the continued influence of 'political and institutional factors on the evolution and structure of laws regulating domestic relationships'.[75] In relation to the factors which might prevent harmonisation of family laws, Bradley suggests that 'tradition, ideology and culture' do not of themselves present insurmountable obstacles, but that, as family laws are part of the 'political economy', they are less open to harmonisation.[76] He continues that central to the function of family law as an aspect of political economy is its role in

72 Hugh Collins, 'Editorial: The Future of European Private Law: An Introduction' (2004) 10 *European Law Journal* 649–52 at 651.
73 Legrand, 'Academic Fallacies and Unreasonable Observations', 66.
74 Pierre Legrand, 'European Legal Systems Are Not Converging' (1996) 45 *International and Comparative Law Quarterly* 52–81 at 59–60.
75 Bradley, 'A Family Law for Europe?', 67.
76 *Ibid.*, 70.

'attempting to establish norms, influence opinion and reinforce a particular system of social organisation'.[77] Principles of the social order are implicit in family laws, such as the privileging of the traditional family or of principles of egalitarianism. At issue will also be approaches to gender equality, to religion and to the state, and family law will also impact on principles of taxation, social and labour market policies. Consequently, Bradley suggests that family law has implications for nothing less than 'income and class equality'.[78] The essential point, he argues, is that 'family law is an indispensable medium to promote political objectives'.[79] Therefore, the construction of a family law for the European Union means 'abandonment of an aspect of national sovereignty'.[80]

This is perhaps best exemplified by the fact that many constitutions of the member states contain provisions relating to families, which necessarily impacts on family law reform debates and possibilities.[81] For example, in Germany, heterosexual cohabitants were excluded from the scope of a partnership law for gay and lesbian couples, supposedly in order to comply with the constitutional safeguard of marriage.[82] Furthermore, reform of family laws, and in particular divorce laws, have generated referendums in at least two member states in recent years.[83] This is evidence of the political, personal and religious significance of these issues.

Bradley precisely captures the nature of family law and why the legal positivist approach to family law and its harmonisation and codification fails to appreciate the wider context of family law reform.[84] Of course, this is also true of other areas of law which are the subject of harmonisation debates. Areas of core economic policy clearly involve tax, social security, competition law and labour market policies and impact most distinctly and deliberately on income and class equality. Thus, while many may dismiss such concerns regarding political and economic contexts, with for example Zweigert and Kötz presenting private law harmonisation as 'relatively "unpolitical"',[85] all fields of law have political and economic ambitions. Duncan Kennedy cogently argues that the view, that 'merely technical' issues of, to use his example, contract law are apolitical, indirectly reinforces

---

77 *Ibid.*, 71.   78 *Ibid.*, 71.   79 *Ibid.*, 71.   80 *Ibid.*, 71.
81 For example, the Portuguese Constitution refers to the family as a 'fundamental institution deserving the support of the State', with the Greek Constitution similarly stating that the family is a 'foundation stone for the preservation and advancement of the nation', as discussed in Eugenia Caracciolo di Torella and Annick Masselot, 'Under Construction: EU Family Law' (2004) 29 *European Law Review* 32–51.
82 Bradley, 'A Family Law for Europe?', 93.
83 In Ireland in 1986 and 1995 and in Italy in 1972, as discussed in Antokolskaia, 'The Harmonisation of Family Law', 31.
84 See also Rebecca Probert and Anne Barlow, 'Displacing Marriage – Diversification and Harmonisation Within Europe' (2000) 12 *Child and Family Law Quarterly* 153–65 at 165, who demonstrate the 'impact of political considerations' on legislation dealing with the rise in cohabitation outside marriage.
85 Zweigert and Kötz, *Comparative Law*, p. 40, discussed in Masha Antokolskaia, 'The "Better Law" Approach and the Harmonisation of Family Law' in Boele-Woelki (ed.), *Unification and Harmonisation of Family Law*, pp. 159–82.

'political centrism against radicalism'.[86] The Study Group on Social Justice in European Private Law provides a welcome antidote to the technical approach to codification with its clear exposition of the 'political significance of private law' both with respect to its 'construction of national identity and in its role of creating foundational values for the market order'.[87]

In essence, therefore, my argument is that harmonisation and codification proposals generally coincide with a belief in law that to all intents and purposes denies any political or ideological content.[88] The desire for unity, cohesion, rationality and the like reinforces the status quo and excludes alternative and often radical approaches to the law. This is not to say that all those who favour codification, particularly in the family law field, are conservatives who wish to reinforce the status quo. But this approach to law militates against alternatives, generally denies connections with other disciplines and contexts and certainly makes radical law reform more difficult. It also lacks, by definition, a real commitment to diversity and plurality, values to be cherished, as chapters 1 and 2 demonstrated. Further, if there was ever an area of law which demanded a broader approach to law, one which took into account the 'irrationality' of feelings, emotions, even instinct and their role in our intimate lives, it is family law.[89]

7.3.3   European family laws: converging or diverse?

It is clear that the family laws of the member states of the Union share many common features. David Bradley argues that general trends towards 'liberty, equality and secularity' can be identified.[90] Walter Pintens suggests that the European Convention on Human Rights has ensured the common recognition of children's rights, the equalisation of illegitimate and legitimate children and equality between women and men.[91] However, beyond such generalities, there is little agreement as to whether or not the family laws of member states are converging or not. This debate is important in that, for many advocating greater harmonisation and/or codification, the argument is made that family laws are converging and that greater harmonisation is largely inevitable. Therefore, it is argued, the drafting of codes and such like should be uncontroversial as it merely speeds up an already existing process.

Masha Antokolskaia claims that the 'infamous diversity of family laws within Europe is mainly a difference in the level of modernity of the family laws in

---

86 Duncan Kennedy, 'The Political Stakes in "Merely Technical" Issues of Contract Law' (2002) 10 *European Review of Private Law* 7–28 at 8.

87 Study Group on Social Justice in European Private Law, 'Social Justice in European Contract Law', 655.

88 This is not always the case. Masha Antokolskaia recognises that value judgments will have to be made in the harmonisation effort: 'The Harmonisation of Family Law', 44.

89 See Alison Diduck, *Law's Families* (London: Butterworths, 2003), p. vi.

90 Bradley, 'A Family Law for Europe?', 81.

91 Pintens, 'Europeanisation of Family Law', 6–7.

various countries across Europe'.[92] Further, the differences in the family laws of member states are directly linked to the differences in the timing of the modernisation of family law.[93] In other words, she is suggesting that there is a common path, from the mediaeval canon law to a modern progressive family law, on which all states can be placed and that all states are moving in the direction of 'modernity'. On this basis, she 'dares to predict' that the 'countries with less modern family law will reach the current level of the vanguard countries in due time'.[94] Convergence here is presented as a 'fact' and one which means that there are few problems with advancing greater harmonisation of family law on the basis of the 'modernised' concept of family law, as all states are approaching that end and will reach it eventually.

By contrast, David Bradley asserts that the convergence thesis in the field of family law is 'misconceived'.[95] The nature of the response to common trends and human rights norms, and the structure of reforms, he suggests, have varied significantly. Similarly, Gunther Teubner rejects the argument of convergence, suggesting on the contrary that the forces of globalisation may be resulting in more fragmented laws, not uniform laws, when viewed on a global scale.[96] In fact, he suggests that the movement towards unification is more likely to produce 'new divergences' as a result of their unintended consequences.[97] This is perhaps most evident in the new divergences between the peoples of Europe with the rise of nationalism and the fear of immigration.

One key area of contention in the divergence/convergence debate is over Nordic co-operation in the family law field. Some commentators argue that Nordic co-operation demonstrates the possibilities of greater harmonisation for the European Union. Walter Pintens and Koen Vanwinckelen suggest that the greater part of Nordic family law is 'unified, sometimes down to the smallest detail'.[98] By contrast, David Bradley maintains that Nordic co-operation in the family law field is in fact representative of the difficulties of harmonisation even within nations which are relatively close in political terms.[99] He concludes that, although, in very general terms, 'liberal laws have been introduced' in the Nordic countries, there is in fact 'little convergence'.[100] Again, we see here a difference in detail. Yes, there is liberalisation in the Nordic states and they can commonly be grouped together as having liberal and progressive family laws in contrast to many other European states. But the details of their laws differ, often considerably.

---

92 Antokolskaia, 'The Harmonisation of Family Law', 41.
93 *Ibid.*, 40–1.
94 Antokolskaia, 'The "Better Law" Approach', 172.
95 Bradley, 'A Family Law for Europe?', 81.
96 Gunther Teubner, 'Legal Irritants: Good Faith in British Law or How Unifying Law Ends Up in New Divergences' (1998) 61 *Modern Law Review* 11–32 at 13.
97 *Ibid.*, 13.
98 Pintens and Vanwinckelen, *European Family Law*, p. 14.
99 Bradley, 'A Family Law for Europe?'.
100 *Ibid.*, 89.

Ignoring such differences, which result from the political choices made in each state, which themselves result from the social, economic and political context of national debates, fails to look behind the text of the laws.[101]

For this reason, Pierre Legrand argues that the convergence thesis is based solely on an examination of 'posited' law, that is, the rules, concepts, substantive law and institutions of the law.[102] He suggests that rules are 'pernicious to the extent that they present but a surface image of a legal system'.[103] Rules and concepts, he continues, do little to disclose that legal systems are but the surface manifestation of legal cultures. In essence, a rule may be the same, but how legal systems came by that rule are likely to diverge considerably, giving the rule itself a different impact, history, ideology and practice. Legrand concludes that 'the law cannot be captured by a set of neatly organised rules' and that there is 'much "law" to be found beyond the rules'.[104] Although it is true, as Gunther Teubner points out, that the ties of laws to society are no longer comprehensive, and vary depending on the rule in question, there remains an undoubted connection between social context and law.[105] In many ways, Legrand's argument is simply a sophisticated rendering of the argument that rules or laws are not the objective, neutral, isolated concepts that many legal positivists so hold, as discussed above. Laws are naturally a product of their environment; they are shaped by social, economic and political pressures. While such an observation is self-evident for many, it requires continued repetition in the harmonisation and codification debates. My aim here is not to attempt to settle the complex 'convergence or not' debate. It is, however, to point out that it is by no means clear that there is convergence of the sort that makes arguments for greater harmonisation or codification of family law more amenable.[106] Convergence cannot be used as a justification for further harmonisation.

7.3.4   Drafting a code: choosing 'better' and 'modern' laws

Even were there to be general agreement that a European code of family law, or the promulgation of common principles of family law, were a positive development, the next challenge is in drafting such provisions. As noted above, the CEFL intends to produce a set of 'Principles of European Family Law' which will serve as a basis for further discussion of harmonisation of family law and become a

---

101 For another example, see Probert and Barlow, 'Displacing Marriage', who outline the common concern among European states regarding the legal issues arising from increasing extra-marital cohabitation and demonstrate the very different approaches to this 'problem' which states have taken, as a result of their differing political, cultural and economic contexts.
102 Legrand, 'European Legal Systems', 55.
103 *Ibid.*, 56.
104 *Ibid.*, 59–60.
105 Teubner, 'Legal Irritants', 18–19.
106 For a clear discussion of the diverse nature of the family policies of the member states, see Linda Hantrais, *Family Policy Matters: Responding to Family Change in Europe* (Bristol: Policy Press, 2004).

reference point for national, European and international legislators when considering reform of family law.[107] The question which arises here is whether drafting should be based on the 'common core' or the 'better law' methods.[108] The 'common core' approach is in many ways the 'simplest' method, requiring the selection of the most common rule among member states.[109] The common core may also require the adoption, not of the particular rule in question, but of a functional approach. That is, although rules may differ in the member states, the function of those rules may be the same or similar in a majority of member states, and that function is adopted as the 'common core', with a particular rule chosen to meet that function.

There are two principal problems with the common core methodology. First, there may not be a common core. There might be such diversity, that there is no core to discover and promote. Secondly, this methodology says nothing about the quality of the rules and whether what represents the common core is actually the 'best' (whatever that may be) method of approaching the particular issue under consideration. To meet these concerns, a 'better law' approach is often advocated.[110] The 'better law' approach demands a choice as to which rules are 'better' and such rules are then used as the basis for harmonisation. Of course, the principal problem with this approach is the justification of the choice of 'better' law. On what basis is the chosen rule 'better'?

Previous harmonisation efforts have adopted a variety of methods. The Unidroit Principles for International Commercial Contracts employed both a common core and a better law approach. In essence, where there was no common core, or irreconcilable differences, a 'better' law was chosen. Little explicit rationale has been put forward for the choice of the better law other than the 'special needs of international trade', whatever they may be.[111] The Lando Commission on European Contract Law took a similar approach, using both methodologies, suggesting a 'better law' where this would provide a 'more satisfactory answer than that which is reached by traditional legal thinking'.[112] The European Group on Tort Law is more explicitly in favour of a better law approach, seeking what

---

107 Similarly, Rene de Groot has proposed the negotiation of a treaty which would attempt to codify the 'basic principles of European family law', quoted in Boele-Woelki, 'The Road Towards a European Family Law'.

108 See further Antokolskaia, 'The "Better Law" Approach'.

109 The common core method is that adopted in the elaboration of the American Restatements. See further Richard Hyland, 'The American Restatements and the Uniform Commercial Code' in Hartkamp *et al.* (eds.), *Towards a European Civil Code*, pp. 55–70 at p. 63, discussed in Antokolskaia, 'The "Better Law" Approach'.

110 As advocated by Antokolskaia, 'The "Better Law" Approach'.

111 Michael Bonell, *An International Restatement of Contract Law – The UNIDROIT Principles of International Commercial Contracts* (New York: Transnational Publications, 1997), p. 16, discussed in Antokolskaia, 'The "Better Law" Approach', 163.

112 See further Ole Lando, 'Optional or Mandatory Europeanisation of Contract Law' (2000) 8 *European Review of Private Law* 59–69 at 65 and Antokolskaia, 'The "Better Law" Approach', 164.

constitutes a more 'modern' set of rules, though without giving any guidance as to what constitutes a 'modern' tort law.[113]

In the family law field, the CEFL has stated that it principally wishes to 'distil common rules', albeit recognising that there will be situations where alternative solutions will be proposed on the basis of 'better law' principles.[114] Assuming that the selection of the common core is unproblematic (a large assumption), on what basis is the better law selected? As already noted, there is an assumption underlying much of this academic work that the promulgation of these harmonised rules is a technical exercise, devoid of political controversy and therefore entailing few problems regarding a choice of better law. In the field of family law, the choices regarding better laws will likely be more highly scrutinised than those in other fields of private law as the ideological nature of family law is more obvious. Masha Antokolskaia accepts that the choice of 'better laws' is an ideological and political choice. She suggests that the principles of the European Convention on Human Rights and the Union Charter of Fundamental Rights 'could provide certain acknowledged reference points to justify the policy-laden choices of the drafters of harmonized family law'.[115] However, such principles, though important, provide only the bare minimum. Accordingly, she suggests that any shared concept of family rights throughout Europe offers little help when drafting better family laws. The recommendation made by Antokolskaia in the end is to 'dare' use a 'better law' approach, based on the 'highest standard of modernity achieved in present-day European family law'.[116]

The problem here is in how one determines what is the more 'modern' law. David Bradley provides many examples to support concerns regarding the 'modern' law thesis. Regarding the establishment of paternity, for example, he details how Sweden and other Nordic countries operate a mandatory paternity procedure whenever a child is born to an unmarried mother, contrasting this with English law where there is no such procedure and only state pressure where the mother is in receipt of state benefits.[117] Bradley suggests that English law may be less egalitarian, but more libertarian, compared with the 'strong state ethic' in the Nordic laws. Which law regarding paternity is the more progressive? It is not at all clear and any choice will depend on a choice of political ideology. Is it not perhaps valid that there are divergences? So long as fathers have the opportunity to establish paternity and to avail themselves of their parental rights, as human rights norms would mandate, is there any problem with a diverse

---

113 Quoted in Antokolskaia, 'The "Better Law" Approach'.
114 Boeli-Woelki, 'Drafting of Principles of a European Family Law', 180.
115 Antokolskaia, 'The "Better Law" Approach', 174.
116 Her proposals are not about 'a crusade aiming to enforce libertarian principles of family law' upon the European population, but to draft principles which could be used by those advocating reform and could form a basis for recommendation and planning of reform: Antokolskaia, 'The "Better Law" Approach', 182.
117 Bradley, 'A Family Law for Europe?', 90–1.

approach to how paternity is established, varying from state to state depending on each state's approach to these issues?

Bradley gives another salient example in relation to divorce law.[118] It appears to be a general 'progressive' view that the abolition of fault as a ground of divorce is appropriate: part of a 'modern' family law. However, Norway recently introduced violent conduct as a ground for divorce as a means of emphasising the seriousness of domestic violence.[119] Which is the more modernised and progressive law on which common principles and harmonisation of family law should be based? How is such a choice to be made? Is it not possible that this divergent approach of Norway is a valuable opportunity to test new approaches to divorce law which may have positive impacts on other areas of law and policy? Might it not be that other states can learn from Norway's example? In a harmonised family law, such options would be extremely limited if not curtailed entirely.

There are many other similar examples which demonstrate that there are no clear answers to the many problems of regulating families and family life. There are a variety of approaches, many of which can claim to be modern and progressive. It is in fact the value of these divergent approaches which should counsel us against greater family law harmonisation and codification. Pluralism of laws should be seen as offering new opportunities. New ideas and new processes can be identified, acting as 'irritants' in national legal systems, moving towards change for the better. This, rather than entrenching a particular vision, should be the way to progress. Legal 'irritants' can 'unleash an evolutionary dynamic in which the external rule's meaning will be reconstructed and the internal context will undergo fundamental change'.[120] There is no automatic transfer of a rule into a national legal system; there is necessarily difference as the rule becomes part of different national laws and legal systems. In this way, European fragmentation is a source of opportunities. Different systems tackle similar problems in different ways and much can be learnt from this. The loss of diversity in a strict system limits innovation.[121] Legal solutions from different countries can be used to create European solutions, but this process is ongoing, experimental and requires a continuous free flow of ideas. Equally, as Roger van den Bergh argues, 'diversity in rules of private law may bring benefits for society as a whole', being better able to satisfy the 'heterogeneous preferences of a large population'.[122]

---

118 *Ibid.*, pp. 96–7.
119 Cited in *ibid.*, 97.
120 Teubner, 'Legal Irritants', 12.
121 For a similar argument in relation to tort and contract law, see Thomas Wilhelmsson, 'Private Law in the EU: Harmonised or Fragmented Europeanisation?' (2002) 10 *European Review of Private Law* 77–94 at 92–3.
122 Roger van den Bergh, 'Subsidiarity as an Economic Demarcation Principle in the Emergence of European Private Law' (1998) 5 *Maastricht Journal of European and Comparative Law* 129–52 at 130.

7.3.5   Market values, family values and codes

For Thomas Wilhelmsson, the adoption of a code would specifically hinder 'democratic pressure for more welfarist norms'.[123] This is for two main reasons. First, he rightly suggests it would mean a shift of power from democratic national legislatures, to the undemocratic, secretive processes of Community law-making. This would more than likely mean that the development of particularly welfarist laws would be limited.[124] And this links to his second concern about moves towards codification. Wilhelmsson claims that the moves towards codification require adherence to a particular political agenda, that of conservative market values.[125] For many, he suggests, this may be a conscious move. But, for those who prefer more welfarist approaches to law, the harmonisation process requires such values to be suppressed. The civil codes of the nineteenth century were drafted at a time of rampant laissez-faire. They were also developed by a dominant social class resolute on pursuing its own agenda, which did not include welfare or social concerns. It is many of these values that would be included in the substance of a code and in its very drafting and promulgation.

It is indeed the language of markets and market integration which is behind many of the calls for greater harmonisation and codification. Thus, despite the fact that the business community has generally not been terribly interested in codification proposals,[126] economic arguments are used to justify a code. It is generally argued that a properly functioning internal market within the Union demands a code.[127] Legal diversity is assumed to be anti-competitive, costly for business and highly risky. Indeed, this approach is affirmed by the Council when it acknowledged that 'differences between national laws may . . . have a negative impact on cross-border transactions and on the functioning of the internal market'.[128] Such arguments are generally presented without evidential support: they are mere assertions.

But, even were this the case for areas of economic law, in the field of family law such discussions and values should have no place. Although there are those who apply an economic analysis to family law,[129] it would be highly regrettable were this approach to hold sway within the Union. However, we have already seen that,

---

123 Wilhelmsson, 'Private Law in the EU', 86. See also Wilhelmsson, 'Varieties of Welfarism in European Contract Law' (2004) 10 *European Law Journal* 712–33.

124 Wilhelmsson details his argument by reference to the codification proposals in relation to contract law. He suggests, for example, that a European contract law based on the Lando Commission principles would have little space for consumer protection legislation: Wilhelmsson, 'Private Law in the EU', 86–7.

125 Wilhelmsson, 'Private Law in the EU', 78.

126 As discussed in Hondius, 'Towards a European *Ius Commune*', 131–2.

127 See many of the contributions to Hartkamp *et al.* (eds.), *Towards a European Civil Code*.

128 Council Report on the need to approximate Member States' legislation in civil matters, Council Report No. 13017/01 of 29 October 2001, adopted on 16 November 2001, para. 2.

129 See, for example: Anthony Dnes and Robert Rowthorn (eds.), *The Law and Economics of Marriage and Divorce* (Cambridge: Cambridge University Press, 2002).

in the development of family law thus far within the Union, the political ambitions for the Union have often been dominant in the drafting and adoption process. It was argued in the last chapter that family law has been instrumentalised within the Community, it being used to support the promotion of a wide range of Community and Union policies, including economic ones. The Council report on the approximation of civil laws did retreat to some extent from this position, stating that 'economic considerations cannot be applied in the same terms' to other fields of private law including family law.[130] This does not mean that there are no economic justifications – just that they are 'not the same'. Indeed, the Council went on to state that the free movement of persons and the desire to create a genuine area of freedom, justice and security could provide a justification for further harmonisation in a field such as family law.[131] While the latter ambition may be primarily political, as well as economic, the free movement of persons has thus far been soundly economic in its ambition and enforcement. True free movement is not a reality for the vast majority of Europeans, even Union citizens. Economics, as well as politics, limit the scope of Community provisions in this area.

Finally, it has been argued throughout this book that current Union law privileges a dominant ideology of the family based on heterosexual marriage, a sexual division of labour and a protectionist approach to children. It is not a modern, egalitarian approach to families and family practices. This ideology of family has been reproduced in many different fields of substantive law, including the Union's incipient family law. The problem is that the adoption of general principles in the area of family policy, and even family law, are not being mooted as part of a European strategy for the modernisation of family life, or the removal of traditional barriers and inequalities. Nor are the harmonisation proposals being advanced on the basis of ensuring the Europe-wide application of the principles of equality, justice, welfare of children (even were this to be possible), or with the aim of promoting fairer regulation of change and conflict in intimate relationships.

They are being proposed as part of an economistic drive to encourage the faster creation of the producers and consumers of the next generation; a concern that changing patterns of family life may endanger fiscal budgets as the population gets older and younger generations are no longer able or willing to care for their elders; a fear that if the birth rate is not increased Europe may lose its footing on the international stage; and as part of a formalistic, technocratic desire for uniformity, efficiency and rationality. None of these ambitions speaks to what should be the basis for laws regulating families and family practices. Perhaps this is because the functions of national family laws, and the principles which govern

---

130 Council Report on the need to approximate Member States' legislation in civil matters, Council Report No. 13017/01 of 29 October 2001, adopted on 16 November 2001, para. 3.
131 *Ibid.*

their adoption and application, can only be fully and fairly effected at a local and individual level. Countless studies have demonstrated that, even on a national scale, the uniform application of a principle of family law can have inequitable outcomes in the complex and often irreconcilable arena of family relationships.[132] Uniform application at a supranational level therefore raises frightening possibilities; adverse outcomes which are clouded when the expressed aims are not justice and fairness, but economistic, demographic and political.

In an analysis of Anglo-Australian law, John Dewar argues that family law is replete with contradictions, is often incoherent and is chaotic.[133] He argues that this does not lead to a diagnosis of crisis, but is a perfectly normal state of affairs as family law deals with contradictory emotions, passions and values and should not be expected to conform to a theoretical rationality of clear rules. Chaos is not therefore a threat to family law, but should be expected. This approach to family law has much to commend it, but is threatened by the centripetal impulses demonstrated by Union law and harmonisation advocates. Not only is the chaotic approach threatened, but so is progressive change in the relationships of women and men and the acceptance of non-traditional families. Accordingly, therefore, a harmonised or codified Union family law is not just a concern for its desire to remove chaos and impose 'order' and 'rationality' which may in fact work against the interests legitimately to be pursued by a family law, but it must also be opposed because of the concept of family values which currently underpins Union law.

7.4   Conclusions: what future for European Union family law?

It would be naïve in the light of the discussion in this and the previous chapter to think or even hope that there would be no future for the European Union's family law. Despite the arguments against further harmonisation and codification raised above, the momentum towards these goals seems ever stronger and increasingly difficult to resist. As is so often the case in European law and politics, the debate now centres on how, and not whether or why.

Nonetheless, what would be the ideal situation? As I have argued throughout this book, human rights principles must form the basis for all family laws and concepts of 'family' throughout the Union. To the extent that this might comprise 'harmonisation' then it is to be welcomed. Thus, there is no room for national isolation; no state can turn its head away from the prevailing norms of a rights-based law and politics. Family law is not so related to culture, political economy

---

132 For a recent analysis of this in English law, see Carol Smart and Bren Neal's discussion of the welfare of the child principle where courts appear to work *to* an abstract principle, rather than working *from* it in individual cases, thus causing unnecessary hardship: *Family Fragments?* (London: Sage, 1999), especially at pp. 186–99.

133 John Dewar, 'The Normal Chaos of Family Law' (1998) 61 *Modern Law Review* 467.

or individual societies that it is immune from challenge on the basis of human rights principles. The core of such human rights principles is to be found in the European Convention and in the jurisprudence of the Court of Human Rights. Although the Convention is a flawed instrument, for the reasons developed in earlier chapters, it remains the commonly accepted foundation for human rights throughout Europe. It has the political legitimacy and support of all member states. The Union's Charter of Fundamental Rights clearly supplements the Convention and does provide more adequate and detailed rights provision in some areas, particularly in relation to children's rights. In interpreting the Charter, and utilising the Convention, the Court of Justice must follow the principles of the Convention, providing 'more extensive' protection where possible, based on the principles of value pluralism.

This is not to suggest that there is no room for common action among states in the family law field. Cross-national family disputes raise very real problems of conflicts of laws. My preferred solution for such problems is the potentially global one, through the work of the Hague Conference. The work of this organisation has served Europe and many other countries extremely well. Its work is collaborative, consensus driven and focuses on the issues of family law and 'family values' at stake, as opposed to the bitter political, economic and ideological battles which characterise Community law-making. It seems that the real needs of families remain a vague and distant concern when Community family law is in debate.

Thus, while Masha Antokolskaia states that, if the European Union is indeed a 'postmodern' state, then there is little future for family law harmonisation, it does not seem that the latter necessarily follows the former.[134] The Union clearly exhibits features of a 'postmodern' state, as discussed in chapter 1, and should be promoting the diversity and plurality of families and family law as argued for in this book. Nonetheless, there does appear to be a future for family law within the Union. Indeed, if it were ever in doubt, the Nice Treaty put paid to that with the first, albeit indirect, reference to family law in the treaties.[135] Furthermore, the European Constitutional Convention explicitly refers to the adoption of 'laws and framework laws concerning family law' and also to the adoption of 'laws and framework laws concerning parental responsibility'.[136] Family law is now part of the Union and Community law landscape.

Accordingly, the choice posited by Pierre Legrand, that of 'legal pluralism versus legal convergence',[137] appears to have been made in favour of the latter. Legrand bemoans the existence of projects across Europe which, rather than being

---

134 Antokolskaia, 'The Harmonisation of Family Law', 44.
135 The new Article 67 of the EC Treaty states that the co-decision legislative procedure will apply in all cases under Article 65 of the EC Treaty 'with the exception of aspects relating to family law'.
136 Article 14(3) of Part II, 14 March 2003, CONV 614/03.
137 Legrand, 'Academic Fallacies and Unreasonable Observations', 61.

aimed at fostering 'deep understanding across legal cultures and legal traditions', in fact are instrumental initiatives purporting to show that, if there are any differences, they are unimportant.[138] These instrumental strategies 'wish to efface difference, to erase it'.[139] This erasure of difference and promotion of harmonisation and codification is a vision of a future for Europe which is divorced from the reality of the European legal order and of the needs for the future. The old ideas of state-building and sovereignty, upon which codification claims are largely based, will not solve the problems or provide the solutions for Europe. For over forty years, the Community, and then the Union, has been based on ideas of liberal legalism, has integrated through law and has harmonised ever more fields of law.

But the disenchantment with Europe, the alienation of its people, has grown ever stronger. This is evidenced not just in the lack of democratic participation in the Union, but also in terms of the rise of nationalism in many member states. The desire to reclaim the local and national is perhaps a reaction against a Europe seen as unwieldy and divorced from the needs and interests of its people. More harmonised laws are not likely to solve this problem. Indeed, they are going to make it worse. The very idea of a unified private law goes against the grain of theoretical thinking about the regulation of Europe and its legal system. It also goes against the empirical evidence of multiplicity, pluralism and diversity. In the final analysis, even positive legal analysis, it also goes against the very concepts of 'closer co-operation', variable geometry, flexibility and subsidiarity in the treaties which speak of a legal system which is not unified and clearly does not wish to be.

138 *Ibid.*, 63.   139 *Ibid.*, 63.

Bibliography

Ackers, Louise (director), *Children, Citizenship and Internal Migration in the European Community* (Project funded by the Nuffield Foundation and the European Commission, project reference 96-10-EET-0122-00)

'From "Best Interests" to Participatory Rights – Children's Involvement in Family Migration Decisions' (2000) 12 *Child and Family Law Quarterly* 167–84

Ackers, Louise and Stalford, Helen, 'Children, Migration and Citizenship in the European Union: Intra-Community Mobility and the Status of Children in EC Law' (1999) 21 *Children and Youth Services Review* 987–1010

A Community for Children? Children, Citizenship and Internal Migration in the EU (Aldershot: Ashgate, 2004)

Alston, Philip, 'The Best Interests Principle: Towards a Reconciliation of Culture and Human Rights' (1994) 8 *International Journal of Law and the Family* 1–25

Antokolskaia, Masha, 'The Harmonization of Family Law: Old and New Dilemmas' (2003) 11 *European Review of Private Law* 28–49

'The "Better Law" Approach and the Harmonization of Family Law' in Boele-Woelki, Katharina (ed.), *Perspectives for the Unification and Harmonisation of Family Law in Europe* (Antwerp: Intersentia, 2003), pp. 159–82

Arber, Sara and Ginn, Jay, 'The Mirage of Gender Equality: Occupational Success in the Labour Market and Within Marriage' (1995) 46 *British Journal of Sociology* 21–43

Archbold, Claire, 'Family Law-Making and Human Rights in the UK' in Maclean, Mavis (ed.), *Making Law for Families* (Oxford: Hart Publishing, 2000), pp. 185–208

Armstrong, Kenneth, 'Tales of the Community: Sexual Orientation Discrimination and EC Law' (1998) 20 *Journal of Social Welfare and Family Law* 455–79

Backstrom, Kirsten, 'The International Human Rights of the Child: Do They Protect the Girl Child?' (1996–7) 30 *George Washington Journal of International Law and Economics* 541–82

Bailey-Harris, Rebecca, 'Law and the Unmarried Couple – Oppression or Liberation?' (1996) 8 *Child and Family Law Quarterly* 137–47

'Third Stonewall Lecture – Lesbian and Gay Family Values and the Law' (1999) 29 *Family Law* 560–70

Bainham, Andrew, 'Family Law in a Pluralistic Society' (1995) 22 *Journal of Law and Society* 234–47

'Family Rights in the Next Millennium' (2000) 53 *Current Legal Problems* 471–503

Bainham, Andrew and Brooks-Gordon, Belinda, 'Reforming the Law on Sexual Offences', in Brooks-Gordon, Belinda *et al.* (eds.), *Sexuality Repositioned* (Oxford: Hart Publishing, 2004), pp. 261–96

Bainham, Andrew, Sclater, Shelley Day and Richards, Martin, 'Introduction' in Bainham, Andrew, Sclater, Shelley Day and Richards, Martin (eds.), *What Is a Parent? A Socio-Legal Analysis* (Oxford: Hart Publishing, 1999), pp. 1–23

Bala, Nicholas and Bromwich, Rebecca Jaremko, 'Context and Inclusivity in Canada's Evolving Definition of the Family' (2002) 16 *International Journal of Law, Policy and the Family* 145–80

Ball, Carlos, 'Moral Foundations for a Discourse on Same Sex Marriage: Looking Beyond Political Liberalism' (1997) 85 *Georgetown Law Journal* 1871–943

Bankowski, Zenon and Christodoulidis, Emilios, 'The European Union as an Essentially Contested Project' (1998) 4 *European Law Journal* 341–54

Bar, Christian von, 'The Study Group on a European Civil Code' in European Parliament Working Paper, *The Private Law Systems in the EU: Discrimination on the Grounds of Nationality and the Need for a European Civil Code* (Luxembourg: European Parliament, 1999), pp. 133–8

'Paving the Way Forward with Principles of European Private Law' in Grundmann, Stefan and Struyck, Jules (eds.), *An Academic Green Paper on European Contract Law* (The Hague: Kluwer, 2002), pp. 137–45

Barbera, Marzia, 'The Unsolved Conflict: Reshaping Family Work and Market Work in the EU Legal Order' in Hervey, Tamara and Kenner, Jeff (eds.), *Economic and Social Rights under the EU Charter of Fundamental Rights – A Legal Perspective* (Oxford: Hart Publishing, 2003), pp. 139–60

Barlow, Anne and Probert, Rebecca, 'Displacing Marriage – Diversification and Harmonisation within Europe' (2000) 12 *Child and Family Law Quarterly* 153–65

Barrett, Michèle, *Women's Oppression Today* (London: Verso, 1980)

Barrett, Michèle and McIntosh, Mary, *The Anti-Social Family* (London: Verso, 1982)

Basedow, Jürgen, 'A Case for a European Contract Act' in Grundmann, Stefan and Struyck, Jules (eds.), *An Academic Green Paper on European Contract Law* (The Hague: Kluwer, 2002), pp. 147–58

Beale, Hugh, Hartkamp, Arthur, Kötz, Hein and Tallon, Denis (eds.), *Contract Law – Casebooks for the Common Law of Europe* (Oxford: Hart Publishing, 2002)

Beaumont, Paul, 'European Court of Justice and Jurisdiction and Enforcement of Judgments in Civil and Commercial Matters' (1999) 48 *International and Comparative Law Quarterly* 223–9

Beaumont, Paul and Moir, Gordon, 'Brussels Convention II: A New Private International Law Instrument in Family Matters for the European Union or European Community?' (1995) 20 *European Law Review* 268–88

Beck, Ulrich and Beck-Gernsheim, Elisabeth, *The Normal Chaos of Love* (Cambridge: Polity Press, 1995)

Bell, Mark, 'Shifting Conceptions of Sexual Discrimination at the Court of Justice: From *P v S* to *Grant v SWT*' (1999) 5 *European Law Journal* 63–81

'Sexual Orientation Discrimination in Employment: An Evolving Role for the European Union' in Wintemute, Robert and Andenas, Mads (eds.), *Legal Recognition of Same Sex Partnerships* (Oxford: Hart Publishing, 2001), pp. 653–76

Anti-Discrimination Law and the European Union (Oxford: Oxford University Press, 2002)

'We Are Family? Same Sex Partners and EU Migration Law' (2004) 9 *Maastricht Journal of European and Comparative Law* 335–55

Benn, Melissa, *Madonna and Child – Towards a New Politics of Motherhood* (London: Jonathan Cape, 1998)

Blake, Nicholas, 'Family Life in Community Law: The Limits of Freedom and Dignity' in Guild, Elspeth (ed.), *The Legal Framework and Social Consequences of Free Movement of Persons in the European Union* (The Hague: Kluwer, 1999), pp. 7–19

Boele-Woelki, Katharina, 'Comparative Research-Based Drafting of Principles of European Family Law' in Faure, Michael, Smits, Jan and Schneider, Hildegard (eds.), *Towards a European Ius Commune in Legal Education and Research* (Antwerp: Intersentia, 2002), pp. 171–89

'The Road Towards a European Family Law' (1997) 1 *Electronic Journal of Comparative Law*, available at http://www.ejcl.org/11/art11-1.html

Boele-Woelki, Katharina, Braat, Bente and Sumner, Ian (eds.), *European Family Law in Action, Volume I: Grounds for Divorce* (Antwerp: Intersentia, 2003)

(eds.), *European Family Law in Action, Volume II: Maintenance Between Former Spouses* (Antwerp: Intersentia, 2003)

Boele-Woelki, Katharina and Fuchs, Angelika (eds.), *Legal Recognition of Same-Sex Couples in Europe* (Antwerp: Intersentia, 2003)

Bogdan, Michael, 'Registered Partnerships and EC Law' in Boele-Woelki, Katharina and Fuchs, Angelika (eds.), *Legal Recognition of Same-Sex Couples in Europe* (Antwerp: Intersentia, 2003), pp. 171–7

Bonell, Michael, *An International Restatement of Contract Law – The UNIDROIT Principles of International Commercial Contracts* (New York: Transnational Publications, 1997)

A New Approach to International Commercial Contracts – The Unidroit Principles of International Commercial Contracts (The Hague: Kluwer, 1999)

Bovis, Christopher and Cnossen, Christine, 'Stereotyped Assumptions Versus Sex Equality: A Socio-Legal Analysis of the Equality Laws in the European Union' (1996) 12 *International Journal of Comparative Labour Law and Industrial Relations* 7–23 and 131–47

Bowlby, John, *Maternal Care and Mental Health* (Geneva: World Health Organization, 1951)

Boyd, Susan, 'Some Postmodernist Challenges to Feminist Analyses of Law, Family and State: Ideology and Discourse in Child Custody Law' (1991) 10 *Canadian Journal of Family Law* 79–113

'Family, Law and Sexuality: Feminist Engagements' (1999) 8 *Social and Legal Studies* 369–90

Bradley, David, 'A Family Law for Europe? Sovereignty, Political Economy and Legit-imation' in Boele-Woelki, Katharina (ed.), *Perspectives for the Unification and Harmonisation of Family Law in Europe* (Antwerp: Intersentia, 2003), pp. 65–104

Bridgeman, Jo and Monk, Daniel (eds.), *Feminist Perspectives on Child Law* (London: Cavendish, 2000)

Brinkmann, Gisbert, 'Family Reunion, Third Country Nationals and the Community's New Powers' in Guild, Elspeth and Harlow, Carol (eds.), *Implementing Amsterdam – Immigration and Asylum Rights in EC Law* (Oxford: Hart Publishing, 2001), pp. 241–66

Búrca, Gráinne de, 'The Drafting of the EU Charter of Fundamental Rights' (2001) 26 *European Law Review* 126–38

Campbell, Tom, 'The Rights of the Minor: As Person, as Child, as Juvenile, as Future Adult' in Alston, Philip, Parker, Stephen and Seymour, John (eds.), *Children, Rights and the Law* (Oxford: Clarendon Press, 1992), pp. 1–23

Camus, Albert, *Resistance, Rebellion and Death* (London: Vintage, 1994)

Canor, Iris, 'Equality for Lesbians and Gay Men in the European Community Legal Order – "They Shall Be Male and Female"' (2000) 7 *Maastricht Journal of European and Comparative Law* 273–99

Caporaso, James, 'The European Union and Forms of the State: Westphalian, Regulatory or Post-Modern' (1996) 34 *Journal of Common Market Studies* 29–52

Cappelletti, Mauro (ed.), *New Perspectives for a Common Law for Europe* (Florence: European University Institute, 1976)

Caracciolo di Torella, Eugenia, 'Childcare, Employment and Equality in the EC: First (False) Steps of the Court' (2000) 25 *European Law Review* 310–16

'The "Family-Friendly" Workplace: The EC Position' (2001) 17 *International Journal of Comparative Labour Law and Industrial Relations* 325–44

Caracciolo di Torella, Eugenia and Masselot, Annick, 'Under Construction: EU Family Law' (2004) 29 *European Law Review* 32–51

Castles, Francis, 'The World Turned Upside Down: Below Replacement Fertility, Chan-ging Preferences and Family Friendly Public Policy in 21 OECD Countries' (2003) 13 *Journal of European Social Policy* 209–27

Chodorow, Nancy, *The Reproduction of Mothering: Psychoanalysis and the Sociology of Gender* (Berkeley: University of California Press, 1978)

Christodoulidis, Emilios, 'Constitutional Irresolution: Law and the Framing of Civil Society' (2003) 9 *European Law Journal* 401–32

Clapham, Andrew and Weiler, Joseph, 'Lesbians and Gay Men in the European Community Legal Order' in Waaldijk, Kees and Clapham, Andrew (eds.), *Homo-sexuality: A European Community Issue* (Dordrecht: Martinus Nijhoff, 1993), pp. 7–69

Claussen, Cathryn, 'Incorporating Women's Reality into Legal Neutrality in the European Community: The Sex Segregation of Labor and the Work–Family Nexus' (1991) 22 *Law and Policy in International Business* 787–813

Cohen, Howard, *Equal Rights for Children* (Totowa, NJ: Littlefield, 1980)

Collier, Richard, ' "Feminising" the Workplace? Law, the "Good Parent" and the "Problem of Men" ' in Morris, Anne and O'Donnell, Therese (eds.), *Feminist Perspectives on Employment Law* (London: Cavendish, 1999), pp. 161–81

Collins, Hugh, 'Editorial: The Future of European Private Law: An Introduction' (2004) 10 *European Law Journal* 649–52

Coppel, Jason and O'Neill, Aidan, 'The European Court of Justice: Taking Rights Seriously?' (1992) 12 *Legal Studies* 227–45

Cossman, Brenda, 'Family Inside/Out' (1994) 44 *University of Toronto Law Journal* 1–39

Costello, Cathryn, 'Gender Equalities and the Charter of Fundamental Rights of the European Union' in Hervey, Tamara and Kenner, Jeff (eds.), *Economic and Social Rights under the EU Charter of Fundamental Rights – A Legal Perspective* (Oxford: Hart Publishing, 2003), pp. 111–38

Cullen, Holly, 'Children's Rights' in Peers, Steve and Ward, Angela (eds.), *The European Union Charter of Fundamental Rights* (Oxford: Hart Publishing, 2004), pp. 323–46

Curtin, Deirdre, *Postnational Democracy: The European Union in Search of a Public Philosophy* (The Hague: Kluwer Law International, 1997)

Dashwood, Alan, 'States in the European Union' (1998) 23 *European Law Review* 201–16

Dewar, John, 'The Normal Chaos of Family Law' (1998) 61 *Modern Law Review* 467

Derrida, Jacques, *The Other Heading: Reflections on Today's Europe* (Bloomington: Indiana University Press, 1992)

Diduck, Alison, *Law's Families* (London: Butterworths, 2003)

Diduck, Alison and Kaganas, Felicity, *Family Law, Gender and the State* (Oxford: Hart Publishing, 1999)

Dnes, Anthony and Rowthorn, Robert (eds.), *The Law and Economics of Marriage and Divorce* (Cambridge: Cambridge University Press, 2002)

Douglas, Gillian, *An Introduction to Family Law* (Oxford: Oxford University Press, 2001)

Dumon, Wilfried, 'Recent Trends and New Prospects for a European Family Policy' in Cavana, Henry (ed.), *The New Citizenship of the Family* (Aldershot: Ashgate, 2000)

Dunne, Gillian (ed.), *Living 'Difference' – Lesbian Perspectives on Work and Family Life* (New York: Harrington Park Press, 1998)

'A Passion for "Sameness"? Sexuality and Gender Accountability' in Silva, Elizabeth and Smart, Carol (eds.), *The New Family?* (London: Sage, 1999), pp. 66–82

Eleftheriadis, Pavlos, 'Cosmopolitan Law' (2003) 9 *European Law Journal* 241–63

Elman, R. Amy, 'The Limits of Citizenship: Migration, Sex Discrimination and Same Sex Partners in EU Law' (2000) 38 *Journal of Common Market Studies* 729–49

'Familiar Orientations: Sex Discrimination, Same Sex Partners and Migration in European Law', paper presented to the American Political Science Association Annual Conference, 1999, quoted in Stychin, Carl, '*Grant*-ing Rights: The Politics of Rights, Sexuality and European Union' (2000) 51 *Northern Ireland Legal Quarterly* 281–302

Eskridge, William, 'The Ideological Structure of the Same Sex Marriage Debate (And Some Postmodern Arguments for Same Sex Marriage)' in Wintemute, Robert and Andenas, Mads (eds.), *Legal Recognition of Same Sex Partnerships* (Oxford: Hart Publishing, 2001), pp. 113–32

Ettelbrick, Paula, 'Since When Is Marriage a Path to Liberation?' in Sherman, Suzanne (ed.), *Lesbian and Gay Marriage: Private Commitments, Public Ceremonies* (Philadelphia: Temple University Press, 1992), pp. 20–7

European Commission, *The Social Situation in the European Union 2003* (Brussels: European Commission, 2003)

European Commission Childcare Network, *Childcare in the European Community 1985–1990* (Brussels: European Commission – Women of Europe Supplement No. 31, August 1990)

    Leave Arrangements for Workers with Children (Brussels: European Commission, 1994)

Eurostat, *Living Conditions in Europe – Statistical Pocketbook* (Luxembourg: European Commission, 2000)

Eyer, Diane, *Mother Infant Bonding – A Scientific Fiction* (New Haven: Yale University Press, 1992)

Fagnani, Jeanne, 'Recent Changes in Family Policy in France' in Drew, Eileen, Emerek, Ruth and Mahon, Evelyn (eds.), *Women, Work and the Family in Europe* (London: Routledge, 1998), pp. 58–65

Fineman, Martha Albertson, *The Neutered Mother, the Sexual Family and Other Twentieth Century Tragedies* (London: Routledge, 1995)

Firestone, Shulamith, *The Dialectic of Sex* (London: Paladin, 1972)

Fitzpatrick, Peter, 'New Europe and Old Stories: Mythology and Legality in the European Union' in Fitzpatrick, Peter and Bergeron, James (eds.), *Europe's Other: European Law Between Modernity and Postmodernity* (Aldershot: Ashgate, 1998), pp. 27–46

Fletcher, George, 'Comparative Law as a Subversive Discipline' (1998) 46 *American Journal of Comparative Law* 683–700

Forder, Caroline, 'Article 8 ECHR: The Utter Limits of "Family Life" and the Law of Parenthood' (1997) 4 *Maastricht Journal of European and Comparative Law* 125–42

Fortin, Jane, *Children's Rights and the Developing Law* (London: Butterworths, 1998)

Fredman, Sandra, 'European Community Discrimination Law: A Critique' (1992) 21 *Industrial Law Journal* 119–34

    Women and the Law (Oxford: Oxford University Press, 1997)

Freeman, Michael, 'Taking Children's Rights More Seriously' (1992) 6 *International Journal of Law and the Family* 52–71

    'Taking Children's Rights More Seriously' in Alston, Philip, Parker, Stephen and Seymour, John (eds.), *Children, Rights and the Law* (Oxford: Clarendon Press, 1992), pp. 52–71

    'The Limits of Children's Rights' in Freeman, Michael and Veerman, Philip (eds.), *The Ideologies of Children's Rights* (Leiden: Martinus Nijhoff, 1992)

Fukuyama, Francis, *The End of History and the Last Man* (London: Penguin, 1992)

Gallagher, Anne, 'Human Rights and the New UN Protocols on Trafficking and Migrant Smuggling: A Preliminary Analysis' (2001) 23 *Human Rights Quarterly* 975–1004

Garry, Hannah, 'Harmonisation of Asylum Law and Policy Within the European Union: A Human Rights Perspective' (2002) 20 *Netherlands Quarterly of Human Rights* 163–84

Giddens, Anthony, *Modernity and Self-Identity: Self and Society in the Late Modern Age* (Cambridge: Polity Press, 1991)

The Transformation of Intimacy (Cambridge: Polity Press, 1992)

Giddens, Anthony and Pierson, Christopher, *Conversations with Anthony Giddens: Making Sense of Modernity* (Cambridge: Polity Press, 1998)

Gittins, Diana, *The Family in Question – Changing Households and Familiar Ideologies* (2nd edn, Basingstoke: Macmillan, 1993)

Glendon, Mary Ann, *Rights Talk: The Impoverishment of Political Discourse* (New York: The Free Press, 1991)

Goonesekere, Savitri, 'Human Rights as a Foundation for Family Law Reform' (2000) 8 *International Journal of Children's Rights* 83–99

Gordley, James, *The Enforceability of Promises in European Contract Law* (Cambridge: Cambridge University Press, 2001)

Gori, Gisella, *Towards an EU Right to Education* (The Hague: Kluwer Law International, 2001)

Griffin, Kate, 'Getting Kids and Keeping Them: Lesbian Motherhood in Europe' in Dunne, Gillian (ed.), *Living 'Difference' – Lesbian Perspectives on Work and Family Life* (New York: Harrington Park Press, 1998), pp. 23–34

Guild, Elspeth, 'Between Persecution and Protection – Refugees and the New European Asylum Policy' (2000) 3 *Cambridge Yearbook of European Legal Studies* 69–198

Habermas, Jürgen, *Between Facts and Norms: Contributions to a Discourse Theory of Law and Democracy* (Cambridge: Polity Press, 1996)

The Postnational Constellation (Cambridge: Polity Press, 2001)

Hamilton, Carolyn and Perry, Alison (eds.), *Family Law in Europe* (2nd edn, London: Butterworths, 2002)

Hantrais, Linda, *Family Policy Matters: Responding to Family Change in Europe* (Bristol: Policy Press, 2004)

Hartkamp, Arthur S. *et al.* (eds.), *Towards a European Civil Code* (2nd edn, The Hague: Kluwer, 1998)

Havel, Václav, *The Art of the Impossible – Politics as Morality in Practice* (New York: Fromm International, 1998)

Heinz, Hans-Joachim, 'The UN Convention and the Network of International Human Rights Protection by the UN' in Freeman, Michael and Veerman, Philip (eds.), *The Ideologies of Children's Rights* (Leiden: Martinus Nijhoff, 1992)

Heringa, Aalt Willem, 'Editorial: Towards an EU Charter of Fundamental Rights?' (2000) 7 *Maastricht Journal of European and Comparative Law* 111–16

Herman, Didi, 'Are We Family? Lesbian Rights and Women's Liberation' (1990) 28 *Osgoode Hall Law Journal* 789–815

Hervey, Tamara and Shaw, Jo, 'Women, Work and Care: Women's Dual Role and Double Burden in EC Sex Equality Law' (1998) 8 *Journal of European Social Policy* 43–63

Hesselink, Martijn, 'The Politics of a European Civil Code' (2004) 10 *European Law Journal* 675–97

Hodson, Loveday, 'Family Values: The Recognition of Same Sex Relationships in International Law' (2004) 22 *Netherlands Quarterly of Human Rights* 33–57

Hondius, Ewoud, 'Towards a European Civil Code' in Hartkamp, Arthur S. *et al.* (eds.), *Towards a European Civil Code* (2nd edn, The Hague: Kluwer, 1998), pp. 3–19

'Towards a European *Ius Commune*: The Current Situation in Other Fields of Private Law' in Boele-Woelki, Katharina (ed.), *Perspectives for the Unification and Harmonisation of Family Law in Europe* (Antwerp: Intersentia, 2003), pp. 118–39

hooks, bell, *Feminist Theory: From Margin to Center* (Boston: South End Press, 1984)

Hoskyns, Catherine, *Integrating Gender – Women, Law and Politics in the European Union* (London: Verso, 1996)

Hunter, Alison, 'Between the Domestic and the International: The Role of the European Union in Providing Protection for Unaccompanied Refugee Children in the United Kingdom' (2001) 3 *European Journal of Migration and Law* 383–410

Hunter, Nan, 'Marriage, Law and Gender: A Feminist Inquiry' (1991) 1 *Law and Sexuality* 9–30

Hyland, Richard, 'The American Restatements and the Uniform Commercial Code' in Hartkamp, Arthur S. *et al.* (eds.), *Towards a European Civil Code* (2nd edn, The Hague: Kluwer, 1998), pp. 55–70

Irwin, Sarah, 'Resourcing the Family: Gendered Claims and Obligations and Issues of Explanation' in Silva, Elizabeth and Smart, Carol (eds.), *The New Family?* (London: Sage, 1999), pp. 31–45

Jagger, Gill and Wright, Caroline, 'Introduction – Changing Family Values' in Jagger, Gill and Wright, Caroline (eds.), *Changing Family Values* (London: Routledge, 1999), pp. 1–16

James, Allison, 'Parents: A Children's Perspective' in Bainham, Andrew, Sclater, Shelley Day and Richards, Martin (eds.), *What Is a Parent? A Socio-Legal Analysis* (Oxford: Hart Publishing, 1999), pp. 181–96

Jamieson, Lynn, 'Intimacy Transformed? A Critical Look at the "Pure" Relationship' (1999) 33 *Sociology* 477–94

Jänterä-Jareborg, Maarit, 'Unification of International Family Law in Europe – A Critical Perspective' in Boele-Woelki, Katharina (ed.), *Perspectives for the Unification and Harmonisation of Family Law in Europe* (Antwerp: Intersentia, 2003), pp. 194–216

Jessurun d'Oliveira, Hans Ulrich, 'Lesbians and Gays and the Freedom of Movement of Persons' in Waaldijk, Kees and Clapham, Andrew (eds.), *Homosexuality: A European Community Issue* (Dordrecht: Martinus Nijhoff, 1993), pp. 289–316

Joerges, Christian, 'Europeanization as Process: Thoughts on the Europeanization of Private Law' (2005) 11 *European Public Law* 63–84

Joshi, Heather and Davies, Hugh, *Childcare and Mothers' Lifetime Earnings – Some European Contrasts (Discussion Paper No. 600)* (London: Centre for Economic Policy Research, 1991)

Karsten, Ian, 'Atypical Families and the Human Rights Act: The Rights of Unmarried Same Sex Couples and Transsexuals' (1999) 2 *European Human Rights Law Review* 195–207

Kennedy, Duncan, 'The Political Stakes in "Merely Technical" Issues of Contract Law' (2002) 10 *European Review of Private Law* 7–28

Kiernan, Kathleen, 'Cohabitation in Western Europe' (1999) 96 *Population Trends* 25–32
  'The Rise of Cohabitation and Childbearing Outside Marriage in Western Europe' (2001) 15 *International Journal of Law, Policy and the Family* 1–21
Kilkelly, Ursula, *The Child and the European Convention on Human Rights* (Aldershot: Ashgate, 1999)
Koppelman, Andrew, 'The Miscegenation Analogy in Europe, or, Lisa Grant Meets Adolf Hitler' in Wintemute, Robert and Andenas, Mads (eds.), *Legal Recognition of Same Sex Partnerships* (Oxford: Hart Publishing, 2001), pp. 623–34
Kostakopoulou, Theodora, 'The "Protective Union": Change and Continuity in Migration Law and Policy in Post-Amsterdam Europe' (2000) 38 *Journal of Common Market Studies* 497–518
Krause, Harry, 'Marriage for the New Millennium: Heterosexual, Same Sex – Or Not at All?' (2000) 34 *Family Law Quarterly* 271–300
Lahey, Kathleen, 'Becoming "Persons" in Canadian Law: Genuine Equality or "Separate but Equal"?' in Wintemute, Robert and Andenas, Mads (eds.), *Legal Recognition of Same Sex Partnerships* (Oxford: Hart Publishing, 2001), pp. 237–78
Lando, Ole, 'The Rules of European Contract Law' in European Parliament Working Paper, *The Private Law Systems in the EU: Discrimination on the Grounds of Nationality and the Need for a European Civil Code* (Luxembourg: European Parliament, 1999), pp. 123–32
  'Optional or Mandatory Europeanisation of Contract Law' (2000) 8 *European Review of Private Law* 59–69
Lando, Ole and Beale, Hugh (eds.), *Principles of European Contract Law – Part I* (Dordrecht: Nijhoff, 1995)
  (eds.), *Principles of European Contract Law – Parts I and II* (The Hague: Kluwer, 2000)
Lavenex, Sandra, 'The Europeanisation of Refugee Policies: Normative Challenges and Institutional Legacies' (2001) 39 *Journal of Common Market Studies* 851–74
Lee, Nick, *Childhood and Society: Growing up in an Age of Uncertainty* (Buckingham: Open University Press, 2001)
Legrand, Pierre, 'European Legal Systems Are Not Converging' (1996) 45 *International and Comparative Law Quarterly* 52–81
  'Against a European Civil Code' (1997) 60 *Modern Law Review* 44–63
  'On the Unbearable Localness of the Law: Academic Fallacies and Unreasonable Observations' (2002) 10 *European Review of Private Law* 61–76
Lewis, Jane, *Marriage, Cohabitation and the Law: Individualism and Obligation (Lord Chancellor's Research Series No. 1/99)* (London: Stationery Office, 1999)
Lewis, Jane, Datta, Jessica and Sarre, Sophie, *Individualism and Commitment in Marriage and Cohabitation (Lord Chancellor's Research Series No. 8/99)* (London: Stationery Office, 1999)
L'Heureux-Dube, Claire, 'What a Difference a Decade Makes: The Canadian Constitution and the Family Since 1991' (2001) 27 *Queen's Law Journal* 361–73
Liddy, Jane, 'The Concept of Family Life under the ECHR' (1998) 1 *European Human Rights Law Review* 15–25

Lowe, Nigel, 'New International Conventions Affecting the Law Relating to Children –
    A Cause for Concern?' (2001) *International Family Law Journal* 171–81
    'The Growing Influence of the European Union on International Family Law –
    A View from the Boundary' (2003) 56 *Current Legal Problems* 439–80
Lynch, M., Roberts, J. and Gordon, M., 'Child Abuse: Early Warning in the Maternity
    Hospital' (1976) 18 *Developmental Medicine and Child Neurology* 759
MacCormick, Neil, *Legal Rights and Social Democracy* (Oxford: Clarendon Press, 1982)
    'Beyond the Sovereign State' (1993) 56 *Modern Law Review* 1–18
Mancini, Federico and Keeling, David, 'From CILFIT to ERT: The Constitutional
    Challenge Facing the European Court' (1991) 11 *Yearbook of European Law* 1–13
Mancini, Giuseppe Federico and O'Leary, Siofra, 'The New Frontiers of Sex Equality Law
    in the European Union' (1999) 24 *European Law Review* 331–53
Martel, Fridiric, *The Pink and the Black: Homosexuals in France Since 1968*, translated by
    Todd, Jane Marie (Stanford: Stanford University Press, 1999)
Mattei, Ugo and di Robilant, Anna, 'The Art and Science of Critical Scholarship. Post-
    modernism and International Style in the Legal Architecture of Europe' (2002) 10
    European Review of Private Law 29–59
McEleavy, Peter, 'The Brussels II Regulation: How the European Community Has Moved
    into Family Law' (2002) 51 *International and Comparative Law Quarterly* 883–908
    'First Steps in the Communitarisation of Family Law: Too Much Haste, Too Little
    Reflection?' in Boele-Woelki, Katharina (ed.), *Perspectives for the Unification and
    Harmonisation of Family Law in Europe* (Antwerp: Intersentia, 2003), pp. 509–26
    'Brussels II*bis*: Matrimonial Matters, Parental Responsibility, Child Abduction and
    Mutual Recognition' (2004) 53 *International and Comparative Law Quarterly*
    503–18
    'The Communitarization of Divorce Rules: What Impact for English and Scottish
    Law?' (2004) 53 *International and Comparative Law Quarterly* 605–42
McGlynn, Clare, 'A Family Law for the European Union?' in Shaw, Jo (ed.), *Social Law
    and Policy in an Evolving European Union* (Oxford: Hart Publishing, 2000), pp.
    223–42
    'Ideologies of Motherhood in European Sex Equality Law' (2000) 6 *European Law
    Journal* 29–44
    'Pregnancy, Parenthood and the Court of Justice in *Abdoulaye*' (2000) 25 *European
    Law Review* 654–62
    'EC Legislation Prohibiting Age Discrimination: "Towards a Europe for All Ages"?'
    (2001) 3 *Cambridge Yearbook of European Legal Studies* 279–99
    'Families and the European Union Charter of Fundamental Rights: Progressive
    Change or Entrenching the Status Quo?' (2001) 26 *European Law Review* 582–98
    'Reclaiming a Feminist Vision: The Reconciliation of Paid Work and Family Life
    in European Union Law and Policy' (2001) 7 *Columbia Journal of European Law*
    241–72
    'Rights for Children? The Potential Impact of the European Charter of Fundamental
    Rights' (2002) 8 *European Public Law* 387–400

McGlynn, Clare and Farrelly, Catherine, 'Equal Pay and the "Protection of Women in Family Life"' (1999) 24 *European Law Review* 202–7

Meulders-Klein, Marie-Therese, 'Towards a European Civil Code on Family Law? Ends and Means' in Boele-Woelki, Katharina (ed.), *Perspectives for the Unification and Harmonisation of Family Law in Europe* (Antwerp: Intersentia, 2003), pp. 105–17

Millar, Jane and Warman, Andrea, *Family Obligations in Europe* (London: Family Policy Studies Centre, 1996)

Minow, Martha, 'All in the Family and in All Families: Membership, Loving and Owing' (1992–3) 95 *West Virginia Law Review* 275–332

Mitchell, Juliet and Goody, Jack, 'Family or Familiarity?' in Bainham, Andrew, Sclater, Shelley Day and Richards, Martin (eds.), *What Is a Parent? A Socio-Legal Analysis* (Oxford: Hart Publishing, 1999), pp. 107–19

Moebius, Isabella and Szyszczak, Erika, 'Of Raising Pigs and Children' (1998) 18 *Yearbook of European Law* 125–56

Moller Okin, Susan, *Justice, Gender and the Family* (New York: Basic Books, 1989)

'Sexual Orientation and Gender: Dichotomizing Differences' in Estlund, David and Nussbaum, Martha (eds.), *Sex, Preference and Family – Essays on Law and Nature* (Oxford: Oxford University Press, 1997), pp. 44–59

'Feminism and Multiculturalism: Some Tensions' (1998) 108 *Ethics* 661–84

Is Multiculturalism Bad for Women? (Princeton: Princeton University Press, 1999)

Monar, Jorg, 'Justice and Home Affairs in the Treaty of Amsterdam: Reform at the Price of Fragmentation' (1998) 23 *European Law Review* 320–35

Monnet Jean, *Memoirs* (London: Doubleday, 1978)

Morgan, David, *Family Connections* (Cambridge: Polity Press, 1996)

'Risk and Family Practices: Accounting for Change and Fluidity in Family Life' in Silva, Elizabeth and Smart, Carol (eds.), *The New Family?* (London: Sage, 1999), pp. 13–30

Moss, Peter, 'Reconciling Employment and Family Responsibilities: A European Perspective' in Lewis, Suzan and Lewis, Jeremy (eds.), *The Work–Family Challenge* (London: Sage, 1996), pp. 20–33

Mostyn, Nicholas, 'Brussels II – The Impact on Forum Disputes' (2001) 31 *Family Law* 359–67

Norrie, Kenneth, 'Sexual Orientation and Family Law' in Scoular, Jane (ed.), *Family Dynamics – Contemporary Issues in Family Law* (London: Butterworths, 2001), pp. 151–75

Nussbaum, Martha, *Sex and Social Justice* (Oxford: Oxford University Press, 1999)

O'Donovan, Katherine, *Family Law Matters* (London: Pluto Press, 1993)

O'Leary, Siofra, *Employment Law at the Court of Justice – Judicial Structures, Policies and Processes* (Oxford: Hart Publishing, 2002)

Oliveira, Castro, 'Workers and Other Persons: Step-by-Step from Movement to Citizenship – Case Law 1995–2001' (2002) 39 *Common Market Law Review* 77–127

O'Neill, Onora, 'Children's Rights and Children's Lives' in Alston, Philip, Parker, Stephen and Seymour, John (eds.), *Children, Rights and the Law* (Oxford: Clarendon Press, 1992), pp. 24–42

Peers, Steve, 'Key Legislative Developments on Migration in the European Union' (2003) 5 *European Journal of Migration and Law* 387–410

'Implementing Equality? The Directive on Long-Term Resident Third-Country Nationals' (2004) 29 *European Law Review* 437–60

Pernice, Ingolf, 'Multilevel Constitutionalism and the Treaty of Amsterdam: European Constitution-Making Revisited' (1999) 36 *Common Market Law Review* 703–50

Pintens, Walter and Vanwinckelen, Koen, *Casebook: European Family Law* (Leuven: Leuven University Press, 2001)

'Europeanisation of Family Law' in Boele-Woelki, Katharina (ed.), *Perspectives for the Unification and Harmonisation of Family Law in Europe* (Antwerp: Intersentia, 2003), pp. 3–33

Polikoff, Nancy, 'We Will Get What We Ask For: Why Legislating Gay and Lesbian Marriage Will Not "Dismantle the Legal Structure of Gender in Every Marriage"' (1993) 79 *Virginia Law Review* 1535–50

Price-Cohen, Cynthia, 'The Relevance of Theories of Natural Law and Legal Positivism' in Freeman, Michael and Veerman, Philip (eds.), *The Ideologies of Children's Rights* (Leiden: Martinus Nijhoff, 1992)

Pringle, Keith, *Children and Social Welfare in Europe* (Buckingham: Open University Press, 1998)

Probert, Rebecca and Barlow, Anne, 'Displacing Marriage – Diversification and Harmonisation Within Europe' (2000) 12 *Child and Family Law Quarterly* 153–65

Rahman, Momin, 'Sexuality and Rights: Problematising Lesbian and Gay Politics' in Carver, Terrell and Mottiers, Véronique (eds.), *Politics of Sexuality: Identity, Gender, Citizenship* (London: Routledge, 1998), pp. 79–88

Rawls, John, 'Kantian Constructivism in Moral Theory' (1980) 77 *Journal of Philosophy* 515–72

'The Idea of an Overlapping Consensus' (1987) 7 *Oxford Journal of Legal Studies* 1–25

Political Liberalism (New York: Columbia University Press, 1993)

The Law of Peoples (Cambridge, MA: Harvard University Press, 1999)

Raz, Joseph, 'Multiculturalism' (1998) 11 *Ratio Juris* 193–205

Reich, Norbert and Harbacevica, Solvita, 'Citizenship and Family on Trial: A Fairly Optimistic Overview of Recent Court Practice with Regard to the Free Movement of Persons' (2003) 40 *Common Market Law Review* 615–38

Remien, Oliver, 'European Private International Law, the European Community and Its Emerging Area of Freedom, Justice and Security' (2001) 38 *Common Market Law Review* 53–86

Rerrich, Maria, 'Modernizing the Patriarchal Family in West Germany' (1996) 3 *European Journal of Women's Studies* 27–37

Reynolds, Jenny and Mansfield, Penny, 'The Effect of Changing Attitudes to Marriage and Its Stability' in *Lord Chancellor's Department Research Series No. 2/99* (2 vols., London: Stationery Office, 1999), Vol. I

Ribbens, Jane, 'Mothers' Images of Children and Their Implication for Material Response' in Brannen, Julia and O'Brien, Margaret (eds.), *Childhood and Parenthood* (London: Institute of Education – University of London, 1995)

Richards, David, 'Introduction – Theoretical Perspectives' in Wintemute, Robert and Andenas, Mads (eds.), *Legal Recognition of Same Sex Partnerships* (Oxford: Hart Publishing, 2001), pp. 25–30

Riley, Denise, '"The Serious Burdens of Love?" Some Questions on Child-Care, Feminism and Socialism' in Segal, Lynne (ed.), *What Is To Be Done About the Family? Crisis in the Eighties* (London: Penguin, 1983), pp. 129–56, reprinted in Phillips, Anne (ed.), *Feminism and Equality* (Oxford: Blackwell, 1987), pp. 176–97

Romito, Patrizia, '"Damned If You Do and Damned If You Don't": Psychological and Social Constraints on Motherhood in Contemporary Europe' in Oakley, Anne and Mitchell, Juliet (eds.), *Who's Afraid of Feminism? Seeing Through the Backlash* (London: Hamish Hamilton, 1997), pp. 162–86

Rowthorn, Robert and Dnes, Anthony (eds.), *The Law and Economics of Marriage and Divorce* (Cambridge: Cambridge University Press, 2002)

Ruddick, Sara, 'The Idea of Fatherhood' in Nelson, Hilde (ed.), *Feminism and Families* (London: Routledge, 1997), pp. 205–20

Ruxton, Sandy, *A Children's Policy for the 21st Century: First Steps* (Brussels: Euronet and the European Commission, 1999)

Sandland, Ralph, 'Crossing and Not Crossing: Gender, Sexuality and Melancholy in the European Court of Human Rights' (2003) 11 *Feminist Legal Studies* 191–209

Schack, Haimo, 'The New International Procedure in Matrimonial Matters in Europe' (2002) 4 *European Journal of Law Reform* 37–56

Schmid, Christoph, 'The Emergence of a Transnational Legal Science in European Private Law' (1999) 19 *Oxford Journal of Legal Studies* 673–89

'Legitimacy Conditions for a European Civil Code' (2001) 8 *Maastricht Journal of European and Comparative Law* 277–98

Schmidt, Marlene, 'Parental Leave: Contested Procedure, Creditable Results' (1997) 13 *International Journal of Comparative Labour Law and Industrial Relations* 113–26

Schulz, Andrea, 'The New Brussels II Regulation and the Hague Conventions of 1980 and 1996' (2004) *International Family Law Journal* 22–6

Schulze, Reiner, 'European Legal History – A New Field of Research in Germany' (1992) 3 *Journal of Legal History* 270–95

Sclater, Shelley Day and Yates, Candida, 'The Psycho-Politics of Post-Divorce Parenting' in Bainham, Andrew, Sclater, Shelley Day and Richards, Martin (eds.), *What Is a Parent? A Socio-Legal Analysis* (Oxford: Hart Publishing, 1999), pp. 271–94

Shah, Prakash, 'Attitudes to Polygamy in English Law' (2003) 52 *International and Comparative Law Quarterly* 369–400

Shaw, Jo, 'Process and Constitutional Discourse in the European Union' (2000) 27 *Journal of Law and Society* 4–37

Siedentop, Larry, *Democracy in Europe* (London: Penguin, 2000)

Silva, Elizabeth and Smart, Carol, 'The "New" Practices and Politics of Family Life' in Silva, Elizabeth and Smart, Carol (eds.), *The New Family?* (London: Sage, 1999), pp. 1–12

Smart, Carol, *The Ties That Bind: Law, Marriage and the Reproduction of Patriarchal Relations* (London: Routledge & Kegan Paul, 1984)

'The "New" Parenthood: Fathers and Mothers After Divorce' in Silva, Elizabeth and Smart, Carol (eds.), *The New Family?* (London: Sage, 1999), pp. 100–14

'Stories of a Family Life: Cohabitation, Marriage and Social Change' (2000) 17 *Canadian Journal of Family Law* 20–53

Smart, Carol and Neale, Bren, *Family Fragments?* (Cambridge: Polity Press, 1999)

Smart, Carol, Neale, Bren and Wade, Amanda, *The Changing Experience of Childhood – Families and Divorce* (Cambridge: Polity Press, 2001)

Smits, Jan, 'A European Private Law as a Mixed Legal System' (1998) 5 *Maastricht Journal of European and Comparative Law* 328–40

Stalford, Helen, 'The Citizenship Status of Children in the European Union' (2000) 8 *International Journal of Children's Rights* 101–31

'The Developing European Agenda on Children's Rights' (2000) 22 *Journal of Social Welfare and Family Law* 229–36

'Transferability of Educational Skills and Qualifications in the European Union: The Case of EU Migrant Children' in Shaw, Jo (ed.), *Social Law and Policy in an Evolving European Union* (Oxford: Hart Publishing, 2001), pp. 243–58

'Concepts of Family under European Union Law: Lessons from the European Convention on Human Rights' (2002) 16 *International Journal of Law, Policy and the Family* 410–34

'Brussels II and Beyond: A Better Deal for Children in the EU?' in Boele-Woelki, Katharina (ed.), *Perspectives for the Unification and Harmonisation of Family Law in Europe* (Antwerp: Intersentia, 2003), pp. 471–88

'Old Problems, New Solutions? – EU Regulations of Cross-National Child Maintenance' (2003) 15 *Child and Family Law Quarterly* 269–78

'Regulating Family Life in Post-Amsterdam Europe' (2003) 28 *European Law Review* 39–52

Steiner, Eva, 'The Spirit of the New French Registered Partnership Law – Promoting Autonomy and Pluralism or Weakening Marriage?' (2000) 12 *Child and Family Law Quarterly* 1–14

Stoddard, Tom, 'Why Gay People Should Seek the Right to Marry' in Sherman, Suzanne (ed.), *Lesbian and Gay Marriage: Private Commitments, Public Ceremonies* (Philadelphia: Temple University Press, 1992), pp. 13–19

'Why Gay People Should Seek the Right to Marry' in Rubenstein, William B. (ed.), *Sexual Orientation Law* (St Paul: West Publishing, 1997)

Study Group on Social Justice in European Private Law, 'Social Justice in European Contract Law: A Manifesto' (2004) 10 *European Law Journal* 653–74

Stychin, Carl, '*Grant*-ing Rights: The Politics of Rights, Sexuality and European Union' (2000) 51 *Northern Ireland Legal Quarterly* 281–302

Governing Sexuality: The Changing Politics of Citizenship and Law Reform (Oxford: Hart Publishing, 2003)

Swithinbank, Andrew, 'The European Union and Social Care' in Munday, Brian and Ely, Peter (eds.), *Social Care in Europe* (Hemel Hempstead: Prentice Hall, 1996), pp. 67–95

Tenreiro, Mario and Ekström, Monika, 'Unification of Private International Law in Family Matters Within the European Union' in Boele-Woelki, Katharina (ed.),

Perspectives for the Unification and Harmonisation of Family Law in Europe (Antwerp: Intersentia, 2003), pp. 185–93

'Recent Developments in EC Judicial Co-operation in the Field of Family Law' (2004) *International Family Law Journal* 30–2

Teubner, Gunther, 'Legal Irritants: Good Faith in British Law or How Unifying Law Ends up in New Divergences' (1998) 61 *Modern Law Review* 11–32

TMC Asser Instituut, *Practical Problems Resulting from the Non-Harmonization of Choice of Law Rules in Divorce Matters* (The Hague: TMC Asser Instituut, 2002)

Toner, Helen, *Partnership Rights, Free Movement and EU Law* (Oxford: Hart Publishing, 2004)

Truex, David, 'Brussels II – It's Here' (2001) 7 *International Family Law Journal* 7–9

Twining, William, *Globalisation and Legal Theory* (London: Butterworths, 2000)

Unger, Roberto, *The Critical Legal Studies Movement* (Cambridge, MA: Harvard University Press, 1986)

Unidroit, *Principles of International Commercial Contracts* (Rome: Unidroit, 1994)

Vaiou, Dina, 'Women's Work and Everyday Life in Southern Europe in the Context of European Integration' in Garcia-Ramon, Maria Dolors and Monk, Janice (eds.), *Women of the European Union – The Politics of Work and Daily Life* (London: Routledge, 1996), pp. 61–73

Van den Berg, Roger, 'Subsidiarity as an Economic Demarcation Principle in the Emergence of European Private Law' (1998) 5 *Maastricht Journal of European and Comparative Law* 129–52

Van Doorne-Huiskes, Anneke, 'Work–Family Arrangements: The Role of the State Versus the Role of the Private Sector' in Baker, Susan and van Doorne-Huiskes, Anneke (eds.), *Women and Public Policy – The Shifting Boundaries Between the Public and the Private Spheres* (Ashgate: Aldershot, 1999)

Van Gerven, Walter, 'The ECJ Case Law as a Means of Unification of Private Law?' in Hartkamp, Arthur S. *et al.* (eds.), *Towards a European Civil Code* (2nd edn, The Hague: Kluwer, 1998), pp. 91–104

'Codifying European Private Law? Yes, If . . . !' (2002) 27 *European Law Review* 156–76

Van Gerven, Walter, Lever, Jeremy and Larouche, Pierre (eds.), *Tort Law – Casebooks for the Common Law of Europe* (Oxford: Hart Publishing, 2000)

Van Gerven, Walter, *et al.* (eds.), *Tort Law: Scope of Protection* (Oxford: Hart Publishing, 1998)

Waaldijk, Kees, 'Free Movement of Same Sex Partners' (1996) 3 *Maastricht Journal of European and Comparative Law* 271–85

'Civil Developments: Patterns of Reform in the Legal Position of Same Sex Partners in Europe' (2000) 17 *Canadian Journal of Family Law* 62–88

'Small Change: How the Road to Same Sex Marriage Got Paved in the Netherlands' in Wintemute, Robert and Andenas, Mads (eds.), *Legal Recognition of Same Sex Partnerships* (Oxford: Hart Publishing, 2001), pp. 437–64

Walby, Sylvia, *Gender Transformations* (London: Routledge, 1997)

Walker, Janet, Timms, Noel and Collier, Richard, 'The Challenge of Social, Legal and Policy Change' in *Lord Chancellor's Department Final Evaluation Report on Information Meetings and Associated Provisions within the Family Law Act 1996* (3 vols., London: Stationery Office, 1999), Vol. I, pp. 5–16

Walker, Kristen, 'United Nations Human Rights Law and Same Sex Relationships: Where to from Here?' in Wintemute, Robert and Andenas, Mads (eds.), *Legal Recognition of Same Sex Partnerships* (Oxford: Hart Publishing, 2001), pp. 743–58

Walker, Neil, 'The Idea of Constitutional Pluralism' (2002) 65 *Modern Law Review* 317–59

Wallace, Chloe and Shaw, Jo, 'Education, Multiculturalism and the Charter of Fundamental Rights of the European Union' in Hervey, Tamara and Kenner, Jeff (eds.), *Economic and Social Rights under the EU Charter of Fundamental Rights – A Legal Perspective* (Oxford: Hart Publishing, 2003), pp. 223–46

Ward, Ian, 'Identity and Difference: The European Union and Postmodernism' in Shaw, Jo and More, Gillian (eds.), *New Legal Dynamics of European Union* (Oxford: Oxford University Press, 1995), pp. 15–28

'Kant and the Transnational Order: Towards a European Community Jurisprudence' (1995) 8 *Ratio Juris* 315–29

'The European Constitution, the Treaty of Amsterdam and the Search for Community' (1999) 27 *Georgia Journal of International and Comparative Law* 519–40

A Critical Introduction to European Law (2nd edn, London: Butterworths, 2003)

'A Decade of Europe? Some Reflections on an Aspiration' (2003) 30 *Journal of Law and Society* 236–57

Warin, Jo, Solomon, Yvette, Lewis, Charlie and Langford, Wendy, *Fathers, Work and Family Life* (London: Family Policy Studies Centre, Joseph Rowntree Foundation, 1999)

Weeks, Jeffrey, Donovan, Catherine and Heaphy, Brian, 'Everyday Experiments: Narratives of Non-Heterosexual Relationships' in Silva, Elizabeth and Smart, Carol (eds.), *The New Family?* (London: Sage, 1999), pp. 83–114

Weiler, Joseph, *The Constitution of Europe* (Cambridge: Cambridge University Press, 1999)

'Editorial: Does the European Union Truly Need a Charter of Rights?' (2000) 6 *European Law Journal* 95–7

Weston, Kath, *Families We Choose* (New York: Columbia University Press, 1991)

Wilhelmsson, Thomas, 'Private Law in the EU: Harmonised or Fragmented Europeanisation?' (2002) 10 *European Review of Private Law* 77–94

'Varieties of Welfarism in European Contract Law' (2004) 10 *European Law Journal* 712–33

Williams, Joan, *Unbending Gender – Why Family and Work Conflict and What To Do About It* (Oxford: Oxford University Press, 2000)

Williams, Patricia, *The Alchemy of Race and Rights* (Cambridge, MA: Harvard University Press, 1991)

Windebank, Jan, 'To What Extent Can Social Policy Challenge the Dominant Ideology of Mothering? A Cross-National Comparison of Sweden, France and Britain' (1996) 6 *Journal of European Social Policy* 147–61

Wintemute, Robert, 'Strasbourg to the Rescue? Same Sex Partners and Parents under the European Convention' in Wintemute, Robert and Andenas, Mads (eds.), *Legal Recognition of Same Sex Partnerships* (Oxford: Hart Publishing, 2001), pp. 713–32

Wintemute, Robert and Andenas, Mads (eds.), *Legal Recognition of Same Sex Partnerships* (Oxford: Hart Publishing, 2001)

Wintersberger, Helmut, 'Work Viewed from a Childhood Perspective' in *Family Observer No. 1* (Luxembourg: European Commission, 1999), pp. 18–24

Woods, Lorna, 'Family Rights in the European Union: Disadvantaging the Disadvantaged?' (1999) 11 *Child and Family Law Quarterly* 17–31

Yeandle, Sue, 'Women, Men and Non-Standard Employment: Breadwinning and Caregiving in Germany, Italy and the UK' in Crompton, Rosemary (ed.), *Restructuring Gender Relations and Employment – The Decline of the Male Breadwinner* (Oxford: Oxford University Press, 1999), pp. 80–104

Young, Claire, 'Spousal Status, Pension Benefits and Tax: *Rosenburg v Canada*' (1998) 6 *Canadian Labour and Employment Law Journal* 435–53

Zimmermann, Reinhard, 'Civil Code and Civil Law – The "Europeanisation" of Private Law Within the European Community and the Re-emergence of a European Legal Science' (1994/5) 1 *Columbia Journal of European Law* 63

'Savigny's Legacy – Legal History, Comparative Law and the Emergence of European Legal Science' (1996) 112 *Law Quarterly Review* 576–605

'Roman Law and European Legal Unity' in Hartkamp, Arthur S. *et al.* (eds.), *Towards a European Civil Code* (2nd edn, The Hague: Kluwer, 1998), pp. 21–39

Zimmermann, Reinhard and Whittaker, Simon, *Good Faith in European Contract Law* (Cambridge: Cambridge University Press, 2000)

Zweigert, Konrad and Kötz, Hein, *An Introduction to Comparative Law*, translated by Weir, Tony (3rd edn, Oxford: Clarendon Press, 1998)

Index

219